as one

as one
Remaking
suede

rodge glass

new modern

new modern

First published in the UK in 2026 by New Modern
An imprint of Putman Publishing
Mermaid House, Puddle Dock, Blackfriars, London, EC4V 3DB

@newmodernbooks
@newmodern_books

Hardback ISBN: 978-1-917923-77-4
eBook ISBN: 978-1-917923-79-8

A CIP catalogue record for this book is available in the British Library.

Publishing and editorial: Pete Selby, James Lilford and Eleanor Porter
Typesetting: Marie Doherty

1 3 5 7 9 10 8 6 4 2

New Modern is an imprint of Putman Publishing

www.newmodernbooks.co.uk
www.putmanpublishing.co.uk

FSC
www.fsc.org
MIX
Paper | Supporting responsible forestry
FSC® C018072

Printed and bound in Great Britain
by Clays Ltd, Elcograf S.p.A.

For Alan Bissett

'From the moment I joined we've been a gang,
and I still see us as a gang now.
I want to present as one being.'

—Richard Oakes

'I may bring in very strongly this quality of
mortality [in my work]. Because the more
violently, more strongly you feel about life,
the more strongly you must be aware of death.'

—Francis Bacon

contents

the band

BRETT ANDERSON – singing

RICHARD OAKES – guitars

NEIL CODLING – synthesisers and piano

MAT OSMAN – electric bass

SIMON GILBERT – drums

introduction
when you were young

'We feel we've been given a second chance ...
and we all want to make the best of it.
That fear, of it going wrong again, is strong.'

—Mat

GREEN TEA AND MAO: 29/1/25

Brett Anderson pours from the kettle, then sits. He's holding a 'She Still Leads Me On' fan club mug named for the love song he wrote for his mum. The song's title is scrawled in his own handwriting, all caps, black on white. 'My only vice,' he says, drily, tapping the mug before taking a sip. 'Almost.' He's comfortable here, in his London flat. Though there's work to do, he's smiling.

As an artist, there are times you're making, times you're preparing to sell, and times you're selling. 'Right now,' Brett says, 'we're moving between the first two,' finishing recording while he works with band photographer Paul Khera on the new album sleeve. It's a response to a photo of the radical gay painter Francis Bacon, taken in Soho in the 1950s, topless, in front of two pig carcasses.* Mat found it at Hatchards

* Deakin's photo was a response to Bacon's painting *Figure with Meat* (1954) which was itself a response to the famous Diego Velázquez painting of Pope Innocent X (1650).

bookshop, in *Portraits of Soho in the Fifties* by John Deakin – 'the most Suede photo I've ever seen,' he says – then pinged it to his singer. (In Suede's version, Brett replaces Bacon, face hidden.) They're trying to obscure his body, while accentuating his bones. Brett and Paul are working on an emblem too, inspired by the celebrated protest artist Gee Vaucher. She did sleeves for the anarcho-punk band Crass, one of Brett's childhood favourites, and he always wanted to work with her.*

So, this week especially, presentation is on his mind.

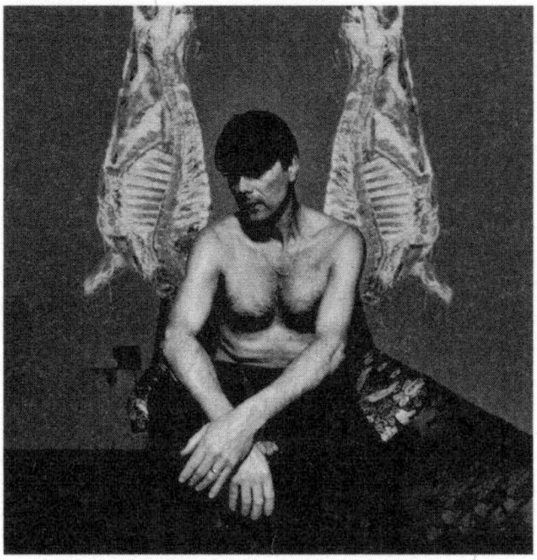

Brett Anderson, with carcasses.
Photo by Paul Khera

This focus on presentation is about music and image, but language too. 'I thought I'd decided the title,' he tells me, 'but now, I'm not so sure.' It's a lonely process, this, though he canvasses the inner circle. His wife, Jodie. The band. Management. Trusted old friends. Jodie's usually upbeat, but she's lukewarm about his working title, 'Broken Music for Broken People', and that's given him pause. Long-time producer

* Suede explored working with Vaucher on *A New Morning*. 'Probably best that didn't happen,' says Brett. 'At least, not then.'

Ed Buller, 'sixth leg of the Suede table', says it 'feels like a description of Suede's entire back catalogue'. That's good, and Brett likes the sound of it, the repetition of 'broken', the rhythm. But he's concerned it's unwieldy – it'll get abbreviated, dismissed – and over green tea he floats an alternative: *Antidepressants,* the title of a new, unreleased song they've been playing live recently. My role is to listen, though I give a view when asked. The process is what I'm here for. My notes suggest we meant to cover other topics, but no matter: this feels like the main business of the day.

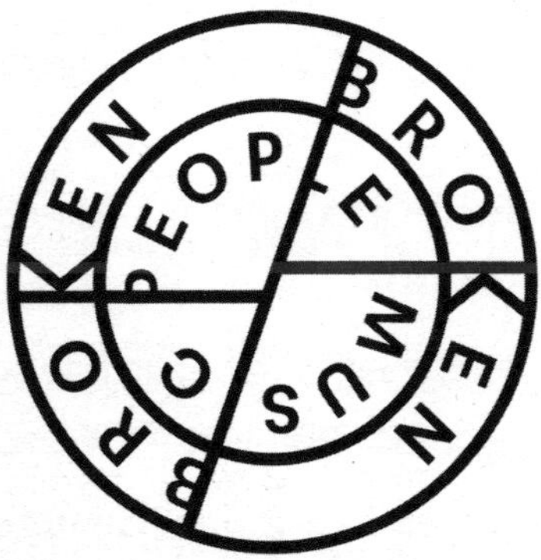

Paul Khera's draft of the 'Broken Music for Broken People' insignia, based on Gee Vaucher's Crass logo.

Brett won't decide for several months. On 27 March he texts me a different suggestion, 'Suppression', with a summary of his thinking, having returned to *Broken Music for Broken People* for a while. Across Zoom meetings, emails and messages, we have a laugh about 'squeaky bum time'. That's Alex Ferguson's quote about the climax of a season, when everyone's knackered and desperate for a holiday, judgement is coming and much remains undecided. Brett canvasses, down to the last. Titles have an outsized impact on the way years of work are seen. The day after suggesting 'Suppression', we talk briefly about Johnny Marr's take on Richard's guitar playing on 'Shadow Self'. Marr's a big fan. On the 29th, Brett texts 'Aaaaaaaaaaargggggggh' at 7 a.m. (Most of his correspondence lands at dawn.) Then he sends me the final title. *Antidepressants*. He got there. It's the right decision.

When I think back to that January day now, one image is clear in my mind: Brett in his front room, Kate Bush on the record player, laughing at his own, absurd comparison. 'What's that line?' he asks. 'You know, about Napoleon?' The one he's grasping for is the infamous, mythic thing Chairman Mao never said: 'It's too early to judge the impact of the French Revolution.' The comedy of equating an album title decision for a bunch of middle-aged rockers with the philosophical war-musings of the architect of the Cultural Revolution isn't lost on him. And yet, it resonates. You can't read the future. To give yourself a chance in the present, all you can do is try and learn from your past. One pompous line always seems ready, on my tongue, to fall out: 'I'm taking this book as seriously as if I was writing a biography of Napoleon,' I tell Brett, when we discuss my project. I need to check myself, resisting that urge to look for approval.

If Brett used to be arrogant, that arrogance is now much reduced. He does occasionally revert to the combative stance of old, but these days those moments are rare. If once he was certain, he now seems more interested in doubt, the mask held up in public for decades now mostly set aside. Or at least, less often reached for. He'll qualify, wonder, speculate. These days he's a war museum nerd obsessed with his gut, a goofy dad who's curious about others, good-humoured, grounded and quick to mock himself. That seemed an unlikely future back when Suede were young. In the '90s, cocksure certainty was not just encouraged, but expected. It's hard to be certain of anything when you're finishing a new album, anyway. You might *think* it's good. You usually do. But Suede know by now – before you mix a new record, you can only wonder what you hold in your hands. If you'll be looking back in your old age, thinking, how could we have thought *that* was a great idea? When Brett gets drawn in deep about Suede, he'll check himself, saying, 'It's only pop music. You can't take it too seriously.' It's one of an army of Brett lines – there's usually some truth in there – but you have to get beyond the line to the man. Anyway. If you get one life, and you make pop music with it, then you *have* to take it seriously, right? And he has. They all have. They still do.

THE PAST IS THE PRESENT

This book is a document of recent history. It takes readers from Suede's break-up in 2003, via an intended one-off reunion gig in 2010, through the making of their next five albums, over the next sixteen years. It examines the lives of the band, management, fans, showing Suede as a live act, in the studio, in private and public. *As One* is a conversation between the past and the present and how those two things, for long-established bands, happen at the same time, all the time. Talking to each other, intertwining. Like the strands, I hope, of this book. The title refers to the band themselves, to their song 'As One', the body of work since 2010, the relationship between band and fans. Even, in Neil's words, to 'our common humanity'. Five letters, like the band name. Five people. Five albums since reunion. It suggests, for me, an underlying effort, an attempt to seem united, even when you're not. It's easy to do a reunion tour, but hard to do a sustained reunion well, never mind for nearly two decades after crashing out. As journalist and long-time Suede fan Simon Price has it:

> The deal between band and audience so often with reunited bands is that you put up with new material in return for the promise of

> old, which reminds you what you used to love, who you used to be, why the band used to matter. Suede are exceptional in that they are releasing some of the finest material of their entire career and they've been doing that for so long now, while being one of the most extraordinary live bands at work anywhere. Everyone should be looking at Suede and thinking, why aren't we doing that? They should shame all the bands of their generation into raising their game.

In this book, I interrogate how Suede have gone about that sustained effort to beat the reunion odds, especially when many of their contemporaries from the '90s were focusing on past glories. I write about the making and sharing of new music, about key moments in the timeline – challenges, setbacks, tensions and small wins – giving in-depth attention to 21st-century Suede for the first time. Along the way, I portrait the band individually and as a unit, examining how they've tried to 'stick together, like a family', as Ed puts it, 'when carrying on feels impossible', in an age when, as Richard tells me, 'downward thumbs are visible, loud and in real time.' Musicians are not gods, after all, though we treat them that way sometimes. They're just people, trying to keep going. Performing can be satisfying. Writing can be satisfying. Recording can be, too, though it's often stressful, as we'll see. Meanwhile, musicians are also trying to keep personal lives together. Work, play, the private, the personal. As you are, in your life. As I am, in mine. For me, nothing is lost by interrogating creativity – pulling music apart, trying to make sense of it, and the lives of those who make it. It only makes it more humane, vulnerable, more magical. Magic, after all, is not something that happens to us, but something we make for ourselves.

My focus on Suede's second creative life goes beyond the release of *Antidepressants* in September 2025; I followed the band from 2023 onwards, finishing a version of the manuscript between gigs on the 2026 UK tour. The band had been working towards *Antidepressants* most of the time I'd been following them, even in the early days touring *Autofiction*, the album that brought so many fans back. Over time, formal interviews have become two-way conversations. That's better. I've been asking individuals to reflect on previous albums from long ago. That changes things, too. It's a moment in time, all this. In the future, we'll look back and see it differently. This is a true version of Suede's second life. But it won't be the only one.

When *Antidepressants* was released, I saw the big promotional push at close quarters. I was there during the band's takeover of the Southbank Centre – five shows, each showing different sides to the band, with different setlists, set-ups, sound. I was there for a last-minute acoustic rehearsal at Richard's place. I was backstage each day, moving between watching, writing and talking to fans. I tried to go largely unseen, 'Casper the Pathologically Friendly Ghost' as I've been called by management. In one photo taken by Paul Khera during soundcheck, you can see me tapping away on my laptop in the distance, in the near-empty Queen Elizabeth Hall, Richard and Brett in the foreground.

With *Antidepressants*, there was genuine jeopardy, nervous tension too. There always is, as, in Brett's words, 'It gets harder every time you come back.' That's another line, but this time it was a different *kind* of hard: the first time Suede ever had a successful album and decided not to take some wild left turn in response. Would Suede X, as the band called it, end up too similar to its predecessor? The first thing Ed said to me at John Henry's studios in April 2024 was, 'We absolutely cannot make *Autofiction* 2. That's the danger.' Well, in the end, would they dodge it?

Since 2010, Suede have gone from barely acknowledged laughing stock (never on the radio, never referenced by other bands, an

Suede soundcheck. Spot the biographer.
Photo by Paul Khera

embarrassing footnote from the '90s) to a genuinely rare, international, late-developing success story. Four reunion albums so far, with another ready to drop, and all this with a line-up few would have bet on, in 2001, when Neil had to leave the band due to ill health. A quarter of a century later, they're still going, Neil and Richard the musical heartbeat of a line-up that's lasted, in total, for twenty-one years and seven albums. This book looks to the present. But let's start by trying to tell the truth about the effect of the long-gone past.

For any long-running band in the 21st century, its old identity is with it constantly, in public, playing on a loop in reels on its Spotify, Instagram, Facebook and TikTok, its worldwide fan groups, private and public: for Suede, that means images of Brett, forever twenty-six, pale, long hair curling over his jawline, giving the camera the come-on in the

'So Young' video as if 1993 was last week. It means an impossibly handsome teenage Richard, fresh out of school, dropped into the shoot for 'We Are the Pigs' on his first day in the job. It means Bernard, forever in the band, forever leaving the band. It's all there, always. Staring back. Saying, over and over, remember me? All this applies particularly if you became famous, as Suede did, overnight, the band completely unprepared for being thunked into the spotlight without warning, when they were still living in poverty. (Suede recouped all £100k, the cost of making their debut album, in the first forty-eight hours after release.)* The way they choose to face that giant of a past, or hide from it, as they get older, is key to their future.

THE MAKING OF THE NEXT THING

'When I think of being in a band,' says Neil, 'it's always focused on making the next thing.' It's that attitude that's helped Suede survive when, 'let's face it, who cares about *any band*'s tenth album?' It's different for Beyoncé: outlandish reinvention is part of the fun, you can drop an album at short notice and global hot takes on the new direction are all part of the promotional campaign. Here comes the dance-floor album! And now the country album! Traditionally, solo artists are sonic cherry pickers, trying to adapt to changing times. Bands rely on what they had in common when they started, fans tend to be less forgiving, and it's harder to shift your ground. Constant graft helps, though. Genuine, humble effort. These things give you a shot.

That focus on the next thing is a recurring theme of this book. As

---

* Soon after, they were back in the red. Suede didn't recoup their outlay from the label again until 1997, around the time of the 'Lazy' single, when *Coming Up* went platinum.

Richard tells me, 'The idea of becoming a straightforward retro act when we play live, simply because it's "what the crowd want", is thoroughly uninspiring to me.' (Those quotation marks do a lot of work. He doesn't think it's what the crowd want at all.) Richard describes himself as 'a bit obsessed' with this issue, and there's always push and pull over what they play. Brett believes 90 per cent of the crowd at *any* Suede gig have never seen the band before: remember that, or risk losing them. That said, there's sustained resistance from the entire Suede camp to the legacy circuit so many acts slip into, like a lukewarm bath. Near-identical setlists. Safe singalongs. Riding the nostalgia train, as grey hairs creep in, knees go, eyes falter. There's no shame in it. Reliving your heyday, without gesturing to the future. It's what happens to almost everyone in the end, if you don't die young, go missing, or die by your own hand, as too many do. This isn't exclusive to any genre, era or culture either. It's adverts on 2020s city-centre streets. The Sex Pistols! Live! With a different singer!* At a punk nostalgia festival! All this is so common, across the spectrum, that it's hard even to notice it. The question is, if you want to avoid that path, can you? If so, how might it be done?

This is a real high-wire act; here, we'll be looking at how it works in practice. As part of this process, I've listened to unheard demos from every era of the band's life. The discarded songs, half-songs, early versions, verses becoming choruses, choruses becoming middle eights. The songs the band loved, then didn't. The songs Ed hated, advocated for, or helped shape anew. I've discussed these with Brett, Neil, Mat and Richard, also many characters involved with every side of the band's life, patching together the timeline. The turning points, the dead ends.

---

* In 2024 and 2025, Sex Pistols original members Glen Matlock, Steve Jones and Paul Cook reformed with Frank Carter, ex of Gallows, on vocals. Carter was born in 1984, six years after the Pistols first disbanded.

The patterns, the tics. What fell by the wayside, and why. What worked, or didn't. What lessons were learned, and how.

THE PRESENT IS THE PAST

Some of this story is about Suede specifically. Who they are, how they work, what they care about, and what difference that makes. They are, in Richard's words, 'five very different personalities', and they've had to work hard to make a life in music together, all over again. But some of this territory might also be about any long-established act, especially a UK guitar band, in the 2020s, trying to face forward. Everyone is living in a slightly different version of the same musical universe. Digital. Fractured. Much more female, more multicultural, thankfully. (Diverse acts were always there, just rarely included in lists of 'great' bands.) We now live in an endless, round-the-clock, round-the-globe music culture where different periods are forever being concertinaed together, then stretched out, then concertinaed again. So much is online, available, all the time. The past is the present. The present is the past. There are opportunities here, as well as traps. But every artist must live with our new world. There's no negotiating with, or avoiding, the times.

One recent example: when Suede arrived at Shanghai airport in 2024 for a festival in Fuyang (late in life, Suede have become Big in China), they were greeted by 150 young fans, in an echo of what they experienced on the long Asian legs of the *Coming Up* tour of 1996–'97. Local teenagers were beside themselves with excitement. Their favourite band, come across the world, to their city. These fans made manga-style drawings to hand over as gifts to their heroes. Not of Suede now, but Suede then. The band were just off a long flight, feeling, frankly, pretty rough. As men of a certain age, conscious of behaving appropriately with excitable, mostly female, fans but trying to respect their enthusiasm, there was a delicate balance to strike. This is common: many fans are younger than the casual observer might expect. (That's not unique to Suede, though their fanbase is more international, more multiracial, than most.) Still, as Richard says, 'Chinese fans are incredibly sweet and generous ... also, they love Suede as an entity, they go just as crazy for "Shadow Self" or "Life Is Golden" as they do for "Animal Nitrate". It feels like a very pure form of appreciation, without the usual baggage and time-warp caveats you get in the UK or Europe. It's liberating.'

So, they signed some drawings. Accepted others, as gifts. Posed for selfies. As Mat recalls, 'They must have known we look nothing like those drawings. But it's *always* 1993 now, same as it's 1963 and the Beatles have just released "She Loves You". That's how modern music works. Even to Chinese teenagers whose favourite song is "Life Is Golden" ... we will always look like those cartoons.' Suede exist in both realms, at the same time. As Mat says, 'Suede straddle not only two versions of itself – the Bernard years, and the Richard/Neil years – but also two versions of popular culture, across time.' To see them clearly, then, you need to hold two worlds in your head at once. One, a pre-internet world with a heavily male-dominated weekly music press and powerful daily tabloid press, where huge album sales, chart countdowns, big publishing deals, hit singles and expensive videos were the norm for bands of Suede's ilk. The other, the world of now.

MAKING IMAGINED THINGS

As One is primarily a book about making. It focuses on elements like resilience, bloody-mindedness, recovery, reconnection, the romance of survival; on growing up, getting sober and getting better at your life's work. It follows the story of a band who dazzled, then threatened to become a cartoon, following the usual trajectory: hope, success, excess, implosion. Who blew it all up, embracing some of the most tired rock clichés along the way, but then managed to make some of their very best work in their fourth decade.

Most Suede fans don't know the story of the band's second life. There's no dominant narrative, no obvious timeline of key dates, moments or beats that people already feel familiar with in the way they might with the first. To even the most dedicated, who queue outside venues for hours to get that front-row spot, using all their annual leave to travel, staying four or five to a hotel room; to those who share Suede memes for every occasion, who scream for rarities at gigs, beg the backline techs or other Suede crew for setlists after lights-up – even for them, there's much that happens out of sight. To these good people, who pay attention to every move the band make and are dedicated beyond any reasonable expectation, the making of Suede's music remains a mystery, even as they snap yet more selfies with Brett, Simon, Neil, Richard and Mat, delighted their heroes learned their names.

There are few assumptions, then, in the band's second life. Fans are likely, though, to have a strong sense of who they think the band *were*, when they were young. This is what Brett calls 'our cartoon past'. The thing about the past is, it can take you over. You can't fight the *Spitting Image* puppet of you from thirty-plus years ago. It's not leaving, and neither is the perception of Britpop, a musical movement that was never a movement at all, but rather shorthand for something that never really existed. That is, a so-called 'British' confidence (for that, read almost exclusively English, white, male, middle-class), presented as a kind of empire on the march. Just look at the magazine covers, and count those Union Jacks.

Where there are assumptions, they suggest maybe there's no story here at all. With a playful laugh, Suede's first biographer David Barnett told me he couldn't imagine anything worse than my new job. 'I mean, what's to say? They grew up, got sober, made some great albums then went to bed at a reasonable time?' Well, that's fair, and it posed me a question. If you take the youth, sex, drugs and cat-fights out of a band's biography, what are you left with? 'Well,' I answered, breaking out into a big grin I could see in the corner of my own Zoom screen. '*Making imagined things*. Now doesn't that sound beautiful to you?' That's what I've been talking to the band about, then, since 2023. Making imagined things.

Hiding under this book there's a well of information that's informed it. Aside from the public stuff – videos, live albums, mountains of YouTube material, articles, podcasts – there have been other Suede books too. Three of the band have published books of their own. Brett alone: two memoirs, though both only lightly gesture, here and there, to recent times. Then there are books by those outside the inner circle, and fanzines produced by private fan group the Insatiable Ones, set up in 2012.* (A newer public fan group, the Mild Ones, was started in Spain in 2022. This has thousands of members around the world, with multiple articles posted daily.†) This has all been critical, as has the wider cultural narrative of Suede's first life – if only because, if you can escape

* As of February 2026, there are 11,700 members. Admins: Samantha Hand, Chiara Fasano, Dominique Tasso, Umberto Picchiotti, Juliet Eckford, Michael Wong, Shawndra Hayes-Budgen. Group created by Sabrina Cipriani, 15 April 2012. Website: theinsatiableones.co.uk. Sam first heard about the Insatiable Ones at a Suede gig in Belgium in 2012. She's been the group's leader since soon after.

† As of April 2026, there are over 15,000 members across the world. José and Sara are admins. Melissa and DeanJean are moderators. This group has a younger profile, with most in countries like Chile (Santiago alone, 13 per cent of group members), Mexico, Argentina and Spain.

seeing everything through the Britpop lens, there's a more complex, nuanced story to tell.

A WAY IN

Brett often says he's looking for 'a way in' to the new music Richard or Neil send him. Some creative starting point, to rev the engine. Biographers need a way in too.

My approach is different from some music writers, as my background is different. I'm not a journalist or an old friend. I'm not part of Quietus Management and not on the payroll. I'm independent – it's not my job to persuade you of anything. Up-close portraiture, that's what I do. I criticise where I think it matters. That said, I pick subjects I value. I've seen this band close-up and feel theirs is a story worth telling. Over three years, I've earned trust, gaining more access with time. That's meant many long conversations, with everyone except Simon, who prefers not to do interviews. That's okay. I respect that.* Neil and Richard's stories were more hidden. Brett and Mat, routinely the public face of the band, are so practised at talking about Suede that it's meant more digging to get past things they've said many times, to many people. Both have hidden stories, too. With Brett in particular, I've learned more over time that's not in the public domain. Trust must be genuine, and hard-earned. If this book gets anywhere near the person rather than just the persona, it's because Brett decided to trust me. Then made himself more vulnerable. Richard and Neil have also done this, in ways that often surprised. Where

---

* I've seen Simon backstage, at soundchecks, in rehearsal, we've exchanged pleasantries and often discussed his contributions with the others. Interviewees talked about Simon, and he's an essential part of the band, of course. I've tried to represent Simon in this book where I can, and he's had right of reply. But he's not gone on record.

relationships have developed, they've developed from scratch. I'm not starry-eyed and I don't tend to get intimidated by fame. I'm earnest, excitable. I like details. I tend to look people in the eye, smile, and do my best. My other books have included novels, biographies of visual artists and writers, a collection of stories and a raw memoir about my nephew's life and my rare blood condition, which I was finishing as I started this one.

In *As One*, I'm often invisible. It's not about me, of course. Suede fans want to learn about the band – though they might wonder what was allowed, what was off-limits, my prejudices or biases. Meanwhile, fans who don't want *any* criticism might also be suspicious of a particular agenda. Again, fair.

I'd been a Suede fan for thirty years before I had any contact with any member of the band. In late 2022, I was just finishing my biography of the maverick Dutch-born novelist Michel Faber. Mat was listening to an audiobook of Faber's *The Crimson Petal and the White* on the tour bus. We got chatting, and it turned out Neil had read one of my previous books. Soon after, I pitched an idea. Others in the band read my stuff, we started talking, doors opened.

And here we are.

ACCESS

I've seen plenty happen in Suedeworld. I've been served chickpea curry by Brett at his place, oven mitts and all. I listened to *Night Thoughts* with Neil as he winced through bits that caused him pain. I sat with Richard in his top-floor home studio as he first mentioned the lost songs from *Night Thoughts*, asked if I wanted to hear them, then played them from his laptop. I followed the band through tours big and small, chatted to Mat through his pre-gig ironing in a space barely big enough for him to stand up in. At the Alexandra Palace gig in London in 2024, I stood watching from the pit in front of the barriers. When Brett came down off the stage above and gave me a hug, it was caught on the big screen. (Biographers should generally go unseen. But it was a nice moment. And from down there, you can hear the band's feet crashing on the stage floor.)

All these are privileges.

I sat in a rehearsal room with the band and Ed, taking notes as Ed conducted proceedings, asking them to consider this or that change, as they played early versions of 'Dancing With the Europeans' and a song that never made it onto the album, 'Why Do I Always Feel So Sad?' (Ed and Brett had a baby row – genuine or not, I'm unsure – about if Brett could hit the falsetto notes. Ed wants Brett to practise singing more. Brett thinks he's doing fine, thanks very much.) For the mixing of *Antidepressants*, I sat with Brett, Neil, Richard, Mat and mix engineer Andrew Scheps at RAK Studios as they went song by song, requesting small improvements as the 2026 tour dates landed in people's phones. I've been at the Paraorchestra gigs – the only time Brett has performed with anyone but Suede since 2013. I attended tiny curiosities – Neil at the Space in Brighton in the depths of winter, early 2024, stands out – a hundred people there, and maybe twenty nationalities in the room. At the only ever event he's done in conversation, by himself. I went to the Imperial War Museum with Brett and his young son Lucian, for fun, discussing the England women's football team, and sat with Ed in his home studio as he played back Simon's drum takes. I heard multiple versions of songs in demo form or partially recorded, the ones that made it and the ones that didn't – including some slated for 'Suede 9.5', an as-yet-unheard lost album I'll be exploring in this book for the first time. Then there are personal photos, Brett's ephemera, as well as extensive, detailed notes sent by Neil as *Antidepressants* was recorded. The lists of what was written, when. How it changed, why. Access to the band's calendars, going back to 2010. I've been lucky. There's plenty I haven't seen, and I'll have missed important details. No matter what trust you build up, you're still an outsider. Meanwhile, I've become invested in *Antidepressants*' success, not least for selfish reasons – that colours my ability to judge the new songs, in particular. These things happen, if you hang around long enough.

Writing any book about a band puts you in a position of unearned power – though most power is an illusion, anyway. You can be tempted into thinking you know it all. You don't. I don't. But let's do our best. I'm not trying to persuade you to like this band. To think this or that song is greatly overlooked, this is a classic, a piece of shit, a mistake ... I will sometimes give my opinion. But for the most part, from now on, I'll let the story tell itself.

CHAPTER 1

the royal albert hall, 2010
an end is a beginning

'Never do a reunion.'
—Brett, 12 February 2010 (forty-two days before the Albert Hall ... and eleven days after the Suede reunion was announced)

THE START

The first thing you hear is a choral chant, ascending and descending – warm, wordless, chilling. It's 'Vessels' by Philip Glass, written for *Koyaanisqatsi* (meaning 'life out of balance' in the indigenous Hopílavayi language).* A camera follows Brett from behind, through the curtain, then onto the stage. The band are in uniform, though the crowd looks thrown together by accident: the Albert Hall, reviewer Luke Turner writes, 'is packed with people straight from the office, ageing fops, young bloods, a group of skinheads'. Above, the world's largest pipe organ (when constructed) hovers like a threat. Below, a fan whirs, cooling the stage. Simon cuts through the backing tape with a double-beat snare, the intro

* *Koyaanisqatsi* was a 1982 cult documentary directed by Godfrey Reggio, exploring the relationship between humans, nature and technology.

music fades, Richard chops once at his guitar, checking it's alive. Then off they go.

They open with 'She', in all its brash confidence. Those shivering guitar stabs that sound like someone's being electrocuted, repeatedly. Neil's menacing falsetto 'la la la's. Next up it's 'Trash', Suede's finest gang lyric, succeeding in doing what so many of their songs try to – invite people in, while claiming outsider status, for everyone. In Suedeworld, you're reminded, everything's romantic, especially if it's mundane. *The litter on the breeze. The lovers on the street.* If you had to strip the back catalogue down to one couplet, you could. The music shifts to that unexpected diminished 'Suede chord'.* Johnny Marr knows a thing or two about patterns in guitar music: 'You don't need to understand anything technical to get the Suede chord,' he says. 'It sends a shiver through the room. Few bands have got a distinctive musical move of their own. Suede have.' As the last chord chimes, Mat releases a grin. 'Filmstar' follows, and it sounds like a twin to 'She'. Stomping, swaggering, shifting from the juddering, sour verse to the sweet-sounding chorus like a gate being thrown open to a different song: 'What to believe in?' Brett asks as, for the first time tonight, he leans into the front row, singing to the roof among a sea of bodies. Then he answers his own question: 'It's impossible to say ...' Occasionally, the band throw each other a glance. But mostly, they're on their own.

That's three from *Coming Up*, and you wonder if there's a policy at work. But no. 'Animal Nitrate' follows. It's been a long time since a big crowd heard the line, 'In your council home, he jumped on your bones / Now you're taking it time after time', but they scream like it was

---

* One for the technical nerds: the 'Suede chord' is a chromatic chord (that's not 'in key'), a twist that sends things off kilter temporarily. See 'Lazy', from *Coming Up*: in the line 'reminding us there's things to be *done*', the Suede chord hits on the final word.

yesterday. Maybe you just need to go away for a while. Or maybe it's nothing to do with time. Maybe it's the songs. 'He's just a fuckin' animal,' Brett sneers, like hundreds of times before, the crowd do the double clap and it's hard to remember what went so horribly wrong. Simon allows himself a quiet smile, and it's straight into 'Heroine', the night's first nod to *Dog Man Star*. A deep cut greeted like a single.

If they were ever dead, these lyrics seem alive again. Tonight's set is full of yearning. Is 'Heroine' approving? Disapproving? Amoral? The Albert Hall sings, 'Hypnotising the silence with her power' – in Suede, women nearly always have the power – and amid all that muscular, stop-start noise, it feels like a reclaiming of something. The desperation the early music is soaked in, the powerlessness, the unlikely victory of the moment, despite the undeniable defeats of ordinary, daily life. After five songs, Brett finally addresses the crowd. 'Good evening. We're Suede,' he says. Voice inflecting slightly upwards, he sounds surprised. Between songs, there's little outward emotion. That won't last.

SOMETHING ELSE TO INVEST IN: 2004–2009

The Albert Hall line-up led radically different lives from 2004 to 2009. They'd lived in each other's pockets for years, as you do, in a band. Invested in the same thing. When it ended, after farewell shows at the Astoria in London in December 2003, everyone struggled to find something else to invest in.

Mat

Mat remembers thinking after the split: 'I'd always seen myself as a member of Suede, not a part of the music industry.' Unlike, say, Simon, he'd only ever really worked with Brett and didn't look for another band.

Mat studied politics at the London School of Economics, once upon a time. In another timeline, who knows what he might have done. But Suede took off, meaning when he had to face the conventional world of work, fourteen years after graduating, he says, 'I wasn't equipped.'

Money drained fast; within a couple of months of the Astoria Mat was driving a van: 'I considered myself a failed musician,' he says. He did keep writing songs – he was more involved in the band's songwriting in the early 2000s – but remembers, 'They just weren't good enough to do anything with. And it's not like those songs [from Suede's last stretch] were loved.' He filled in occasionally in Brett's solo band when his old friend was stuck, playing bass on Brett's solo single 'Back to You' in 2007. There was no terrible fracture. But he was lost, and casting around.

Mat had wanted to write fiction for years but knew little of the writing world, or how to earn while practising his craft. He didn't know if he was good enough. What he might have to say. The world is full of aspiring writers; most get nowhere. It's hard to make a living from fiction. Also, successful writers tend to start early or have a financial cushion. Mat had potential, but his creativity had, so far, been filtered through Brett's public persona. This is true for so many rhythm sections. They stand in the shadows, while the singer speaks for everyone. When you're so used to that voice, writing or playing for someone else, how do you find one of your own? Once Mat was writing every day, it began to nag at him. So, he started writing short stories, sitting at the computer most days and either picking up a bass, or starting to write:

> Like many, many writers, I was in thrall to David Mitchell's *Cloud Atlas* and the way it interwove different stories and genres to create something [like the] loose cohesion of a concept album. When I had a stack of stories, I decided to interlace them to create my own

> *Cloud Atlas*. It was terrible. *Cloud Atlas* is the result of years of careful study, research and plotting. My book, tentatively (and terribly) titled *The Worldwide Shortage of Tears* was an ad hoc Frankenstein's monster of unrelated fluff. But ... it was about 80,000 words, so at least it looked like a novel.

This was a start, but little more. In the mid-2000s Mat moved between jobs, looking for direction. It was slow going. He worked in an office, at Amazon, writing copy, doing menial online stuff. He was the London editor of *le cool*, which recommended arty things to do in European cities. Though it was a different kind of writing, it was publishing experience, and he was well placed.*

Mat didn't leave his old life behind completely. He wrote music for TV programmes like *8 Out of 10 Cats* and *The Marriage Ref*. Also, the Mat-penned final Suede single from 2003, 'Golden Gun'† became the theme music for the Channel 4 series *You Have Been Watching*. In China, one of the Suede songs he wrote for *A New Morning*, 'Lost in TV', was proving popular. He'd written 'Europe Is Our Playground', too, one of the band's most celebrated rarities, featured on B-sides album *Sci-Fi Lullabies*, though that legacy was hardly enough to live on. In six years, post-Astoria, Mat described being an ex-member of Suede as 'like being invisible, like our whole history had been disappeared'. He never heard Suede's music in a bar or on the move. He never heard them namechecked or stumbled across a mention. In the office, people knew who he was, but they didn't say anything. No one mentioned Suede at all.

---

* Mat spent nine months with his then partner (now wife) Anissa in New York, working with Anissa's dad and writing that first novel manuscript.

† Technically it was a double A-side single, with 'Attitude', though 'Attitude' got played on the radio.

Simon

Simon had been talking about moving for years, telling his old friend Mike Christie that he'd relocate to Thailand when Suede split. The band had a history there. They'd first played Bangkok in March 1995 as a four-piece, returned in 1997 and 1999, then played Chiang Mai, in the north, in 2003. After the Astoria, Simon was true to his word, buying a home out there. He became fluent in Thai. He didn't want to be one of those ex-pats who couldn't speak the language.

Simon immersed himself in Thai music, too. Soon he joined another band, playing drums for Futon, a Bangkok-based act he saw headline a Thai music festival and told to ditch their drum machine (their debut album *Never Mind the Botox* had gone big in Thailand in 2003). This was the second time he'd replaced a drum machine, Suede being the first. Simon recorded two albums with them, *Love Bites* (2005) and *Pain Killer* (2007). Futon toured widely and had a punky, good-time, party sound – a multilingual version of Iggy Pop's 'I Wanna Be Your Dog' got heavy rotation in their drum machine days. Songs like 'Fuck Machine', 'Strap It On' and 'High' give a sense of the territory. When Futon fell apart, Goo was born 'out of the ashes', in 2009. They were doing initial recordings by the end of the year, Simon part of a line-up including Thai musicians Oh+ on bass and vocals, and Tuan on guitar.* But Goo didn't last long.

Brett

Only one member of Suede recorded and performed constantly in the in-between years. Within days of the Astoria, Brett was talking to Bernard, who had left Suede in 1994, about a new project.

---

* The mini-album *Sniffin' Goo* was released on 10 April 2010.

This became the Tears. It started out in secret, but things moved fast, Anderson and Butler recruiting bassist Nathan Fisher, Mako Sakamoto, the distinctive Japanese drummer known for his work with McAlmont & Butler, and keyboard player Will Foster. In contrast to Suede's long, slow end, demos came fast, and just six months later they were recording. The Tears went public in October 2004 and were playing live by December, their first single out the following April. The ultimatum that saw Bernard leave Suede was rooted in a disagreement over production duties. No debates this time: Bernard produced the record. *Here Come the Tears* was released in June 2005.

The Tears were a good idea at the wrong time. Though Anderson–Butler was once considered an elite songwriting team comparable, say, to Morrissey–Marr of the Smiths, the Tears formed with Suede's reputation at its lowest ebb and Butler's star on the wane: Bernard's first solo album did very well, but the follow-up, *Friends & Lovers*, flopped. He was an uncomfortable frontman, his label Creation Records folded in 2000 and, as he's said, when the '90s were over he felt people just wanted him to go away. That made it hard for this new band rooted in the previous decade to find its own space. Also, Brett and Bernard were still the same two men who had fallen out many times before. Perhaps it was always destined to be short-lived.

This period is often forgotten now, like some kind of Suede-fantasist's fever dream – did Brett and Bernard really get back together? – but the album went to number fifteen in the UK, and first single 'Refugees' went top ten, meaning they were back on *Top of the Pops*. The song had a chamber pop, soul-influenced sound – the difference split between McAlmont & Butler and Suede, trademark Butler guitars competing with Anderson singing a line over the top about Bonnie and Clyde. And all of us, really, being outsiders. 'Refugees' was a song of identification with new arrivals to London in the early 2000s.

The return was hard going. Under pressure to play the early material that made their reputation – Bernard refused, until finally agreeing to air one early Suede B-side, 'The Living Dead'* – the Tears only lasted a year or two before the label dropped them. What a contrast. A decade earlier the appetite had been huge, while interest in Brett and Bernard's personal relationship threatened to crowd out the music. Many Suede fans never even heard about the Tears. No sooner had it begun than it ended. And who cared? After the Tears, Brett worked at a furious pace. Looking for a new manager, he agreed to work with Ian Grenfell, who he'd crossed briefly in 2000 when guesting on a record by Swedish singer-songwriter Stina Nordenstam, one of Ian's artists.†

In six years, as well as the Tears' album Brett made three solo records – *Brett Anderson* (2007), *Wilderness* (2008, mostly recorded as-live, with cellist and friend Amy Langley‡) and *Slow Attack* (2009, co-written with Leo Abrahams, known for work with Regina Spektor, Brian Eno and David Byrne). Now drug-free and healthy, working solo allowed Brett to experiment with different genres. Often spare, often downbeat, Anderson solo shows happened in intimate venues. The music's impact was slight. As Ian recalls now, 'The first record especially was upsetting for us both. We believed in that music. I still like it a great deal. But few others did.' The

* As of 2026, Bernard has occasionally played 'The Wild Ones' and 'The Next Life' when performing solo.

† Ian was general manager of East West Records before joining a management company. For *This Is Stina Nordenstam* Brett guested on the songs 'Trainsurfing' and 'Keen Yellow Planet'. Then-Suede manager Charlie Charlton wanted a meeting about Ian's plan for the record. They met at the Cock and Bottle pub in west London – Charlie, Brett, Stina, Ian. Brett was edgy with Charlie, Ian recalls now, but still, 'there was something about Brett's personality that appealed to me.'

‡ Amy Langley played on Brett's *Wilderness* album, toured that record with him as a duo, and is 'part of Suede's family'. She played at the *Dog Man Star* twentieth anniversary show with the Dirty Pretty Strings alongside her sister Gita, who sang the lullaby at the end of 'Learning to Be' on *Night Thoughts*.

first review in *Vox* magazine was damning. Others followed, similarly. To give a sense of the scale: Brett's self-titled debut solo record charted at number fifty-four. Neither *Wilderness* nor *Slow Attack* broke the top hundred. Given Suede's 2003 *A New Morning* going in at twenty-four had been seen as a shocking disaster, this rather puts things in perspective.

In 2007, Brett started dating Jodie. They first met back in 2000, in Ibiza, where Jodie rented a flat. She loved dance music, raves and gay discos back in London, and when she moved to Ibiza in 1998, she'd barely heard of Suede. 'We thought we were pirates,' she remembers, of the period, 'we thought we were the coolest cats in the world.' The first time she clocked Brett she tutted and walked away, irritated her then-boyfriend was hanging out with 'pasty coked-up Londoners'. (Far better to be sun-kissed E-heads, in her view.) Ibiza was full of the famous and infamous, the notorious and the numb. At the time she was having a fun summer romance with a mutual friend, dismissing Brett as 'my boyfriend's annoying mate from London from some indie band that was not on my radar at all.'

In 2001 Brett was back visiting Ibiza again, blond highlights in, cleaning his life up. Jodie's friend Jesse was getting close to Brett. This meant they crossed paths again, Jesse and Brett renting a place together close by. By now, Jodie was jointly running a club night at the Manumission hotel. Jodie didn't even recognise him from the year before. Conversation was brief. Brett tried, and failed, to impress. By the time they reconnected in June 2007, Jodie was now mum to toddler Jack, born in 2004. She and Jack's dad had split amicably; Jodie moved back to England but kept her place in Ibiza. One day her friend Nicole encouraged her to work a wedding with her. Jack wasn't quite so little any more. It was time to get out of the house. Nicole said there'd be lots of people Jodie knew there, including Jesse. And Brett.

In this story, Jesse matters. Jodie describes him as being: 'a fabulous influence on Brett ... a wonderful, vivacious character. Feminine, masculine, he'd been a model – he giggled the whole time, he was so warm, people loved having him around and he was good at bringing Brett out of himself. He put Brett through "Jesse's finishing school".' Brett was a different person to the one Jodie ignored in 2000: 'He'd slowed down,' she said, 'become obsessed with his health.' Brett was now thirty-nine, in this fabulous Notting Hill townhouse, where friends Jesse and Sarah lived with him for free. Jodie was 'relieved and surprised Brett no longer had a drug habit.' Many don't get through to the other side.

Brett's most comfortable talking in small groups. Off duty, he doesn't peacock. After the wedding, wearing a smart suit ('I'm not into pathetic aesthetic,' says Jodie), he and the group of friends sat around chatting. There was an attraction there, and Brett had recently split from his previous girlfriend – but he misheard, thinking Jodie said she was 'married', not 'separated'. When they spoke on the phone a week later, she clarified. 'Oh!' he said. 'Right! Well!' Then came a first date. Dinner, walk in the park. That summer, they wrote each other long letters back and forth, Jodie still spending most of her time in Ibiza. 'It was a beautiful, slow courtship,' she remembers now. 'I remember us both laughing later [after Jodie moved back to London] because he'd just put out his first solo album ... he felt like he was starting again, but so was I. I was just going back to college, living in this little flat with Jack. We both had these big chapters in our lives that had fallen apart.' Jodie now says, 'I missed phase one [of Brett's life] completely. Timing is so important. In a way, I think that helped us both.'

Brett and Jodie moved slowly, six months passing before Brett met Jack. There were no other Suede kids. He was from a small family. His big sister Blandine didn't have any either. But Brett took to caring for Jack straight away, teaching him to read, playing with him freely: 'He made it clear from the beginning,' says Jodie, now, 'that he was keen [to be with Jack too]. I could just tell he wasn't going to be difficult. Not annoying or pushy. He was so genuine, so different to what you'd think a famous person in a band would be like. I met him, and got to know him, away from persona mode.' In 2008, they got engaged. 'We were both quite keen to do things properly,' says Jodie. 'We'd both lived these crazy, liberal lives. We'd both seen the bullshit, the nonsense, the brokenness that leads to. We'd both been surrounded by drugs. We were ready for something more conventional.'

Soon after, the seed of something: Brett did a solo session for the Teenage Cancer Trust's 'Love Music Love Food' campaign, the playful photo shoot marking the start of the tenth year of the Teenage Cancer Trust. (Blueberry juice dripping down Brett's arms, for the camera. Blueberry juice in syringes, in splashes on a crisp white shirt. In one of his sillier interview answers he said, 'I've never written about food, but I did write a song called "Everything Will Flow". And I suppose, if you eat enough fruit, then everything *will* flow.')* Why the Teenage Cancer Trust? Brett's mum Sandra died of cancer when he was still at college. When he was barely out of his own teenage years.†

After the session with photographer Patrice de Villiers, Ian's assistant Andrea Mills asked Patrice who they might talk to at the Teenage Cancer Trust about a potential Suede reunion. The event producer was Des Murphy (who was also in a band called Penguin Cafe with Neil):

---

* *Love Music Love Food: The Rock Star Cookbook*, was eventually published in 2011, curated and authored by Patrice de Villiers.

† As Des Murphy explains, TCT actively support the families of people with cancer, as well as teenagers affected by cancer more broadly. In other words, Brett might have benefitted from the TCT when his own mum died, had it existed then.

'It wouldn't have occurred to Des I wanted to talk to him about Suede,' Ian says. 'No one was talking about Suede.' Des describes this as 'like being offered something you'd bite someone's hand off for ... there was no doubt in my mind that they'd smash it.' When asked by Ian if the Teenage Cancer Trust would be interested in a one-off Suede reunion show, Des replied with a yes, and two questions. One, will they agree to it? And two: Is Neil involved?* Though no one had agreed to anything yet, or even knew about the idea, Ian said yes to the first question. They'd sort out the details later.

On 23 May 2009, Simon spent his forty-fourth birthday at Brett and Jodie's wedding. Mat and his long-term partner Anissa were there, as was close friend John Brandham, Brett's driver for many years. Brett's old friend Alan, with him throughout the '90s, was best man. The wedding party lunched at Scott's, the posh fish restaurant in London. Brett's ex-girlfriend Sam, subject of the Suede song of the same name, wrote the best man's speech for Alan, having been present for so many of the earlier, good times. (Jodie and Brett maintained good relationships with past partners. Both had exes at the wedding.) But then Alan was too nervous to give it, Jesse stepping in with something off-the-cuff to warm applause instead, 'backing Alan up, like a true friend'. After the wedding, Jodie, Jack and Brett embarked on 'a sweet life, without big overheads'. 'It wasn't expensive, really, so it didn't feel like it mattered too much how successful Brett's solo career was.' When he was doing it, Jodie recalls, 'he was fully immersed in it all. He has this immense grit and resilience.' But he wasn't doing it all the time.

---

* It would have been awkward had Neil not been involved, but Des kept it secret for the time being and didn't discuss anything with Neil, one of his closest friends. (They sat on stage next to each other for Penguin Cafe gigs. Meanwhile, Des didn't actively push Ian for Neil to be in the Suede line-up.)

Jesse giving the speech at Brett's wedding, with Alan and Jodie's son Jack.
Photo courtesy of Jodie Anderson

In 2009 Brett recorded *Slow Attack*, feeling he was getting somewhere as a songwriter, but did anyone care? Brett knew better than anyone; the band that made his name were deeply unfashionable. Meanwhile, towards the end of that year, the joyful, friendship-filled life of recent years took a dark turn. The record was due out on 9 November, but in September Jesse suddenly took ill with hypomania. Everyone was consumed with worry as he suffered delusions, the fun-loving centre of the room who indirectly brought Jodie and Brett together now delicate and in need. It was confusing, destabilising, for everyone. By December Jesse was hospitalised. By release in early January, his parents were taking turns to care for him.

Richard

Mat wasn't the only one unsure what to do after the Astoria. Richard had recently bought a home in a part of west London with no underground station, and rather drifted: 'There was no falling out as such, it just stopped being fun, we weren't on the same page creatively and I had as little idea of where to take Suede as Brett did. Once it was over, there was simply no need for us to be in each other's lives any more.' Another kind of personality might have formed another band. Richard was still just twenty-seven – the same age as Brett when Richard joined the band in October 1994. Now, he didn't have to live in the shadow of another guitarist. He could have made his own way. Even on a smaller scale, like Brett or Simon, he could have. Why didn't he just pick himself up and go do something else? Or leave London? Or travel? Or anything?

Richard's confidence was shattered, and he'd never started anything from scratch before. Thrown into the media firepit as a teenager, he'd been tasked with giving a high-profile band new identity. Which he did, and then some, writing much of the band's most popular music. 'Trash'. 'Filmstar'. Their biggest hit worldwide, 'Beautiful Ones'. 'Saturday Night'. The band moved away from him with *Head Music*, further with *A New Morning*, and he couldn't cope. He wasn't into drugs, taking quiet refuge in drinking instead. Once the band split, he was paralysed by depression and anxiety. Old Suede manager Charlie Charlton checked in on Richard regularly. There was occasionally hangover Suede business, and a couple of offers did come in, though in 2004 he took 'a deliberate break from music' to move house. From 2005, he sometimes wrote at home. But he didn't want to perform, release anything, be seen. Out there, Brett was touring with the Tears, then constantly moving, solo. Brett's response to every setback was the same – keep pushing, try something else, make your case. But Richard was a very different personality.

By early 2008 it was four years since the Astoria. Then, Richard and his partner split. They met when he was just twenty, still new to the band. His only adult relationship was over. He remembers: 'My self-esteem was pretty much at rock bottom.' He needed something to focus on. Then, producer Sean McGhee got in touch. Sean says now, 'I just found it staggering that he wasn't doing anything. No one seemed to appreciate him.' A friend of Sean's knew Richard's brother Stephen; Stephen put Sean in touch, via Charlie. What followed were baby steps, but critical. Richard says now: 'Even a year after my break-up, which was just horrible, I was still picking up the pieces from that ... so it came at a really good time.'

More than anyone else in the band, Richard was in personal recovery, but in recovery from Suede, too. So much so that he didn't even call his new venture a band at all. No, it was to be a 'project', Artmagic: another indicator of just how ill at ease Richard was, even as working with Sean was restorative, fun, low-pressure. After the Astoria, Richard was protected from financial precarity due to his writing credits. But that was double-edged. Unlike, say, Mat, he wasn't forced to adapt. Richard's sensitivity is crucial to his playing; it's what makes him a considerate presence in a room. But in his twenties, he didn't have the resilience or life experience of the others. He'd joined the band direct from school and spent much of his time in studios, at gigs, on planes, on the move: 'There's always a crew around ... you're not expected to act like a grown-up.' Between Suede's last gig and the phone ringing six years later, Richard did not play one show, or release one note of music.

Sean started out as a programmer and mixer for Robyn, Britney Spears and Alanis Morissette in the early 2000s, but by 2008 he was producer and musical director for electronic rock act Temposhark. There was no juggernaut behind him and Richard, no official timetable, publishing deal, live band, website, touring schedule or public profile. In other words, they were free. Richard remembers: 'By late 2009 I had been writing with Sean for about a year – we were amassing an album's worth of material and that was my only creative outlet. I was inspired by how different it was working with Sean, but we were still a way off finishing or releasing anything, and he had other projects going on.'

Sean describes himself as being 'keen to please' – his admiration was genuine, feeling 'Richard needed the support of someone who valued him for who he was.' Sean's experience with pop acts meant he was 'used to coming into a room cold, then getting straight to work.' Sean is down-to-earth, understated. Though the singer in Artmagic, he'd spent most of his working life in the background. This meant he was flexible, not precious, and this project didn't hold any pressure for him, either. Sean created an atmosphere where Richard could just come up with ideas in response to his own, in the moment. Back then, this was new to Richard, and frightening. Progress was slow, occasional, and essential to building Richard's confidence. He was only just starting to recover from the Suede fallout. When the phone rang, he might have reasonably thought, why would I get involved with that thing again now? And with the people I was recovering from in the first place?

Neil

Neil also went largely unseen. Given he and Richard had been responsible for writing much of Suede's music across their commercial peak, including some of their finest songs, it seems incredible both had this experience. Though it was for different reasons, in different ways.

It all ended for Neil sooner than the others. Initially, he was simply trying to get back to good health, having been diagnosed with post-viral fatigue after contracting glandular fever back in 1997. The root cause remained a mystery:

> Every test came out normal. No doctor I saw would diagnose me, with anything. That didn't help, because I'd see a doctor, the doctor

> would tell Charlie, 'There's nothing wrong with him, he'll be fine' and Charlie would tell the rest of the band 'He'll be fine.' As time went on, this created tension, frustration and accusations of malingering. It must be psychosomatic, and my getting better was simply a case of mind over matter, so why was I letting everybody down? Why wasn't I trying harder? In '98, '99, there were long periods I couldn't get out of bed, let alone confront an illness or actively try to turn things around with a health kick. One doctor in Hong Kong told me to stop drinking Lucozade and I'd be fine (I never touched the stuff), and a personal trainer Charlie got for me recommended I smoke weed and just … chill out. What I needed was to cut all this bullshit out of my life and only then could I begin to heal.

Neil continued in Suede for four more years, but eventually his health declined 'to the point where I couldn't contribute properly to the band and convalesce at the same time'. After initial demos were done for *A New Morning* in early 2001, he resigned, leaving Brett, to use his own word, 'furious'. He'd held the band together, he felt, for years. People were always leaving. Here he was having to cope with that again, and why? Neil was quickly replaced by Alex Lee and the band continued recording. Brett told the *NME*, 'He couldn't help it, I know, but I did feel let down … more at the universe than at Neil.' Neil wrote a public letter to fans thanking them for their support and wishing Suede well. But it was hard.

By August 2001 Brett was describing Alex's arrival as giving Suede a 'shot in the arm', and the new songs as having a 'celebratory' feel. Neil recalls now: 'It all sounded like Suede were doing better without me, that the new album was going to be great, and I wasn't missed.' Of course, Brett was just making it *sound* like Suede were winning. But Neil was out in the cold, for reasons unclear, the implication being it was his own fault. In late 2001, he was coming to terms with being out of the band, trying to understand his health and its consequences, while *A New Morning* racked up bills and producers, getting less celebratory over time.

Neil's years outside the band began with an unexpected three-year tax bill – Suede's accountant Frank Dixon, also representing the likes of Primal Scream, had been pretending to pay Suede's bills since 1997. (Dixon was finally imprisoned for this, over a decade later, when much damage had been done.) In 2003, there was a further complication, when Sony Records refused to pay Neil an advance for the Suede *Singles* album, though as a co-writer on four songs, he was entitled. Downplaying it now, he says: 'The stress and legal fees to put that right didn't help matters.'

In 2001 Neil wrote part of the soundtrack for *Far from China*, directed by C.S. Leigh, starring Aurélia Thiérrée and featuring Marianne Faithfull. (He left the soundtrack unfinished; Saul Freeman, ex-Thieves, finished it after his departure.)* Neil was a multi-instrumentalist; he could read and write music; he had technical skills and was well used to complementing or developing others' ideas. As a child, he'd loved 10cc; all four members of that band wrote, sang and produced. All were multi-instrumentalists, and he thought of himself, like them, as most comfortable looking for what individual pieces of music needed from him, rather than sticking to one instrument or approach. Neil wondered if he might be able to segue into a parallel career. He says now that 'much of the aughts was a write-off' for him, but that doesn't mean he wasn't working.

At first, Neil made music for short films, but 'was dropped for more experienced composers when directors got bigger budgets.' He wrote the theme for a prime-time BBC show that got mothballed. (It resurfaced five years later, with different music.) He made music for a horror film

* In 2001, Freeman was half of the trip-hop duo Mandalay, whom Charlie Charlton also managed.

that got mothballed. (It emerged five years later, with different music.) As Neil recalls, 'I spent Christmas Day 2005 writing a theme tune for ITV's Formula One coverage to meet a tight deadline, only to be told later that they'd settled on a Moby track before everyone broke for the holiday.' This work had to be done 'on spec' – this meant working full time making music but often ending up unpaid, his income sporadic. Neil recalls:

> I made music for adverts on MTV and ITV for clients from the *Daily Telegraph* to *Loaded*, for Ted Baker, Coca-Cola, for Swarovski and baked beans, for barbecue marinade in the US, and for a series of animated Argos ads. I wrote and recorded music for a Disney documentary about Lapland, for plays at the Arcola Theatre in Hackney, and stuff for Radio 4. There was music for corporate videos about risk management, and music for amusement park queues, but all this wasn't enough to make a living, and by 2008 I was putting mortgage payments on a credit card.

All this paints a radically different picture from the one sometimes assumed: that Neil's only ever been in Suede. Couldn't be bothered to get well. Didn't get out of bed for a decade. On the contrary, he was hustling hard, despite his health.

It was 2004, after seven years of chronic fatigue, before Neil was able to play live again: 'To keep my oar in, I played in bands with friends in pubs, and in marquees for weddings and birthdays. I played bass in Pearl Lowe's solo band throughout 2004 [previously of Powder and Lodger, now a noted fashion and textile designer], keyboards in Natalie Imbruglia's band on various tours in 2005, guitar in Wolfman and the Side Effects in 2007.' Like Mat, he also played keys for Brett in 2007, even appearing in Brett's band at the same time as Mat once, putting three-fifths of Suede on stage together. But these were one-offs. In 2007, in between all the film music, adverts and documentary work, Neil was scoped out for other roles in well-known bands, variously on bass or keyboards, and he auditioned as a touring musician 'for bands I didn't fit, and for bands that didn't fit me'. It felt like looking for scraps: 'I failed auditions for up-and-coming artists who saw I could play, but turned me down because in truth I didn't look like I belonged in a band any more,' Neil remembers now. 'I was a has-been. I never gave up on music, but it seemed music was giving up on me.'

It was 2009 before Neil joined another band. This was Penguin Cafe, for whom he played piano, guitar, cuatro and ukulele. That year, they were working towards their first album, a kind of continuation/reinvention of the Penguin Cafe Orchestra, the chamber pop band put together by founding member Arthur Jeffes' father, Simon, in the 1970s. Their first release, *Music from the Penguin Cafe, Live at the Royal Albert Hall*, drawing mostly on the Penguin Cafe Orchestra's '70s material, was released in 2009.* There's a bizarre edit of this show intercut with interviews on YouTube, Neil playing away close to Des Murphy while the (possibly hungover) production manager Steve Allen, trapped in a penguin suit, nods along approvingly in the middle row of the otherwise empty Albert Hall. Soon, this space would be crucial to Neil's future. But for now, he had an audience of one.

Alex

Alex Lee had to move on too. He usually only gets a line or two in the Suede history, his tenure in the band dismissed by fans and commentators as it coincided with their most disappointing record. Speaking to

* The new Penguin Cafe line-up 'recorded some studio tracks to add to the live ones (at Air-Edel in Marylebone) on 09/09/09, mostly old stuff from the Penguin Cafe Orchestra, but with one new tune, too.'

me now, Alex is gracious. He knows he joined Suede when things were going wrong – as a newbie, he was in no position to do anything about that – but he also accepts the music he wrote wasn't as strong as the band's previous output. Pre-Suede, Alex had been in the Blue Aeroplanes and Strangelove. His post-Suede life is rich and various. These days, he plays guitar in Massive Attack's live band, and in recent years he's worked as musical director for Florence + The Machine. He's worked with the Royal Shakespeare Company on multiple productions.

After the Astoria, Alex went on to play a part in the lives of several of Suede's contemporaries. Having joined initially as part of the Suede live band, he says, 'I thought, I see a way forward here. I felt like this suited me, to concentrate on just playing music, in the background.' By 2006–7, he was a touring guitarist with Placebo on their mammoth *Meds* tour, headlining Wembley Arena, playing thirty-three US shows, and no fewer than twenty-five shows in France alone in a single year. After that, other opportunities came. He toured with Goldfrapp from 2008, playing guitar on their next three albums. For Alex, the end of Suede was just a beginning. He's been happy in the shadows.

It wasn't just Alex. To most onlookers, *all* members of Suede, past and present, may as well have been invisible for most of this period. Everyone was forced to face real life.

THE MIDDLE

The opening wash of cymbals introduce you to 'Pantomime Horse' as the lights turn red, then dim. Tonight, it sounds *big*. One moment the hall's silent, full of space. Then the noise builds, the distorted guitar figure leading up to the notorious, repeat line: 'Have you ever tried it that way?' First, it's sung low and haunting. Then, an octave higher. Early in the song, the odd line is slightly off-key, like Brett's searching for each note rather than hitting it. But by the end it soars, and he delivers the coda from his knees, Mat behind him, swaying, eyes closed.

The first notes of 'Can't Get Enough' are greeted with a cheer that seems to surprise everyone. It's played with furious energy, faster, harder than on record. In the intro, Brett's pogoing like a kid. Richard's guitars stretch and moan. The words in 'Can't Get Enough' are plainly ridiculous. But they're delivered with such joy, the tension contained and released, contained and released, that it somehow gets away with making no sense. Something about Buddha. Something about a teenage tough. By the time the applause rings out Brett's dropped his cool act. As 'Everything Will Flow' begins he makes a face at the others, as if to say, well, they liked that one, eh? Tonight could have been a disaster, but by this point, the good feeling is catching.

A START WILL BE AN ENDING

It was only supposed to be a one-off. 'We thought it'd be cool to lose money on it,' remembers Mat. 'Suede had ended with a whimper. It would be good to correct that ending, we thought. Just one gig, then back to our lives.' When Brett was approached with the idea of a one-off reunion for the Teenage Cancer Trust at the Albert Hall, he was unsure how to respond. As we've seen, Ian had been working behind the scenes, trying to orchestrate an approach to the band, in the hope that if the right invite was there, Brett might consider it. (A hypothetical was no use, though this meant a balancing act for Ian, who pitched the reunion before knowing if Brett, or anyone, would agree.) Even in their 2003 split announcement, Suede hinted they might return, one day. Still, in summer 2009 there was serious concern there might be no audience. Brett had been working hard on his solo career for years, Ian feeling like 'you couldn't even *mention* Suede for much of that time, it was like talking about a dead parent ...' They knew how Suede were seen. Though Ian hoped, anyway. It might look from the outside that Roger Daltrey of the Who, figurehead at the Teenage Cancer Trust, simply called Brett and asked him to put the band back together, but no. Ian and others worked for months behind the scenes to engineer something presented to Brett as a *fait accompli*.

After talking it over with Ian, Brett called Mat first. He was, tentatively, on board. Mat says if he'd been asked if he wanted to reform Suede properly in that call – new songs, new album, full commitment – he'd have said no. 'I didn't like the idea of starting again,' he recalls, 'but as it was just one gig, at a venue where we had a strong emotional connection, I could see why it might be good.' (Suede had played there before, as a four-piece, in 1995. Brett's dad, a Franz Liszt obsessive, had taken him to the Albert Hall to see classical music as a child.) Brett Skyped Simon in Thailand. He'd fly back for rehearsals, he said, if Brett could persuade others. That was half a band. But Brett and Mat both feared depleting Suede's already shrunken reputation, doing the thing they thought, deep down, that great bands probably shouldn't do.

Few reunions improved a band's story. The Sex Pistols, a constant reference for Brett and Mat since childhood, reunited for the Filthy Lucre world tour in the mid-'90s, only reducing themselves in the process. Mat saw the Velvet Underground live in 1993 (they played Glastonbury that year, while Suede headlined the *NME* tent) and was underwhelmed. Then there was money; neither Brett nor Mat wanted to do anything that might look like – or *be* – cashing in, while appearing desperate to regain lost attention. At least a charity gig couldn't be accused of being a money-spinner. But even if people came, who'd be on stage?

In an often-repeated line, Brett once joked that Suede involved a 'cast of thousands',* the band's history being 'like a pram that's been pushed down a hill'. Not quite thousands, but 1989 to 2003 Suede was an ever-changing line-up, and the last featured Alex Lee. Would they return to Alex? (He was recording Goldfrapp's album *Head First* at the time.) Or was Neil a better fit? If they thought so, would he be up to it? Or willing?

Then the most vexed question: guitarist. For some hardcore fans, Suede was over once Bernard Butler left. For many others, even after rapprochement in the 2000s, the idea of a Bernard return seemed silly, obviously unworkable. Famously, Bernard had declared he had 'grown to hate' the early Suede material shortly after it was released – in the years since, he'd worked with David McAlmont, made solo albums, become a producer (most significantly, on the multi-award-winning Duffy album *Rockferry*) and even preferred to start a *new* band with Brett instead of returning to the old one. Under pressure to play songs they'd written as young men, the Tears disbanded. Already that reconnection was several years in the rear-view mirror now, with Bernard back to working off stage. He'd made a career from his restlessness. Would he really, fifteen years after declaring himself sick of 'The Drowners', return to play that, along with Richard's hits? If he didn't play anything of Richard's, was return even viable? At this point Bernard and Brett were friendly, but Bernard only ever acknowledged Richard to call him a 'talentless clone'. Surely any new Suede show would have to include their most popular songs – which, bluntly put, were Richard's. But would Richard be interested?

---

* The full quote, to *NME* in 1994: 'The history of this fucking band is ridiculous. It's like Machiavelli rewriting *Fear and Loathing in Las Vegas*. It involves a cast of thousands. It should star Charlton Heston ... it's like a pram that's been pushed down a hill. It's always been fiery and tempestuous and really on the edge and it never stops. I don't think it ever will.'

In Jodie's words, 'Brett thought Richard might not do it. It had probably been a nightmare to be in a band with crack-head Brett. Why go back?' There was no way of knowing whether he would.

Brett called Richard in July 2009. They hadn't spoken since that final Astoria show. There had been very occasional emails, but that was all. Richard was surprised. For him, the last eighteen months of the band, 2002 to 2003, were a trial:

> I felt I got a disproportionate amount of blame from the band and management for why Suede's fortunes had taken such a drastic turn downwards after the failure of *A New Morning* and it gradually sapped my ambition. I ended up with no real desire to be in the band any more and was just marking time, trying to deflect attention ... When Brett told me about the Teenage Cancer Trust gig offer, the very first thing I asked was whether he'd thought about putting the old line-up back together.

This was typically self-effacing; also a sign of Richard's self-esteem. Either way, he must have known he was suggesting something impossible. Brett responded by saying he thought the *Coming Up*-era line-up was the one he thought functioned best and had the most potential for a reunion. Richard asked how the others felt; they were willing, if he was. This was encouraging, but also applied pressure. When the call came, Richard says, 'I discussed it with Sean as closely as I did with family and friends – I felt like I needed a lot of advice on whether to say yes or no.' Richard doesn't rush into things. He turned over the possibilities, meaning the others didn't have an answer for weeks. Roger Daltrey, curator of the Albert Hall series, had to wait too. In 2025, looking back on the band's long second life, Mat laughs, 'I mean, in that time, what if Paul McCartney had offered to step in?'

Richard knew a reunion gig ignoring the first two albums wasn't viable, but as he remembers now, he agonised over it: 'I started bargaining about what I would and wouldn't play. It seems ridiculous now, but it reflects the emotional battle I was going through to prepare myself to be a part of Suede again.' That said, he acknowledges the band were 'very patient and agreeable to my conditions'. No one seemed to underestimate what it meant for Richard to step back into a world that had come to represent difficulty, pressure, even a kind of suppression of his own identity. Despite never meeting, he and Bernard were kind of haunted by each other's existence.* No wonder Richard took his time.

Sean played an important role here, not least in supporting Richard to re-engage with his previous life, rather than complaining or seeing it as some kind of betrayal. All these years later, Richard emphasises that Sean approached him when no one else would: 'Sean was pivotal in helping me restart my career, getting me creative and collaborative again, and ultimately giving me enough confidence to agree to be part of Suede again.' After consulting with Sean, family and friends, and after much deliberation, Richard responded to Brett. A month after he'd been asked, Richard agreed to join the reunion. Suede were pencilled for the first night of the Teenage Cancer Trust shows.†

---

* Bernard discussed his perspective on this with collaborator Ben Watt, of Everything But the Girl, in 2017: 'Ben Watt (Everything But the Girl) Talks with Bernard Butler', *Talkhouse Music Podcast*. They did eventually meet, once, by chance, shaking hands when they found themselves in the same rehearsal studio.

† Discussions around this time were impacted by the possible 'coup' act that might be included in the final bill on the Saturday night. This ended up being Arctic Monkeys. Noel Gallagher did two nights, fresh out of the Oasis split, too. First night might have made a bigger splash for Suede, given it was the major press night. In the end, this slot went to Them Crooked Vultures and Suede played the third date on the Wednesday.

He wasn't alone in being unsure of his place in the one-off reunion. Would Neil be invited to take part? Brett admits now that back in 2001 he didn't understand Neil's condition, taking it as a kind of personal rejection. A lot had happened since. With the passage of time, a change in culture too, there was more understanding now that Neil's struggle deserved respect, rather than being seen as the result of too much partying on the *Coming Up* tours. Come 2009, Neil was not a part of the decision-making process. This was led by Brett, with Richard's inclusion being the main focus. Neil remembers now: 'I didn't know I'd be part of it [the Albert Hall]. Brett could have had Alex [Lee] or just Richard. You never know do you, so it was nice to be asked. I kind of had unfinished business cos I left them in a difficult way, and it wasn't my choice. I just got sick and had to leave.'

He didn't assume the phone would ring for any future Suede reunion, but from Brett's perspective, Neil was integral. As Brett saw it, Suede started to fall apart when Neil stepped down. Also, Brett had been hugely energised by Neil's potential to make the band more modern, more versatile, after he joined. Despite not being able to contribute easily during the writing of *Head Music,* Neil was responsible for some of its finest moments – co-writing 'Electricity', 'Can't Get Enough' (sometimes assumed to be a Richard composition), 'She's in Fashion' and 'He's Gone', all examples of where Neil and Richard worked well together. Brett remembers, 'My instinct was that they were the best team we had. And before it had gone wrong, those had been the happiest days of the band. I always wanted Neil to be involved, even if it was for just one gig.'

For Neil, his 'unfinished business' was reason enough to agree, even if the question of anything longer term could be postponed for another time.

Caveats in place, Brett had the 1995–2001 line-up in full. It was time to respond to the invite.

'WE'VE NOT FINISHED YET'

After 'Everything Will Flow' comes to an end, Brett's demeanour shifts. The crowd quieten.

'There's one person who can't be here tonight,' he says, stuttering slightly. 'Who I miss very dearly. My good friend Jesse, who died three weeks ago.' Up in the box seats, Jesse's mum Anthea is sitting with Jodie, Jodie's mum and John Brandham: 'The whole thing was a party,' Jodie remembers now. 'Then, Brett changed the mood so quickly. [During "He's Gone"] we were all crying our eyes out. It was new to us all. My mum said, "Wow! I did not expect that!" It was like, where did that come from? Where did Clark Kent go? Because he's not an extrovert at home. I suddenly got to see this Suede persona flick on, like a switch. I was so proud. I just remember thinking, oh, thank God I like it!' While Jodie's in the box, Ian Grenfell is down at the sound desk, 'nervous as hell', Roger Daltrey close by, 'freaking out because they were playing too loud.' They *were* too loud. With the Albert Hall's excellent acoustics, you don't need to push. But, Ian says, 'It was great, irreverent, punk – in that space, they didn't really fit.'

Though he often goes full throttle at gigs, Brett's rarely overly sentimental. He doesn't make long speeches. There's no beating of the chest here, no over-the-top emoting in the name of his lost friend – though you'd forgive him for it, raw as the event still is. But the lyrics of 'He's Gone' do the work:

And like the leaves on the trees
Like the Carpenters' song
Like the planes, and the trains, and the lives that were young
He's gone, and it feels like the words to a song.

It's sad, but not sentimental. Universal, but not cheesy. As Brett has said, 'Sometimes you only work out what a song is about years after you've written it. Sometimes you have to wait for life to happen around it, to work it out.' The end of 'He's Gone' sees Richard teasing out the last distorted sounds as Brett looks down at the stage floor. He stays there, Brett and Neil performing 'The Next Life', Brett's first ode to his mum, as a duo.

Few would have come to the Albert Hall expecting to hear 'The Asphalt World'. On record, it's a nine-and-a-half-minute epic exploring obsession and sexual jealousy from the perspective of a man imagining his girlfriend and her own girlfriend together, alone, contained in their 'asphalt world'. For many who love the dramatic side of Suede, this song represents their musical high point – though it's also notorious for contributing to the near-breaking of the band. That history is hard to escape, and tonight they dodge the challenge by playing just the first third of it, replacing the move into the instrumental break with a cute jump cut into 'So Young'. That gets a grand cheer, but some are disappointed too. Negotiating the band's previous lives is tricky.

As 'Metal Mickey' clatters to its familiar ending, something strange happens. The crowd roars, as you'd expect, but then they roar some more, and keep roaring themselves into a spontaneous standing ovation. The band look at each other. They can't work out why it's happening – but it is still happening. After a while, Brett smiles wide and the rest of the band follow suit. Mat's laughing again. They take it in. Brett looks upwards, around the upper circle. Even Neil finally breaks his studied expression. They wait for the noise to die down. It doesn't. They wonder what to do with themselves. Eventually, Brett says, in that flat way: 'We haven't finished yet.' There's a potential double meaning here. It's an end-of-gig outpouring, come too early. But it's obvious, the impact this reception has. The sheer surprise of it. The enjoyment of playing these songs again. The sense that the band hasn't totally been erased. And that people are enjoying themselves.

WE'RE DOING THE RIGHT THING, RIGHT?

Brett drove out to South Buckinghamshire on a hot, late summer day to see Ian at home. By now, they'd built up plenty of trust but, as Ian recalls, 'his confidence had been so knocked that I think he just wanted me to look him in the eye and get reassurances. To see I didn't have any doubts ... He said, "We are doing the right thing, aren't we? Because if this goes wrong it'll be worse than doing nothing."' Ian looked at Brett and replied: 'It's going to be fine. Don't worry.' With agreement from the band and a date set, they scheduled in rehearsals and discussed announcing the return. There were still months of the unknown ahead, but seeing Ian in person helped. For now.

In late 2009, the band began preparations: Brett, Mat, Richard and Neil all in London, and Simon, arriving from Thailand. The first rehearsal was at the Grove in North Kensington on 22 December, between Grenfell Tower and Wormwood Scrubs. Richard's memories suggest how far outside the world of rock stardom he'd been. The day before, he spent time with Peter Sissons, Suede's guitar tech from his first audition right through until the split. The two of them 'dug out the old equipment from a lock-up somewhere', taking it to the Grove to see if it was usable. The instruments were dusty, strings dulled by rust, but when they switched things on, they worked. Guitars can always be set up, new strings fitted, dust wiped away. Richard had used a couple of guitars for recent Artmagic recordings, but almost everything he owned had been in lock-up since December 2003 and needed maintenance. He remembers:

> It was pretty surreal to set up the same amps in the corner, just as I had done in the old days, and play with the volume turned up. For the intervening years I hadn't been on stage at all, and only played at home. But it was good for me to get used to that before I saw everyone else the next day, and talking to Peter about the whole thing made me a lot more comfortable.

The following day it was a little awkward, the band all in the same space for the first time in so long, but as Richard remembers, 'very quickly that was overcome.' In a rehearsal room, unlike on stage, you face each other. That makes it harder to avoid discomfort, also the passage of time. Brett, the others joked, had no right to be so skinny – arguably, he looked younger than their heyday, given he was much healthier now – while Mat was teased for losing hair, Richard for a bit of a paunch. Neil seemed in good health, Peter Pan-esque, like Brett. The band always shared a dry sense of humour, which kicked back in, fast. Neil's presence made a difference to Richard from the start:

> I remember it feeling totally natural to have Neil there – I think he was the only member of the band I had seen socially during any of those years, though not all that often. Although I had very much enjoyed being in a band with Alex (apart from his highly skilled musicianship, he was also a voice of sanity and reason during the dark period of 2002–3, and a lot of fun to be on the road with!), we were obviously going to be playing mostly material that Neil had recorded with us, so it felt right he was there.

On that first day, the band were not quite alone. Mike Christie was there, with his camera. Mike had been present since the very early days of the band and was now a distinguished film-maker. He knew how to stay out of the way. Still, this was a reminder that people were looking again.

The first song they rehearsed was 'Filmstar', which set a positive tone. Brett remembers: 'Instantly, it sounded like us again.' Others echo that it felt easy rehearsing that first song, as if it had been weeks or months, not years. They gradually worked their way through the back catalogue and Richard was surprised to find that, once he was doing it rather than just thinking about it, he had no problem playing material written before he was in the band. As he says now, 'It all just seemed to merge together and flow. Any unsureness I'd felt about those songs just evaporated.'

Different band members had different gaps in their memories about how this or that bit went, or particular sounds, but gaps filled fast. The first day went as well as anyone could have hoped, personally and in terms of piecing together the songs. After rehearsal, Brett, Mat, Simon, Neil and Richard went for a curry at the Star of Bombay on Westbourne Grove and shared how their lives had been going the last six years. Scoping each other out. Tuning back into old dynamics. The second day of rehearsals, Paul Khera came to the Grove on Brett's request: 'He didn't explain much. He just said, "Come around, take the pictures. We're rehearsing. And, you know, it's me back in Suede. We're just doing one show. I just want some documentation." There was no specific project, but it was felt that even if nothing was made public, Brett might want a record of this, one day. They all might.'

In rehearsal, Brett ran the sessions. He'd say what to try next, how he wanted things to sound, while they discussed potential setlists as they went. Brett had played some of these songs recently with his solo band. They'd all reconvene in the new year, to get ready. A few days later, Richard went down to Dorset for Christmas, confident that dealing with the rest of the band was going to be fine: 'Dealing with the public and media for the first time since 2003, though,' he remembers. 'That was a whole different set of anxieties.'

Neil looking on as Brett writes potential setlists on the wall in rehearsal.
Photo by Paul Khera

While Brett was on tour there was a hiatus of two months. On 22 January he played the Shepherd's Bush Empire again, drawing exclusively from his solo albums. (That wasn't a given: in 2008 and 2009, playing in Chile, Peru, Greece, Germany and Sweden, two-thirds of the set was Suede material.) These shows were promoting *Slow Attack*, though, so that made sense. Following a twelve-date European tour he returned to small venues in the UK. Brett was touring with a full band now, including Didz Hammond on bass – Didz had been the bassist in the Dirty Pretty Things (alongside the Libertines' Carl Barât) and the Cooper Temple Clause before that. The sound was louder, more expansive. Brett said he still loved the old songs, and was proud of them, but needed a break from Suede material for a while. Perhaps he imagined a longer break. This solo tour was more raucous – he got his time away from Suede, though briefly, and might have wondered if he was building something, only to turn away just as it was getting going. Maybe they'd underestimated the interest, though, in the Albert Hall. Were Suede really just going to do one gig and disappear?

The band reconvened on 17 February, back in the Grove, for five days. The following week, a warm-up gig at the Ritz in Manchester was announced (capacity 1,500), followed shortly after by the 100 Club (capacity 320).* The 100 Club was first. It's no coincidence they went for these kinds of venues. At Mat put it later, 'the reunion had to feel like five boys playing the Southampton Joiners Arms.† To hide behind anything would have been cheating.' That Southampton gig was Suede legend, one of the first times the crowd jumped on stage, when the band were first blowing up. What Mat meant was, no gimmicks, not too much protection. Suede played the 100 Club just once before, in September 1992. That was the week 'Metal Mickey' saw them break the top twenty for the first time. It had been a long time since they'd played somewhere that small.

The week after rehearsals, awful news: Jesse had taken his own life. Brett, Jodie and friends felt this keenly – anyone who survives a

* The 100 Club often hosts secret/warm-up shows for major bands. Their website mentions Suede as a highlight from the '90s; also the Sex Pistols and the Clash from the '70s.

† Legendary Suede gig. Mat's future publisher and fellow writer Tariq Goddard was there.

life of addiction loses too many people. Brett was devastated by the loss, but he had to carry on. Anyway, there was no backing out now. Preparations were completed in the shadow of Jesse's death. Richard had lobbied hard for including 'He's Gone'. It was already in the setlist. Now it seemed essential.

A REMINDER OF WHAT YOU'VE MISSED: THE 100 CLUB AND THE RITZ

A few days after Jesse's funeral, on 20 March, the band packed their gear and headed off to soundcheck for their first gig as a five-piece in nine years.

As far as most fans are concerned, the reunion was the Albert Hall – in part, because it's so often referred to as the start of this era, in part because it was later made into a film. But for Richard, the 100 Club was more nerve-wracking. One of the things he'd appreciated was being able to 'disappear from public view and live an entirely private life, not have to be photographed and filmed, gawped at and discussed'. That was about to change, and he felt a sense of foreboding. The 100 Club being a small venue made no difference.

Returning to playing live with Suede was intense for Richard in a way it wasn't for others. Brett, who'd gigged through most of the year so far. Simon, drumming across the world. Neil may also have felt pressure, but he'd performed live plenty recently and tends to show little externally. Live, Neil was known for concentrating on the music. This, for some, was part of his appeal. A distanced, elevated cool. At times, it seemed like he didn't notice the crowd at all. As for Mat, he never used to get anxious and was looking forward to the reunion. But, looking back now, Mat says he'd 'pretty much forgotten how much I valued playing live. The sounds you hear on stage, the amp at your back. The way you forget yourself and just do it.' He was about to get a reminder of what he'd missed.

In those first weeks of 2010, Richard experienced more stress than ever; for the first time, he sought medical help for anxiety. This wasn't about people. Or music. As he remembers: 'I was quite simply terrified of stepping back on stage again.' He didn't necessarily think he'd *never* perform again, though at times he might have wondered. It was more that, as a natural introvert, he'd always struggled, and the passing years only seemed to increase his fear. On joining the band in 1994, though outwardly he seemed unfazed – he was, after all, a teenage guitar virtuoso, skill never in question – he felt the pressure of judgement, comparison, potential dismissal. Brett's pressure was of a different kind, especially once news of the reunion got out via an *NME* article published shortly before the Teenage Cancer Trust's official announcement on 1 February.

Mat contrasts the expectations placed on musicians now and then. Previously, there was more of an expectation of confidence, a pose that most guitar bands struck as a way of coping. Bands were expected to put each other down. They were asked in interviews about who they hated and often said things they now wince at. For extroverts, for alphas, that came more naturally. But not for Richard:

> I always considered myself a musician, not a pop star, and I was happily terrible at the latter. At school I had no idea how to be cool and didn't think it was at all important. So learning in '94 that as a member of Suede I couldn't just stand at the back and concentrate on my playing, I had to quickly learn to be some sort of show-off, was hard enough. But having to face that again in my thirties, after such a long break from public life, and with a whole new set of grown-up anxieties, was much more difficult.

The 100 Club suggested he could overcome those difficulties. They trialled an Albert Hall setlist and the opening salvo, from 'She' through to 'Pantomime Horse', felt right. They tried out 'She's in Fashion', too. This was Jodie's very first experience of a Suede gig, and on the night there was little anxiety around. That said, for Richard, 'the whole thing for me was a blur of foreboding, panic, adrenaline and extreme relief once it was over.' He was light-headed after coming off stage, describing the experience as something he had 'survived'. Someone made a dumb joke and he laughed for minutes, mildly hysterical. Reviews of the night were more positive than expected: Kevin Harley in the *Independent* called 'She' 'panther-sleek', 'Can't Get Enough' 'rampaging' and Brett was described as throwing himself into the occasion 'with glorious abandon'. Overall, he wrote, the gig was in 'the spirit of celebration, earned in rivers of sweat'. The crowd contained many for whom Suede were not just a band, but an essential part of their identities. Future leader of Suede fan group the Insatiable Ones Sam Hand recalls the 100 Club gig, saying that night felt like a kind of rebirth. 'I'd lost my dad to cancer six weeks before and I was in a dark place. That night magic happened and I felt hope, passion and comfort through Suede's performance. That night I vowed to follow Suede as much as I could.' She wasn't alone.

Next was Manchester. They opened with a curveball – the much-loved 'Europe Is Our Playground'. Otherwise, they played most of the set from the night before. The quiet, plaintive piano-and-vocal of 'The Next Life' appeared in place of 'She's in Fashion'. They'd rehearsed both 'Lost in TV' and 'Obsessions' at the Grove, and in the two-song encore they played 'Obsessions' first, Neil having bought a chromatic harmonica so he could play Alex's part from the record. They finished with *Dog Man Star* album track, 'The 2 of Us'. Though over half the set was rooted in the band's early days, Richard was happy:

> The Ritz was a much more enjoyable experience for me personally, as I was in control of my emotions by then and able to concentrate fully on performing well. Plus, for all these shows there was a network of support backstage, old and trusted friends such as Mike ... Peter [the guitar tech], Donald [the hairdresser] and Tania [make-up] who eased my nerves and made me feel part of a team, a family.

Richard had lived with Mike as a teenager, after joining the band and moving to London. All these years later, his presence made a difference. Some performers always experience stage fright. What might be freeing can be torture to others, every time. The sweats, the shakes. Still others perform for years with no problem, then get stage fright and it sticks, before one day evaporating again, without warning. For Richard, the 100 Club was like an instant cure, and the Ritz, just twenty-four hours later, was easy. They were nearly ready. In the van after the gig, for the first time ever, Suede were able to get instant feedback – this was a new world, now – checking Twitter and searching 'Suede Ritz' to find the response. Once again, it was encouraging.

The big show was three days later. For this one there were family, friends, as well as the inner circle. Mike had been tasked with capturing the band backstage – for what, no one knew yet – using Simon's camcorder, while Matt Askem filmed the whole show. So there would be at least one record of the night, though of course no one knew if this was a full stop, or a mistake. But they had a sense, after the two warm-ups, that they sounded good. The Albert Hall had sold out 'in nanoseconds', tickets exchanging for crazy sums outside the venue to the last moment.

The setlist had been an ongoing discussion. 'The Living Dead', an early favourite Brett could play himself, acoustic, was back in. 'She's in Fashion' and 'Europe Is Our Playground' were out. So too, 'Obsessions'

– several say they 'got cold feet' when it came to including anything off *A New Morning*. Neil recalls material from that period 'wasn't *verboten*' from day one, it was 'more like some of these things calcified as time went on'. Perhaps the level of stigma associated with the record – for band, audience, critics – was ultimately too much to face down.

As the Albert Hall approached, Ian noticed Brett was increasingly twitchy. Suede were just one of nine consecutive nights of Teenage Cancer Trust shows, with Noel Gallagher, Arctic Monkeys and the Specials also appearing, before the Who on the final night. Two nights before Suede it was Them Crooked Vultures, the hard rock supergroup featuring Dave Grohl (Nirvana/Foo Fighters), Josh Homme (Queens of the Stone Age) and Led Zeppelin's John Paul Jones, in the same venue. Ian and Brett arrived late and conspicuous, their guest tickets at the very lip of the stage. They didn't stay long, but they noticed the huge rug on the stage, band quite far back, creating more of 'a jamming vibe'. Brett said to Ian, 'We can't do that. Tell Charlie [previous band manager back on board as tour manager] we have to move everything as close to the front as possible.' In every respect, they wanted to lean *forward*. A couple of nights later, it was Suede's turn. By now, Ian's phone was ringing; they'd had an offer to play the Smukfest in Denmark, where Suede remained a big draw. Would they take it? Ian didn't even mention the invite yet. Backstage before the show, he heard the band agreeing it was going to take a lot for them to do any more than this.

THE END OF THE START

The rest of the gig rushes by. They follow 'Metal Mickey' with a trio of singles – 'The Wild Ones', 'New Generation' and finally 'Beautiful Ones'. 'Thank you, you're beautiful,' says Brett, before leaving the stage. It's not the end, though. There'll be an encore. Of course there will. Brett comes out from behind the curtain alone, with an acoustic guitar. Sitting on a stool at the front of the stage, almost emptied out, he plays 'The Living Dead', the line 'could have walked in the sky but we stare at the wall' delivered a cappella. Then he's joined by the others, and they play 'The 2 of Us'.

Brett gives no sense he's planning on making this a habit. Addressing the crowd, it seems like he's guarding against emotion, or trying to be genuine, but struggling to express himself: 'I don't have anything to say about all this except it's been a lot of fun,' he tells the crowd before final song, 'Saturday Night', Suede's most hopeful moment. 'And you've been absolutely wonderful, and, I feel very happy to be here tonight.' (Truly, he doesn't sound all that happy. You wonder if there's a joke coming. It doesn't.) Then he adds the same line he used at the 100 Club: 'Let's do it again in seven years.' Look closely at Mat, Simon, Richard or Neil in this moment, searching for whether they know something the audience doesn't, and you'll notice, there's not a flicker.

Backstage after the gig, as Mike films, energy is high and the verdict is in. Celebration, joy. They ask each other, could you believe that ovation after 'Metal Mickey'? In the moment, Richard said, he thought someone had wandered onto the stage or something. He looks around, says to the room, 'Right, what's next?'

They couldn't have hoped for more.

UPDATING THE WIKIPEDIA ENTRY: AFTER THE ALBERT HALL

Well, we didn't know then, but that wasn't it.

Journalist and Suede fan Luke Turner attended all three gigs, reviewing them for the *NME* and the *Quietus*. Something written within hours of a gig has a different energy from something written years later, in the knowledge of what happened next. Turner wrote:

> It's not yet clear whether there will be any further Suede gigs. In a way, it'd be perfect if there weren't, if these three special nights in Manchester and London would make for Suede's epitaph, a final vindication and celebration for band and for us, and sod the rest of 'em ... Yet a rejuvenated Suede are on such astounding form that you can't help but hope they do give it another go, and silence the doubters with a dose of this wonderful, beautiful, love and poison.

An epitaph is a kind of full stop; if that's what this was going to be, then they'd done what Mat hoped for. As he put it, with a half-laugh, 'altering the end of that Wikipedia entry, you know?' But it wasn't a full stop, or an epitaph. As they were already saying to each other, that was too good not to do again.

The Albert Hall show proved this version of Suede had decent self-awareness. The balance they'd strike for the next few years was already evident. Sets were divided between a selection of Butler-era and Oakes–Codling era favourites, but not necessarily singles. ('Electricity', for example, was a top-five hit, but Brett didn't like it. 'Stay Together', a top-three hit, was jettisoned too.) You could argue with individual choices, but they generally had a keener sense of what was good about the first era, and also what should quietly be left behind. This was the approach, then: singles complemented with a sprinkling of tried and tested, fan-favourite deep cuts. 'Killing of a Flashboy' was welcomed regularly in sets like an old hit – while they routinely ignored *A New Morning*. When they played songs from *Head Music*, they selected the ones that, well ... sounded the most like Suede.

The Albert Hall can be intimidating for many experienced artists, but Richard wasn't bothered. In fact, by this point he was probably less nervous than others. He remembers: 'The gig went fantastically well, we had that famous couple of minutes of standing ovation, and I remember being unable to stop myself grinning. Surreal as it was, it was still the moment when I knew it had been the right thing to be involved with the reunion, and that I could actually enjoy the public side of my job again. I guess you could say my self-esteem finally started to climb after that.' The Albert Hall was also crucial for Brett. It really was a new beginning. As captured by Mike on camera, after coming off stage, Brett said to the rest of the band: 'I've taken a lot of drugs in my life, and nothing compares to that.'

It's tempting to overstate the importance of the Albert Hall. Press articles, interviews and broadsheet pieces on the band's recent albums (these days, most reviews are also overviews in brief of a band's 'official narrative') now routinely report the history in a few lines. The Teenage Cancer Trust was a one-off, then the 'Metal Mickey' ovation happened, then they set off to make beautiful new music together. Not so. Anyway, it was three gigs. And it was an incremental process that spooled out over the next couple of years. Later in 2010, Brett was touring solo – Hong Kong, China, Japan. When he announced, 'Here's an old one,' he had to qualify, responding to excitement in the audience – 'No, not that old.' During that tour, he'd already begun writing and recording *Black Rainbows*, which was released the following year. In 2010, emboldened, Richard also came out of hibernation with Artmagic. Their first shows were in June 2010, a few months after the Albert Hall. Neil popped up with Penguin Cafe, as well, on Radio 3 that September, back at the Albert Hall as part of the Proms. Quite the tone shift from the reunion.

Genuinely taken aback by the response, Suede decided to do more later in the year, too. The key, everyone agreed, was to try and keep it special. Not to set off on an endless tour around the world hawking the old material, becoming exhausted and tired of each other, of the old music too, but rather to spend a little time appreciating it. There wasn't the whole band infrastructure in place again yet, anyway. The first show was that Smukfest show in Denmark, the country that stayed most loyal in the early 2000s, when most other places had switched off. In October and November, they played the 200-year-old Élysée Montmartre in Paris and the polygon-shaped Cirque Royal in Brussels, as a warm-up for the O2. The tour grew a little, but not much. In each place, they were pleasantly surprised by the reaction.

On 1 November 2010 the double album *The Best of Suede* was released, put together by Brett, and Bernard too. The first disc was singles-only (no 'Positivity' or 'Attitude', from 2002–3, though all the others made it), while the second largely concentrated on early years, album tracks and B-sides like 'She', 'This Hollywood Life', 'By the Sea' and 'Still Life'. The album went to number thirty-one in the UK – there was little expectation of massive success, there being no new music to promote – though it was enough to be encouraging, and the critical reception showed a kind of slow, quiet rehabilitation. Reviews were often written by people astonished to find Suede weren't a shit '90s punchline after all. Again, incremental, baby-steps success came through being selective. Realising what was good about the band the first time around. Curating carefully. There were no left-field attempts to persuade crowds to love songs they didn't love. *The Best of Suede* was a response to what people had loved about the band, as much as it was a presentation of the band's view of what constituted their 'best' music.

Anyone that tells you everyone in the band immediately changed course the morning after the Albert Hall, refocusing on Suede, is forgetting things. Most were multitasking, unsure how things would play out. Not just occasionally doing other things, but pursuing them. There was no talk of new music in public in 2010, either. That said, in Simon's words, 'the Royal Albert Hall was the best show we had ever done. We came off stage afterwards and thought, we can't possibly stop now, not after that.' More offers arrived, and within limits, they started saying yes. Bit by bit, by the close of the year, the band were inching towards something. Return.

CHAPTER 2

bloodsports
'too much is not enough'

'We had an aim with the record to do two things. First: reconnect with people who had bought the records previously. And second: for it to be worthy of a contemporary artist. It had to be worthy of being taken on its own terms as something of value. We had to remind people of what Suede was, but also show people where we were at now.'

—Neil

SORRY, BLOB – JANUARY 2012

'I love them. But I had to tell them,' says Ed Buller. He's wincing and smiling. 'I was probably a bit harsh. I can be. But I think that's what they want me for. On some level they might know it's not good enough, but they don't always want to tell each other ... I tell them, "Sorry Blob, but that's just shit!"' Ed shrugs, grins. Says, 'Then we knock heads for a bit.'

Swivelling in the big chair at the desk of his home studio, Ed is looking back on the process of making *Bloodsports*. His energy is infectious, knowledge encyclopaedic. He's forthright, animated, the biggest Suede fan in any room, their regular 'first listener', the 'expert in course correction' who prides himself on being alert to the wrong move, when he feels it might be made. Okay, so he's likely to forget the bass player's name, he might lose the odd recorded part somewhere, he's getting more irritable with age in the studio, and he always thinks he knows best. But Ed is every bit as invested in the band's success as they are. He cares too much and can't stop himself from saying what he thinks. It's that approach, the evidence suggests, that gets shit done. And well.

It's easier to laugh now. The early days of the reunion are history already. Also, Ed's dominance – Brett says it 'probably went too far, but then, we probably needed it' – doesn't seem as important now as it would have done when they were all knocking heads. Not only that, but Ed set the pattern for a way of working that has largely held since. So long after they first worked together on their debut single in early 1992, he's still deeply proud of his connection to, and influence on, the band.

Ed has a reputation independent of Suede. He's also known for his work on Pulp's breakthrough *His 'n' Hers* in the '90s for instance, three albums with White Lies, and plenty of others too – but few producers are so closely associated with one band. These days Ed is the oft-derided, oft-indulged 'Imperial Thumb' who grants his benevolence – or doesn't – when that thumb goes up or down at some new part that reminds him – or doesn't remind him enough – of something they recorded together, way back when. He's continually referencing '70s records they don't like or know. He's always making the case, pushing for change, wondering how they might get back on the radio. (He's just spitballing. He has no idea, really. None of them does.) Move on. Become something new. He's the grumpy uncle who only wants the best for you, if only you'd just *listen* properly.

That's how things are now. In 2012, though, they were very different. Buller and Suede were working together for the first time in sixteen years – 'which is a *million* music years,' he tells me – and, in the period from 1996 to 2011, everyone's lives had changed beyond recognition. For starters, the used-to-be kids of the band, Richard and Neil, had grown up and up-skilled. If Ed was the sixth leg of the Suede table, it's worth remembering that table hadn't had all its legs since Brett got clean, or since Suede fell out of fashion, hard. Wounds were raw from the end of the band's first life and everyone understood they'd only get one chance to start afresh. That meant nerves. Suede have always operated with a small inner circle, returning to the same trusted faces. But was this really the right move, going back, to go forward? Were they being sentimental? Or coming back to Ed Buller for more because they didn't know what else to do?

As Ed sees it, there are two kinds of people in his line of work. First, there are engineer–producers. They facilitate recordings, support a band's vision but don't challenge it, listening to what the musicians say they want, even if they don't really understand anything about the recording process. These people try to put that plan into action in good faith, no matter what. Then there are producer–engineers. That's people like him. People who question the artist's intentions, influence sound and instrumentation, lean into conflict, refuse to record songs they don't like, and make themselves an active part of the process from the first drum take onwards. In part, Ed believes, 'Suede want someone like me *because* I'm a producer–engineer – everyone accepts this means they will be challenged. They *want* to be. But being challenged is still fucking hard.' When they asked if he'd produce their reunion album, in late 2011, Suede had already spent half a year making new music. They'd had a good time doing it. They felt positive. Optimistic about recording once more. Then, in their first serious meeting, Ed poured cold water over every note.

'They had these ... *songs*,' says Ed now, the word 'songs' delivered like a swear word. 'But they could ruin them all over again. There was no way I was going to let that happen.' He winces again, considering alternative, disastrous timelines. How it all could have been so different. Then adds, leaning forward, 'So I didn't.'

ONE OF THOSE BANDS

In autumn 2010, Suede toured the UK and Europe, leading up to one of the biggest shows of their career at the O2 Arena in London on 7 December. Suede were never an arena band. Even in their heyday, they never operated at that level. And yet, all these years later, here they were. For one night, at least. Now there was no wondering if there was an audience. They'd been seeing that audience all year, singing at the top of their lungs. But was it purely a nod to the past, or evidence of a potential future?

The autumn had been good to everyone. On 14 October, Artmagic played their first proper headline London show at the Hoxton Underbelly, the 220-capacity venue 'absolutely rammed and fizzing with genuine excitement'. David Barnett, doing the guest list for Richard, recalls there was 'an audible gasp when Brett, Neil and Simon sneaked in near the beginning of the set ... all in regulation black Suedewear with newly dyed hair, really looking like a band.' A little breathless, David wrote in his diary, 'I'd forgotten how charming Brett can be. Neil looked about 22.' The Suede tour kicked off later that month at Bush Hall, a few England dates followed by Spain, France, Belgium and Sweden.

Five days before the O2 they played the Paradiso, the grand ex-church known as Amsterdam's 'pop temple', famous for Pink Floyd playing there in 1968 just after Syd Barrett's departure. Brett spoke to Neil before that show, scoping out how he felt about making a new record. He also spoke to Richard, one on one. They'd all seen enough since March to try, though for everyone this meant commitment-shuffling. Brett wasn't cancelling his next solo album (he was recording in early 2011, writing with Leo Abrahams again). Richard wasn't abandoning Artmagic (he and Sean had nearly a full album of material now). Penguin Cafe's album *A Matter of Life* ... was coming out in January 2011, too. They agreed to regroup, after a break, to start writing together. No announcement, no pressure. At the O2 they delivered an expanded set, the reaction described in the *Independent* as 'rabidly celebratory', Brett taking the stage 'like a wronged man scenting vindication'. Andy Gill wrote, '[I]f they can't feel renewed fire in their bellies after a night like this, what are they doing it for?' Twelve months earlier, Richard's guitars had been in a lock-up, under six years of dust. A lot had changed in a year.

No one knew what a new Suede album might sound like, but look at the 2010 setlists and you could take an educated guess. 'What we wanted,' Mat remembers, 'was a record that simply said this is what you've been missing. We wanted a reminder of what was great about the band.' No wild new experiments, no avant-garde left turns. Band discussions focused on finding the best version of their past. But no one wanted a poor imitation of what they used to be. How to tell people what they'd been missing, without just repeating themselves?

In between side projects Suede played a handful of spring shows, and the context got them thinking. 'Everyone seemed to be reforming,' says Mat, 'Bands of different generations, genres, from America especially.' Even just within American hard rock, many '90s big hitters were coming back around. In 2010, Rage Against the Machine reformed, teasing new material that never came. Soundgarden were back, touring old songs. Guns N' Roses. Jane's Addiction. 'One of the things we noticed,' says Mat, 'was the tendency to bombast, like they weren't particularly sure about their powers.' Of course, Suede weren't sure either. But they knew they didn't want to come across as what Mat calls 'another one of *those bands*.' Over-performing, trying too hard, making like they still had it. They wanted to avoid what Brett called 'the living death of playing exclusively old songs, forever'. But also, they didn't want to try making a new album, then back out. Or worse, deliver something bad, then tour it, grim-faced. They'd done that before. No thanks.

In April 2011 they played Coachella in California, billed as the London Suede. (They were sued by an obscure jazz singer already using the 'Suede' moniker, way back when, and the restriction still applies today.) It was a strange lead-up, with Mat's visa delayed, the band unsure whether he'd be allowed into the country. (His name had been problematic before. Two of the 9/11 bombers had been Usmans, and the band's travel history made the US tricky.) That year, several legacy acts were at Coachella. Leftfield (last record 1995, reunited 2010). Lauryn Hill (last album, 1998, with only a couple of one-off singles since self-imposed exile). There were reunion gigs for Wire and Duran Duran, too, as well as a surprise Mars Volta/At the Drive-In reunion, with Cedric Bixler-Zavala joining Omar Rodríguez-López on stage for his whole 'solo' slot.

It seemed like there were plenty of examples of what they wanted to avoid, then, and precious few good models. (Back home, the Stone Roses were 2011's great reunion gone wrong, much fanfare followed by a couple of terrible singles and an abandoned new album, then quietly disbanding again.) In the end, Mat never made Coachella; that visa didn't come through and the others had to scramble for a plan. With typical understatement, Neil simply switched to bass and, in a sign of how little what a band does is noticed sometimes, literally nobody asked why Suede had become a four-piece. (Lyndsey Parker's *NME* blog detailing the '12 Most Memorable Moments' from Coachella that year put Suede at a lofty number two, saying they 'gave a masterclass in how to stage a proper Coachella comeback' – but made no mention at all of Mat's absence.)

The experience was energising. It was a mostly empty tent, though Brett, who loves a crisis, accepted the circumstances as a challenge. This felt good. They could adapt! Persevere! Triumph over visa adversity, even! In Brett's words, 'You never cancel a gig. You always find a way. Then you feel good that you found a way.' But it also made them determined not to coast. In May, they played three sold-out nights at the Brixton Academy promoting the album reissues, where the crowds were absolutely jumping, way more than expected. By now they'd had a glut of opportunities to notice they'd been remembered. At the Jisan Valley Festival in South Korea for example, in July 2011, Suede headlined the third night, with Arctic Monkeys and the Chemical Brothers the other headliners. They drove way out into this forest venue that seemed so far from anywhere on the other side of the world, playing, randomly, after Incubus, in the driving rain. They showed up expecting very little, only to find literally thousands of people bouncing to 'Beautiful Ones', the entire ground shaking. Wow, they thought. There might be life in this thing yet. Enough to actually make it sustainable. With these experiences fresh in the mind, Suede looked around and realised that if they didn't want to be pegged as one of *those kinds of bands*, it was time to stop hawking the old stuff, and make something new.

NO PLAN, NO AGENDA, NO TIMELINE

At first, Brett led the process. Given they were coming in cold, after so long, he suggested just trying some ideas out – no plan, agenda or timeline. Richard recalls, 'I was fine with that, but had no real sense of whether we could come up with anything decent. It took me a while to join in as I was busy with a lot of Artmagic stuff in 2011, and my head was in that world.' The first ideas came from Neil, Brett and Mat. Around this time, Neil and Brett had been in the studio remastering *Coming Up*, *Head Music* and *A New Morning*, for rereleased, expanded versions. (Brett wrote self-critical liner notes for remasters of all the first five albums.) Everyone expected it to take a while to 'get the chakras spinning' in Neil's words, or 'the muscle strengthened', in Richard's. But it was fun to write together again. Not nerve-wracking, as nothing was at stake. Not yet, anyway. Not really.

Richard remembers the first song that caught his ear was 'I Don't Know Why', written by Neil and Brett in summer 2011. There was also 'a lot of darker, more gothy stuff floating around too,' he recalls. 'I remember Brett was experimenting with a more Peter Murphy-like approach back then' (Murphy of Bauhaus, the hugely influential goth pioneers). Encouraged, Richard started pitching in when they moved from writing demos to getting together as a five-piece in London that autumn. The first song he wrote with Brett since 2003 was called 'Someone Better'. 'It was pretty unremarkable,' he recalls now, 'but it had a good energy, and when we began rehearsing at the Grove towards the end of 2011, we'd always start with that.'

Along with these, there were several other songs rehearsed at the Grove too, including a Mat demo, 'Gothtopus', retitled 'Bloodsport' after Brett's part was added on April Fool's Day 2011.* Even Simon was coming up with ideas, recording a couple of demos on a little keyboard he borrowed from Mat, including one that became 'Falling Planes'.† Then

---

* NB: There was also a song called 'Blood Sports', written on 29/7/12 to a tune written by Neil and Richard called '(Here's Looking at) Euclid'.

† Simon was chuffed Brett had written something to his first idea, but when nothing happened with his second one, he didn't do any more. In Neil's words: '50 per cent demo-to-song conversion rate? Elite numbers.'

there were Neil pieces like 'Future Nightmare' (post-punk, angular, noisy) and 'Cold War' (more indie rock). Richard remembers another dark, moody demo written by Neil called 'Evensong' that became 'Sabotage'. 'It sounded like a winner to all of us,' he says, 'a recognisably Suede sound but not an obvious copy of something we'd already done.' Brett remembers his frustration feeding into the music:

> I remember coming up with a couple of vocal ideas at Neil's but then I took the music away thinking, no ... I often find that if I'm writing vocal ideas in someone else's presence, then they're just good melodically, but I have to take them away and let myself go, really let rip as a singer, push my voice ... So that was 'Sabotage'. I wrote something at Neil's, and I took it away. Then brought it back, better.

In a sense, Richard playing catch-up is typical of his story: he usually takes longer to get going than others, no matter the task. But it's also different. Everyone else writing, with Richard unintentionally sidelined, didn't fit how they'd done things at the height of their powers. It was fine everyone contributing but they'd done this once before, with no real core writing team, towards the end of their first life, and that led to a lack of identity in the music. (There were seven different writing combinations used on the *A New Morning* sessions.) Also, others wondered if Richard was going to take a lead, as on *Coming Up*. He had, after all, gone quiet before. (On *Head Music*, Richard wrote 'Everything Will Flow', one of the album's best songs, plus B-sides like 'Leaving', though at the time Brett was more interested in writing his own music. *A New Morning* featured just two Anderson–Oakes songs.) As with the Albert Hall, the rest of the band were patient, waiting to see if Richard would warm to writing again, as he'd warmed to playing together.

Richard remembers this period as idyllic. They rehearsed at the Grove every week, turning up on their bikes in the rain, playing exclusively new ideas, then packing down at the end of the day. In his words, 'It was pretty much like starting again as a new band, and a world away from the glamour of playing old hits on a big festival stage somewhere in Europe.' The quiet, hard work was good practice for what was coming, and operating this way appealed to Richard's personality: for now, they were protected from any response. Was that healthy though? Also, Richard found it frustrating that once he did start coming up with things, most of his ideas were quickly discarded: 'I couldn't seem to find a common ground for inspiration with Brett,' he says. 'But listening back to that music now, I can hear that it was simply un-Suede-like. I needed time to find that style again.'

The year 2011 was fragmented: building other lives made it challenging to then re-prioritise Suede. Artmagic did live gigs in February, May and October, all in London. The show at the Windmill Brixton, the night before the Suede three-night residency round the corner, was the launch for Richard and Sean's first EP, *I Keep on Walking*,* and they recorded their debut album, *Become the One You Love*, over the summer. In the first half of 2011, meanwhile, Brett recorded *Black Rainbows*; it was released in September in the UK. After that he was touring, doing promotion, interviews, a now-rare TV appearance on Jools Holland where he performed the single 'Brittle Heart'. He was busy.

The critical reception to *Black Rainbows* was a muted improvement. There were exceptions (the *NME* called it 'his best solo work to date'), but plenty of publications with quite different readerships (*Clash*, the

* David Barnett was on the merch stall, selling CDs, as documented in his diary.

Independent, Record Collector) were damning. It's fair to say, then, that Brett's focus was elsewhere for part of 2011. He must have wondered what his chances were, after four middlingly reviewed records with dwindling sales, of getting a better reception in future, if he kept going it alone. Quietly, Brett's view was changing: he confided to Jodie that he felt like his solo work was 'becoming a vanity project', realising 'this wasn't going to see him into old age'. The timing of the switch to Suede was perfect. Brett and Jodie had been together for four years. They wanted to have a child.

When Suede did work together in 2011, part of that time was spent on the road. That year they played thirty-five shows in twenty countries, on four continents, places like Turkey, Indonesia, South Korea, Ireland and Japan. It was enjoyable, and not quite like the relentless schedules of yesteryear, but touring took time and energy away from writing. The *Pitchfork* review of *Black Rainbows* said Suede clearly had 'no intention of recording new material'. (Though that wasn't true, they hadn't told anyone, so understandably audiences and critics thought they were just another old band taking a victory lap.) As it happened, Suede thought they *did* have new songs. And they wanted to test them out live.

But first, they wanted to get a producer on board for the new record. It was tricky. The band machinery was in transition, for a start. Ian Grenfell had been Brett's manager since 2006 – now he became Suede's, too. His company, Quietus Management, was bought by Live Nation in 2011, also representing bands like the Pretenders. Didz Hammond, a key presence in Brett's live set-up, was charged with a new day job: looking after Suede from a new London office. 'Some pivot,' as Brett recalls. 'And at the time, a risk.' Meanwhile, Suede didn't have a record deal, and they'd been out of circulation forever. What to do, then? Who to approach?

From their first life, they knew they'd never go back to producers they'd used after Ed. Steve Osborne, widely known for his work with U2, Placebo and New Order, produced *Head Music*; despite some good songs, the atmosphere had been poor, and the combination of personalities hadn't worked. *A New Morning* had multiple producers: first, Tony Hoffer. (That didn't go well.) Then Stephen Street, widely respected for his work with the Smiths, the Pretenders and closely associated with Blur, for whom he produced four albums. Also, John Leckie, producer of the Stone Roses – though there was little love for *A New Morning*, nor any desire to go back to those who worked on it.

Suede weren't well connected or in touch. They couldn't just call up a younger name producer to make them sound more modern (that would probably be a mistake, anyway). How much would a 'name' producer cost, and where would the money come from? At this stage, things were still ad hoc, on faith, and the band could see they'd have to operate differently to get back up on their feet. Less money. Less studio time. Making better demos, themselves. If they were to have a chance at making this work in a fast-changing music landscape where album sales no longer dominated, that was non-negotiable. Everything led back to the producer question. There was only one person who would work with Suede without knowing how long it was going to go on for, what it would cost, in time, energy, money. Without even knowing if they had any songs. Ed's own reputation had fluctuated in the in-between years too, and he'd moved back and forth to the US more than once. But recently, he'd been rehabilitated in the eyes of some who had written him off, owing to the White Lies album *To Lose My Life ...*, a recent UK number one. That aside, Suede knew Ed. They trusted him. And his work with Suede was unquestioned. Neil recalls, 'We needed to get whatever mojo we'd lost back. That meant calling Ed. We'd made our best records with Ed.'

Brett kept it simple. He just said, 'Want to make another Suede record?' Ed agreed immediately. He, like the band, had something to prove.

STRESS-TESTING AT BELOW FREEZING

It's December 2011.

Before Christmas, the band leave home for two low-key shows – the Glav club in St Petersburg, then Blastfest in Moscow. The idea is to stress-test songs they've been practising recently at the Grove, without songs leaking or being reviewed back home. They think they may have the bulk of a good new record, or at least part of one. In advance of the trip, Mat exudes his usual press confidence, declaring this represents the end of the on–off reunion tour that's been going since the Albert Hall: 'We're gonna be good,' he tells the *Moscow Times*. 'It's up to the audience to make it an amazing show.'

In St Petersburg on 16 December, below freezing outside, they open with a trio of live debuts for new songs 'The Only', 'Someone Better' and 'I Don't Know Why', the latter a Neil and Brett collaboration Richard describes as 'harking back to classic, *Coming Up*-style singles', featuring 'twisted but romantic-sounding chords'. They see it as a key potential comeback song. Everyone has to concentrate; some of this material is just weeks old, Brett holding the lyrics to the new songs on sheets of A4 as he sings. Between hits and deep cuts, they weave four more new songs into the rest of the set – Simon's ballad 'Falling Planes', then another back-to-back trio towards the end of the gig: 'Future Nightmare', 'Cold War' and lastly 'Sabotage', only demoed in November.*

---

* Neil: 'Brett didn't introduce "Future Nightmare", so people online had to guess at the song title from the lyrics. The chorus went 'You are the colour of woman, you are

'Sabotage' is the first reunion song where Brett sounds like himself. It's full of longing and the suggestion of secrecy at work in a relationship gone sour: 'I touch her things when I think I'm alone / With self-control that approaches mania'. 'Positivity' it's not. But it's also not parody. Towards the song's end the narrative takes a turn, and we might be listening to something off *Dog Man Star*: 'Alone in the climate of her greed / Her love is the shape of mother'. The guitars open out splendidly at the close. In St Petersburg, though, it falls flat, as all the other new songs do. Neil looks out and sees people just standing there, unmoved.

Two days later in Moscow, just two new songs survive – 'The Only', played first again, and 'Falling Planes'. This in a set more tailored to Blastfest, a Russian festival chosen as Brett played there in 2008, with Mat on bass. The reception was good then; after the show Brett told Mat they should have played Moscow with Suede, though tonight the response to the new songs is polite at best. Richard is trying so hard to remember his new parts that he hardly registers the reception. This show is less important, as it's a festival. The St Petersburg show was the one that mattered. They leave Russia wondering what it all means; if it means anything at all.

At home, the band check the feedback. Richard remembers: 'We read online reactions from fans afterwards, and it was very sobering to hear how unimpressed they were with all of it. It made us realise we had a lot of work to do before we could think about recording anything new.' But they still hope they have *something* to work with. Anyway: would this response be the same everywhere? Live, audiences usually

---

my future nightmare.' On the suede.co.uk forum, these lines were often misheard, the title sometimes assumed to be 'Cannibal Woman'. Or worse.

want to hear songs they already love. So what if St Petersburg didn't respond immediately?

This, then, is where we are at the start of 2012. There's no schedule. Ed isn't being paid. In the meeting with Brett, Neil and Richard he announces *all* the Russia songs should be ditched and they should start again. Even 'Sabotage' doesn't impress the Imperial Thumb. Where's the chorus, he asks? It keeps sounding like it's headed towards one, but never quite gets there. If Suede are going to come back, they need to come back with bangers. To have any chance of being taken seriously as a going concern rather than as a nostalgia act, they're going to need ten of them.

At first, the band are unsure about ditching the Russia songs, but Ed argues too much of the new material belies a lack of confidence. That's understandable, after all this time away, but he encourages them to work through it. There's plenty of attitude in there, he thinks. That's something. They're forceful in places and hit some Suede lyrical and musical beats. But they sound like they're trying too hard. Too many of the choruses alternate between two or three notes; they're just not memorable to the ear. Even 'Falling Planes', which has a descending, repetitive melody line, isn't catchy. It's too simple, too straightforward, too ordinary. If they come back with these, Ed fears, they'll be laughed at. They don't want to be one of those bands.

Listening back to the demos for the first time in over a decade, in Brighton in 2024, Neil recognises what Ed was talking about, explaining what wasn't there in 2011:

> Think of 'Yesterday' by Paul McCartney, the melody of that song is all over the place. Or the verse of 'Trash' – the melodic line of the verse takes a long time to resolve and start repeating. Some of those early things we wrote suffered from weak melodies ... Sometimes

> Brett wasn't confident about where he could go or something in the music wasn't inspiring him. Brett doesn't think in technical terms – 'it's just two alternating notes, where's my melodic line?' – he just opens his mouth and it comes out. But for him to be able to make it work, it's our job to give him what he needs.

What seems obvious now seemed harsh then. But as Richard remembers, there was something clarifying about Ed's diagnosis. 'Basically, he argued we needed to find our own individual strengths again as writers and performers.' Brett, Richard and Neil didn't want to compromise the band further. They'd come back to 'Sabotage' later. But overall, they knew Ed was right.

ED PLACES A ROCKET

It's not just about songs, he says, it's about songwriters. This time, Ed says, they need to do things differently.

Ed's had a long time to think about Suede. He's got strong feelings about what they're good at, and what's required if they're ever to find the old magic. As he puts it, 'One problem with *Head Music* and *A New Morning* was Brett spreading himself too thin, [writing] not just melody and lyrics but music too,' something he believes he's simply not as good at. Ed points to the five songs Brett wrote alone on *Head Music*, the likes of the much-derided 'Savoir Faire', the controversial 'Head Music', replete with 'give me head, give me head' refrain he says Steve Osborne should have refused to work on (Osborne *did* initially refuse, then relented), also Anderson-only songs from *A New Morning* 'One Hit to the Body' and '... Morning', as well as others that later surfaced as forgettable extras.

Is this fair? Brett would say himself he's not as sophisticated a musician as Neil or Richard. His guitar and piano playing are comparatively basic – he jokes about this whenever he whips the acoustic out at Suede gigs, claiming he 'can only play three songs'. That's an exaggeration; in the 2000s, Brett sometimes performed live at the piano, alone. But his palette is more limited, the point objectively fair. Brett responds to sound instinctively, not technically. He excels when it comes to aspects of songwriting the others can't touch: arresting imagery, soaring melody, delivering lines with conviction. He has a distinctive voice, sensibility and vocabulary all his own, incredibly rare for any frontman. In part, it's what built the band. Brett's personal appeal, especially live, remains a large part of Suede's appeal. But let's be honest, it's a different skill set.

Making his pitch in 2012, Ed said he wanted to exploit Brett's best assets. He believed Brett's primary strength was *responding* to musical ideas; it was no shame to admit his own just weren't as fresh. That was chastening to hear for a singer who'd made five albums since Suede split up and was used to being in charge. Never mind the reception, Brett believed *Black Rainbows* was his best solo work yet. Who was Ed to say what he was allowed to write? When Suede first approached Ed to work with them again, Brett sent a selection of his solo material by email, though he doesn't think he even listened to the songs; it didn't seem relevant to Ed that Brett had this whole other musical life. But maybe, Brett thought, it was worth considering this approach, if this whole reunion thing was going to work.

In the discussions that followed, in Neil's words, Ed 'put a rocket up us'. Ed argued Suede could only be at their best if there was a clear demarcation of responsibilities, Neil and Richard writing the music while Brett concentrated on the top line, and no more of this chopping and changing. They needed a system, with Richard and Neil the musical engine of the band. Crucially, he meant Richard and Neil *working together*. Not separately, as they had done in the '90s, or the last six months. Now, Ed felt the writing team needed to be in the same room, responding to each other's ideas in real time. Churning out new songs until there were enough good ones. All this even though, until recently, Richard and Neil hadn't written together, or spent much time together, for over a decade. In recent months, neither of them had written anything Ed rated. Which begs the question: why was he so confident that was about to change?

The answer is partly about focus, partly about chemistry and partly about creating an atmosphere where better work can flourish. Ed believes once everyone focuses more on attuning to the way others work rather than getting on incrementally at a distance between other projects, then quality will improve. It also brings everyone closer, which is good for the band. Neil's laughing: 'If he was there then he could say don't do that, do that,' he says now. 'Ed didn't really trust us to come up with good stuff on our own!' So that was the new system. There was a long road ahead, and no one assumed they'd get there. Out of all that experimentation at the Grove, they had, maybe, one song. Or none, if Ed got his way. Had they really been a new band, as Richard enjoyed imagining, they wouldn't have ever got off the ground. Neil says, 'We didn't talk about it. But I suppose we wondered if we were up to the task.'

It wasn't just this specific combination of Neil, Richard and Brett that Ed wanted to set to work; he also wanted them at his home, for full days. For as long as it took. Like a full-time job: another adjustment. Was it really going to be better writing at Ed's, hovering over each other as they tried to come up with ideas, in real time? Richard was nervous. And what about Brett – was he going to have to come up with lyrics and melodies on the spot? What if it didn't work? Didn't he hate that? Well, said Ed. Did they want this or not? The Artmagic album, *Become the One*

You Love, was put back till July 2012, so Richard had time. Neil's commitments with Penguin Cafe were minimal. Brett had a couple of *Black Rainbows* commitments left, the record's North American release coming in February 2012 – but he was done touring, and home in London. In the months to come, then, this is what they'd do. Go round to Ed's. Write. And see if they could do it.

It's not quite true to say they were starting again from scratch here. As well as 'Sabotage', there was one other early demo with promise. From this point on they would usually bring in Mat and Simon once ideas had been developed, others cast aside. But towards the end of 2011 the full band came up with something in rehearsal, Neil starting to play a verse part on guitar before the others joined in and a chorus part was added. Brett wrote a vocal on 1 December, the early demo of 'Always' only slightly suggestive of the atmosphere the song would one day develop. It wasn't ready for Russia, but they'd come back to it in the new year.

Everything else went in the bin.

IMPROVING AT ED'S

When they reconvened, things immediately improved. The first new idea was 'Faultlines', written on 13 January, with key song 'Sometimes I Feel I'll Float Away' later the same month, on the 28th. Richard wrote the verse and bridge at home, then, he says, 'I brought it to Ed's and wrote the chorus in the room.' This was the first Anderson–Oakes song in a decade that sounded like it could stand up next to old material. Meanwhile, Brett told the band Jodie was pregnant – they were expecting a child, late May or early June. No pressure, then, to make progress quickly.

The demo of 'Sometimes I Feel I'll Float Away' shows it initially had a choppier, Neil Young-esque guitar line. It was slow, overdriven. That early version didn't immediately announce itself as a standout, but Brett's lyric, inspired by a line from the series *Mad Men*, was exactly the kind of soaring, dramatic mini-narrative they'd been looking for. (After her philandering husband has moved out, Betty Draper wonders if she can cope alone: 'Sometimes I feel like I'll float away,' she says, 'if Don isn't holding me down.' Brett scribbled the words, while watching TV.)* This hinted at the theme of coercive control also explored in 'Sabotage' – a disguised way for Brett to talk about 'my need for love ... my inability to function without it.' Brett thought this 'a beautiful way to describe co-dependency' and the line became the song's 'lyrical anchor'. 'I've always seen myself as mildly co-dependent,' he says now, 'that sense that experiences are only beautiful when they are shared. I thought it was new and interesting territory for a rock song, most of which are about loss or longing or dominance. The song contained Brett's favourite new lyric, 'And I count to ten as the race begins round your hairpin bends', while the music was plaintive and sweet, then twisted and dark, before opening out into a more expansive, melodic chorus and an unrestrained Richard guitar line. It also saw the reappearance of the Suede chord, the repeated words 'float away' matched with that unexpected change beneath.

This felt like recognisably Suedey territory, without being a duplicate of past work. Now they had a couple of songs with their own sound, their own characters, too. In 'Sometimes I Feel I'll Float Away', the narrator confesses they 'need you more than you need to be needed', the object of love seen as superior, even superhuman: 'All the colours in the rainbow don't compare with one look in your impossible eyes', Brett sings at the outset. Like Betty in *Mad Men*, facing what her life might be like if she's no longer subject to Don's neglect or abuse, the narrator shrinks from

---

* 'The Inheritance', Season 2, Episode 10, *Mad Men* (2008).

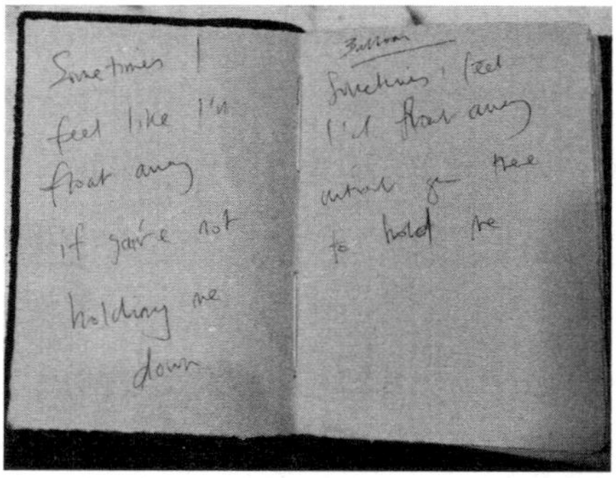

'Sometimes I feel like I'll float away if you're not holding me down / Sometimes I feel I'll float away without you there to hold me,' scribbled while watching Mad Men, *2012.*

that potential freedom, fearing they can't live without the security that comes from being suffocated. Here was a song, everyone thought, that could soar.

January's progress was encouraging, but they were working on some average ideas, too. Also, both 'Faultlines' and 'Sometimes I Feel I'll Float Away' were big ballads. As was 'Always'; even 'Sabotage' was slow-paced. That posed a challenge; even as they saw the system starting to work, the imbalance was clear. Each working day in January, Ed, Richard, Neil and Brett moved between ideas, working on something for a while, then changing things up, Brett sometimes responding in the moment, sometimes taking notes or singing along. The best ideas all sounded like songs for Side Two of a record. That was fine, but they also wanted singles. There was no big moment of breakthrough here, only more work. Neil remembers, 'Sometimes we forgot about an idea, while working on other things – so it fell down the pecking order. Then someone would ask, what about that other one? And we'd go back to it, forgetting others.'

At Ed's, sometimes Neil and Richard wrote together, live, from scratch. Sometimes they brought along things they'd been working on alone, sharing them in the room. Ed responding. Brett responding. Play that again. No, the other one. What's that, Blob? Is this anything? (They all call each other 'Blob'. Dumb, affectionate, dismissive, insulting. This has gone on forever.) Sometimes Brett would scurry away, come back with a top line, then start modifying it in rehearsal. Even after 'Sometimes I Feel I'll Float Away', no one yet had a clear sense of what they were trying to achieve, except, as Ed puts it, 'a vague desire to write somewhere in the space between *Dog Man Star* and *Coming Up*.' Understandably, that led to some second-guessing, less risk-taking. Richard remembers, 'You come up with an idea then almost immediately think – is that too Suedey? Or not Suedey enough?' He laughs, then delivers the next line in his ever-so-English way. 'It's enough to drive you a little bit maaaad.'

This often felt like impossible guesswork. In writing, they couldn't just freely do whatever they liked, drawing on influences or sounds picked up in the last decade; the job was to tune back in to something from long ago, continually being on the lookout for slipping into self-parody or drifting too far from what fans might want. It's all very well playing celebratory sets all around the world, drawing entirely on songs people already adore. You've simply to pick the right ones, and deliver them. It's quite another to make something new that might fit seamlessly into one of those sets without everyone making a break for the bar.

Across this process, Neil and Richard produced a mountain of music, along with individual sections that moved in and out of favour, some of these parts being dropped into, and out of, other songs, looking to change up intros, verses, choruses and middle eights that might work in combination. They wanted quality control, but there was too much to remember. Both men are meticulous with records. Every idea has a demo nickname (sometimes these working titles get remembered long after the actual songs are forgotten). They help to crystallise in the mind which idea is which. But it's messy, and it can feel like, on any given day, how on earth do you know what to concentrate on?

Push, push. On, on. Dead ends. Half-ideas. Things with promise, things that got stuck. At the start of February, Brett immediately responded to a revolving guitar riff, becoming animated in the room at Richard's demo 'Satan Bug', putting his vocal together quickly soon after. This became 'For the Strangers', inspired by Public Image Ltd's 'Rise'.* (He'd often refer to this Richard guitar part in future, using it as an example. Not an obvious lead guitar line *competing* with the vocal, but more of a *complement*, leaving space for him to find himself in it.) The day they wrote 'For the Strangers', Ed told his wife Laura, 'they're back, they're back!',† but it was another few weeks of hard work – what Neil calls 'the doldrums, where you just get stuck' – before they came up with the next decent song; this time, they had something that, in Neil's words, 'immediately sounded poppy enough that it could be a single'. He wrote the music, Brett the top line. The basics came together quickly. That's usually a good sign.

The original demo of 'It Starts and Ends With You' was sunny, simple, quite '60s, with Neil strumming an acoustic throughout. In Neil's words, it was 'a bit stoned-sounding', Brett's starting point being Echo & the Bunnymen's album *Ocean Rain*. (He always loved 'The Killing Moon'.) The lead line was Richard's, the intro riff Neil's. There was potential here, but they needed to clear space to find it. Once identified as a potential

---

* Brett has long been a huge fan – several songs on *Black Rainbows* were inspired by 'Rise', too.

† Ed: Before 'Strangers' I thought, it's like one out of every fifteen songs is good – shit, maybe we don't have this any more. But then I remember telling Laura that night, they're back, they're back, they've got 'For the Strangers'.

single, 'It Starts and Ends With You' sped up, out came the acoustic, the electric guitars became harder, and the song went up a level once the rhythm section came in.

By spring 2012, the punkier-sounding Russia songs had been replaced by a clutch that sounded more recognisably mid-'90s Suede. Neil remembers what it felt like, a few months into writing at Ed's:

> You get on a hot streak ... those moments are so important in records, where you feel like you've got a direction. You hear something and think, yeah, we want more of *this*. The dynamic of making records can be that maybe you go a year and get nothing, then you hit on something and you might get down three songs in a week. When you're writing music it's so instinctual, you can't intellectualise ... you have to use the instinctual part of your brain to make things happen. Only then can you step back and see what you've got.

There was no single, clarifying moment, rather a consistent effort to find the best of the mountain of material, then improve it. A reshaped single-ish thing here. An upbeat, old-school-sounding song there. A couple of big, sweeping ballads. They kept pushing. Looking back now, Mat recalls the goal was 'simply to pick the ten best songs – making it as much like a new "greatest hits" as we could.' Trying to be as objective as possible about quality, then insisting on it. Everyone was driven by the mistakes of *Head Music* and *A New Morning*, albums that could have been different had they been more unforgiving during the process, rather than allowing things to drift. This was their chance to right that, and frankly, they were afraid of failure.

That said, no one can be truly objective, and anyway, quality wasn't the only criterion. Good demos were discarded because there was no space for more slow songs. (In February, for instance, Neil wrote a beautiful instrumental called 'Underwater Bond'. It would resurface five years later, but for now they already had too many ballads.) Other ideas were discarded because they sounded similar to things they already had, or not similar enough. Variety, then, was important too, also a desire to have Side One punchier than Side Two. Even in the digital age, this is how they thought: Side One and Side Two of a vinyl record.

Often, all this worrying and self-selection happened before ideas got to Mat and Simon. Mat was less involved in writing now, though his contributions once they were working as a band were as important as ever. Simon was getting used to flying in from Thailand, but his role was reduced, too. Or at least, the band were finding a way to operate as a four-piece when their drummer was six thousand miles away. When the writing team were confident, they sent ideas by email, Mat and Simon's responses influencing whether ideas got pursued. Neil learned to approximate Simon's drum style for demos, adding drum parts in the meantime at Ed's or at home, in the knowledge that, if songs survived, then Simon could make them his own.

No individual idea could be sure to make the cut, but working this way was better. In the '90s, Neil or Richard might spend a week working on something, send it to Brett on tape, then wait. Back then, most ideas got written to. Now, Brett had this avalanche of material, couldn't write to everything anyway, but had more freedom to dismiss ideas. Brett's response to new pieces was often indifference, followed by 'Have you got anything else?' This could be maddening, and it put Brett in an elevated position – if he wrote to something, it was more likely to get finished. If he struggled, or didn't want to respond, then it didn't. But this was more of a team effort, with more clearly defined roles. It also meant Richard and Neil having to be less precious about their ideas.

Less precious, and more accepting, too. For Richard and Neil, they soon learned that multiple musical ideas, maybe many of their own personal favourites, might never lead anywhere. 'There's no point pouring your heart and soul into something that might come to nothing', says Neil. 'It's not that we didn't care what happened. We cared, a lot. It's just ... it becomes a bit more of a factory. We all wanted to make one more good Suede record, and we realised that, with only about one in ten ideas good enough, we had to set aside egos, to work in a way that meant that we could each deal with it if our own ideas got discarded. In fact, it was best not to think of them as "belonging" to anyone at all.'

TAKING SHAPE, IN AND OUT OF THE STUDIO

By early March, something was taking shape. One morning Richard woke with a new verse riff in his head, then sang it into his phone, before working out how to play it on guitar – this became 'Snowblind', which was completed on 7 March. A term for temporary blindness sometimes assumed to be a cocaine reference by fans, 'Snowblind' was big, bold and had three proper choruses. The lyrics sketched the moment when two people who are 'too beautiful to really care what's right' become infatuated with each other, finding themselves 'frozen by the moment' on the tube in 'those first intoxicating moments of lust'. Brett was fond of the line, 'We find our keys on the kitchen table and forget what's done'. In writing the lyric, he imagined 'the awkward morning after the night before, the gathering of possessions, hesitant goodbyes, facing up to the day.' All this was very Suede – but not too Suedey. It was also another Anderson–Oakes song, with Richard now more tuned in, the writing evening out between him and Neil.

With the baby due soon the band had another few months to finish the album; babies wait for no creative process. At least there was momentum now. Of 'Snowblind', Brett says, 'I immediately thought it was right up there with the best things the band had written, at any time. I still do.' They booked rehearsals, pre-production time, studio time in May, with mixing in June (by which time, Brett might be a father). But they also decided to keep writing, looking for more songs to change the emphasis of the record, making it more upbeat. One or two more like 'Snowblind'. Amazingly, there were no fewer than 124 pieces of music written for the album – sixty-five complete songs, as well as fifty-nine instrumental demos that got no top line.*

As Ed recalls, 'Some days, looking at Richard's expression – oh! The poor guy. He just looked ... *defeated*. Or like he was trying *really hard* to carry on. There were times it *was* fun. When you come up with a great idea, everyone smiles. But we really worked Richard like hell.' Ed is uniquely placed to observe how each person in Suede operates. Then and now, Richard wears his emotion on his face. He'd committed to this way of working – writing until it was good enough. But it was also a strain, especially as nearly everything he crafted was junked. 'It really was like a factory,' he recalls now. 'Just churning out more stuff, to go who knows where.' He laughs. 'The bin!'

As on stage, so in private, Neil gives less away. He shows frustration quietly, operating less with emotion and more as a technically minded problem solver: 'Okay,' he'll say, 'so that's no good – fine. Well, what about this, then? Better?' Neil moves between instruments, playing with different sounds, searching for different ways into ideas. Brett

* Of the sixty-five songs there were ten album tracks, eight extra tracks/B-sides, forty-seven unused songs and then the further fifty-nine demos not written to.

meanwhile, operates, Ed says, in three main modes, moving between: Mr Cold Water (dismissing ideas others worked hard on, often on a whim), Mr Enthusiastic (everything is great, let's go, we're the best band in the fucking world) or Mr Disengaged (I don't know how to deal with this problem, I'm stuck, so I'm withdrawing). 'The challenge for us,' Ed says, 'is to find Mr Enthusiastic, but rein him in for long enough to move songs forward, before he gets bored again.'

The next good song was another quiet one, the heartbreak of 'What Are You Not Telling Me?' – again, concerning secrecy and power dynamics in relationships. In fact, this was the quietest of the lot, a gorgeous song of desperation featuring just a spare piano and keyboard accompaniment to Brett's raw, echo-laden vocal in the first half – 'Just bread for the birds in second hand furs / An occasional touch, an occasional word' – before a lonely guitar line joins for the song's end. That was completed on 24 April. (Calendar nerds will notice that's a full six weeks work since the last complete song worth mentioning, 'Snowblind'.) They repaired from Ed's place in Highgate, where he'd been at the computer while they wrote,* to Sarm Studios in Notting Hill in May 2012, to record.

They thought they had around ten songs for the album and maybe six extras, though this kept evolving. Working in a vacuum, they had no idea how realistic it was – was that all in the past? – but they were trying to come up with more direct, shorter, faster songs that sounded like they *could* be singles, if singles were still a thing. Soon, that paid dividends. Next came an early version of 'Barriers', which took time after the original verse was written. 'Barriers' might have been on *Coming Up* – lighter, poppier, more optimistic, uplifting, it was based around a very simple

* Neil: 'Often we'd have a really rudimentary one-bar loop that Ed would lay down and we'd be playing over it. Just enough to get the basic ideas down.'

metaphor (a relationship overcoming obstacles). Suede chords? Plenty of them. 'Oh-ho' singalong? Yes indeed. It might even work as an album opener. Time was running short, patience wearing thinner, but maybe they were nearly there. There were occasional breaks for gigs in June, then July.

These happened either side of the birth of Brett's son Lucian Jesse, named for the great portrait painter Lucian Freud, and for Brett's much-missed friend. Lucian was born on 5 June 2012, in a birthing pool at Brett and Jodie's Notting Hill home. Laughing now, Jodie says, 'When people meet Brett, they have one of two responses. Even at a home birth! Some, who have no idea who he is, or couldn't care less. And others, like the second midwife who arrived at our house, who was a Suede fan ... Her jaw dropped when she realised whose baby she was there to deliver ... "I'll have to put my professional hat on!" she said.' The whole thing was surreal. The birth itself was quick; baby Lucian was tiny and delicate. Brett was 'hilarious', according to Jodie. Immediately devoted, as with young Jack, who had to adapt to the new arrival. Brett was incredibly gentle. (Sometimes he wouldn't put Lucian into his clothes properly as he feared hurting him by putting his arm through the Babygro.) At first, Brett was troubled by how Lucian looked – born with a big nose, the thinnest lips, his eyes closed for a long time – though that passed soon enough. The sleep deprivation comes for everyone, but Brett was a natural when it came to talking to and playing with kids. Imaginary games. Early mornings. Late nights. They wanted it, though Jodie had forgotten how hard it was to have a newborn.

So this was quite a manic period, personally and professionally. Between a show in Kent on 1 July and a festival in Yokohama, Japan, on the 16th, an old demo called 'Victim' was 'cut 'n' shut' (a regular term the band use, like with a welded car) to a new chorus, becoming 'Hit Me'.

'Barriers' got a new chorus on 21 July, the same day Neil played with Penguin Cafe at Somerset House. Still, they wondered if they had enough, so Neil and Richard kept going, even as recording continued, between summer festivals (one in Spain, one in Simon's adopted home of Thailand), where the one new song in the set was 'Sabotage'. The only survivor from the start of the writing process, it was also the song they wanted to use to trail the album live. Meanwhile, they kept working on 'Hit Me', the most straightforward of those in contention and, like 'Barriers', based on an easy-to-understand relationship metaphor. Once pegged as a potential single, Brett rewrote his original darker lyrics for it, replacing these with something brighter.* 'Hit Me' sounded shiny, kind of disposable. But maybe that's what they were looking for?

Recording was finished, the band exhausted, and Brett was mostly away from work, in the earliest all-consuming days of fatherhood. But the process was not over yet. Ed was keen for the album to be mixed by a specialist with a strong track record, who could make it sound *big*. Andy Wallace, one of the world's most respected mixers, best known for his work with Patti Smith and Jeff Buckley, also on Nirvana's era-defining *Nevermind*, was approached. Wallace's records were alternative, but commercial. He agreed to work with the band from the US. This meant mixing by email, which was frustrating. Any time someone asked to hear this or that element of a song differently, they had to email Andy and wait for a reply. Decisions that might have taken seconds in the room took days. By the time it was over, everyone was knackered and sick of the songs, swearing they'd never work this way again.

---

* Originally called 'Victim', it used to go, 'I'm not a victim of your suffering, I'm not a victim of all that whispering / Sometimes bruises don't show, and even your best friends don't know I know'. Once retitled 'Hit Me', the violence was repurposed as a positive.

THE *BLOODSPORTS* NARRATIVE

Brett started to think about possible track lists. If 'Barriers', 'Snowblind', 'It Starts and Ends with You', 'Sabotage' and 'For the Strangers' went back-to-back, then that was a whole Side One. And the slower songs on Side Two, after 'Hit Me'. Okay, so now they had an album. Probably. Maybe. A new Suede record was happening now, no backing out. Last time was a disaster. What if the same happened? What if nobody bought it? What if, what if, what if? But signs were promising. Taking a punt on Suede at a time when few reunited bands of the era were making new music, Warner Brothers signed them for a single record; release was scheduled for the following year, with Latin American gigs in autumn 2012. Brett, Jodie, Jack and baby Lucian made for Ibiza, where the family often spent summers anyway. (Praise be, the sun helped Lucian sleep.) August, September and early October were clear. In mid-October, the band called friends and fans to the studio. David Barnett wrote in his diary on the 12th: 'We went in to do handclaps on the new Suede album the other day ... people keep asking me what it sounds like. It sounds like Suede.' Well, that was the aim. But good Suede or bad? By the end of the year, plans were in place for pre-album singles, a release in March, then a handful of dates, the main *Bloodsports* tour scheduled in for autumn 2013.

Once an album is recorded, Brett turns his attentions to how he'll pitch it. For both him and Mat, doing the promo, there was the challenge of trying to make sense of the work in a way that felt true but also presented the band in the most positive light. Almost like they knew what they were doing. Mat is articulate, on behalf of everyone. But ultimately, Brett has to choose how to present the story of the album. Neil says, 'After the smoke clears, Brett has to say to people, this is what we were thinking' – which means the lyrical content. That was going to be hard.

How to present a hundred-plus songs cut to ten in an atmosphere of desperation to avoid repeating the mistakes of the past, without either lying, or otherwise sounding anxious or deluded? In stolen moments in the first few months of fatherhood, Brett started to think about how he was going to make sense of the record to others.

With any new album, there are several opportunities to present something clear and coherent. The first is title: Brett chose *Bloodsports,* as it suggested violence, play and romance at once. His next task was to work out what to say the album was *about.* When curating something based on so many other variables, the lyrics that end up on a record can feel a bit random. The only real conscious attempt here had been to reconnect with what the band sounded like, back when they were popular. But you can't say that in public.

Brett arranged the songs in an order inspired by the philosopher Alain de Botton's book *Essays in Love,* which tracks a relationship from start to finish.* Once he had the idea of *Bloodsports* following a similar arc, a narrative started to emerge: this meant moving from the opening, breezy hope of 'Barriers' and the dizzying 'Snowblind' moments of early desire, through the hope and commitment of 'It Starts and Ends With You', on to the self-destruction of 'Sabotage', the desperate co-dependence of 'Sometimes I Feel I'll Float Away', then the dark, twisted ending in which the consequences of all that secrecy and lies play out, on 'Always' and finally 'Faultlines'. In truth, this didn't really stand up to scrutiny; 'Faultlines' in particular is a lovely song, though at best it's lyrically confused. Still, the priority was to show Suede were back, and Brett Anderson knew what he was doing. So the relationship narrative arc it was.

---

* Brett on de Botton: 'I don't care that he's a "pop philosopher" or whatever and probably considered lightweight by intellectual snobs, I find his work fascinating and the whole School of Life project is an embarrassment of riches.'

APPRECIATION, FAR FROM HOME

In October, after a proper break, the band did a further handful of dates. This was the first Suede tour of Latin America* taking in Mexico, Brazil (a festival and a TV appearance, where they played 'Animal Nitrate', 'Filmstar' and 'Metal Mickey'), Chile and Argentina. Amazingly, they'd never played there, despite the size of their following. Sometimes it's assumed Suede could only make sense in the context of English working-class life, or a particular corner of the past. But touring reminds us that fans in different countries see different stories in the same band. Songs are interpreted in ways you can't imagine, by people you'll never know. Even after a couple of years of these shows playing old music, Suede could still occasionally be surprised by fans' depth of feeling in places they barely knew or understood.

Bloodsports material was held back at these gigs, where fans who hardly ever got to see their heroes responded in a way you rarely see at home. In the UK, people might expect their favourite acts to come around every couple of years. But Latin American audiences knew this might be a one-off and responded as if they'd never see the band again. By now, Suede's return was no longer news. They weren't promoting anything old, or anything new. This made it more surprising when they got an outsized reaction for doing the same thing they were doing everywhere.

On 21 October 2012 Suede played the Teatro Vorterix in Buenos Aires, in a show that even now stands out as wild in the memories of several of the band. It was a rainy, humid Monday night, with (as was sometimes the case in Argentina in those days, before tragedies tightened up the rules) over 2,000 fans packed into a venue that, for legal

---

* Brett had toured there, solo.

reasons, newspapers had to say contained 1,500. Before Suede were even on stage, the level of screaming was overwhelming. The band were taken aback. Writing in the Argentinian *Página 12* newspaper, Facundo Enrique Soler wrote up the gig as 'one of the best concerts of the year'.

In fact, in a sign of its significance, *Página 12* ran two reviews of this gig, the other being written by the great Argentinian novelist Mariana Enríquez, also an experienced rock journalist.* Looking back on this show over a decade later, she was keen to impress on me the impact of Suede in her home country, especially how much the working-class outlook of Brett's lyrics in particular 'did not need to be explained' to people in Argentina, 'because we live it every day.' She recalls: 'If you look across Suede lyrics, they are a code for a life that millions of people recognise. That language is in our bones. So ... the reason we felt so strongly about Suede was because it was so rare to hear our lives being projected back at us. It didn't matter [they were from] London, or [musical] movements of the time. You listen to a song like "Saturday Night" and it could be a song of redemption and escape for the workers of Buenos Aires. When the band finally came to Argentina, we wanted to show them what it meant. We wanted them to remember this was a place where Suede meant something.'

During the show, Brett praised the crowd, repeatedly. They played 'My Dark Star', the line 'she will come from Argentina / With her cemetery eyes' receiving a roar of recognition. The last encore was 'Saturday Night', and the dangerously over-full Teatro Vorterix sang every word. The final line of Soler's review was, 'Outside, the streets of Colegiales

---

* Enríquez is one of the most celebrated international writers of her generation, in any country. She wrote her own 2023 Suede book exploring fan culture, obsession, mania and desire, published in Spanish, in Chile: *Porque demasiado no es suficiente. Mi historia de amor con Suede* (*Because Too Much is Never Enough: My Love Affair with Suede*).

promised an endless rain, worthy of a postcard to close the most London night of the year.' Along with key shows like Jisan Valley, the Albert Hall and the three Brixton Academy shows celebrating the first three albums, this was one of the best receptions the band ever had, anywhere. They wouldn't forget it.

THE FUTURE SEEMS POSSIBLE: FIRST RELEASES, AND LIVE RETURN

The first new song was released in January 2013. This was 'Barriers' – not quite a single, rather a 'free download', in a sign of how much the industry had changed. In a sense, this was a safe bet. There's no chart position for a free download, and 'Barriers' was a good indicator of what *Bloodsports* was all about. Suede chords in the chorus: check. Return to trademark sound: check. Lyrics about togetherness, romance and triumph over adversity: check. And no lyrical or musical clangers. As early fan and author of *The Illustrated A to Z of Suede Lyrics* Rachel Apps later put it, '"Barriers" immediately sounded like a call to arms to fans, to come rushing back.' In short, the reaction they were hoping for.

'Barriers' isn't many Suede fans' favourite song, but it did what it was supposed to: announce the band's return, get them back on the radio (in the UK, this now meant 6 Music, where many of the old alternative Radio 1 DJs from the '90s moved to), and let people know an album was coming. The reception to 'Barriers' was positive, if guarded, though by the time the first single proper, 'It Starts and Ends With You' was released on 4 February, momentum was building. The song wasn't going to be a 'hit' in the way that Suede used to have hits, though perhaps that was to be expected. Rather, like the Albert Hall, comeback tours and *Best Of* album, it contributed to a sense the band were being rehabilitated. On 11 February, Suede did a live session for 6 Music where they played

'Barriers', 'It Starts and Ends With You', 'For the Strangers', 'Sabotage' and a handful of classics. The very fact this was happening suggested the release of a new Suede record was an event.*

On the red carpet at the *NME* Awards later that month Brett was relaxed, describing himself as 'buzzing' about Suede being back and how much he was looking forward to the Ally Pally show in a few weeks' time. Joking with an Absolute Radio reporter about Simon keeping Suede's awards to himself, along with a stack of their laminated press cuttings – 'what a sad fucker!' – Brett said what he'd be saying, in different ways, to journalists over the months ahead: 'We have a lot of history to rewrite ... we just want to make sure we don't fuck up again.' Also, that he believed *Bloodsports* was 'right up there with our best stuff'.

Two weeks before the album dropped, Suede played the Barfly in London, the first of forty-four shows that year. It was not quite the 'smallest venue they've ever played', as the XFM MC claimed, but close enough to be exciting for those with tickets. This was what they'd been working towards: an opportunity to survive on their wits, new songs, and not much else. No tricks or overblown hype. Reviewing the gig for *Louder Than War*, David Barnett, who'd been watching the band for long enough to know the difference, identified 'a new-found vigour and none of the vim of the sex, drugs, and more drugs Suede of popular legend.'

This was what Suede fans would be getting now: confident, sober, clean, loud, even youthful-looking. The band all in black jeans and T-shirts (no frills there, either), with Brett in a 'fresh white shirt'. They opened with 'Barriers' and played 'For the Strangers', 'Hit Me', 'Sabotage' and 'It Starts and Ends With You', picking smartly from the back catalogue.

---

* Several other indicators suggested they could reach a more significant audience than 6 Music allowed. For example, in March 2013 Brett, Neil and Richard played 'It Starts and Ends With You' acoustic on BBC2's *The Review Show*.

They played ten singles. Any residual queasiness about early Suede seemed to be a non-issue, and the set was all the better for it: 'He's Dead' just one example, that night, of how much 'new blood and passion' Oakes could pour into a song once thought of as quintessentially Butler. Somehow, fans down the front knew the words to 'For the Strangers' already, and the age range in the audience suggested this wasn't just people searching out their own youth. Sure, there were some of those, but half the audience were toddlers during the early '90s. How did they even know who Suede were? Where had they come from? They finished with the now-traditional 'Beautiful Ones', and Barnett described the Barfly as being like 'one giant human trampoline'. A slightly giddy feeling took over. A future seemed possible.

BLOODSPORTS: RELEASE AND RECEPTION

Finally, release time was here, and the cover image for *Bloodsports* was confirmed. Like the title of the new record, this explored danger and play. The final version showed a blurred, gender-ambiguous couple, one holding the other down. The band didn't want to come across as polite or safe. Whether a sex game or an attack isn't clear, but it encourages viewers to see the potential for both. Few bands are as closely associated with the bedroom or the mattress; both *Dog Man Star* and *Coming Up* featured mattresses as a backdrop, in different kinds of squalor. Here was another version of that, but one different enough to feel fresh, and relevant to this album.

Timing is everything. Very Suede, then, that the week before *Bloodsports* was released it was overshadowed by David Bowie, who surprised everyone by dropping his first album in ten years, overnight. *The Next Day* was the best Bowie album in a long time; it shot to number one, making international news. It's what almost anyone interested in alternative music was talking about in March 2013, which put Suede's return in the shade, especially as their debt to Bowie was so commonly referenced.

In this context, no one was quite sure what to expect. They wanted something to build on, that indicated this reunion might be the beginning of something. But how much was enough to build on? Bowie or no Bowie, hopes were realistic, but was top twenty too much to hope for? *Bloodsports* was released on 18 March. At first, it looked like they were teetering on the edge of the top ten, before later news suggested they might land just outside it. In the chart mix there was Bowie, Justin Timberlake and Pink in the top five, while Suede competed with Bon Jovi (also on the comeback trail), the Lumineers and Mumford & Sons at the lower end of the top ten. Come Sunday, *Bloodsports* landed at number ten, just. This was a victory, one Brett felt was 'satisfying'. After a decade in the wilderness, it made Richard feel like 'punching the sky'. Though the band knew the chart position was down to a hard core of around 10,000 fans turning up to buy old-school hard copies, on vinyl or CD, the album likely to plunge the following week, they now got to call *Bloodsports* a top-ten album. For good. They were no longer a band who ended with a whimper.

The review coverage, if not exactly breathless, was mostly positive. Part of this may simply be about a different generation of listeners coming along, while a few old fans returned. Certainly, that was a factor; but even if old listeners were receptive, you still needed to give them something to fall for. This may be a sign of low expectations, but when faced with a slew of 7/10 reviews from the likes of *Rolling Stone* and *Uncut* (as well as four-star reviews in the *Guardian*, *Mojo* and *Q*), with some very good reviews in the US too, the band were generally happy, as relieved by the critical reception as they had been by the chart position. *Pitchfork*, then a fast-growing, international taste-making site with increasing heft, gave it a 7.6/10, a marked improvement on their review of Brett's *Black Rainbows* not long before.

Most coverage was fair. Yes, reviewers noted some Suede-by-numbers elements at work. Oohs and la la la's, aping 'Beautiful Ones', for example. (This is the kind of thing the band dislike now, an attempt by Ed to recreate the end of 'Hot Love' by T. Rex, or 'Starman' by David Bowie.) Classic Suede imagery – 'Barriers' featuring 'aniseed kisses' and 'lipstick traces', phrases straight from the Suede Thesaurus. The sound was determinedly aimed at bringing in as many old fans as possible, too, rather than reaching into new territory. But that's what they wanted. The pacing of the record – as much downbeat as upbeat material – may have been slightly wonky, but then, Suede were always good at the dark torch song.

Despite this, the odd response rankled. When Helen Brown reviewed the album for the *Telegraph* she said they were 'back on yelping, yearning ... electrifying top form'. But there was, perhaps, a lingering sense among those who remembered late '90s/early 2000s Suede that Brett was a bad lyricist. This applied even when his words were simply misheard. 'There are some dodgy lyrics,' wrote Brown. 'I'm not sure what he means by "like a cog without a martyr" on lead single "It Starts and Ends With You".' Well, that would have been confusing, but the line was 'like a *cause* without a martyr' – which makes more sense in a song about a relationship with a hole at its heart. Going back to that review now, it strikes me as extremely positive: 'Sixth album *Bloodsports* finds the wheels of that pram sparking on their rims' (in reference to the oft-used image of the out-of-control pram). 'It's romantic, menacing and carnal. And it sets the tone for a drama and vitality that Suede sustain across the ten exhilarating tracks.' But Brett wasn't the only one seen in a way he wanted to shake off.

Richard's contribution was still seen via the legacy of his predecessor. In the end, Richard really stepped up on *Bloodsports*, co-writing eight of the ten songs, often as part of that three-person team, working at Ed's. But he also wrote two of the album's key songs with Brett, as a duo: 'Snowblind' and 'Sometimes I Feel I'll Float Away'. Still. Even when praised, he was nearly always praised as the man not producing ideas of his own, but doing an impression of someone else's, Brown writing: 'guitarist Richard Oakes ploughing into some unabashedly Butler-esque riffs, it sounds almost like it could be a lost record from the band's electrifying mid-'90s period.'* Of course, the guitarist from the band's mid-'90s period was ... Richard Oakes. But he often gets overlooked or misunderstood, even in the very best reviews.

No one in the band remembers the rest of this review now, nor the writer, and some have forgotten the publication. But they all still regularly refer to it as an example of how Brett has been unfairly maligned as a lyricist.

THE ARTIFICIAL GRIT: BRETT'S REFLECTIONS ON *BLOODSPORTS*

Brett feels more able to appraise the album now than he was at the time. Before one of our early interviews, he went back to the record, listening to it from beginning to end for the first time in years: 'I can immediately identify what would have improved it,' he says. 'For starters, the last three

* In fact, this was only half the quote. The cheesy sign-off from Brown's review marked out 'It Starts and Ends With You' for praise: 'I like the seedy, suburban decay of the following line: "Like a hairline crack in the radiator / Leaking life". No cracks in the new Suede, though. *Bloodsports* is bleeding good.'

songs didn't work. We still ended up with too many slow songs.' The way Brett discusses all the Suede records displays a mixture of confidence, genuine self-knowledge but also harsh self-critique that sometimes can seem *too* critical.

Anyway, Brett's not alone in being dismissive about good songs they worked hard on, some of which are loved by fans. The emblematic example the band keep coming back to is 'Always', the song that started out in the rehearsal room and grew into a big, soaring ballad with a real sense of threat. Not big enough, or soaring enough, though. In conversation, both Neil and Brett used exactly the same words here, describing it as being 'simply not good enough', the building end section 'like a poorer version of "The Asphalt World"' according to Brett. 'We didn't have the courage to either extend it further musically, à la "Asphalt World", or take it somewhere else entirely,' he said, leaving a kind of 'half-arsed' song which was kind of in similar territory to that *kind* of Suede song – expansive, dank, disturbing lyrically – but not quite big enough to have the desired impact. At the start of the breakdown section of 'Always', it sounds like it's about to open into a huge instrumental that never arrives. It's easy to imagine what that 'braver' version might have sounded like, understandable why it frustrates them, as a kind of symbol of how they were too contained. But it's still a very good song. And it doesn't mean the whole back end of the album doesn't work.

Reflecting on the record, Brett doesn't immediately concentrate on the songs themselves, but rather the period of his life he was in and how that fed into the process. 'The craziness that a new baby brings to everyone's lives hadn't kicked in in my life,' he recalls. 'I was still writing about my pre-fatherhood life, which was pretty harmonious. You know, I think I was looking for grit in the lens, and looking back now, it feels like the grit is slightly, *artificial*. I hadn't found anything interesting to write about. So I [relied on this] vaguely sort of Gothic, poetic stuff that I don't think really stands as my best. Apart from the best song on that record. Which is, without a doubt, "... Float Away".'

Sometimes I'll ask a question in person, and Brett will mull on it, then reach out soon after, either to clarify, or just to expand on something. He's reaching for the right wording. After we talked over *Bloodsports*, he emailed some follow-up thoughts, having had the chance to think about what bothered him:

> Possibly I was too content ... Life was balanced and charmed and sometimes that can numb you. I think the album lacks cynicism, it needs a more slanted, sour take, its optimism kind of grates and makes it lightweight for me. Musically [as well], I find it a little indebted to phase one Suede. Richard hadn't yet found his own identity. Still, it's a fine record which I'm very proud of, and it contains some of our best post-ref songs – 'For the Strangers', 'Sometimes I Feel I'll Float Away', 'Snowblind', 'Sabotage'.

This answer made me curious. It seemed like both a defence of a good chunk of the songs, while seeing Brett being dismissive of his own contribution, and not only his own.

In a sense, the desire to reimagine how *Bloodsports* might have been improved is standard. Brett has always speculated publicly over how each Suede album could have been improved, from *Suede* onwards. ('Moving', 'Animal Lover' – delete. 'To the Birds', 'My Insatiable One' – include.) In our emails, Brett points to the omission of 'Dawn Chorus' from the standard running order as being a 'regret'. He doesn't flinch from that word, 'regret'. He uses it about the whole of *A New Morning*. Plenty. He uses it about the years of his life spent on drugs. So the word stands out, and shows how seriously he reflects on these selections. But there's something going on with *Bloodsports* that doesn't apply elsewhere. It was the point at which the second life of the band was as yet unknown. They were testing out whether they could do this again – and if so, how? Brett recalls: 'It's interesting how proximity to work can sometimes cloud your judgement. I think it would have been a much stronger record had we not tried to go for the epic, three-ballad ending. It's a fine idea if the songs are strong enough (see *Dog Man Star*) but in *Bloodsports'* case, [those three] just weren't.'*

This is more interesting to me than, say, Brett's previous dismissals of chunks of *Head Music*, or the entirety of *A New Morning*. In those cases, he'd been subject to ridicule for songs or lyrics in the press – 'She live in a house / She stupid as a mouse' from *Head Music*'s 'Savoir Faire' being an obvious, oft-repeated example which seemed to represent Suede lyrically succumbing to self-parody. But in this case, there's no reason for him to be critical except his own self-awareness, self-reflection. *Bloodsports* did well. It was, as he says, a period of happiness and optimism personally – without it, the band's second life wouldn't have come to be. So why so harsh, especially lyrically?

I think Brett's assessment is too critical – those three ballads, 'What Are You Not Telling Me?', 'Always' and 'Faultlines' – are all good songs. They also contain plenty of the sourness Brett says is lacking. 'Always', especially. Maybe Brett was aware that sourness, darkness, discomfort, were essential parts of the Suede vocabulary he needed to access to make a Suede comeback album work – though he found it hard to access in a way that now feels too obvious. *Bloodsports* was promoted as a concept album, one moving from the heady, exciting early days of love and ending

* BA, email to RG, 4/1/24.

in a relationship's broken, twisted ending. Though it came at a time when he was happily married, excited to be a dad in his forties. Reflecting on how harsh I say he is about his own music, he writes to me, 'I know I can seem too harsh on our music sometimes. But that's how we get better.'

'Hit Me' came and went as a single, accompanied by an expensive video featuring a couple flirting in an art gallery while violently destroying the art, though the band were cooling on the song already. By the time 'For the Strangers' was released on 21 October 2013 – the video a black-and-white offering filmed at their celebratory homecoming Ally Pally show earlier that year – the band were trying to uncover the next thing. Next time, things would be different. But for now, they could enjoy that they hadn't fucked up. As Brett got in the habit of saying, 'It was the hardest record we've ever made. But also, the most satisfying.' It was good to be back in Suede.

CHAPTER 3

night thoughts
'i don't know how to reach you'

'In general, men like us – of a certain generation – are very very *happy expressing our emotions playing guitars and very* very *unhappy expressing them any other way.'*

—Mat

KINDS OF COMMUNICATION

There are different kinds of communication. You can be expert at one kind, and amateur at another.

The members of Suede know their strengths and aren't afraid to admit weakness. They're proud in public and work hard in private. When writing, they're able to articulate what they want, like, dislike. They're self-critical and don't eviscerate each other when upset. Rather, they operate by in-joke and withering aside, a reliable shorthand developed over the years. That's fine in some contexts, but communicating thoughts and feelings is hard. For all their evident self-reflection and emotional intelligence, Suede are still men of a certain age, moulded by an industry where tensions were routinely suppressed, grievances withheld – and rarely does suppression work out. You're ill equipped to face down problems, or spot future ones coming.

Even when things are going well the band don't really connect emotionally with each other. (Simon is the most open, friendly, popular. But then, he's not driving anything. And he's not always there.) They don't tend to celebrate or console; they don't get too high after a success; they don't cry, talk about hopes and dreams. Despite a lifetime of investment in the same thing they don't get physically close, make eye contact on stage, hug or kiss, either as performance or real human intimacy, in private moments. Rather, they get on with things, heads down. When Brett connects, it's usually with a crowd. As he's so often the focus of attention, that can make it seem like they're the kind of band who put all hands into the centre of a circle and give a speech about how they always believed in each other. Sure, there are band meetings *after* gigs, congratulations or commiserations, brief reflections over pizza, for those that eat it. But they're not overtly emotional.

In spring 2013, there was no big discussion about whether to carry on. Brett wasn't about to return to solo records, but didn't say so, and no one asked. Same for Richard and Artmagic. Neil was still in Penguin Cafe, though it went unspoken that Suede came first. The return to new material was not going to be a one-off, though – bluntly put, the business model didn't allow for years on the beach. But again, this went unsaid. When I asked how they came to make a second Suede reunion record, answers were muted or avoidant. As Neil has said, 'There was no five-year plan or anything. We just kind of looked at each other and went, "Do another one? Yeah, go on then."' Then he paused, for comic effect. 'I think that's partly to do with our inability to communicate with each other.' That inability might sometimes have felt like a joke, but during the making of Suede #7 it was also serious.

By the time *Bloodsports* went top ten, things were changing; as the band were getting re-established, so was the back office led by Ian and run by Didz, with ex-manager Charlie back on board as long-term tour manager. Suede were about to hit the road for their biggest tour in many years – a proper bus and everything. This would cross the UK, with extended visits to Europe, Asia and festivals too. On 30 March they played Ally Pally in high spirits, starting with the opening trio from *Bloodsports*. In April they were on *Later ... With Jools Holland*, *The Jonathan Ross Show* and did an Absolute Radio gig at Abbey Road Studios. In May and June there was a smattering of one-offs: Norway, Denmark, Spain, but commitments were sporadic or scheduled for autumn. That left gaps; also opportunities. Ed's role was essential here. If they thought he was needed before, that had just been proved once more. This year, then, Suede would tour the new album, using space between live dates to write the next one, Ed on board from day one this time – emboldened, and a core part of the set-up.

HAMINADOS AMBITION

On 31 May 2013, Brett, Ed, Neil and Richard met in Haminados, a Greek café on Chepstow Road near Brett's place in Notting Hill. It was a sunny day and there was, as Neil recalls, 'a welcome sense of possibility' in the air. Ed's recalls, 'The mood was for pushing on ... to keep building momentum.' There were two things to decide: musical direction, and approach. The first might have been difficult but turned out to be easy. The second might have been easy but, in Brett's words, 'It turned out to be a fucking nightmare.'*

---

* Richard also used exactly these words, 'a fucking nightmare', when describing his experience to me.

For Richard, the initial reception to *Bloodsports* had been crucial for his confidence, but he knew they'd been straightforward musically. 'This time,' Richard says, 'we all wanted to create something that had more of a narrative arc and was more ambitious.' New things meant bigger things, more complex things, more range, working towards one long 'overall journey'. Counterintuitive as ever – Suede can be brought together by feeling they're working against something – everyone wanted to make a determinedly interconnected record for the age of bits-and-pieces streaming services, which was taking off. In Mat's words, 'The success of *Bloodsports* gave us all the confidence to look forward to the next thing, together, and hope.' Early references were Pink Floyd's *Wish You Were Here* and Talk Talk's *Spirit of Eden*, Richard and Neil thinking in terms of writing motifs that might appear, then reappear, periodically.

L to R: *Ed, Brett and Richard in Haminados, Chepstow Road, 31 May 2013.*
Photo by Neil

There were two main reasons for this shift. The artistic reason was a desire to stretch out, pursuing the more expansive, ambitious side of Suede's music – 'ambitious' being the most used word in that first meeting – but with Richard and Neil defining the band's sound anew, together. (If 'Always' hadn't been ambitious enough, then here was an opportunity to remedy that.) In Ed's words: 'I wanted to get away from this piecemeal thing ... [writing a] single, [then a] not quite single ... I said straight away: Richard and Neil have earned the opportunity to have a musical statement of their own. Something more adventurous and cohesive.'

The practical reason was related to the artistic one. *Bloodsports* pleased all, in part, because expectations were low – but dreams of being back on Radio 1 in the UK, or making global pop playlists, were clearly in the past. Okay, there was a bigger core Suede audience than expected. Enough to keep the band afloat, maybe – a new two-album deal with Warners suggested they had label support too. But the days of sustained airplay were probably gone; they may never have a charting single again.* Fashions change, sounds change, culture shifts. Suede remained, if noticed at all, a relic of a previous decade, and they were only going to grow more distant from the current moment with age. Still, with acceptance comes liberation. Those already listening responded strongly to the grandeur on *Bloodsports*, the bigger sound on Side Two that was less radio-friendly but contained more depth.

Suede had plenty of musical tensions in the first era, but there seemed little chance of making that mistake now. Richard recalls: 'Though we'll often disagree on individual pieces, the band do genuinely tend to agree

* They haven't. Their last charting single was 'Attitude' in October 2003, peaking at number fourteen. This suggests chart placing doesn't necessarily define whether a song will be remembered, or valued, by fans or the public. But it's a salutary detail. Not one song from the Suede reunion era has charted as a single.

on direction. That's partly because we know how destructive it has been [in the past] ... on *Head Music* I might have been too young or lacking confidence to say I wanted to expand on the *Coming Up* sound, push harder with a guitar-led album – but I didn't know how to, and pulling in different directions led to a weaker result.' No different directions this time, then.

The second decision was not about *what* to make, but *how* to make it.

Richard and Neil had just spent eighteen months writing much more than almost any band would to produce a single album. The prospect of continuing that way was terrifying to Richard. 'It was like, here's the mountain, you've just scaled a massive one – now here's another, get climbing! Oh God, you know? This time we thought, let's just work on stuff we think is *great* ... We were gonna have this multi-layered, multi-mood musical journey with recurring themes. Give it to Brett and say, now your turn.' Ed also wanted a change. '[The *Bloodsports* approach] was just the antithesis of what I thought we should be doing on the next record,' he says. There was also the hardcore fanbase, who might appreciate a leftward move – the best move anyway, if the old rules of their previous life no longer applied. This mattered. In a band you're trying to sell something, and Suede had the fans in mind: 'We wanted something they could get more out of, to not hear everything on the first listen, and albums like *Wish You Were Here* are like that. Whatever you think about prog rock – and it's a horrible word, even the sound of it is horrible! – they made records where they thought, this is going to be a world of our own, it's going to take you somewhere. We had a strong mindset, like that. We wanted *an album*.' Richard was energised, Neil too, but Ed led from the front.

Instead of swamping Brett with two or three ideas a day, this time they'd move faster *and* slower, with each idea more developed, more time spent on it.* Ed remembers Brett being unsure, though others thought him enthusiastic, both about direction and the weight of material coming his way. Brett wanted to sharpen up lyrically; more time on each piece might help that. He was getting older. He couldn't write the old love and poison songs forever. But what else was there? Since becoming a father the year before, he'd experienced a new kind of love – often sitting with an acoustic guitar at dawn with baby Lucian, playing him sweet little songs – but also a new fear, and he wondered how to feed this into his songwriting while dodging cringe sentimentality. 'People writing about their children is usually so bad,' he says now. 'But I'm awkward, stubborn. I thought I could do it better than most.' Maybe if he was given a complete album's worth of music he could write a coherent suite of lyrics to go with it, one that explored the terror of parenthood. He mentioned the idea to Mat, who demurred. It was probably a terrible idea. People writing about their children is usually *so bad*.† Over the summer, Brett was in Ibiza on and off for a couple of months with Jodie and the family. The plan was, write the album with Ed directing and send the music to Brett in September, giving him two months to come up with parts. 'We thought of it as an experiment,' recalls Richard now. 'Ed may have been certain, but that's not how Neil and I are. We thought it was worth trying. I did wonder, at the back of my mind, whether it would work out.'

---

* Neil explains the process: 'The songs were rather more involved and convoluted than the music for BS or AF [*Bloodsports* or *Autofiction*]. With BS (and later with AF and AD [*Antidepressants*]), if a demo proved tricky to write to, it would often not become a song, and the demos that did become songs would be relatively simple, less twisty. We consciously wanted NT to be more complex, the music more meandering, the chord progressions more tricksy than BS.'

† Joking, Mat has said many times that he would have advised against many of Brett's most successful evolutions as a lyricist in recent years.

At this time, Ed says he was 'a bit obsessed by *Dog Man Star*', thinking this 'another album #2 that could play into similar musical territory, led by Neil and Richard', though hopefully without the fracture that followed. The band disagreed. *Dog Man Star* was twenty years old. They didn't sit around discussing how to emulate the past. Despite the much-documented drama around the making of Suede's second album, Ed felt this kind of return could not have been their first statement upon reforming, but represented a perfect second move. In Richard's words, 'Though Ed hated [making *Dog Man Star*] and still had nightmares about it, he still thinks that horrific tension was really creative and exciting.' So, he tried to recreate it. Perhaps *Bloodsports*, in Ed's mind, was Suede's debut repeated, a new version of the old band, starting anew. Now they had to follow it with the difficult second album. Again.

Dog Man Star was made in a different world. Back then demos were written by Bernard then shared on tape, with Brett adding vocals after. Then they'd go into the studio, working songs up in rehearsal. In the early days, they wrote twenty songs and released them all. The hit rate was high, in part because they felt like kings of the world, in part because they didn't have much history yet and didn't fear repeating themselves. Music first, top line second was simple, it produced results, and minimised singer–guitarist interaction. It also coincided with Bernard having the confidence of youth, opportunity and immediate success. But a different Suede line-up had literally just made a record the opposite way, led by Ed, to *avoid* first-era mistakes. Why reverse that now?

Ed pushes the band to experiment, but he's also always harked back to Suede's early days. Even now, after Suede's tenth album, his favourite recording is still 'My Insatiable One', the B-side to 'The Drowners', recorded fast, for a few quid, in 1992. That iteration of the band saw its first breakthrough; you're only young once, and it's special. But *Dog Man Star* almost broke the band. Bernard left after giving the others an explicit ultimatum: it's Ed or me. So, it's unlikely Ed would want to recreate *Dog Man Star* conditions at a time of harmony and optimism. Rather, he was interested in recreating aspects of the atmosphere, making space for signature new sounds, but still sounding recognisably Suede. Perhaps, if made under similar conditions, this music might be a kind of partner to *Dog Man Star*. All with Brett writing as he had in the early '90s.

One example shows how Old Suede – whether or how it would reappear – was part of Ed's thinking at the time. One afternoon, he floated the idea of knitting the record together with a collage of rerecorded moments from the first three Suede albums, 'almost like memories'. It was only one afternoon, Ed himself says the idea was 'rightly torpedoed', and it was never discussed again, but still, it's notable. Brett was set against the idea and, though Ed mentioned it to Neil, it never got as far as Richard. (It was reported to Richard by Brett, after the fact.) In practice, how would this have worked? Richard playing Bernard's old parts on a new Suede album? Songs credited to Anderson–Butler–Oakes–Codling? A snatch of 'Animal Nitrate', or 'Beautiful Ones', fed through the time machine, before switching to something new? Surely it would have been an acknowledgement that the band's best days were in the past.* The nature of recording means ideas are constantly being floated and shot down, floated and shot down. It feels cruel to dwell on this. But the idea of a callback did jar, and for some it was representative of Ed's fondness for looking to Suede's history. (In fact, there is precedent for Suede

---

* Neil: 'We scoffed at Ed's idea, of course, but done in the right way, like a sweep on an analogue radio picking up bits of old tunes [exactly like 'Wish You Were Here' by Pink Floyd] it might actually have sounded okay, but how could you start a song with the riff from "Beautiful Ones" and then switch to something else without it sounding deflating? Or can you imagine a Suede song featuring a little nod to the riff from "Animal Nitrate" or something and it being credited to Anderson–Butler–Oakes? No way.'

callbacks: on the extended, unedited version of 'The Asphalt World' you can make out Bernard playing a slowed, sarcastic version of his part to 'The Drowners' at the end. But it's like he's blowing a raspberry. It's not a tribute to earlier, good times.)

As for Brett's new, further reduced role in writing: it's one thing to make every song work in your twenties. It's quite another two decades later, when the songwriting team is different, the tech means you don't *need* to work that way and you've covered so much ground it's hard to find new territory. Brett explained his reservations, but Ed believed you don't make your best work when comfortable. With *Bloodsports*, Brett could discard musical ideas quickly, the 'schoolmaster' often 'pouring cold water on good ideas'. If Brett was made to do this, wouldn't he have to make it work? He was prepared to give it a go.

'A BODY OF WORK WE CONSIDERED AN ALBUM': EARLY BULLSEYES

They got started after the Barcelona gig on 5 July 2013, and on day one, the very first piece of music they wrote excited everyone. This was 'I Don't Know How to Reach You', featuring a drum part the early-days Suede drummer Justin Welch, later of Elastica, called the 'Suede bossa nova'.* 'It was like hitting the bullseye, first time,' says Mat. 'We couldn't believe it. We thought, this is gonna be easy!'

Neil also uses the bullseye metaphor: 'Normally ... you write stuff for a year and none of that is kept. So to start with an anchor track, it felt like beginner's luck, you just casually walk up to the dartboard – oh, bullseye!' For Brett too, this felt fresh. The lyric was filled with charged imagery:

---

* This is a tradition that goes back to 1992's 'He's Dead' and has surfaced in different iterations since. Justin was in Suede for 'about three weeks' but has remained on good terms. His band Aircooled supported Suede on tour in 2023.

I'd steal a shadow for you
I'd love you like a knife
From the towers, I try to call you
From the depths of the power lines
Tell me the things that scare you
Touch me with terror's flame
Fill me with hesitation
Again.

Devotion, desperation, fear. The chorus explored emotional distance, the speaker reflecting on a long-gone closeness, now stuck in regretful memory, unable to connect. All these things would recur in the rest of the album's lyrics. All were there from the start.

Looking back now, Mat identifies 'I Don't Know How to Reach You' as critical: 'It represents a shift – that's when Brett started writing about family. Also, there's something quite gnarly and un-single-ish about it.' Gnarly was what they were looking for. '"... Reach You" I think is musically interesting,' says Ed, playing the song back in his home studio. 'Richard and Neil start in these chromatic shifts, these horrible little changes, the devil's interval is in there a couple of times – it goes to the places that you wouldn't particularly want to. The fact that everyone liked it meant we could just release the strictures a bit. There didn't need to be this *Coming Up*-style directness to everything. That became a huge influence on the record. ["... Reach You" showed] we didn't mind going further.'

Good material came fast. Richard and Neil worked at Ed's new place, which was near Suicide Bridge in north London. They arrived each morning and Ed, in his enthusiasm, would play stuff before they began, saying, 'Let's do something like this!' Some were strange little things – 'He was trying to get a certain musical flavour out of us that he thought he could see in each song we were working on,' says Richard. One day, he played a Thompson Twins track. Another day, Alice Cooper. 'He's excitable and he wants to play you stuff,' says Richard. 'It can be infectious. But it's also often not stuff we like.' On days Brett was there, he might be the one saying, 'Err, can you turn that off?' Last time out, Richard 'felt like a performing seal' having to come up with ideas on the spot; but now he *wanted* to work that way.* Neil can also respond in the room, but Ed describes their contrasting approaches: 'Neil is very painstaking,' he says. 'He feels his way around, wants to do things that aren't obvious ... He can't get an idea till he gets a sound, and he can't get a sound until he gets an idea.'

The songs written in this first rush included the ballad 'I Can't Give Her What She Wants' – Richard wrote the guitar part in the room – and the more pleading, full-band 'What I'm Trying to Tell You'. This excited Ed because it was the closest thing to a poppy-sounding single so far. 'I loved the chorus on that!' he says now. 'Brett just came up with the chorus, bang, so suddenly – it was funky, it reminded me of something from *Station to Station*, the way the groove works ... there's lots of real inventiveness on there.' The slow, grandiose 'The Fur and the Feathers' came next, born as a Neil piano riff, which he and Richard then developed. Brett also wrote to 'Pale Snow' right away, the demo cut 'n' shut together by Neil from 'the most successful parts of two very different songs' – the end of 'Something in Me Breaks' and the start of 'I've Seen

---

* Richard: 'You basically sit and strum away at a guitar until someone says, "That's good!" Until then, music had been my small bit of self-expression, my genius I send when it's done – that's my statement. Totally different to coming up with a riff in the room.'

the Way That You Look at Her'.* This proved working on fewer ideas for longer *was* faster, even when ideas were refashioned. Ed again: 'When they were together in the man cave in my old flat, the songs were painted in this beautiful way – we hadn't done that for ages. Brett was there for the first bit too. He was on great form. He'd walk around with his little Dictaphone and would then go away to do his work, head buzzing with ideas.'

Over July and August, working at Ed's – sometimes with Brett there, sometimes keeping in touch from Ibiza – Richard and Neil wrote a whole album of music. The songs above were all agreed on, with Brett's contributions suggesting an emerging theme. Even the titles of 'I Don't Know How to Reach You', 'I Can't Give Her What She Wants' and 'What I'm Trying to Tell You' suggested a preoccupation with trying to bridge some unbridgeable emotional gap. (The nature of the relationships explored was often ambiguous. Were they between lovers? Parents and children? If so, was the 'I' of the songs the child, or parent, or both?) Along with these five there were another half-dozen that, Richard says, 'we thought were equally brilliant'. He saw the possibility of finally putting more of his own stamp on a Suede record, one he could be hugely proud of.

Richard remembers, 'We came up with a body of work we considered an album, pretty quickly.' This contained all Richard, Neil and Ed had hoped for in those initial conversations, before writing a note. Intricacy. Motifs weaving throughout. A big sound. More complex, layered musical sections. Even a suite of short pieces at the end that they referred to as 'Abbey Road', given its structural similarity to the closing suite on the Beatles album of the same name, and the fact that it was supposed to

---

* 'This was a thing I loved so much about this record,' remembers Ed. 'The amount of keyboards that were on it – nice orchestration, and the keyboards and guitars really responded to each other.'

go at the end. Given the complications of the previous few years, it's surprising the album was written so quickly, Richard and Neil able to conjure their 'ambitious, cinematic' new sound as if pouring water into a cup. You want a *Wish You Were Here*? Sure, no problem, Blob. Here it is. Experiment successful.

Well, Brett tried.

It's been said in the past, when the tricksy process of making this album has been hinted at (they've been extremely guarded about this in public),* that Brett simply declared he 'couldn't write' to some of the material the others produced. It's more nuanced, though. That suggests a whole tranche of instrumentals somewhere on a hard drive, waiting for vocals that never came. That's not true. Brett worked hard to come up with parts for nearly all these songs over several months, and no one expected a bullseye every time anyway.

These writing sessions were broken up by a short run of gigs in August taking in South Korea, Spain, Romania, Northern Ireland and one back home. It's hard to imagine Suede agreeing in the '90s to a gig curated by English Heritage, but now they played the 'stately and faintly preposterous' Kenwood House in a 'Live by the Lake' gig 'in the north-eastern armpit of Hampstead Heath', close to Highgate, the part of London much of *Dog Man Star* was written in. So, a typically Suede mixture of the gutter and the stars, then. Fans pissed in the bushes, the band opened with early favourite 'The Big Time', while they intercut *Bloodsports* with songs from their debut on its twentieth anniversary. Reviewers noted some other '90s lead singers had become more like

---

* Interviews to promote *Night Thoughts* (e.g. a track-by-track series of videos with the band and Ed together, now available on their website) either hugely played down or simply didn't mention any of these struggles. There were only very occasional mentions of it being hard, and of the three recording blocks covered in this chapter.

caricatures, while Brett – once *such* a caricature – seemed to have stopped being one. He was energetic, healthier looking, pogoing like a kid, seemingly delighted to be back in Suede.

After returning from Ibiza, Ed says Brett seemed to have cooled on the approach to Suede #7. When I asked about timing, he gave a broader answer, seeing connections between past and present challenges: 'By the time we got to *Bloodsports*, Brett had got used to relying on the instant chemistry he has when he reacts to a piece of music. It had yielded dividends for him, so he believed in it ... He'd go home, put on some headphones and try and try to come up with something. It was a very private thing he did, none of us got to see it. He had to somehow ignite the material – and if it didn't catch fire he'd say, "I can't get anything out of that, what else have you got?"' Unable to find that instant chemistry with this new material, after Kenwood House he said, 'Okay, what else have we got?' Soon after, he tried again: 'What if we've only got half an album of material?' To which Ed answered, 'That's the album, Blob. That's the album! You have to bloody write to it!'

Rarely is a neat story true. As we've seen, Richard and Neil sent or shared pieces as they went, Ed's response sometimes affecting whether they progressed. It was all very well talking about 'a single piece of music', but that music would inevitably be made up of songs. The question of *how* it would all come together was set aside, though the process was more familiar than imagined at that first meeting. Maybe this wouldn't work? Ed believed pressuring Brett was the only way to find out. Maybe some of that tension might find its way into the music – but for now, it was time to get back on the tour bus. Before they left, Richard and Neil sent songs and instrumental pieces to Mat and Simon to rehearse.

Over the next six weeks, Suede gigged hard. After starting out in Turkey, Singapore, then a tour of China and Japan, they came home to a stiflingly hot gig in the 600-capacity Garage in Highbury,* before embarking on a quick eight-date sweep around the UK and Ireland. After that it was sixteen dates in Europe: the Czech Republic, France, Portugal, Germany. Responses were good, the band were efficient, sharp, and smart about song selection, rewarding fans with deep cuts. (Sometimes they opened with the *Bloodsports* closer, 'Faultlines'. But they were as likely to start with 'Still Life', 'Daddy's Speeding' or 'Europe Is Our Playground' as with anything new.) For Richard the tour was fun, despite the relentless schedule and background anxieties – also, despite deciding to make a change to his performance routine. More worried about his hearing now, he started to play with earplugs in. (At first, it was like 'having a bath with your socks on', he says. 'But I couldn't play without them now.')†

On tour, the band practised new music in soundcheck ahead of recording. Since getting clean, Brett survives travel by following a strict routine, meaning sleep, food and focus are all-important. It's how he maintains energy at shows. That means downtime, either side of performance. The others have got plenty to think about, but they don't whirl around for ninety minutes, the focus of the room. So, while Brett was resting or in the dressing room, Simon, Mat, Neil and Richard trialled the likes of 'Pale Snow', 'I Don't Know How to Reach You', 'Enemies' or 'Abbey Road'. Not since the band's earliest days had they rehearsed new

---

* Neil recalls: 'They had to open the load-in doors at the back of the stage to keep the audience (and the band) from fainting.'

† Richard says he once left his earplugs at the hotel before a gig and 'felt like my head was exploding'. He'd changed routine mid-tour once before, in 2002. He used to wear glasses and take them off for gigs: 'I didn't want to look like a nerd, so the audience would be a blur. I'm quite myopic; I was blind on stage, I had to squint to see the setlist. That was normal for me, for years. Then I got contact lenses and could suddenly see the audience. I was so uncomfortable.'

songs on tour. But they didn't have long for pre-production, being due at ICP Studios in Brussels in November. They had to be ready. The same month, Suede also put out a new box set of the band's studio albums plus *Sci-Fi Lullabies* on vinyl, re-contextualising the band's past.

'YOU DON'T WANT TO TURN PEOPLE INTO ENEMIES'

Suede played their last gig of 2013 in Amsterdam on 23 November, the whole tour considered a success. That's no small thing, though this was now taken for granted – that they were a good, improving live act. They came home to prep for ICP, Brett's unease building. He asked, 'Should we be doing this when I don't have anything good enough for half of these songs?' Mat felt, quietly, that it was risky to spend money on recordings without the singer, when the singer kept saying he was struggling. But he didn't demand plans change, neither did anyone else, and again the chorus came back from Ed to Brett, 'Blob, the music's fucking fantastic. You just need to *write* to it.' Brett and Ed were increasingly at loggerheads, with the other less confrontational members of the band waiting for something to give.

Despite the atmosphere, Ed remembers this time as productive: 'When we went to Brussels the first time there was this awful tension and cloud hanging over everybody. At some point I had to go in the studio and conduct. Brett's mood had an effect on Simon and Mat, they could see his frustration, but we actually got *tons* done. We recorded the bulk of the backing tracks in three days!' Reflecting on Brett's role now, Ed is put in mind of the relationship between actors and the films they've starred in, having little sense of overall effect until first screening. 'They're involved, but they've got no idea what they're taking part in,' he says. 'Brett felt that way, but Neil, Richard and I knew how it knitted together. We knew how strong the atmosphere was. It had a real aroma to it. But Brett's headspace was, you know – I've got no melody for this bit, I don't know what to do here.'

Richard found this hard. 'I don't like being in the middle of conflict,' he explains, 'and I felt that at times Ed was fabricating conflict ... Neil and I were very proud of [the music], but I don't remember us ever feeling belligerent – it's not our style to be so direct, whereas it *is* Ed's way. You know, there was no single moment where I thought, I've done my job and I'm now going to hang up my guitar until the next album.' Ed is thoughtful when we discuss this response of Richard's. 'Some part of me was looking to create drama in an otherwise happy band set-up,' he says. 'Like, somehow I thought generating conflict would also generate great songs.' Richard again: 'We're in a *band*. We're trying to work *together*. You don't want to turn people into enemies. And Neil and I are, when it comes to confrontation, we don't get stuck in. We're pretty passive.'

It's easy to say someone should have stepped in here. Yes, if there'd been a more open, honest meeting pre-Brussels, and if others had spoken up, then things could have played out differently. But then, there were mitigating factors. One of the few major studios in the heart of a major European city, ICP is also an old Belgian factory. It was Ed's favourite place to record, which meant it was cheaper than recording in London. They knew it well, it had great gear, a good atmosphere; at ICP, you can roll out of bed and start recording. It had to be booked months in advance, too, so they were locked in long before the sessions came around. It was reasonable to think they might be ready. Also, there was half a record ready to go that everyone was behind. Had Brett come up with top lines for, say, another two or three more songs, it might have felt like a healthier exercise. But as it was, the band were all crossing their fingers, while Ed's line remained: 'Blob, you know what to do. Your job.'

At ICP, when they clashed, Ed told Brett that not every part needed vocals. Maybe a few instrumentals, or at least more instrumental sections, might be fine. (They'd done this before, with 'Still Life' for example, on *Dog Man Star*, though that started as a conventional song. Only later was Brett happy to step back and allow an extended instrumental section.) Brett sometimes wondered if there was space for him here – whether these songs were in fact, instrumentals. Richard says, 'Obviously I hoped he'd find a way, but I thought Brett's approach was fair enough. After all, what is Suede to people? It's Brett. It's him, at the front of the stage. If we release something that doesn't feature Brett then it's not really Suede, is it?'

After Christmas most of the band returned to Belgium, all twelve songs recorded in full by 19 January 2014. If anything, this period only made Richard surer that what they'd written was new, exciting territory. He loved his parts and the idea of the album, but the more Brett tried to work on the likes of 'Abbey Road', the less it felt possible. Around this time, Brett and Didz visited Belgium, Didz sleeping on the studio sofa – the management couldn't force Brett to magic up parts, but couldn't make the band start again either. By mid-January, Ed aimed to have most of the album down, though they knew they might have to go back and do more. Richard and Neil met with manager Ian in Mayfair on the 21st to see if they could keep going this way. They felt that meeting ended positively, though after another session in Musikbox in Kentish Town on the 23rd, further email discussions followed. What to do? Ed suggested pushing on for another couple of weeks with these songs, then maybe trying to write a single, with everyone still hoping Brett would come good in the end.

DON'T NAME YOUR PETS: RICHARD'S HOME ARCHIVE

On the top floor of Richard's house is a room with guitars and a mini-studio, where sometimes the band write or rehearse. During Covid lockdowns, with little to do, Richard went back to the very first demo he recorded as a teenager, on 26 April 1995, and digitised the whole of his Suede history. One day at his, when I asked him how he felt back in January 2014 during these difficulties making Suede #7, we went up and he played me the unused music. He scrolled through files, occasionally giving a quiet sigh. He cued up the first song. 'Don't name your pets ...' he muttered, with a half-laugh. 'Because one by one they'll all die! I got too attached to all this.' Then again, a little more slowly. 'Tooooo attached.' Richard's archive contains the entire 'body of work' that was Suede #7, original version.

'Enemies' opens with a classical piano figure then moves towards a big, fuzzy guitar-heavy chorus. It's intricate, layered and knotty, and couldn't have appeared on any previous Suede album. 'One of my favourite pieces of music we've made,' said Richard, turning it up. 'There was a vision for a musical journey here.' He shuffled in the chair and pointed out little features, saying 'You'll hear that later,' or 'This returns on "Abbey Road".' 'Enemies' sounds like mid-'70s Pink Floyd fed through a Suede song generator. Which song on *Wish You Were Here* did Richard think 'Enemies' sounded like? 'All of them!' he grinned, inspecting the folders, close-up. 'Enemies' Brett couldn't nail. There was a full lyric and melody, delivered tentatively, the vocal searching for a home: 'Death is your ambition, love is just a scheme,' goes one line, though it sounds forced, confused. Richard leaned back, in his happy place, listening.

Like the Beatles melange it's named for, 'Abbey Road' is several short chunks in one – this sounds even more Floyd than 'Enemies'. 'We wanted the end to be bombastic,' Richard said, pointing at the screen each time a motif from 'Enemies' reappeared. Did they try to repurpose these ideas further down the line? 'Oh yes. Well, having lost this, we may have been *forced* to attempt something similar again next time.' As we talked, the end of 'The Waves', an alternative version of 'Where the Pigeons Go',* opened out into this exquisite guitar riff, recognisable from 'When You Are/Were Young'. They might have discarded half an album here, but they also went back to pick the bones out of it.†

While the sun came through the skylight on the top floor, Richard clicked more files last opened a decade ago. 'I've Seen the Way You Look at Her.'‡ 'Something in Me Breaks'.§ The Manics-esque guitars of 'Month of Sundays'.¶ Richard played songs from later sessions, too, lost songs including 'You're Gonna Hurt Me Again'. 'Oh, this one!' 'Oh, this!' He listened for a long time. Though clearly pained, he was happy. When he finally left the laptop, walking down the bright rainbow-coloured stairs to the floors below, Richard coughed. 'Like I say. Don't. Name. Your. Pets.'

Richard and Neil began looking for another half an album. In

---

* 'Described by Neil as 'a stately, quiet–loud song along the lines of "Sometimes I Feel I'll Float Away",' 'Where the Pigeons Go' was supposed run into 'Abbey Road'. Featuring the Suede chord, this song had a spidery guitar line that reappeared, in another context, later on.

† Brett liked the concept of 'The Waves' enough to hone the idea for 'Tides', on Suede's next album. 'The Waves' was once tried as a potential penultimate track on Suede #7 before a 'When You Were Young' reprise. It was also considered as an album closer: 'Oh how I shivered that day, when I stepped in from the rain / and put my suitcase away'. They stare into 'the oblivion' of the mirror: 'I will turn my face / and no one sees me.'

‡ One of two pieces that became 'Pale Snow', this is much faster, and has different lyrics.

§ Full of unexpected, thoughtful musical changes, this contains a placeholder vocal. The end of the song was lifted for the other part of 'Pale Snow'.

¶ Rooted in the demo 'Eat the Teacher', Richard says only Ed liked this song, really, though memories differ. Brett didn't like it at first. Then he wrote a lyric and *did*, but by then everyone else had gone off it.

Richard's words, 'We were just writing and writing, back to the scatter-gun approach of *Bloodsports*, just hoping something would appear.' Neil buried himself in the details, but Richard struggled: 'I felt I'd tried hard to spread my wings, be ambitious – and look what happened. I was bitter and angry. I carried on because I felt I had to, but none of the songs we wrote were any good.' A pity, not least because the band had booked more studio time, once again in hope, in Sarm Studios close to Brett's place. This session was a creative low point: they wrote songs like 'Playground Words', 'Exit', 'Polkadots', 'Command Me' and 'Shame',* songs Richard says 'were all written at Ed's', that might have been finished off if they'd been in the right headspace for it, though they also recorded some vocals and other sounds used later on.† Of these, 'Shame' was generally considered the best. It's not terrible – 'the choice of weapons is more than half the battle' is a nice line, while the rolling toms and Joy Division bass line are enticing. But as a whole 'Shame' is too reliant on tired ideas and old imagery; the band were stuck. In other cases, there was disagreement over quality. Richard didn't like 'You're Gonna Hurt Me Again', though Mat and Brett rated it. Richard kept trying to work with the song, as he remembers now, changing the chords and trying new versions 'to please please please others' – but he was miserable. They tried bringing it back a few times, then that, too, got put to one side.

Around this time, some possible work came Ed's way. Ed and Hans Zimmer had been friends since school. These days Zimmer is a film composer and music producer with over 150 film credits, two Oscars and a slew of other awards. He's one of the most celebrated film composers

---

* This sounded a little like 'It's Always the Quiet Ones' on *Autofiction*.

† Some of the sounds in 'The Fur and the Feathers' were recorded by Ed, the sound of children coming from the playground of Colville Primary School, a little further south on Portobello Road.

alive. But he played keyboards in London in various outfits around the time young Ed was starting out, also as a keyboard player, touring with the Psychedelic Furs. In spring 2014, Hans was heading up a stable of composers and asked Ed if he'd be interested in movies.* Working for Hans might mean moving to California – though he didn't know yet how much work there might be, or if it would just be short term. Meanwhile, there were lots of Suede meetings. Some at Ed's. Some at Brett's. But no solution was found to the impasse. After March/April 2014 the band began writing without Ed.

The problem was compounded by an upcoming twentieth-anniversary celebration of *Dog Man Star*.† After seeing them at their recent Ally Pally show, Noel Gallagher invited Suede to return to the Albert Hall for another Teenage Cancer Trust fundraiser, while they also agreed to a handful of far-flung dates. Had they been thriving, making the finishing touches to their 21st-century Neil-and-Richard-led art rock masterpiece, this might have felt like a victory lap. There was much pride in *Dog Man Star* for those who made it, and Richard was more open to the idea than some expected. (At this point, he still felt like he owed something to Suede's past lives.) In a rare one-off, they were due to play with the Dirty Pretty Strings, (featuring Ellie Stanford, also sisters Amy, Gita and Rosie Langley), the string quartet joining the band for half a dozen key songs. But did they really want this *now*? Towards the end of March the band spent three days in Sarm recording 'Shame', 'Command Me' and 'Playground Words', which no one thought were working, before they had to switch modes,

* Ed remembers: 'I wasn't moving to America – then out of nowhere got a call from Hans. We'd had this casual friendship, I first met him when I was fourteen ... he belongs to a group of people I knew when I was a schoolboy. He's very clever. We'd been hanging out, he wanted a synthesiser I'd designed. Then he offered for me to come to LA.'

† There was new artwork and packaging planned for a *Dog Man Star* re-release and live album, designed by Paul Khera.

with only two days of rehearsal booked for the *Dog Man Star* shows. No progress, then. More money spent. Not a little sense of panic.

A warm-up was booked at the O2 Academy in Oxford, two nights before the Albert Hall. Ian came down to discuss the new record. Soundcheck ran as normal, then everyone went for dinner in a nearby restaurant. Ian had seen bands fall out over making albums many times, had little patience for Suede eating themselves again, and plenty else on his mind that day, anyway. He put it to the band: *Bloodsports* had turned out so well, what was the problem? To understand what happened next, you have to know how Suede talk to each other, or don't. If in doubt they just keep working, though to work effectively you need a plan, and without one, something had to give. But what?

When discussion turned to what they were trying to do differently this time around, they used the language they'd been using for a year now. About doing something more complex, dramatic, darker, more ambitious. But to Brett, at least in the moment, that might have sounded like a criticism of *Bloodsports*. (By this point, others had cooled on that record, while Brett didn't yet want to admit, even indirectly, to its flaws.) Brett banged the table: '*Bloodsports* was a fucking great album!' It was typical of him to stand four-square behind the last thing he'd made, but this felt like he was trying too hard to sell it to those he made it with, as if that would somehow make sense of what they had to do next.

As the meal went on Brett became more defensive, saying he'd *told* everyone they only had half an album and that this approach wouldn't work, then they went ahead anyway. Spent the money. Recorded the parts. When the problem didn't magically solve itself, he didn't want to be blamed for the fallout. In another band, this argument might have escalated. But neither Richard nor Neil point fingers or scream. Meanwhile, neither Mat nor Simon drive the creative process; they're not aggressive or dominant personalities either. They've seen worse and come through it. Anyway, Suede don't have shouting matches – even Brett and Ed are more like an old bickering married couple than two people filled with hatred. (Everyone agrees they respect each other, even when things are at their worst.) In Richard's words, when band meetings go wrong, 'Everyone just waits for it to be over rather than getting stuck in with both fists.' After the meal, nothing was resolved. All they'd done was admit they didn't know what to do. But Ian understood just how strained things were, how unhappy Brett was, too. After dinner, everyone headed back to the venue. It doesn't matter what happens before a gig. When doors open, fans file in and the lights go down, you just do it. Which they did. Richard again: 'It was fine! In a way, performing is the safest thing we can do. We know what we're all for. You just stand in your spot. Switch on. And make it work.'

Two nights later, they really made it work.

The *Dog Man Star* anniversary show at the Albert Hall with the Dirty Pretty Strings was a success, in part because the band set aside differences in the here and now. Playing these songs was sometimes complicated – but one curiosity of Suede's reunion years is that the band seem more at peace with its legacy. What made the 2014 return hard was not the album itself, nor 1994's shadow, but simply the fact that, having put the band back together so many times since, Suede were struggling, yet again, to keep going. In Richard's words, 'We were doing this thing celebrating the past when we couldn't make a future.'

SAVING THE SUEDE REUNION

The band returned to China and Japan in April and May, including stops in Beijing, Tokyo and Osaka. *Dog Man Star*-branded shows filled rooms around the world, and they might have done more. But these were short trips. With Ed working on another project in Prague, Neil and Richard were back to writing. Rather than being the focused group of people they were at the start of writing Suede #7, they were starting to drift apart. Richard recalls: 'I'd been there before. I had an older head on my shoulders, but it was a different version of the same old thing. Feeling powerless. Not knowing what to write. You think, what am I doing this for? Why am I in this band? I was resentful. It's terrible, but I just thought: fuck this, I'm going to switch my focus to other parts of my life. This is a mess, let someone else clean it up.' That meant Neil and Brett doing the cleaning. Neil reverted to writing alone – no change in direction, though it was unclear what they were looking for. 'Neil is much more philosophical,' Richard says now. 'When things go wrong, I retreat, but he stays on task.' On 23 May Richard went away for two weeks with his partner, leaving Neil at work with Brett, regularly going round to his place. They'd been stuck for nearly six months, five songs going stale since December.

Brett and Neil got things going again. One new song was 'Tightrope', another 'When You Are Young', which had the potential to open the record. Richard was sent demos and liked both, though he was conscious of backing away. Come July and August the band were travelling again, doing festivals, and Richard got some energy back. 'I realised I needed to contribute to finishing this album. Or else when it came out people would say, you're not really on this thing, are you? I wasn't sure I could handle that happening again.' By the time they began writing once more, Richard was determined to change. He was strict with himself. He'd go round to Neil's each day, making sure he had at least one idea recorded on his phone to share, so they were never short of something new to work with.

Between the end of August and the end of October, they turned it around. Back in the same room, collaborating. Again, no big discussion. (When I put it to Neil that Richard said he was working without his songwriting partner that summer, he simply said, 'I don't remember feeling alone at any point.') Rather, in Neil's version of events, it was just obvious that eventually they were going to have to get their shit together – and no one wanted to fail. To return to his mantra, 'The answer is always more work.'

By now they were writing hard. They played Ed the demo of 'My Imaginary Friend'. He remembers, 'The bridge was brilliant – but otherwise ... I told him [Brett], "I don't like that, Blob! Why are you doing that?"' – but they were getting somewhere. 'I love it when they get the chords shifting under the melodies,' says Ed, evangelising. 'When Suede are pop they never sound like bland pop – and when Brett gets it right you get this timeless, edgy pop thing, it just feels classic in the best way. So I kept saying to him, "That's the best bit, work with that!" He'd sometimes play me new bits down the phone. He'd say, "Check your email! I've sent you a new verse!"' When there were suddenly several good ideas on the go, Ed remembers a meeting where 'it was agreed we had most of the record; with two or three new songs we had it. Brett walked in that day thinking it was half a record, but when he walked out, he was saying it was nearly there.' The impossible, after a few good days, felt possible.

They also wrote the delicate 'Easter Day' (this would return later in another form), plus a few more, all resurrected as titles for completely different songs further down the line: 'Wasteland', 'There Is No Me If There Is No You' and 'The Quiet Ones', written in October, came when they were looking for more noisy material. Those spots ended up being taken by 'Outsiders', which came from a backing track Neil had been working on, and the Banshees-esque grind of 'No Tomorrow'. (The demo's title,

'Underground', was a reference to the Siouxsie and the Banshees song 'Overground' from 1978's *The Scream.*) Going through multiple versions after Neil's initial chugging demo 'Superblues', 'Outsiders' almost never was. This was the latest in the tradition of Suede songs romanticising love between people brought together by a sense of unbelonging. It was also one of those Brett immediately thought emblematic for the band, one of the strongest they'd written since reforming.

French-Algerian novelist and philosopher Albert Camus had popped up in Suede's work before – most obviously in *A New Morning*'s 'Obsessions' ('It's the way you don't read Camus, or Bret Easton Ellis'), but this was a more meaningful reference, Camus' 1942 novella *The Outsider* being one a handful of books Brett's returned to repeatedly as an adult.* Brett had drawn on *The Outsider* for years. Alienation. The consequences of violence. The absurd nature of reality. But was literally calling a song 'Outsiders' pompous, self-important? Brett was unsure:

> Sometimes when I'm deep in writing mode I get lost in the labyrinths and corridors and can't see things with much perspective. Basically, I can be guilty of playing too many mind games with myself. As a writer of pop songs, sometimes you need to shake yourself free of all that and try and access that which will go straight to the gut of the audience. Using a clearly Suede-adjacent term like 'outsiders' could have come across as crass, but the melody and the music and the detail was strong enough to create something special.

---

* Other enduring inspirations for Anderson include *Birdsong* by Sebastian Faulks, Ian McEwan's *Atonement*, Orwell's *1984*, *Rebecca* by Daphne du Maurier, *Standard Deviation* and *Early Morning Riser* by Katherine Heiny, Cormac McCarthy's *The Road* and Louise Doughty's thriller *Apple Tree Yard*.

Brett thought of the song's protagonists as his own parents. He tells me, 'They were definitely considered oddballs in our little council estate – the Liszt-obsessed taxi driver and the frustrated artist who like to sunbathe nude in the garden.' Despite their many difficulties, Brett's parents were romanticised, celebrated, in the lyric, while the chorus's change of perspective – 'She puts her faith in the moment, outsiders / He puts his faith in the moment, outsiders' – seemed as emblematic of Suede to Brett as, say, 'We're the litter on the breeze'. The way the title was delivered like a call to arms gave it lift-off. And he got to say something deeply personal, without listeners having any idea who or what he was drawing from.

Parts being written and rewritten, junked and remade. Sped up, slowed down, moods changed completely. Most of the best music that eventually made it onto Suede #7 was the result of several very different versions of songs, or parts that used to be elsewhere. As for that bridge from 'My Imaginary Friend', it got glued to new sections Richard recorded, transforming it into 'Like Kids'. Typically, Ed was buzzing over that one, as it sounded to him like a single, but was also dark enough. 'That song came out of something I took to Neil's one day on my phone,' says Richard now. 'After that, I think he thought we had it. We were all really into it – it seemed like the finishing piece of the jigsaw.' If everything in a band moves in cycles, it felt like the wheel was finally turning again. 'It was a disciplined time,' says Richard now, 'I just realised [that] ... when I was young, with something like *Head Music* or *A New Morning*, I didn't really fight to be on those records. This time, I did. It wasn't about feeling competitive with Neil, like I might have done in the early days.*

---

* Richard: 'In the '90s it was more a case of pitching ideas against each other. When Brett said to Neil "why don't you try writing" and he did the demo for "Starcrazy" I remember thinking, *oh, I'm going to have up my game!* When Neil joined, he brought

It was more about trying to contribute, together, and me being able to take pride in my contributions.'

Ed was still in the UK, unsure if the work with Hans might come, or when. This time was crucial, with November 2014's new recordings bringing the album into focus: 'Outsiders', 'Tightrope', 'No Tomorrow', 'Learning to Be', 'When You Are Young', its sister song 'When You Were Young', and 'Like Kids' were all laid down. Brett wrote to me recently: 'If you wanted to be melodramatic about it, you could say these are the songs – "Outsiders" especially – that saved the Suede reunion.' Whether or not we accept that, and not everyone saw things this way, the atmosphere was improving. Richard was re-engaged, the finish line in sight. Tensions started to dissipate. Then, on 6 December, Ed got a phone call from Hans asking if he could start, right away. Ed emailed to check with the band; they wished him well, then discussions turned to what they could do before Ed left (and what they might do afterwards, to tidy things up). A plan was hatched to draw all the files together, with Andy Hughes an important connection. (Andy, a trusted hand, had been one of the engineers for *Bloodsports*.)

In mid-December track listing was still being hotly debated. (Emails show, for example, that 'I Can't Give Her What She Wants' was almost left off, Brett cooling on it at the last.) It kept shifting even after Ed spent his last couple of days in the country with Andy Hughes in Sarm. Then he left for LA, on 14 December. He was only supposed to be there until March at the latest, in the first instance.* The band would keep working

---

a sense of pop and soul to proceedings, Dusty Springfield and Northern Soul. I was more Pistols, Floyd... so at the start, maybe it felt like competition. But by now, even if I was withdrawn, I never felt in competition with Neil. It was more about making my own mark.'

* Ed returned on 14 February 2015, though earlier emails with Andy on booking time in to work with the band suggested he was initially expected back in March.

in the meantime, Andy going through the drives with Richard and Neil at Ed's place.

THESE RABBIT MACHINES

Ed left behind a hard drive of songs to mix. But when Neil and Richard met up to go through the files, there were bits they couldn't find. Some overdubbed guitar parts recorded at Ed's place were missing. Most of the keyboard parts Neil recorded at home were gone, too. The more they looked, the more they found gaps. Neil says: 'How Ed managed to lose so much in consolidating everything for mixing is anybody's guess.' 'I Can't Give Her What She Wants' had gone through structural changes in recording and those seemed to have disappeared. What initially seemed a complete jigsaw began to feel like one with pieces missing. Ed remained in contact with Neil and Richard by email; they'd all had to respond incredibly fast to Ed going to LA. Ed had been around for months longer than expected, though unfortunately that was when the band were stuck. But still, there was a challenge here. Richard and Neil got to work.

They liked what the track 'Voices of Old People' added to the 1968 Simon & Garfunkel record *Bookends*, and Brett took it upon himself to add something similar. After leaving Neil's one January afternoon Brett went to L'Étoile on Westbourne Grove, ordered tea and chatted to an elderly customer while he recorded their conversation. By chance, the lady started talking about the loss of politeness and personal connection in the real world. 'Some places you'll go and they don't even say "Good morning" or "Hello",' she told Brett. 'And all this computer work ... these rabbit machines ... When you're young, you know, when you're in that age, you've got all the time in the world.' Had she really used the phrase 'when you are young'? Brett clipped the chat and emailed it to Neil. That serendipity led Richard and Neil, that same week, to write the start of 'When You Were Young'. Listen closely to the album and you can hear the sounds of Westbourne Grove that Friday afternoon.

Looking back now, Ed acknowledges Neil's contribution: 'Neil put "When You Were Young" into a place, gave it a setting, added the little ingredients that made it the song I wanted, this portentous thing – he's a real craftsman.' Memories conflict, and it's tricky to reconstruct events all these years later, but as January became February, Richard and Neil kept going. From Ed's perspective, he'd done everything right and, besides, he was back from LA already. Maybe there was some communication breakdown: Ed thought the band had all they needed, and he wasn't included in the work from this point on. Neil and Richard wanted to push on. This meant filling in some gaps, but they also felt able to add to the record, improving it overall. Neil recorded one piece in Queen's Park, with children playing, for the end of 'Learning to Be'. That was a Sunday morning, 1 February. In a bizarre sign of the times, then-mayor of London Boris Johnson was playing tennis in the background, on a nearby court.

On 18 February, Suede played a six-song set at the *NME* Awards in London where they picked up a 'Godlike Genius' Award (2002's hopeless losers were now being lauded once more), debuting 'What I'm Trying to Tell You' among the hits. This in a ceremony where a young Charli XCX also performed, an illustration of how much time had passed since they were the hot young things themselves. In a nice touch, comedian Ricky Gervais, briefly Suede's co-manager in 1991, recorded a video message for broadcast before their performance, in which he built his part in their history, dismissed it, and complained about the name of the award, all within a single minute. Brett was in swaggering form, enjoying the band's moment back in the spotlight at a show mostly focused on the work of artists who were kids, if born at all, when Suede started out. The photos from the night made Richard seem especially glum, pale, even ill – there's nothing he hates more than a red carpet – while Neil looked somewhat distracted. Maybe the photos are just a bit unforgiving. On collecting their award from New Order's Bernard Sumner, Brett reflected on Suede's life so far, saying, 'It's been a long, strange, heartbreaking journey, but well worth it.' That word 'heartbreaking' stands out, now, given it was a celebration.

Now came the business of adding various elements into the record to 'give a hint of the cinematic', calling in favours left and right to finish the job. Neil got fellow Penguin Cafe member, violinist and arranger Oli Langford, to record strings. In his own studio on Turnpike Lane, Oli added parts for 'When You Are Young' for the album's opening, also the middle eight of 'Tightrope' and 'When You Were Young', near the end. This was a reprise of the album's opening, reworked, to give the whole record 'a uniting effect'. New parts. More changes. More additions. The results lifted the sound – now *there* was that ambition they'd all been talking about – but Oli's partner of the time, Sophia del Pizzo, had her own take on how long this was all drawing out. On Oli's mouse mat one day she wrote, 'SUEDE HAVE STOLEN MY BOYFRIEND'.*

The running order may have been set, but the songs didn't run into each other yet. Over twenty-two days Neil painstakingly set about trying to make the album feel like a single piece of music, intended to be experienced in order, one song seamlessly becoming the next. These were 'interstitials', intended to go between individual songs on a record. Some

---

* Neil bumped into Sophia in August 2025 and asked permission to name her here. She had forgotten this detail, but found it very funny, and gave her blessing. Thank you, Sophia.

were like the L'Étoile recording, captured on the fly. Others contained snatches of music. Still others, both.

For the start of the low, atmospheric 'Learning to Be', Brett's stepson Jack was recorded reading from the Bible, inspired by the intro to 'Reality Asylum' by Crass, a song that 'fascinated and terrified' Brett as an adolescent. For the song's end, Amy Langley's sister Gita, who had recently played with the band at that *Dog Man Star* anniversary show, was drafted in to sing before the drum fill that announces 'Like Kids' with, in Neil's words, 'the sound of a pot simmering on a stove ... children playing outside, and someone on the radio talking about the skull hidden in Hans Holbein the Younger's painting *The Ambassadors*.' Lean in and you can hear Gita's nursery rhyme-style 'la la las' interrupted by Lucian, then just a toddler, shouting, 'Stop singing!' (The melody of these 'la la las' was from a song Brett wrote for Lucian when he was a baby, called 'Who's the Bear?' Gita tried singing it with Brett's words, but this failed the sickly-sweet test – so they reverted to no words for the recording.) At the end of the intro to 'When You Are Young' you can also hear Lucian saying, 'Here comes the spider!'* Fascination. Fear. Family. Love. Horror. Abjection. The power of the lullaby, sung in the dark.

By the end of February, Brett saw the new record as pretty much done – though he didn't need to be elbows-deep in the minutiae and didn't understand the final technicalities as Neil and Richard patched the album back together. Brett saw that Neil was getting rather too caught up in the work and suggested he step back from it all. 'Keep your chin up,' he said, as he left Neil's place.

* This reappears, the phrase elongated during the piano section of 'When You Were Young', under Brett's singing.

THE FILM

The word 'cinematic' kept coming up and the interstitials only seemed to suggest a filmic approach even more. Lessons had been learned from *Bloodsports*, and Mat felt that they might as well do something artistically interesting that was also more economical, rather than doing expensive, conventional videos. If the album was one long piece of music, Mat thought, might a film stretch out over it, too?

It seemed like mad recklessness, but exciting, if done right, and the record felt lyrically coherent enough for it. A commissioned film, everyone agreed, should be shaped by the film-maker, who could then choose how to respond to the album's themes themselves. Better that than the band hovering like helicopter parents, telling them they were interpreting the album wrong.

From this point on, things only got busier. Didz accompanied Neil to Decoy Studios where mixing began in early March, Cenzo Townshend at the helm.* Mixing usually happens once recording is signed off, the band present or more involved, but while Cenzo was at work, Richard and Neil were still recording synth and guitar parts over at Neil's place, then sending them over, working till the last. In mid-April Neil emailed Ed, offering to come round and play him the album. Meanwhile, they thought they'd found a film-maker. In discussions, one name kept coming up.

Roger Sargent had made music videos Mat felt were as Suede as they come: 'Just watch thirty seconds of the Fat White Family song "Touch the Leather",' he said. 'That explains all you need to know.' (It's simply one long shot of singer Lias Saoudi smoking a cigarette in the foreground,

---

* Cenzo started working as an assistant to Alan Moulder in the late '80s and went on to work with the likes of U2, the Rolling Stones, Florence + The Machine and many more.

full of attitude, while a man's bare arse slides back and forth across the screen behind him, gaping for the camera, in slow motion.) In his younger days Roger had photographed Suede at gigs and festivals, and was recently reintroduced to the band when he took promo shots for *Bloodsports*. Now he was tasked with making a complete 45-minute-long narrative film. Sargent had also worked with the Prodigy, Baxter Dury and Sleaford Mods, acts who in their own ways were radical, confrontational, unconventionally masculine – and very English. The common sensibility was clear. They wanted something dark, murky, moody, something immediately recognisable as Suede's aesthetic. Roger understood that. But then, this was also an entire album about children, vulnerability, internal worry, anxiety. 'Not very chase the dragon'.

The album was finally signed off almost exactly two years since the first meeting in the Greek café near Brett's when they'd resolved to keep building momentum by making the next record fast. Does the interwoven nature of the music matter now? Neil says, 'I had the bit between my teeth and everyone just let me get on with it ... This was the first Suede record where I had access to all of the recorded parts at home, and *carte blanche* to do what I wanted with it.' In fact, Neil led crucial parts of the process. For whatever reason, they didn't go back to Ed on his return, and Suede had no other members who had the skills or, frankly, the willingness, to painstakingly go through the album, then spend five months finishing it off.

To me, this process seemed torturous. Neil didn't recognise that description though, saying this was simply 'the nature of the work'. Also, they see that work differently now, post-reunion: 'This time around,' he says, 'we understand our privilege, don't take things for granted, and don't act like pampered musicians. It's our job, and it can be frustrating. But making records is a joy.' Not always, though, and not equally, for all.

Arguably, Neil had been preparing for this task since leaving the band in 2001. He was finally finding a more prominent, essential role, one he couldn't have envisaged when the call came for the Albert Hall in 2009, and this was energising, even when others were struggling. Maybe it had been coming since his first *Coming Up* sessions in 1995, where he began observing Ed's approach to production.

Paul Khera was asked to do the album photo shoot and record design. This was more of a group discussion than with other Suede albums, but Brett found an image for the sleeve. This time, he spent 'countless hours and days trawling through banks of online images and art books looking for something to steal'. Something avant-garde, maybe, something classic, something amateur – 'anything that suggests a "Suede" image we could either use directly or appropriate.' This time, Brett selected a stunning photo taken by the pioneer American war and fashion photographer Toni Frissell.* In 'Lady in the Water', the photograph shows a woman in a white dress from underneath the surface, body at the top of the frame. Only her face is out of the picture – it's presented as if in another world, on the other side of the water's surface. Frissell published her photo, taken in Weeki Wachee Springs, Florida, in *Harper's Magazine* in 1947.

The idea of recreating a modern 'Lady in the Water' appealed to all: though many others have done their own copies since, the photo was quite unknown at the time. Brett, Mat and Neil were all there for the photo shoot, which took place in Woodside Park Pool, part of a secondary

* Frissell was the official photographer for the American Red Cross for a time during the Second World War. Her archive of 340,000 images is now held in the Library of Congress. The *Atlantic* described her as a 'pioneer in her field' when publishing a selection of her photos, including 'Lady in the Water', in 2018.

school in Southgate.* Given the demands of the shoot, Paul drafted in several others to make the image construction work, and identical twins were hired. (They swapped places when one got too cold and needed a break from the water. No one knows which twin was used in the final cover.) The underwater photographer Lucy Ray was at the bottom of the pool while Paul and others stood on the sidelines trying to make the twins look more lifeless. In Frissell's original, the detail of the world beneath the surface is rich and clear, the Florida landscape visible. In Suede's version, the entire underwater world is blackened, as if taking place in a nightmare. Frissell's white dress is made into a luminous blue. Frissell's full-of-life figure, the lower half of the body drifting slightly beneath the water, is replaced by an image with both arms and legs below the water, knees pointed downwards, in an unsettling parallel.

Brett scrawling lyrics to 'The Fur and the Feathers' on walls of a building site, for the inside sleeve of Suede #7.

Despite the album's exuberant moments, the novelist Ever Dundas, a friend of Mat's, describes *Night Thoughts* as an album full of 'a kind of fraught intensity'. (Ever lost her sister Rachel a few years before the

* Richard had been at the album mastering at Metropolis with engineer Tony Cousins the day before. Some remembered Richard being at the photo shoot too, but he wasn't there.

album's release, and was processing that when she first saw Sargent's film.) By chance, she had a copy of Toni Frissell's photo on her wall for years before *Night Thoughts* was released, so it was already meaningful. Ever contrasts the Frissell original and Suede's version:

> It looks like the person has no face; it reminds me of the extremely discomforting moments in the *Under the Skin* film [starring Scarlett Johansson, based on Michel Faber's novel]. Also, the way their body is angled down it feels more fraught than the Frissell, like there's the risk they'll sink/be pulled under, into the darkness. But because it's a frozen moment where their face is still just above water there's also a feeling of hope. But then because of the no face/distortion of the reflection, it's not a straightforward hope; there's an uncanny and unnerving element.

That sense of the uncanny fitted with the emerging film too; these disparate elements were coming together. By now, those involved in making *Night Thoughts* were more inclined to be generous about the process, crediting each other for work done under difficult circumstances, the record being 'such a fucking pain to do'. In emails, sometimes Ed was the more affectionate 'Teddy'. (Though mostly, it was 'Blob'.) Having been sent the final record, Ed replied on 26 July: 'I really am blown away by this record ... you should all be very proud ... a brutal journey but what a result! ... might be the best yet.'

'A FINAL GIFT TO THE MIND'

Roger Sargent had six stepfathers. His happiest childhood period was with his mum and one of these men, who was from West Wales – from when Roger was five, during the mid-1970s, they lived there, close to the beach, in a caravan on Newport Sands. When he was nine his mum had her first breakdown, his stepdad left, and they left too. But he never forgot the place.

In 2015, Roger was relatively new to video work. The *Guardian* once called him 'the UK's most important music photographer' and the *NME* awarded him the Outstanding Contribution to Music Photography Award in 2012. He'd directed a documentary about the first, fitful reunion of the Libertines in 2011, *There Are No Innocent Bystanders*. By the mid-2010s Roger was working with the Prodigy on their single 'Ibiza' when he was approached. 'I loved Suede,' he recalls, 'and I'd recently become a father myself ... [it appealed to me], the idea of an album circling the terror of new parenthood, how it connects to the terror of childhood and fear of abandonment. I thought, here was a chance to make a twin to the album.' When he heard the music, he was sold: 'It was incredible – bolder and better than anything they made in the '90s. Even before I got to think about what to do with it visually, a song like "Pale Snow" ... I just thought God, this is *so beautiful*.' In April, Mat met Roger at the old Phoenix Brewery to discuss the project while the others were in Suffolk, mixing with Cenzo. The following day, Brett finally emailed the band and management, telling them the title: *Night Thoughts*.

This referred to Brett's fear of something awful happening to Lucian, 'the kind of thing that keeps you up in the dark' and has 'any parent imagining the worst ... if they'd ever survive it, should it come to pass'. The phrase itself pre-dated these fears by decades. Brett knew the poem 'The Complaint: Or, Night Thoughts on Life, Death & Immortality', by Edward Young, for years. First published in nine parts (or nine 'nights') between 1742 and 1745, 'The Complaint' featured engravings by the polymath William Blake. But it had a more personal relevance for Brett, one he forgot, then remembered: 'When Justine and I were together,' he wrote to me, 'we would sit and smoke and chat shit all night like most pretentious students.* If the subjects got too dark she would often turn to me before we went to sleep and say half-jokingly, "Hmmm, night thoughts." I always thought that was quite funny. Anyway, the blackly comic term stayed with me and very much resonated with my new role as a father – awake in the small hours worrying about whooping cough and life insurance and catchment areas.'

For many years Roger's mum lived in Spain, but in 2014 she returned to the UK and told her son she wanted to go back to where they'd been happiest. She was fragile. She was usually in recovery from 'a volcanic, difficult childhood' and had psychosomatic epilepsy (seizures triggered by stress or trauma). Roger's stepfathers came from different places; as a child sometimes he and his mum had been dependent on them for somewhere to live. This meant they were often moving, each the other's only common denominator across the years. 'It was like taking a pilgrimage,' Roger says, of their return to West Wales. 'We went to all the old spots. Me, her and my own son.' This three-generation trip reminded him of the area's beauty and was good for his mum's mental health, but hope was short-lived: 'Four months later she was dead,' Roger recalls now. 'I realised early on that we had to film *Night Thoughts* there, though I don't think I realised just how much her loss influenced the making of

---

* Justine Frischmann and Brett met in 1988. They fell in love and were together during the early days of Suede, Justine playing rhythm guitar between 1989 and 1991. She was an essential part of the band during this period, crossing over with Bernard Butler, who joined late in 1989, after Brett, Mat and Justine advertised in the *NME* for a lead guitarist. Justine remained in Suede beyond the end of her relationship with Brett in 1991, leaving before the band's breakout year. Justine went on to great success as the frontwoman of the band Elastica, especially with their debut self-titled album in 1995, at the time the fastest-selling debut album in UK music history. After retiring from music, Justine moved to the US and became a successful painter.

the film until it was done. The story, the decisions we made. The places and the scenes we shot.'

In Roger's first meeting with Suede, still in the early days of grief and fatherhood, he found it hard to articulate his idea. He tried to explain: this man walks into the sea to take his own life as 'When You Are Young' plays, then the body of the film traces what the man thinks about as he drowns. Fragments of memory, snapshots, glitches, each accessing the past that led him here.

The partnership seemed an easy fit, between kindred spirits: 'They are the least difficult people I've ever worked with,' Roger says of Suede. 'The thing that joins us together, I think, is we're a bit fucked up and misfitted into this world. It felt like they recognised something in me and trusted me.' Mat recalls Roger being so full of ideas that the film's original shape had to be honed. What interested Roger most? 'I got really into this idea that when you die the brain releases a chemical that is like a kindness,' he says now, 'like a gift, to the mind. It makes people feel like their life is flashing before their eyes – DMT is a natural psychedelic, you can take it, but the brain produces it in your final moments. My idea was that this father gets to see his son and the mother of his child one more time before he goes – they're summoned, by his mind, at the last.' *Night Thoughts* tracks the relationship history between Bryn and Sasha, and the life of their young child, Cian. When Cian dies in a seaside accident, Bryn and Sasha tear themselves and each other apart in the aftermath. The main narrative, as seen through Bryn's fear, guilt and regret, is interleaved with the light of the main beach near Fishguard, fields of wheat where the family run and play in happier times, as well as the narrow suburban streets of Cardiff.

By 2015, the music industry had gone through transformational change; in the not-too-distant past a budget of £15,000 to £30,000 was typical for a single promo video. Now, Roger had to stretch £45,000 to make a 45-minute story without words. If they were going to get this done, they'd need to be fast and nimble. That meant no reshoots. No days to lose. Long hours. Roger had never worked with a script before. He was anxious and hated being away from his young son, describing himself as 'in awe of Suede, especially Brett'. But Roger felt Brett got it: 'He had a real, patient understanding. He wanted to make the whole thing more raw, more gritty. Brett knew what I was trying to do; I had imposter syndrome, but he never made me feel like I wasn't up to it.'

Night Thoughts was made over two and a half weeks in West Wales. The cast was small: Alex Walton (Bryn), Jane Walsh (Sasha) and Gabe Trimble (Cian) had not met before filming began, and the writer, Stephanie de Giorgio, just twenty-three, a 'powerful, positive force' involved in her first production, was often frustrated by the process and said so.* Producers Alex Ashman and Janna Bartlett, and editor Elena Carmen, all had to hustle, securing access to locations and necessary props on the fly. Brett's lyrics loomed large here, the music providing a foreboding atmosphere, the shape of the story evolving in the making. 'To make a film with an intricate narrative but no dialogue felt really freeing,' says Roger now. 'Though also terrifying. ... we could just change things when they didn't work ... as long as we could think of another idea in time.' Most shooting happened at night, which meant sleeping during the day, on set. Roger described this as 'a kind of weird jet lag ... you feel like you're moving slowly, but you know moving slow isn't good enough.' For Roger this wasn't just another project, but rather a necessary, if disguised,

---

* I tried, without success, to find Stephanie de Giorgio. *Night Thoughts* seems to be her only writing credit. I understand Stephanie was frankly sick of the music, not really a fan of Suede and not connected to its themes and concerns as Roger was. Though I'm reluctant to be critical without giving Stephanie right of reply.

response to his own personal history. He believed this was Suede's best record, throwing all he could at giving his own contribution the kind of emotional potency the soundtrack provided him.

While the film was being made, Suede left Roger's team to it. On 27 June they had a rare Glastonbury appearance, playing a hits-heavy set on the sweaty, smaller John Peel Stage. What a contrast to Suede's last Glastonbury in 2003, where they'd opened with career low 'Love the Way You Love' just months before falling apart.

THE ROUNDHOUSE

With album and film ready, plans were hatched for something special. The release of *Night Thoughts* was kicked into January 2016 – post-Christmas. January is a 'soft chart', and they wanted to build on the first week of *Bloodsports*. But 'Outsiders' was made available to radio on 24 September: in Brett's words, 'Outsiders' was a 'pivotal song ... with a commercial dimension other songs on the album just didn't have'.* The two back-to-back nights at the Roundhouse on 13 and 14 November could be used to premiere Roger's film while the band performed the music: part-screening, part-gig. But how? Simon didn't play to a click track – unlike many bands, Suede never use one – and trying to follow the beats of the film might have been comically bad.† What would they do? Watch the film as they played, trying to keep in sync?

* BA, email to RG, 24/10/25: '"Outsiders" was a flagship song – anthemic and placed firmly in Suedeworld but wiry and new somehow. Possibly most importantly its post-punk feel pointed us in the direction of AF and AD, suggesting a new way of being Suede. That's what I think. Who knows what would have happened had we not written it. Maybe we would have come up with something else, giving up isn't really in our DNA.'

† Recent screenings of *Jaws* at the Albert Hall had used a click track and an orchestra and this was briefly floated. But none of the band was willing.

Long-serving Suede set designer and lighting director Jip Nipius, with the band since 1997, suggested they lead the film, rather than the other way around. Jip says, 'For *Night Thoughts* I tried to figure out the best way to combine the two art forms, film and music, and do justice to both.' Jip's plan was 'to have the band in an orchestra pit, like you would have seen in the days of the silent film, early 1900s.' In discussions they decided not *only* to play *Night Thoughts,* then end the gig. (Brett thought people would feel cheated if the show was only forty-five minutes, without any Suede songs they knew.) In that case, if Suede were to play what Didz called a 'hits and treats' set too, Jip realised moving the backline from the orchestra pit with all the gear to the main stage was necessary, but impossible. (This was also going to tour, hopefully, so it wasn't only about the Roundhouse.) Then Jip suggested putting the band *behind* the screen and a plan fell into place. Punters would be encouraged to watch the film, not the band. This allowed band members to appear and disappear by utilising a sharkstooth gauze, an old theatrical technique that looks opaque when lit from the front but can create intricate effects from behind. In Jip's words, this allowed 'the band [to] ghost into and out of the movie' – Brett's outstretched arm visible for a moment here, Mat's bass for a moment there. During an intermission, Jip and the team removed the gauze. As for the film speed, Svend the video operator was tasked with adjusting, or cutting to the next section, should the band get out of sync. (They usually play fast songs faster live than on record, and slow songs slower, so it was likely they'd slip out of time.) Neil would trigger the interstitials from his laptop, on stage. The 'spit and sawdust' section of 'hits and treats' was easy. But the rest? Not so much.

Neil remembers the plan: 'If something went wrong, we couldn't just laugh it off, go back and start a song again: it would've broken the spell, and there was no way to relay to Svend if there was a problem anyway.' Neil had a guitar pedalboard synced up to his on-stage laptop, which meant more opportunities for things to go wrong. Before *Night Thoughts,* Neil was essentially a rhythm guitarist: 'This record involved more intricate playing, with my taking lead lines occasionally,' he says, 'Richard and I interweaving around each other.' In production rehearsal, Neil had to work out levels for new keyboard sounds and the interstitials with his tech Jef, and Shaun the front-of-house sound guy: 'We had none of us been involved in a production like this ... Svend had a jog wheel* ... but how on earth could he know if we were playing too fast for the film or too slow? Even now, thinking of all the ways it could've gone wrong makes me shudder.'

In principle the screen idea was exciting, but not equally so for all. Brett liked experimenting – he also enjoyed declaring Suede *different* from other bands – but the reality of doing things differently sometimes chafed. For him, the screen provided a literal barrier: what was his job? What was he to do while singing? Work with the shadow or ignore the screen? That might feel more like a rehearsal, without the intensity needed for a great show. Was the screen a mistake, or a worthwhile, playful innovation? For Neil, it was nerve-wracking to play forty-five minutes of new music that had to be played seamlessly, though Richard loved the experience, sitting down, able to focus completely on playing an album he'd wondered if they'd ever finish, without having to think about a crowd. Ah, the freedom! For Mat, this meant staying close to Simon; as usual, Simon followed Brett's lead.

Soundcheck is usually stop–start, a run-through of songs dropped late into the set, things the band don't usually play, testing out particular

* This allows the operator to speed up or slow down the track in order to get it in sync when necessary.

instruments and sounds. They might play half a dozen songs or half-songs, if they're checking a specific part. But on the day of the first Roundhouse show, nerves jangling, the band ran through the whole album. Behind the curtain, Neil and Richard sat, without the usual distractions of a gig: people, lights, noise. (Richard remembers this being easier, though for Neil it was harder.) Like any London show, they had friends and family coming along. Roger was there too, emotional at seeing his film projected this way. This was album unveiling, film screening and experimental theatre all in one, quite different from the usual pre-gig energy. No one know how it would go.

Somehow, it went to plan. Just. In Neil's words, 'Much of the show looked and felt like we were playing to a solid wall, and we were only sparsely and occasionally lit. We could sense the crowd there, but really couldn't see much of them, and they were looking at the film as much as Brett or the band.' At no point did they have to stop and admit, ah shit, this has all got out of whack. If crowds were holding their breath at times, that contributed to an eventual release. Neil again: 'I think that's one reason why the *Night Thoughts* shows went down so well in general: there was a feeling of sheer relief after the end of the film, both for fans and the band. The screen could be flown out, the literal and figurative darkness of the film could be forgotten, and the stage properly lit. For the second half we could play some songs everybody knew and everyone could jump around.' No two-song encore, this. They played a sixteen-song set, leaning heavily on early material.

Playing under the film changed the relationship some of the band had to the music – Richard recalls, 'I only really felt like I completely got a song like "Tightrope" when we were playing it behind the screen, with the kites flying above [the characters], on the beach. I thought, yes, I feel this now ... Something similar happened with "I Can't Give Her

What She Wants". The song just seemed to have way more depth, it made more sense to me. I love "Tightrope" as a song now. That kid going into the sea, it's so uncomfortable and emotional. You can't stop him drifting away. I realised I really wanted to get those kinds of experiences from playing live more.' By the end of the show, the atmosphere was euphoric. They could take this on tour. It might have been bolder to play the new record and leave, but Brett was right: those who stood silently watching the film and the shadows had earned the right to dance.

When Suede came off stage, things soured quickly when they learned there'd just been a horrific attack at the Bataclan, a famous Parisian gig venue, where Eagles of Death Metal were playing that night. The rock venue became the site of a mass shooting as well as a hostage site. Ninety people were killed in the Bataclan alone. When police raided the theatre, the attackers detonated suicide vests. This was just one of a series of co-ordinated attacks, another at the Stade de France, and others on the streets, attackers spraying bullets across restaurants and Parisian cafés. Europe was shaken. For Neil this was personal; someone close to him was taking a group to Paris Photo* that weekend; a student of theirs was in one of the restaurants that was attacked. This meant 'much of that night was spent trying to make sure they were all right. There was no time to digest anything.' Charlie had to respond fast. Cancellation of night two was never considered. Instead, suddenly there was increased security; contingency measures too. This was also deeply affecting for the crew. They all found out when they arrived at the hotel lobby after walking back from the Roundhouse. Jip recalls, 'We were shocked, because we all knew some of the crew in the Bataclan

* Founded in 1997, Paris Photo is the world's largest international fair dedicated to photography and image-based art.

who were killed.' It was horrendous. The following night, Suede's crew put the French flag up on screen, as well as red, white and blue lights in the venue, in solidarity.

The second day's prep meant walking through security preparations most knew would be ill equipped to combat a similar situation, if terrorists decided to break into the Roundhouse. Given the co-ordinated nature of the attacks the day before, it felt possible there might be more. Probably not in their venue, but surely that would have seemed an impossibility to Eagles of Death Metal too, until it wasn't. On the second night at the Roundhouse, Suede mixed up the show's second half, adding songs like the rarely heard 'Heroin' and 'Animal Lover'. With so many security concerns, they started late. In an unusual move, Camden Council let Suede breach the usual curfew. Neil recalls the evening 'had an air of defiance' about it.

The Roundhouse shows saw a clutch of great reviews. The *Independent*'s Roisín O'Donnell described this as 'a gig format that feels utterly original', calling the first-half behind-the-screen show a 'scintillating performance'. In the *Telegraph*, Neil McCormick's review, headlined 'Have Suede Reinvented the Album?' opened with the line, 'Few fans go to see old bands hoping to hear new songs', then went on to frame this night as an exception. Andre Paine of the *Evening Standard* wrote that playing a new record in its entirety weeks before it's even released 'implied an unshakeable confidence', a line those involved in making *Night Thoughts* enjoy. That's often Suede's way – to look confident, even when they're not. Especially when they're not.

Some of these reviews read differently now. The *Evening Standard* marked 'Like Kids' as a standout, calling it 'such a satisfying throwback it might just as well have been called "Trashy Beautiful Ones".' It was a compliment, and there was plenty of enthusiasm in the camp at the time – Didz pushed hard for 'Like Kids' as a single, for instance – but the band wanted to move into new territory and they'd soon disown the song for exactly that reason. With *Night Thoughts,* they'd done the same thing as last time, just in a different way. Pushing for a few more songs at the end of the process that sounded more like singles. Even on an album that didn't want to have any.

Along with the release of the album, the band did a series of screenings and Q&A events with Roger Sargent in places like Cardiff, Manchester and London – more than the film-maker expected when the project began. 'It was very emotional, doing those events,' Roger remembers. 'The sheer amount of people that came up to me saying "I lost a child" ... I had no idea how deeply it would resonate with people. It was catharsis. It was a beautiful gift.' What started out as Brett's imagined fear of parental loss – as he later put it, 'unlike fear for your own mortality, fear for your child's mortality is a thousand times worse' – the *Night Thoughts* film ended up being cathartic for those who really had lived through that kind of loss.

RELEASE

In a strange serendipity, David Bowie once again played a part in release week, performing a kind of tragic magic trick that was also a work of art. Bowie released his final album, *Blackstar,* on his sixty-ninth birthday – 8 January 2016 – and died two days later, having kept his liver cancer secret for eighteen months. Naturally, Bowie's huge legacy dominated conversation and his music sold widely in the early weeks of 2016. Even in death Suede were, once again, in his shadow. Just as they were about to release their own most radical statement, one of the most celebrated alternative artists of the past fifty years released his best album in a quarter of a century – an experimental jazz epic – then expired in a puff of smoke. All within forty-eight hours.

This meant *Night Thoughts* came out when the usual rules didn't apply. Clearly, no one anticipated this when they planned a 22 January release. Between *Blackstar* at number one and various 'best ofs' and classics (*Hunky Dory, The Rise and Fall of Ziggy Stardust and the Spiders from Mars*), Bowie occupied half the top ten. And yet, there in the middle was *Night Thoughts*, at number six, four places better than *Bloodsports*. That felt like vindication. So too, the coverage: last time out they'd sometimes struggled for media profile, but now they landed several major laudatory, in-depth reviews. The Roundhouse shows signalled intent, and here the album landed with the impact they'd hoped for, the film too, positioning Suede no longer as yesterday's band, but rather as vital, confident, inventive. After all that discussion of Richard and Neil's own musical statement, the sustained effort to make *Night Thoughts* distinct, some review coverage went all *Dog Man Star* anyway, contrasting the band's early promise, in all its drama and conflict, with the seemingly calm later life in which they were continuing to beat the odds. In a sense, this only reaffirmed the elevated place of *Dog Man Star* in the Suede canon. But there was more recognition of Richard and Neil's contribution, and more respect for Brett's lyrical sharpness, even if much of the framing looked towards a long-gone version of the band. Not quite out of the shadow, then. But heading towards the light.

Night Thoughts stood alone as a body of work, so this time Suede didn't bother with 'proper' singles, extra tracks or expanded editions. This meant anything else from the period was discarded, those earlier songs from *Night Thoughts* Mark 1 gone for good. Instead, they released an entirely instrumental version of the album, inspired by Mercury Rev doing the same with their late-'90s alternative classic *Deserter's Songs*.

(This is funny, given the album's history, and Brett's place on it. Though perhaps a little-noticed Brett-free version was enough of a curiosity not to matter. It did sound oddly complete without vocals.) 'Like Kids' was released as a standalone digital track on 1 December; thankfully, someone noticed it might be problematic to write SUEDE LIKE KIDS in big letters on the artwork, so that was changed just in time. But there was no physical release. The tour was short, just twelve shows with the screen, in carefully selected European venues. It was expensive to do. It was some undertaking. But it dazzled wherever it went.

Brett and Neil at DR Koncerthuset, Copenhagen, Denmark, 1 February 2016.
Photo by Paul Khera

'WE GOT THERE IN THE END'

A decade on, Ed is keen to record his reflections, and he does so in his trademark upbeat way. Even when reporting mistakes, hard times, the strain on those he cares about, he does so as if unburdened. 'My relationship with Brett is the relationship of my career,' he says now. 'So it matters to me ... Despite the tensions, up to that point, *Night Thoughts* was my favourite Suede record. I played it two months ago,' he told me, 'and I'm so fucking pleased I got to finish that record – we were doing a lot of yelling, but that's the great thing about Brett, really. It's ring-fenced, it's about the music, it's never personal. I don't really get to Brett until we're really at loggerheads about something. We have this running joke about him being quite school-mastery ... but he also has this enormous trust.' Does he regret the way they went about making the album? 'Yes. I regret enormously putting Brett in a position where he felt he was being cornered – especially closer to us going off to Belgium to start recording. He got more and more agitated. He gets anxious, he needs reassurance, and if I can't reassure him, he gets really miserable.'

When discussing Suede matters at Ed's home studio, he rarely concentrates on a single period, even if that period is the focus of conversation. Rather, he draws from the experience of their relationship over three and a half decades, exploring what he feels he's learned: 'You need Brett to be excited by a record ... [When he's] concerned I can always say, "don't worry we can fix it"; they're usually valid concerns. But if he's disappointed or doesn't like a song it's usually its death knell. With *Night Thoughts*, we wouldn't let him kill the songs and I pushed too hard for that way of working. But we got there in the end.'

By release time the band were once again looking forward. As for Brett, he was doing his usual in public – full throttle, declaring *Night Thoughts* the band's best work, portraying confidence. With Brett, it takes longer for him to become critical, but when he does, he can be brutal. He told me in 2024: '*Night Thoughts* is an album with only one banger on it ["Outsiders"] – the other two singles are Suede-by-numbers crap ["What

I'm Trying to Tell You" and "Like Kids"]. But though I don't think the songs are as good as *Bloodsports,* I do think it's a more coherent album.' Given how critical he's also been about *Bloodsports,* that's surprising. *Night Thoughts* didn't give him much of what he wanted for a Suede gig. But it did have some of their best songs and represented a crucial change in his lyrical approach. Neil's view is partially shaped by Brett's: 'These days Brett doesn't like the songwriting on much of the album,' he says, 'but thinks *Night Thoughts* gets any plaudits it does because it flows well as a record. Maybe, then, all the work I did on it wasn't wasted.'

That's typically deadpan. Brett's take, when pressed, is more nuanced than simply thinking the album's best feature was its 'flow', but there is something to this. Brett *is* quite dismissive about *Night Thoughts,* and it *is* striking how well the record knits together. Perhaps the issue is more about how it works live, divided up into small chunks. In Ed's words: 'If a gig's going well, everyone's looking at him. And if a gig's going badly, then everyone's looking at him.' That applies a pressure only Brett has to deal with. 'Brett's layered state,' says Ed, 'now comes out a different way. Instead of through drugs, it's from being on his hands and knees headbanging and screaming, down in the crowd. He needs that. Neil, Richard and Mat want to do different types of shows.' For Brett, the most important change with *Night Thoughts* was lyrical: that, as he's said, he was starting to use parenthood as 'a motor to generate ideas'.

When I listened back to the album on vinyl at Quietus HQ with Neil in 2024, he was the most uncomfortable I've ever seen him. Tutting, troubled by this or that minute detail, regretful about small decisions that seemingly prevented him from being able to enjoy the experience of listening back to this thing he worked on so long after it was 'done', he seemed in genuine pain while listening. (Neil is unfailingly polite to outsiders like me, even when uncomfortable. At times, I wondered if he was only staying in his seat because he felt it would be rude to leave.) Listening back to my recording afterwards, I noticed he only ever spoke up between or during songs to express frustration. He didn't express pride, or pleasure, or identify a single moment that made him smile. When I suggested it was a shame such a monumental effort seemed to provide him so little satisfaction, even at this many years' distance, he explained himself not exactly via *Night Thoughts*, but rather, his approach to all making: 'The most fascinating thing for me about being in a band is the mechanics of making the records, making sounds. At the end, what you're left with is just some music that can be aural wallpaper in a way. The creating of it is more important. Everyone else can look at it as an artefact, but to us it's a long three-year process of getting to that point.'

Despite Brett or Neil's reflections, the record stands tall. With *Night Thoughts*, Suede just about pulled off their big cinematic single-piece statement and a show to match it. Through all those failures to communicate, they managed to produce their most celebrated album in twenty years. But they were also unsure how much of that new material, so well received, worked at Suede gigs.

This time, they got away with it, just about. But next time?

CHAPTER 4

the blue hour
'our own suedeworld'

'Trust Brett to find the hypodermic needle in the haystack.'
– Neil, responding to his bandmate's idyllic move to the countryside

A WHOLE NEW FRIENDSHIP

Mike Christie is one of a handful of people who've been in Suedeworld since the very early days. Mike was especially close to Simon, the two of them filming hundreds of hours of footage and talking about making a Suede film one day. When Richard joined the band and needed somewhere to live, they set him up with then 24-year-old Mike as flatmate, 'the closest thing to an adult any of them knew'. He's navigated relationships on all sides; he was, for example, the only member of the Suede entourage at Bernard's wedding.

Close to the Pet Shop Boys and others around the '90s London music scene, Mike is upbeat, full of charisma, stories and anecdotes, but also has that sliver of ice a director needs for skewering his subjects. These days, he's an in-demand film-maker, not always close to Suede but often returning at key moments. He was at the final show of the first era, in 2003. He was at Albert Hall rehearsals in 2010, filming backstage on the night. He's Lucian's godfather. Recent projects, such as a *Wham! Ten Days in China* documentary and *Nick Cave's Veiled World* give a sense of the scale he works at.

In June 2015 Suede played a Glastonbury warm-up in Bexhill-on-Sea, to a faithful 'who gathered in throngs from across all corners of the world'. Mike went along that night. It had been a while since he and Brett were regularly in each other's lives. Chatting backstage afterwards, Brett said he and Jodie were buying a place in Somerset. They'd been going mad with their neighbours drilling down to make a second basement, a nightmare with a toddler. 'It felt like the noisiest place in London,' Brett recalls. 'I had to drive Lucian to Hyde Park every day so he could nap in the quiet.' So they were getting out. 'Oh, where are you moving to?' When Brett showed Mike the listing, he did a double take; it was literally down the road from his place. Nearly a quarter of a century on from when they first crossed paths, both would soon have places in London and Somerset, travelling regularly between them. Mike beams: 'It was a whole new adult relationship, twenty years later. A whole new type of friendship.' The coming change in Brett's life would charge Suede's next album, and Mike would find himself an integral part of Suede #8. In the next few years, they'd be seeing much more of each other.

THE RIGHT TO STRETCH OUT

There's no repair more effective than success, and Suede were now enjoying a second post-reunion uptick, a rare thing in a world of precious few good comebacks. There was no doubting how tough things had been, but now? Brett recalls, 'We'd earned the right to stretch out a bit, to explore the darker, more complex side of our music. If *Night Thoughts* was a road, we wanted to head further down it.' Neil recalls also wanting to go further personally: 'What I did in the latter stages of *Night Thoughts* was just putting a bow on it, proof-of-concept that I could have a vision for something and see it through.' After the Roundhouse gig, the band met with Ed to scope out whether they could work together again. Ed recalls that 'Brett (love him) just wanted to do *Night Thoughts* Part 2. I said that was a mistake.'

Any band is a tiny speck in the musical landscape; ''90s band makes third reunion record' is not a story, and with each return it gets harder to gain or hold the attention of casual observers. Brett, Neil and Richard knew they'd have to keep working in a similar way: trying to keep a hold of that bloody-minded quality control, to have a chance at being noticed as a going concern. Delivering music for Brett to write to had led to half a great album, but proved too brittle, making the whole Suede edifice shake. So: back to the mountain of material it was. This time, with experience and focus, the mountain might be a little smaller?

THE ROPE AND THE DARKNESS

Change is constant, but it presents differently for everyone, partly based on personal lives, partly on recent experience, and partly on how each band member is perceived. In 2016, for the core writing team, things were shifting personally and professionally, which made for new possibilities.

Brett had found a way to channel his present preoccupations, avoiding the pitfalls of trying to write like a young man, also dodging self-parody and sentimentality. Now he wanted to develop that with a more complete narrative, pushing the music ever-darker. As he's said, 'It was like lowering ourselves into a well. That's what we were ready for. The rope, and the darkness.' Ropes, roads, going down, sinking into something: these metaphors came up repeatedly in our conversations. Brett saw going down into that well as connecting with some inner part of himself, as yet untapped, but also reconnecting with fans. The *Night Thoughts* screen had been a barrier. He wanted barriers down.

Neil's role was changing. He'd evolved beyond keyboards and secondary guitar and shown himself able to turn a record into something greater than the sum of its parts. This time Neil wanted to record demos to a higher standard. Do it himself. Be all over it, 'from soup to nuts'. Richard's role was also changing, though in a different way. *Night Thoughts* had been liberating. After a youth often seen within the framing of Bernard's work, then a period of sustained mental struggle after the band split in 2003 and a tentative start to returning to 'the best and worst thing that ever happened to me', Richard was an essential part of Suede's renaissance. But he was still trying to avoid discomfort. Largely the band's post-reunion system had worked. Two monster egos in any band is usually one too many, and Brett gives enough lead-singer energy to fill three bands. That's what made this work. Brett: in spotlight. Richard and Neil: in the shadows. Richard was willing to play early Suede songs, but wanted to stretch himself, too.

More seemed possible now. The idea that leaning into more left-field albums might, counterintuitively perhaps, make the band more radical *and* more likely to endure was exciting (rather than, say, the risky, dead-end business of chasing catchy singles which would never chart). As so often in the past, Richard's personal life was still stuck in a rut. But *Night Thoughts* suggested how he might be more creatively fulfilled. Richard says those 2016 shows 'gave me a glimpse of a whole different way of performing that I wanted to explore further ... All of us wanted the follow-up to create our own "Suedeworld", reflected even in the cover art and bits of video and photos.'*

At the end of February, Brett, Neil and Richard met Ed again, back in London during one of his trips home, by which time they knew *Night Thoughts* had landed well, band and producer more closely associated than ever. In the band's view, last time they'd ended up with a good but 'chewier *Bloodsports*'; there was deeper they could go. Ed said they should make 'a gnarly, stripped-back rock record like something by Iggy Pop'. But the band's instincts were otherwise. Perhaps if they'd been in sync, they might have found a way. Perhaps if confidence was lower; if they'd felt more vulnerable, as they had done in, say, 2011. But 2011 was a long time ago now.

TENNIS COURTS: *THE BLUE HOUR* MANIFESTO

Brett, Neil and Richard met up to discuss next moves in early March. In Richard's words, 'We felt we were able to conceive, write, record and complete an album all on our own.' He remembers realising how Suede were now perceived: 'We felt free enough to map out the whole concept before we started writing ... We started to genuinely see ourselves as an "albums band". I remember I started listening closely to Kate Bush and Talk Talk. Initially that was to get on the same page as Brett and Neil, but I soon became obsessed with both artists, and they became the soundtrack to my life.'

* The next line of this quote is: 'At this point, the idea of writing a song like "Fifteen Again" [from 2022's *Autofiction*] was totally alien to us.'

At a follow-up meeting shortly afterwards they made a detailed plan for Suede #8. They wanted longer songs, more complex, with multiple sections. To tell a coherent story, leaning into elements that bound the songs together. They wanted spoken-word sections. More field recordings. This meant working against the playlist-led, algorithm thinking of the fast-mushrooming Spotify era, which partly selects songs on length and on being standalone pieces. In other words, Suede were purposely committing to being playlisted even *less*. Listened to less. Except, that is, by those prepared to buy into a whole record intended to be experienced beginning to end. Brett made a list of bullet points as they talked, titling his notebook page 'Tennis Courts'. (That was an in-joke. After *Bloodsports* was followed by the rhyming *Night Thoughts*, maybe *Tennis Courts* might be next up? To date, *Tennis Courts* remains, tragically, unrealised.)

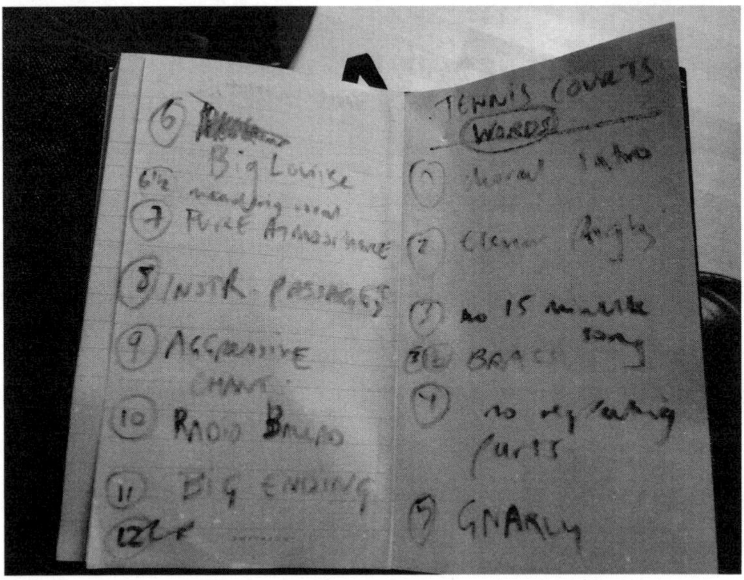

These pages read: '1. Choral Intro. 2. 'Elenor [sic] Rigby' (referencing the Beatles song – strings-only). 3. 15-minute song. 4. No repeating parts. 5. GNARLY. 6. 'Big Louise' (referencing the Scott Walker song). 6½. meandering vocal. 7. PURE ATMOSPHERE. 8. INSTRUMENTAL PASSAGES. 9. AGGRESSIVE CHANT. 10. RADIO BALLAD. 11. BIG ENDING.'

There was one more thing too: the idea that, in Richard's words, 'The songs should put us in mind of Neil's fridge magnet of [Rudyard] Kipling's black and white illustration for his story "The Cat That Walked By Himself",' the animal seen entering wintry woodland, tail up, heading into the unknown. They wanted a cold, unsparing record. If the cat was Suede, it had its tail up, anticipating what it might find in there.

I laugh when I see this list, wondering, say, how a Saul Galpern figure (Nude label boss who signed Suede in 1992) might have responded, at their commercial peak, to the suggestion of fifteen-minute songs, no repeating parts, meandering vocals, instrumentals and aggressive chants. Suede had no presence in their inner circle like that now, and few immediate commercial pressures. They had another album to deliver on their Warners contract, signed pre-*Night Thoughts*, but no one at the label was round the table at a creative band meeting – certainly they had no one to persuade of their new musical direction. Their process, they felt, could be trusted. Ian and Didz filled a similar-*ish* role to Galpern's, 'grown-up musical ears one step removed from the band and therefore slightly more objective', but the style of both men is to support, selectively. (If sent three demos, they might celebrate one, not mentioning others – but they'd never be negative about a song or critique a musical direction. Quick responses to songs they love are taken seriously.)* Effectively, Suede had become their own A&R.† Didz and Ian remained consistent, 'trying to encourage, but also to encourage them to be hard on themselves'.

---

* Didz started out as effectively Ian's assistant, though by *The Blue Hour* he was more experienced. Several others have worked alongside him on Suede business since 2011, but his is one of several critical, consistent voices in the camp.

† Ian, backstage at Suede's Folkestone gig, 30/1/26: 'They've got five A&R guys in the same band.'

This is largely forgotten now, but initially playfulness was a factor. The band even considered each learning a new instrument, Richard recalls, 'to give a different feel to the live performances'. He remembers sitting in Neil's kitchen in west London trying to picture it: 'We discussed how it would look on stage, and we toyed with the idea of costumes. (I recall a "plague doctor" look.) The whole mood was, okay, we've done two successful albums under Ed's guidance, so now we can do it on our own, indulge ourselves with our artistic grace period.' The plague doctor idea was a joke, but there's more movement across instruments in Suede than casual observers might imagine. Neil plays everything. Mat and Brett wrote an album's worth of unused *Bloodsports* material on keyboards. How this might have worked in practice, who knows? – perhaps they'd have written on their usual instruments, then switched – but either way, when bands are insecure, they're more conservative. Willingness to be vulnerable usually comes with confidence. Confidence, that is, for things to go horribly wrong in some new, as-yet-unimagined way.

SOMERSET AND SUBURBIA

As Simon Price puts it, 'Suede have always been a band concerned with exploring real British lives as they are lived.' For those attracted to that theme, the evidence has been consistent, through many musical reinventions. But up to 2016 Suede had always been considered very much a band of a *certain kind* of British lives: marginal lives almost exclusively lived out in cities and suburbs, roads, lay-bys, car parks. Much of the world Brett presented, even in the post-reunion era so far, concerned people in a suffocating, narrow world, tied to their kitchen sinks or partners, behind closed doors. In his youth, Brett stirred that in with androgyny, violence and drugs, the potency of the imagery juxtaposing love and different kinds of danger, whether drug-induced, sex-obsessed or mundane. More recently, he'd performed the same trick with love and fatherhood. But even that was in a recognisably Suede geography. What would he make of country life? And if you take Suede out of London, well, what's left? What if Brett got to Somerset and was, well, *happy*?

Jodie and Brett first saw their new house in December 2014, when travelling to Devon to see Brett's sister Blandine at Christmas, stopping off 'to see this great big, beautiful Regency place with wraparound garden' on the way. But they didn't move until early 2016. (Not a single other prospective buyer viewed the house, while they were struggling to sell their place in London.) The noise from below ground next door dragged on, through 2015. Jodie let her place in Ibiza go. The process was stressful and slow.

When they finally moved, Jodie recalls it being not quite the release they'd hoped for. 'Brett really fucking hated it,' she says now. 'We don't argue, but it made us argue – I thought, how can you not like it? I wanted him to be grateful we were in this amazing position. I thought, just get on with it! Brett is a homing pigeon; he'd lived within the same few streets for twenty-five years. I wonder if, without me, he'd still be there.' He certainly missed the city's culture and wondered at first what to do with himself in all those quiet hours. Jodie didn't have that longing, but Brett felt an acute absence. 'I fixated on this ghost existence,' he says now, 'where I kept thinking, how would things be if we were still in London?' Jodie suggested Brett could live back there Monday to Friday, returning on weekends – but he wanted to be together. Do ordinary, mundane parenting. There was a creative scene in that corner of Somerset, but that meant a lot of parties; Brett and Jodie were, in Jodie's words, 'always the first to go home, and not as wild'. They quickly got a reputation 'for being a bit boring' among creatives living it up in the private members' clubs close by. All that was alienating, Brett 'oddly displaced'. If they were going to make this work, it would be by finding peace in the house, the countryside. A routine. A balance, between family life and work.

The distance between the imagined reality of living ten miles from the Glastonbury festival site and actual reality was stark. Brett struggled with the quiet, the wind, the isolation, the long, cold winters. But this also represented the realisation of a dream. The boys were put into local schools and he did the school run daily, trying to focus on 'small moments of wonder'. In between drop-off and pick-up, he'd do a run of around 5 to 10k a day, headphones in, and write. There was usually something to work on. There was always Suede business. He saw Mike regularly, who felt his friend's new home, even in those early days, was different: 'If you got the Brett persona in London,' he says now, 'you got Brett the person in Somerset.'

By 2016, Brett had lived through multiple material changes since becoming a public figure, with six key romantic relationships over several decades. He'd survived years on drugs then made a sustained effort to get clean, learning to channel energies elsewhere. He'd experienced fame, then what happens when fame fades. Marriage. Becoming a stepdad then finding himself, against all odds, an outwardly conventional, adoring dad at the school gates in his forties, increasingly prone to reflection on his own early life and the legacies of his own parents' lives. His mum, an artist who made clothes for her children and foraged in the woods for food when they had none. His dad, an abrasive eccentric who played classical music at top volume and insisted on swearing on Liszt's biography in court when called for jury duty.

Yes, Brett's childhood was suburban, but it was also as much in the wilds as it was in what people might think of when they conjure that word, 'suburban'. Brett recalled eating rabbit caught out the back of the house, when the family were short. That makes sense of his drive to escape, also of getting sucked into the capital from Haywards Heath, between London and Brighton. But it could also help make sense of why Brett might have envisioned a move to the country as a kind of return home, too. In his words, 'I wanted my son to have the kind of idyllic childhood I'd felt the lack of when I was small.' Where he'd been used to precarity, worn home-made clothes and eaten cuts of meat so cheap he couldn't chew them (he sometimes cried at the table, before food was thrown away), he wanted Jack and Lucian to grow up in more rarefied air. Somerset offered that, though would he ever get used to it? 'It was an idyllic life,' he says now, 'but also felt like pretend. Safe. Secure. Away from everything. I wondered whether making that move really was doing right by the kids.'

In 2016, Brett and Mike often did long drives to London and back, 130 miles each way: 'Brett would jump in the car and we'd talk about music the whole way.' On these journeys they shared enthusiasms, reminisced and looked forward. At twenty-four, Mike had started his own business. At twenty-four, Brett was the singer in an unsigned band, going nowhere – but they'd both somehow made a whole life out of art, and were thriving. They still talked about making a Suede film sometimes; until recently, '90s bands were considered 'too young' by TV execs for long-form documentaries. Mike was told he was too early. Though that was changing.

It was on one of these journeys that Mike played Brett a song that gave him an idea.

'MISTRESS' AND NARRATIVE BEGINNINGS

'Love is a Catastrophe' is a little-noticed track from the Pet Shop Boys' 2002 album *Release*. Suede are rarely compared to them – it's easier to lump them in with so-called Britpop acts whose music draws from very different traditions and sounds. But there's plenty of crossover. Mike started out in event and concert production with both bands when he was working with Derek Jarman. An ability to mix a distinct, English poppy sensibility with an instinct for the darkness – sexual, manipulative, violent, marginal – fuels many of both acts' best songs. Neil Tennant has long been an influence on Brett, and they'd performed together before, too. So when Mike wanted to play Brett a Pet Shop Boys deep cut he'd never heard in the car one day, he was willing to listen.

Unusually for them, 'Love Is a Catastrophe' is rooted in a winding, slow guitar figure and has no keyboards. Set amid a rural backdrop of 'high wind through the trees' and 'falling November leaves', the narrator is realising something awful for the first time. It starts out like a simple heartbreak song but builds slowly, a sense of confusion, panic and fear taking over as it reaches its final lines. What draws the listener in, seeming light at first, turns undeniably dark:

To think I could believe
In love as the kindest law
not as a declaration of war
on my life and sanity

Much remains ambiguous but there's devastating conflict here, no redemption possible.

It's too neat to say this song provided a template for Suede #8: the haunting dangers of the countryside, a terrible realisation played out – all the darkness of Suedeworld, applied to a fresh, rural backdrop. But Brett was intrigued by the approach. Soon after, he played 'Love Is a Catastrophe' to Richard and Neil; 'Mistress' was the first good song demoed for Suede #8, with music written on acoustic guitar by Richard in early May 2016, Brett's lyric added mid-June. The heart of the song, like 'Love Is a Catastrophe', is a realisation the speaker is only just coming to. There's a kind of sister guitar line, too – a clipped, winding arpeggio.

Mat says that for him there was something crystallising about 'Mistress', his favourite song from this period. The story sees a child realise one of their parents is having an affair. The lyrics build a sense of creeping threat, but also childish vulnerability, steering well clear of the dreaded sweetness: 'There's something wonderfully confusing about whose viewpoint this is. It shifts around ... It's about a child watching something happening with his parents, but there's something non-moralistic about it, because you're never really sure whose side the protagonist is on.'

That ambiguity is at its most powerful in the chorus. It isn't a plaintive, 'Mistress / leave him', or similar. It's 'Mistress / stay with him'. The killer line isn't, 'You're all that he's got', it's, 'You're not all that he's got, but you're all that he wants'. (After all, the subject in the song is a parent – though their child thinks they're not valued.) All this turns a simple cry of anguish – the discovery of shameful, parental betrayal – into something more complex and surprising. The child seems to recognise, despite their own pain, that whatever this affair is, it's meaningful, and they promise not to expose it: 'I won't tell the neighbours / they don't mean a thing / now you're in love'. The final line here is repeated, like an echo. It doesn't sound like someone who wants his parents to be faithful in any conventional sense. It suggests, quietly, a crucial absence. The line isn't 'You're in love again'. It's 'Now you're in love'.

From that kernel of the May demo of 'Mistress' came the idea of writing more from a child's perspective, inverting the *Night Thoughts* approach, the child in 'Mistress' running away after discovering this affair. The idea of a search party out looking for the child in 'the blue hour', the time when light fades in the countryside and the night draws in. Once set, this would influence everything.

ANNA AND RICHARD FALL IN LOVE (AGAIN)

On the *Coming Up* tour in 1996, a young Swedish woman called Anna Granath wanted to see Suede live but couldn't afford to, so went along to their free in-store in Stockholm instead. As she stood around, not queuing to meet the band, Charlotta from Sony asked if she and her friend wanted to see the band DJ. That night, sharing a similar sense of humour, Anna and Mat became friends instantly. He put Anna on the guest list for the two Stockholm gigs, between which she took the band sightseeing and drank pink champagne. During this brief period, Anna fell for Richard: 'He was so innocent, so shy. I knew I was in love, though everyone thought I was crazy.' In those days there were no smartphones, no way of contacting a band on the move – they were on an eighteen-month world tour. 'When they left for Germany, we said goodbye and I was so sad because I would never see them again,' she remembers. 'I felt like I'd always known him. Like we were siblings or something, that met for the first time. When he left, I cried and cried.'

To say this was unusual for Richard is an understatement. Over the next two decades, Richard was only in two relationships: one for twelve years, another for six. Typically untypical, even in the early days he didn't indulge in one-night stands or the usual rock cliché behaviour. (This when he was young, hot and in demand.) The band felt he always seemed to be with someone who didn't like him: perhaps there's a relationship here between lack of confidence in his private life, an inability to say what he needed and hold to it, and the difficulty he found advocating for himself professionally when things were hard.

By 2016, Richard was miserable at home, unsure how to handle being 'in a six-year relationship going nowhere.' In June Suede played a one-off gig in Gröna Lund amusement park in Stockholm. They'd last played the city, the full *Night Thoughts* show, only a few months before. Anna was in the audience then, at Cirkus, expecting the screen to rise after a song or two. She was back again tonight. Over the years, Anna had regularly been at Suede shows in Stockholm. But she was self-conscious about seeing Richard again. He wasn't often at after-parties anyway. In 1998, Anna had met the father of her children and lived with him for seventeen years: 'My brief romance with Richard,' she remembers, 'had become a nostalgic sweet memory, that's all.'

In the intervening years, Anna – confident, forthright, focused – developed an extraordinary career, becoming famous in Sweden. Starting out performing in musicals, she moved into stand-up comedy, then TV – 'that was the goal', she says now. She wrote for comedy shows, then moved in front of the camera, becoming a writer–actress splitting her time fifty–fifty between the two disciplines. By 2016, the bright-eyed teenager was long gone. She was acclaimed in her own right. But she was still a Suede fan, and when the band were in the country, she went along to see her friend Mat backstage.

After the Gröna Lund show, twenty years on from their first meeting, she and Richard were drawn together once more. Anna had been separated for about a year, trying to find a new balance between family, work and personal life. She wasn't looking for a new partner, but her friend suggested they talk to Richard, anyway. When they approached, he didn't immediately recognise them. As Richard 'began to download the memory', Anna's children wanted to leave to go on the rides at the Tivoli, so she had to go. It didn't feel like a wow moment.

The wow came later. Richard sent her 'this cute message' via

Facebook, apologising for not recognising her, saying he remembered that week in 1996 well and how she made him feel. 'Let's have a drink next time we're in Stockholm,' he wrote. Soon they began writing long messages, daily. Richard remembers: 'We instantly fell in love.' This made his personal life complicated, but also gave him hope. In Anna's words: 'It was frustrating. There was all this longing. We wrote for months and I fell head over heels in love with him again. He opened up, we talked about everything in our lives, though he was scared. He's not shy when he's writing. He felt safe with me and I felt safe with him.' But still, 'he felt scared [by his situation], he wasn't free.' Richard was consumed by guilt. 'It felt,' Anna said, 'like our friendship was becoming something else, so I said I would try and respect that, just friends, that I was just glad to have him back in my life. But that didn't last.'

Richard and Neil made the trip out to Somerset to try writing at Brett's place. During this session Richard's 'head was spinning out of control with emotion ... I remember sitting in Brett's dining room, feeling very cold (even though it was June), the room seeming sunny and unreal, and being unable to take my eyes off my phone in case Anna messaged me.' Anna's text landed twenty-four hours after they'd promised to restrain themselves: 'Hi friend, how's it going with you?' He texted back, 'I'm with the boys and I'm trying to write.' 'We were suffering!' Anna laughs now. Neil and Brett, Richard remembers, knew something was wrong. But they didn't know what it was.

That day, 21 June, they worked on several different pieces. Richard liked a song called 'Mother', but 'As One' was the breakthrough. With the lyric added two days later, Neil remembers: '"As One" ... was written on Midsummer's Day in Brett's light, sunny piano room in Somerset on his baby grand piano but it had a tense, wintery, haunted quality that pointed the way for much of what came after it.' These were the song's bare bones, written with the three men clustered together: Neil on piano, Richard on acoustic, Brett standing close-in. Perhaps the setting helped. It didn't become a regular practice to write in Brett's new back yard, but seeing the place, even briefly, helped Richard and Neil imagine the Suedeworld they would create using that setting. Mat immediately considered this new song a potential album opener. The fast staccato strings on the demo came from Neil thinking about music 'with a wintry feel' written specifically for children. (Children, after all, learn danger in storytelling, the better to manage it in real life.)

Neil remembered a piece called 'The Snow Is Dancing' from *Children's Corner*, a piano suite Debussy wrote in 1906–8 for his young daughter, Claude-Emma. 'The Snow is Dancing' begins with a fast piano figure; if you slow that piece down, change the key, play it lower 'so it sounds more menacing' and switch the piano out for strings, you pretty much have the cello and bass viol lines for 'As One'. Neil added this to the bare bones piece written at Brett's, the 'fast run' of cellos and double basses going right to the song's climax.* Richard remembers it was Neil who had such ambitious plans for songs like 'As One', considering how the songs might correspond to Brett's notebook list.

Richard had to face his personal situation, sure he wanted to be with Anna and knowing it wasn't right to drag things out at home. 'I tried to painlessly end things with my then-partner,' he remembers, 'but handled it very badly, and my house became a war zone for a few months towards the end of 2016,' when she finally moved out. When I asked if this made it harder to focus, he suggested it wasn't that simple: 'As much as these events turned my world upside down temporarily, I don't think it interfered with my focus on writing – it just meant I was a troubled soul

---

* Neil, Mat and Richard discuss this on *The Blue Hour* audio commentary.

when we were coming up with that material.' Richard poured himself into writing not just with Suede, but also with Sean, starting work on a second Artmagic album. In the same way that Jodie can hear Brett's life, disguised, in Suede's lyrics, Anna says she can hear Richard's in the music he made during that period.

Across thousands of messages, Richard and Anna began to talk about the future, also how Richard might face his shame and discomfort at the attention he'd received over the years. Anna recalls:

> We worked together on him *owning* his success. Before, he would say he was just lucky, that him being in Suede was just luck. But if he hadn't spent all those hours practising, hadn't sent in his demo, hadn't written all these songs since then, worked so hard and done so much for the band – you know, he *is* worthy of this success. He is such a good person. It has taken a long time, but I have helped make him more confident. He's never stepped on anyone's toes. He deserves credit.

This isn't Anna putting herself at the centre of Richard's development; she too has grown into confidence, consciously working towards this for years. Richard, meanwhile, sees Anna's contribution as central. Everyone sees it in action, all the time. It was hard for a while. It was messy. But Anna's arrival in Richard's life was also transformative. The shy, uneasy anti-rock star who never quite grew up or valued himself was changing.

BRETT'S 'WASTELANDS' OBSESSION

There were plenty of demos, but overall progress felt slow. Next was the music for 'Wastelands' written in late September by Richard, the hypnotic arpeggiated lead guitar line influenced by Johnny Marr. (The two had a mutual appreciation society going.) Once Brett wrote a top line at the end of November, he became utterly captivated, saying, 'For a while, I thought "Wastelands" was Suede's best song in twenty years. The best since "Everything Will Flow".' (Again: the others don't agree. But when Brett gets intoxicated by a song, he really loses himself in it.)

These days Brett listened to the band's music-in-progress on the move, coming up with ideas on the daily run, though with 'Wastelands' he was compelled to listen for pleasure. By his own count, Brett heard the demo at least 200 times, over about nine months. The band discussed shortening it, or 'teasing something else out'; Brett now suggests 'that might have been more likely had Ed been involved'. But these days there was 'no filterless voice' telling them what they thought about the music as it was being written. Once established, this made ideas hard to shift. Sometimes, it was hard to retain emotional distance. Brett was devoted to 'Wastelands' as it was first written, so the song's structure became set and he resisted any change. It clocked in at five and a half minutes, with a long intro and outro.

'Wastelands' was the latest Suede bossa nova, the off-beat rhythm, melody and guitar line becoming addictive to Brett. In it, he sensed a way to present this new rural world as suffocating, something like a suburban bedsit. In 'Wastelands' the weather talks, encouraging people to break out of their societal strictures together: 'And the wind is calling us / and the pleasantries will chain us no more'. In Suedeworld, the wastelands are a place to run to, a desolate place of glorious escape for young protagonists for whom 'the world is much too much'. 'When the snow is all there is and words sound different', 'fear will fade away', and language comes back to life. It's a kind of freedom. A place where, as the last line of the chorus goes, 'Where the children in us play'. Crucially, Brett started to envision how the countryside might be presented as a neglected, filth-laden tip, but nevertheless beautiful, in spite of itself.

There were a couple more gigs in October, then towards the end of November Suede played two back-to-back shows in Mexico City. They wrote the main body of 'Flytipping' the day after Neil's birthday, on 6 December, lyric and melody following shortly after. It had raw promise, the title coming from this strangely Suedey word Brett noticed on rural Somerset tracks warning against people dumping rubbish and running away. The heart of the lyric, though, as so often, came from visual art: Brett had seen an exhibition years before by the artist Michael Landy called *Breakdown*, in which he, in Brett's words, 'systematically destroyed all of his worldly possessions as a comment on consumerism.' Brett looked for a home for this idea for years – it's common for people who grow up poor, then escape poverty, to wonder at the value of multiplying possessions. What would it be like to *own nothing*, he wondered. 'There was a spark of something that fascinated me,' he recalls now. 'When we moved to the countryside, like any move it involved a kind of assessment of worldly possessions as we boxed them up to be relocated. I remember feeling a distinct sense of glut.' In 'Flytipping', the protagonists are liberated by 'getting rid of all their shit', though it destroys the untouched beauty of their surroundings for others. 'What is mine and what is yours?' the chorus asks, 'Do we own these things? What has it all been for?' 'Romantic and idealistic,' says Brett now, 'but strangely attractive in this age of crushing materialism.' With 'Flytipping', Neil once again had ideas here, the high drama of the song's subjects 'casting their possessions to the breeze' offering plenty of potential for expansion. Around this time, they also wrote the music for 'The Invisibles', lyrics and melody coming the next day. Richard remembers these 'starting out fairly simple and organic, then Neil would work on writing extra parts for them, later ... He did a great job,' he remembers, 'during a period where I was very preoccupied.'

Despite having written for most of 2016, they only really had a few good songs so far, though they clearly represented a desirable sonic evolution. What they'd learned was: be patient. Keep working. This time round there was less anxiety, less conflict, more focus. Throughout Suede's history, there'd only been one previous year without live commitments, but in 2017 they'd do one thing only: make the world of this album as potent as could be.

Good new ideas came in a rush, though the next notable one was rooted in the past. In 2012 'Underwater Bond' came to nothing as it hadn't fitted the *Bloodsports* brief, but now Neil re-sent the demo to Brett. This time he wrote to it, making it 'All the Wild Places'. As with 'Wastelands', much of the old Suede vocabulary was recycled: simply moving Brett's preoccupations to the countryside gave them a new charge. In the verses, the speaker is drawn by some outside force into the unknown:

Take her cold hands
Place the snowdrops in her palms
And pushing through the wire
I have no choice but to follow you
Feel the weak sunlight on my skin
As I take my spade and place her
Forever by the birch trees.

Is it a burial? Of an animal? A person? The chorus is a looped prayer: 'Oh, of all the wild places I love / you are the most desolate'.

Next, Neil wrote two demos that seemed to want to go together. First, the Pistols-y 'Cold Hands', updated with a new chorus in early February.

'The 'cold hands' of 'All the Wild Places' reappeared here, Brett amused by having a singalong chorus featuring the line, 'Now I want to curl up and die'. Counterintuitive, maybe. But catchy. Then the atmospheric half-song 'Chalk Circles', later the same month, with music, lyrics and melody again written in quick succession. On 9 March they recorded two more together: the music for a promising ballad, and Richard's 'Manipulation', a more raucous, upbeat song.* Exciting but out of place.† When Brett was adding parts now, they were soaring. If it felt like they were warming up to something, then the following day showed what they were warming up to. The day after the ballad demo was laid down Brett added a crucial top line. Here was a song for the heart of the album. Maybe, for the heart of the whole reunion era.

'LIFE IS GOLDEN': A WISH FOR THE FUTURE

If Brett had been writing indirectly about parenthood, this represented him being more direct. No indirect allusions or filtering experience through imagined others: here, undisguised, was Lucian's song. It drew on recent experience, writing about parental love, picking angular images and partnering them with a sunny melody. In the way that, say, 'The Wild Ones', 'Saturday Night' or 'Life Is Golden' is painted in primary colours. The lyric uses repetition to draw close the connections between father and son, though it avoids anything soft-focus:

---

* 'Manipulation' (the only extra track on the deluxe edition of *The Blue Hour*) was completed on 15/3/17.

† Brett says of 'Manipulation': 'Stupidly, we always do this with extra tracks. We don't realise how good they are – and that was a real kind of garagey thing, and I think we didn't put it on the record because it just didn't fit with the sound. But it really influenced what we did next.'

The same blood runs through your veins
The same strange way of talking
The same thoughts sink through your pillow
The same crooked smile.

What they have in common is not something sweet like eye colour, but rather that 'crooked smile'. It's not innocence; even with Lucian so young, it's their oddness, sharpness, their curious, shared thoughts in the dark. 'Life Is Golden' is a song of connection, the chorus unashamed celebration: 'You're not alone, look up to the sky and be calm / Not alone, look into the light and be heard / You're never alone, your life is golden, golden'. In an album of determined coldness, it's a blast of heat.

'Life Is Golden' is a wish for the future, a song for fathers to sing far from home, and a new take on the Suede song of unity, reinvented for family love. Brett is private about his marriage and rarely discusses it with the band, never mind the public. Jodie is in Suede's music in disguise. But here, a notable exception. In the second verse, she appears for the first time, unquestionably, within a Suede song: 'The same blood runs through your veins / But you, you have the light of your mother / She holds her love to her tender breast'. Mat believed this was something emblematic Brett had been working towards for a long time, now in powerful miniature.

By now, they had more songs, though Richard wanted 'something more wind[ing], dark, hard.' That led to another rush, including 'White Widow', named after a strain of weed. Though abandoned in its original form, this ended up being important.* Richard liked its hardness, but it didn't feel complete to others. He remembers: 'The thing they liked

---

* Not to be confused with another discarded song from this era, '*The* White Widow' (my italics).

most was the verse guitar part. So we lifted that from the song, changed the key and made it heavier and slower. Then we used it as the opening riff for "As One".'

NEIL'S 'FLYTIPPING' IDEA

Neil's focus was on Suede, but he was still in Penguin Cafe, and hearing what the City of Prague Philharmonic Orchestra added to their new album *The Imperfect Sea* made him think Suede might be able to attempt something similar, without breaking the bank.* On 21 March, string arranger Oli and Brett were heading to Neil's to work up ideas for a spoken-word piece. Brett and Neil loved the whispered 'Widow's Peak' by Bat for Lashes from her recent concept album *The Bride*. That day in March, Brett's train from Somerset was cancelled and he didn't make it. Instead, Neil improvised, using a combination of Oli's spontaneous violin playing and studio effects to make the background music for what became 'Roadkill'. 'What you hear on the record,' says Neil, 'is what Oli and I came up with that day'. Brett loved the results. Channelling *The Bride*, also the Velvet Underground's spoken-word 'The Gift', this became nailed-on well before some of the more conventional songs on *The Blue Hour*.†

March was good. Also that month, Neil had an idea – to add a second half to 'Flytipping', turning it from a conventional-length song to the longest Suede piece post-reunion, with extended musical coda.‡

---

* Neil played his last Penguin Cafe gig at the Union Chapel in December of 2017. He appeared on two songs on *The Imperfect Sea*, playing kalimba on 'Franz Schubert' and ukulele on album closer 'Wheels Within Wheels'.

† They played 'Roadkill' every single night of the 2018 European tour, even at an HMV in-store performance on Oxford Street in London, on 23/9/18.

‡ Original 'Flytipping' written 8/12/16. Music written 6/12/16. Second half (from after the line '... by the underpass' onwards) written on 21/7/17.

Neil recalls, 'Richard and I spent an afternoon sparking off each other, adding each section, coming back out of the woods of *The Blue Hour* layer by layer, the guitars at the album's close mirroring those at the beginning.' This was the two of them, at their best, 'a joyful couple of hours of true collaboration'. Those extra two and a half minutes added drama and gave Richard a chance to shine. When Anna heard 'Flytipping' it instantly became her favourite Suede song; she could see Richard growing in confidence and range, in the band as well as out of it.*

The band met on Skype with Ed again. He invited them to record the album in the US – he believed 'it could be done quickly'. They'd shared the best songs so far with him; clearly this was not that stripped-back record they'd discussed – but they still explored working together. In the end, the band were reluctant to record in the US, while they also thought they'd likely need more, not less time.

THE UNDERPAINTING

Brett's not the only one who needs an 'entry point'. Richard's approach is led, as Brett has it, 'by his instinctive response'. He's intelligent, sensitive, he gets moved by a piece and wants to write from a place of emotional unawareness. Too much thinking and he freezes. Neil's approach is a mixture of emotional response combined with a study of what he's making. This might occur in the moment or be something he turns over as songs evolve. It's a different kind of warmth. He's looking for ways to get emotionally involved, using storytelling from other forms.

---

* Around this time, the music for 'Roadkill' (demo title 'Mood Piece') was written at Neil's on 21 March, 'Tides' ('Digital Rug') on the 24th. Alongside 'Flytipping', Anna believed that 'Tides' in particular represented a growth in Richard's confidence.

Brett's move to Somerset presented Neil with an opportunity. Though he'd lived in London since joining the band, he grew up two minutes' bike ride from rural Warwickshire, surrounded by a similar landscape. Listening to Brett's lyrics, he recognised that world and began to see commonalities with Suede's urban writing, too. Outsiderdom, alienation, character pieces exploring fear, love and the hinge between the two, just in a different landscape. It was no marginal detail, but the environment of the whole record.

It's too easy to say if a musician reads a book then they're an 'intellectual'. That comes from the lazy assumption that musicians are dumb animals channelling some mysterious force, guided by nothing but three chords and the truth, having no curiosity, interests or hinterland. Most are led by other art forms they come across, taking inspiration in widely. To adapt Mat's wording, all new art responds to old art, and no rule says you're only allowed to be influenced by your own form. But how does this work in practice?

When Neil's interested, he goes deep. Brett flags this about Neil: he'll embrace discussions about influences or references. This moves the writing forward: 'It's something I just love about Neil,' he says, 'as a person, but also as someone to work with. I can talk about the most obscure book, and he would know all about it, in much more depth than me. You can talk about anything to do with classical music or jazz and he'll understand. He's got an encyclopaedic memory and knowledge of these things.' This period was probably, more than any other time in the reunion era, when Neil and Brett were most in tune.

When Brett said he was channelling Somerset, Neil knew this meant the *dark* side of country life: he immersed himself in folk-horror films, considered what kind of writing might complement that, how interstitials and snippets of dialogue might be used. He thought of the 1977 film *Capricorn One*, where Brenda Vaccaro reads Dr. Seuss to her children; also cult Polish film-maker Jerzy Skolimowski's folk-horror *The Shout* (1978). At one point, he wanted to use dialogue from *And Soon the Darkness*, from the early '70s. As Neil puts it, 'In these films, rural life isn't bucolic or idyllic: it's sinister, full of threat.' Much of this work was either made in the 1970s or influenced by that decade. (Born in 1967, Brett was six in 1973, similar to the child at the heart of this Suede album, and to Lucian when it was made. Neil was born in 1973.)

In Alan Garner's fantasy novel *Red Shift*, also published in 1973, Neil found a story where, 'the adult world, viewed from a young person's eyes, is one of chaos and threat'. That seemed to speak to L.P. Hartley's novel *The Go-Between*, in which protagonist Leo accesses a suppressed memory from when he was young, via a found diary, rediscovered in the middle of what Hartley calls 'this hideous century'. That novel is now remembered for its opening line: 'The past is a foreign country: they do things differently there.' The point here is not about borrowing from any film, novel or piece of music. It's about atmosphere. Brett remembers Neil asking what he was writing about, then responding by immersing himself in works across genre and form that explored the dark side of rural life, what Neil says now, with a laugh, might be described as Brett's 'hypodermic needle in the haystack'. This speaks to a point of connection with what Suede have done before; a way for new music to respond to old.

It was natural for Brett to go looking for life at the margins. He'd always done so. It meant the songs felt like they were written by the same band, with concerns that made sense to listeners. Okay, you're still exploring alienation, but now it's rural, through a child's eyes. The child is Lucian, but it's also Brett. It's the 21st century, but it's also the 1970s. Somerset, but also some other world, an alternative version of the English countryside, something in common with the wilds behind Brett's own childhood home. These, then, were Neil's ways into the emotional heart of the record-in-progress. Some of this is about what Neil carries all the time. But some of it is specific to this particular record, and might be seen differently now.

When I asked Neil about the references in his audio commentary for *The Blue Hour*, many skipped over so quickly that most listeners wouldn't be able to make them out, I began to realise just how many of these there were. There's a lot of depth and seriousness that goes unseen; it's the underpainting of *The Blue Hour*. I was curious about the horror Neil referenced, so much of it concerned with the impossible gulf between parents and children, with memory and suppression – stuff he described as 'hauntological'.* Around 2016, Neil was also watching *The Wicker Man*, David Rudkin's 1974 TV play *Penda's Fen, The Blood on Satan's Claw, The Witch, Valerie and Her Week of Wonders*:

> Perhaps I'm just a magpie, feathering the nest with cultural clutter. I think *The Blue Hour* had an inherent depth that allowed me to lean into that tendency of mine a bit more. If I tried to sneak French impressionist music into a three-minute post-punk song I'd be given short shrift. But on *The Blue Hour* everything was so dense and symphonic I don't think anyone noticed what I put in there ...

The word 'clutter' is self-deprecating. It's a way of pointing to something while waving away its importance. (If you do this, it means people can't accuse you of being 'clever', or trying hard. In rock music, for all its evolution, there's still little worse than being seen to have *tried*.) But in

---

* That's a word that squishes together 'haunting' and 'ontology' – the term, rooted in the work of Jacques Derrida, being as much about lost time as lost souls. No, I didn't think French philosophy would get so much attention in this book either.

fact, Neil *is* serious about these influences, and they do have a concrete impact. You don't need to know anything about *The Wicker Man* to spot it, though it contributes to the depth of Suedeworld.

The thing that stands out to me most on relistening to *The Blue Hour* is not the folk horror, or literary references; it's the orchestral music: some of this intersects with Neil's long-held, hidden interest in modernism across culture. (Some listeners will notice 'Wastelands' is a similar title to T.S. Eliot's modernist epic 'The Waste Land'.) Mostly that influence is irrelevant for Suede records. Neil is agile enough to shift from orchestral to aggressive post-punk, ever-keen to fill the next hole. But for this record, the late Romantic and Impressionist influence was everywhere. Stravinsky's *Rite of Spring* was key: widely considered one of the first modernist pieces of music, it had a riot-inducing debut in Paris in 1913, being 'noted for its brutality, its barbaric rhythms, and its dissonance.' (The piece ends with the protagonist dancing herself to death, so it's not short on the darkness.) Ravel's *L'enfant et les sortilèges*, 'an opera about a child who won't do his homework', was an influence too: this opera about a rebellious child ending with the same woodwind line with which it begins.

All this is arguably the deepest of Suede rabbit holes. It's tempting to dive in, as the entire period is a kind of rabbit hole, in which more can be found if you're prepared to look. I'll soon have to back out into the light, for fear of disappearing, but the connections are real. The circular nature of the music, like Ravel's woodwind, is rooted in Neil wanting to 'make *The Blue Hour* a ricorso'. That is, a piece that ends where it began. There are plenty of examples of this, but for Neil the key reference was James Joyce's modernist novel *Finnegans Wake*, which he'd been reading between January and May 2016. (A more obscure reference, *Berg*, by Brighton-born experimental writer Ann Quin, published in 1964, also influenced Neil, doing a version of the same thing.) With *Finnegans*

Wake in mind, starting and ending in the middle of the same sentence – *The Wall* by Pink Floyd does this too – the echoes across 'As One' and 'Flytipping' make more sense. Listeners who don't register these things consciously might be more likely to think of the music as being one complete experience rather than a collection of random bits of sound, dumped in any old order. That's intentional: *Night Thoughts* had been 'a move in this direction', but now they wanted to dial it up.

GETTING THE RELUCTANT ENGINEER–PRODUCER ON BOARD

Once they were ready, Alan Moulder was approached to produce. Brett had worked with him on one song as a solo artist, so there was a slight connection, and he'd worked with Ian too, on other projects. Alan is one of the biggest names there is, but having come up initially in the late '80s, he was 'never quite in the same social or musical circles as Suede', giving a bit of distance. If Ed is a producer–engineer, Alan is very much an engineer–producer; in Alan they'd be getting someone whose approach would be to trust, listen, facilitate rather than push or provoke. Richard especially was keen to get the kinds of hard, uncompromising guitar sounds he'd loved on Moulder records he remembered from being a kid, such as Ride's *Going Blank Again* and My Bloody Valentine's *Loveless*.

Though Alan worked on many records they admired (by the Killers, Foals, Interpol, Beach House) and was a Suede fan, initially he was reluctant. He told Ian he was used to being one part of a duo alongside Flood*, with whom he'd set up Assault & Battery Studios. They usually came as a team: Alan mixing, Flood on production. Also, in Alan's words: 'I had

* Alan Moulder and Flood are perhaps more known for their work with the likes of U2, Smashing Pumpkins and Nine Inch Nails, though these weren't a reference for Suede.

an opinion of what I thought Ed would have given them. And I didn't think I could give them that. His kind of musicality and arrangement skills, I'm not that kind of producer, so I was a bit nervous about them expecting something I couldn't deliver.' Ian persuaded him these demos were so evolved that 'they weren't really looking for any big changes.' Alan was told: 'It's all pretty much there – we just need it recorded and we need someone who's good at recording guitars. Can you do that?' He thought *yeah, I can do that* ... though he was 'very conscious of how well *Night Thoughts* had been received. I thought I was coming in, you know [laughs], for – peak, peak, crash!'

The management sent Alan 'Life Is Golden' and 'Flytipping'. These were the highest-quality demos Suede had ever prepared pre-studio. Scoping out is standard; producers like to have an idea of the territory they'll be working in. Even when bands are well known, well established, the next record might take some new, off-putting direction – and producers live by their reputation as much as bands do. Here, demos really mattered. By this point, Suede had done a lot of the difficult stuff many bands do further down the line. Alan again: 'The demos gave me a sense of how dark and potent the material was ... and it was great. But also, I could see just how central Neil was to the band's process. I don't think I appreciated that before. I don't think it's seen at all, really. His contribution.'

On this evidence, especially excited by 'Flytipping', he agreed. Neil would act like a kind of shadow producer and Alan would record, an occasional voice in the room. He'd also feed in much of what Neil had prepped on spoken-word pieces like 'Roadkill', 'Dead Bird' and the interstitials. Songs were selected, parts worked out, arrangements set, lyrics done. The work was mostly in weaving everything together, then considering additions afterwards. Assault & Battery Studios were booked for six weeks, from September to October 2017. Richard was looking forward to a different atmosphere: 'Alan is very calm, not remotely confrontational or reactionary like Ed is, so it was a very different atmosphere recording with him. I think he was quite happy to record the songs as we had written and demoed them, let us be in charge of arrangements (something Ed would never do, he likes to get forensic with songs and sometimes even alter their DNA). We are a very hands-on group, we like to be there all the way through a mix and all offer our opinions and advice all the time.'

RECORDING *THE BLUE HOUR*: 'VERY HAPPY TO BE MAKING A TERRIFYING RECORD'

With a grin, Alan remembers *The Blue Hour* as being 'one of the most pleasant recording experiences I've ever had.' He knows he's describing an album laden with doom, but from the producer's perspective, the process was comically idyllic. Brett, Mat and Richard cycled into the studio in north-west London daily, while Neil preferred to walk. Good humour abounded. Though they didn't have the same long history they had with Ed, no in-jokes or experience of having done it before, everyone got on well and it felt low risk. Perhaps because much of the hard work had been done and 'they all turned up fresh as daisies every morning,' in Alan's words, 'ready to go'.

The sessions started with Simon. (The others joked they spent several years working on *The Blue Hour*, while he 'turned up for about an hour and a half'. For an hour and a half, read just shy of four days?)* According to Alan, 'The drums just sounded fantastic from the very start, which meant we were on a firm foundation. After that, everything just

* They started with 'Wastelands', late afternoon 18 September, with Simon done by 12.30 on the 21st. (It would have been quicker, but they re-recorded the drums for 'Beyond the Outskirts' at a brisker tempo on the Thursday.)

went really well together.' Alan tried not to overthink: 'It's an emotional album,' he says, 'so it made sense to respond to it that way. All the songs are incredibly strong emotionally. Very dark, dark stuff. Which is, again, [why] it was quite funny thinking about the recording.' Moulder has worked with some of the industry's biggest egos. He's too polite to name names. But it's clear he found the contrast amusing between some of his previous work and weeks spent with these nice men who seemed very happy to be making a terrifying record. Over a sandwich one day, chatting to Flood, Alan described the ominous, choral 'As One' – now so far removed from that simple piano idea born at Brett's new place – saying it sounded like 'the devil wanting to take over the world'. (A good thing. Obviously.) To Alan, Suede even seemed to be (whisper it) emotionally mature. Respectful about each other's ideas, able to dispute or challenge something that wasn't working, without things blowing up.

I pushed back. Was this really the same band as had made, well, all their previous records? The closest I got to the admission of professional or personal tension was this, from Richard: 'There were one or two occasions where [us being around for everything] got on Alan's nerves, and he would turn around to us and calmly suggest that we all go home for a few hours and let him get on with his work. Which is totally fair enough!' Well, if that's your problem, then you don't have problems. But what if, in all this pleasantness and maturity, they'd lost an essential edge? I pressed Alan on whether the band were too comfortable. In his view it wasn't about comfort, but rather clarity of purpose, and confidence in that purpose. Alan believes Suede are unusual in having experience and restlessness in equal measure:

> Unless you're gonna become a pantomime version of yourself, that's what you've got to be, driven, or else it gets boring. And they're not

> the sort of people that just do anything. They're not making these albums just so they can go out and tour and make money. They're making albums because they want to make something incredible. To make art, that's their legacy. So they want it to be as good as it can be. But it's great they've got the confidence that means they're willing to try things. At the end of it if it doesn't work, okay, but you've got to be willing to try.

Great, but were they just repeating what they'd done with demos, in a studio, unthinkingly? Alan says there was plenty of experimentation. 'They knew the songs they wanted, but they kept changing as we recorded. Well beyond initial recordings, they were looking for ideas to help those songs shine. You can see that, if you look at all they did afterwards.' The band thought Alan's input essential, though Alan routinely talks down his own contribution, insisting he wasn't so much producing as turning things on and watching, for pleasure. I asked what he felt he *added* as producer. Alan's answer was: 'Neil produced the album more than I did. It was all done. All we were doing was doing it properly, in a proper studio.' Then he described why he loves 'Tides'.

Mat felt 'Tides' grew in the studio, thanks to Alan:

> I think it's the best-produced thing on *The Blue Hour*, it's the kind of thing Alan does brilliantly. It's quite linear, it just builds each time, there's no middle eight or anything like that – very straightforward. Nothing clever going on. We're constantly trying to capture that feral live side of the band, and this is the opposite of that. It was made in the studio. What he does is, at every step the track *widens*. You listen to it and each time something else, a sound or instrument, comes in higher up and lower down and you just get this sense of it being more expansive. A lot of doing that kind of building song is

> about either speeding it up or making it louder. Which is a band's way of doing it. What Alan does in that track is he widens it all the way through. Suddenly it goes from this tight little wiry thing and by the end you're in this huge wide expanse.

Recording 'Life Is Golden', there was real excitement. Mat remembers: 'We all thought, oh! This is gonna be like "The Wild Ones", this is gonna be our encore, forever ...' Meanwhile, for 'The Invisibles', the band toyed with Oli or Neil doing the string arrangement, as the idea of it being a single set in. With that in mind – it being the first thing fans would hear – they decided to return to 'the gravitas and experience' of Craig Armstrong. Craig arranged strings for 'She', 'The Chemistry Between Us' and 'Beautiful Ones' (unused) for *Coming Up* in 1996. More recently, Brett and Craig worked together on 'Crash' for Armstrong's album, *It's Nearly Tomorrow*. Yet again, then, the band were returning to trusted people.

Neil considers 'Flytipping' 'emblematic of *The Blue Hour*', in part because of the versions it went through. Originally, it finished at the line, '... by the underpass'. For Neil this would have 'closed the album rather like "Faultlines" did *Bloodsports*.' This time, they pushed further. 'At first it was a bit too pretty for its subject matter,' says Neil. 'I re-demoed it to de-prettify it and give it more space: a de-cluttering to mirror its subject matter. When I suggested to Brett that it could be doubled in length with an instrumental passage I didn't get an enthusiastic response, so Richard and I had to show him what it could be. Even then, Brett – and later Alan – looked rather nonplussed when they first heard the ending. I'm glad we put the second half on there, though.' There was more work to do. But most of the album was down. And now it ended on 'a fittingly dramatic note'.

Neil wasn't the only one hiding things away during recording. Deliberately low in the mix on 'As One', Brett's hidden lyrics suggest new meaning. The song starts out with that choral part, first mooted the year before – for this, Neil assembled a choir, the Hackney Wick Women's Chorus, from members of the Victoria Park Singers, for the album's opening and closing tracks. Of the 'As One' part, Neil remembers: 'We wanted something dark and sinister, like the choir in Carl Orff's *Carmina Burana*.' Neil scored the parts, mirroring the piano and guitar riff with the added lyrics.

The line before Brett's hidden lyric comes in is, 'When he smiles, he looks like a fox / but when he holds me we will be as one'. The dancing, sinister orchestral part comes in with the choir, while underneath Brett's main vocal – 'Here I am / Talking to my shadow' – there's a hint this child abduction might be abuse by a member of the local community:

The nettles by the underpass
the nail waiting in the grass
The sound of distant violence
two figures waiting by the fence
The faces at the window
the way the restless wind blows
My father's friend creeps in
And says unusual things
The faces at the window
The way the savage wind blows
My father's friend creeps in
And takes me by the hand again.

The search party takes over: 'Sonny! Sonny!' Then in comes the opening riff of 'Wastelands'. As so often in Anderson's lyrics, the natural is scary

– the wind is not just blowing, it's restless, it's savage. Violence is never far away. It sounds like these lines are delivered by a child in danger. No wonder they kept it low in the mix.

'[Alan] never got wound up by anything,' Richard remembers. 'Even when I decided to bring Anna and her kids (I was only just starting to get to know them in 2017) down to the studio to sit quietly and probably get bored while we were recording the guitars for "Wastelands". Looking back, that was an odd decision of mine, but I wanted the kids [Liv, then eleven, Jona, then six] to see me "at work" so they could understand what I do a little better! Liv is now a very talented musician and songwriter, at college in Stockholm on a songwriting course, so maybe being at Assault & Battery watching Suede recording when she was only eleven had a positive effect on her!' This was Richard asserting himself. If he wanted to take the children into the studio for a day, well, why shouldn't they see him play?

Mat looks back now on what Alan contributed with fondness, comparing *The Blue Hour* to Suede's other work: 'The records we've done without Ed,' he says, 'are kind of outliers. *The Blue Hour* is an outlier because it meanders in a way our records don't usually. Weirdly, the records made without Ed are less well known, but it doesn't mean the production is lacking in any way. The production on "Tides" and "Flytipping" have a kind of widescreen-ness to the songs that we haven't got before. Of all the records since we've come back that's the one that's gone furthest into new territory.'

LITTLE WINS AND HIGH STANDARDS: MAT'S CHANGING ROLE

Readers might wonder about Mat's changing role. He did too. He was still half of the public face of Suede, he and Brett doing interviews together for decades, fans therefore seeing him as the backbone of the band. He was still an essential live presence, of course. It's hard to imagine Suede without him. But by 2017 he was a more marginal creative presence. In a sense, this was good news – the band's songwriting engine was humming; Mat loved the recent material and the reunion was going well. Still, he was needed less, and this posed a question: what to do with his own creativity? By now, Mat had harboured hopes of publishing his writing for over a decade: 'I've always had a romantic idea of the writing life; I love the idea that if you are interesting enough you can make a living without encumbrances or bosses, just you, a pen and paper, and an idea ... Its magic is the same as making music – you start the day with nothing – empty audio tape, a blank sheet of paper – and end with (hopefully) something beautiful.' Writing gave Mat an outlet and an aim, even if he wasn't publishing yet. He wasn't the only Osman moving into writing either. After Mat, over the next couple of years his younger brother Richard, long-time co-host of the TV quiz *Pointless*, started writing, too, with instant international success.

Seeing his role shrinking, as Richard and Neil matured and with Simon often absent, Mat tried writing a long-form book again. It was a struggle, but he persevered:

> The sheer scale of a novel is daunting: the acres of blank pages, the many ways to take a wrong turning. But every record we've made since we've come back has had a moment where it seemed like it might collapse. It's only the knowledge that you've been through this before and found a way out that keeps you going. That attitude – a combination of stubbornness, self-belief, and dedication – was so inspiring to me in the (many, many) moments where I thought that what I was writing had no worth. When people talk about

> making art, any art, it's usually the ineffable, magical parts of the process that are seen as the most important. Moments of inspiration, songs that seem to drop out of thin air, tracks recorded in one take. But much of making an album, or writing a book, is work. When things were going awry I saw how Brett, Richard and Neil doubled down. They wrote more, rewrote more, and tried things in different ways. Anything to get just one more good song. Little wins and high standards – if they could do it so could I.

Mat's new fiction concerned a band, with some similarities to Suede but plenty of differences too. Drawing on a world he knew, Mat began to expand a short story into what would become his debut novel, *The Ruins*.* It grew 'like a fungus', over several years, while *The Blue Hour* evolved, too. As he worked, Mat talked to award-winning author, friend and publisher Tariq Goddard of Repeater Books, whom he'd known since Suede's early days. 'I wanted to write about how it feels to make music,' he recalls, 'not about style. But I also wanted to write about an unsuccessful musician. Because most artists are unsuccessful.' In the first draft, the protagonist Brandon hated Suede, giving Mat a mouthpiece to slag off his own band – though thankfully the author thought better of that self-referential wink before *The Ruins* was contracted to Repeater in the UK.

Most of the band were trying out something new. Throughout 2017, Richard was also working on the second Artmagic record, *The Songs of Other England* (he self-funded this, and they recorded it in bits, release scheduled for June 2018),† while Brett, hunkering down in Somerset

---

* Mat completed the full manuscript then sent himself a copy in June 2018. He looked for agents, sent it to Tariq to read. He wanted to publish it.

† The Artmagic story may seem marginal to some. They have a very small following. They've not played live or released anything since 2019. Even many hardcore Suede fans don't know Artmagic exist. At the time of writing, they have no website, meaning

over the winters, with not much to do, was writing prose too. The obvious move was a memoir about Suede's heyday. But he chose to focus on his early life instead, *Coal Black Mornings* determinedly stopping before Suede's first single proper. That meant more focus on his upbringing, mum and dad, early life in Haywards Heath, also his early relationships with Justine and Bernard. Brett spent several months describing the small home he grew up in, drawing on memories he's reimagined so much since in Suede's music. All these side projects saw individual Suede members stretching out, mostly without commercial pressure or expectation. What Brett, or Mat, or Richard, were doing creatively was for its own sake. It was a while until *The Blue Hour* was due, and it wasn't finished yet. But together and apart, the next couple of years would be busy for everyone.

RICHARD'S BAND MEETING

The orchestration took months to prepare. Again, Neil was hustling. Going to Prague was 20 per cent of the cost of working with an orchestra in England, but he still needed to call in favours.

The father of Penguin Cafe's creative manager, Lucy Protheroe, is Guy Protheroe. He's a vastly experienced conductor and arranger who worked on the Who's *Tommy* as chorus master, pursuing a glittering career since. Neil approached Guy to help, with James Fitzpatrick acting as fixer. Neil ran his arrangements past violinist Clementine Brown from Penguin Cafe, then spent a day at Guy's checking the parts. James

limited online presence, while review coverage of their albums was occasional, found in marginal spaces, and usually down to Richard's Suede profile. But focusing on the band's size misses the point of its value to Richard, and also its importance in the Suede story.

worked on the ground in Prague with the recording engineer for the orchestra, Vítek Král, and translator, recording supervisor and violinist Stanja Vomáčková. (Neil recalls, 'Stanja stayed in the control room and translated our notes and requests for the orchestra, and spoke to them out in the live room via a microphone.') They had just one single day in February booked, with Guy as conductor, to make this work.

Initially Neil was due to go to Prague alone, much of his focus on 'The Invisibles' and 'All the Wild Places', with the other songs having a more 'salt and pepper' occasional approach to orchestration. Then Mike wanted to come. His long-mooted Suede film had just been commissioned, after the big success of his recent documentary for Sky *Hansa Studios: By the Wall 1976–1990*.* After *Hansa*, the Sky execs asked, what did he want to do next? 'Well,' he answered. 'There's this film I've been wanting to make for years ...' Mike thought the Prague trip worth documenting. Once he was going, with a camera and an eye on the documentary, Brett decided to tag along and observe. It was all quite last minute, no harm intended, but no one thought to tell Richard. That made for a tense band meeting in which Richard threatened to quit if something like this ever happened again. On reflection, Richard felt he pushed back too hard, and he's understandably squeamish about this being mentioned at all, years later, in this book. It was, perhaps, a sign of lingering insecurity. Could he, after all these years, still be forgotten? Wasn't he supposed to be involved in all things musical? For his part, Brett felt no member of Suede should be able to hold that over the heads of the others. Fuck-ups happened. This was their creative livelihoods, and no one meant to exclude Richard.

---

* *Hansa Studios: By the Wall* was first broadcast by Sky in January 2018 and was nominated for Best Arts Documentary at the Grierson Awards. The trip to Prague happened a few weeks later.

Speak to the band now and mostly people are just mortified this happened. Also, Didz has been keen to claim responsibility for not telling Richard the plans. But given Richard was starting to assert himself more, it's notable that this, of all things, was the one time in over twenty-five years in Suede he ever called a band meeting. The language might have been regrettable, the situation curious (after all, this was a trip with nothing much for the band to do). But it was a reminder Richard was not to be taken for granted. In any event, Mike got some shots of Brett dressed like a middle-aged music teacher, looking on pensively as the City of Prague Philharmonic ran through exquisite-sounding orchestral parts. The final pieces of *The Blue Hour* were in place, with Alan mixing the album and mastering taking place at Abbey Road.

LUCIAN AND THE SNOW MACHINE: *THE BLUE HOUR* COVER

Surprisingly, the album cover was shot in London, not Somerset. '*The Blue Hour* is a creative triumph,' says Didz, 'but it's a macabre record, insanely depressing – and incredibly cold, too. That presentation was deliberate. It's supposed to be icy, the whole thing.' Yes, it's cold, but beautiful. Paul hired a snow machine and treated the sky in the photos so it looked freezing. He designed the artwork, for multiple formats. This time, the cover star was Lucian himself, the lost boy presented half in shadow, Brett's young son disguised, like so much on the record, that you might miss him completely.

The cover idea came from Suede's first tour in the US in the '90s, when Brett had seen 'an incredibly haunting sight in Washington ... a family who had clearly just been made homeless sitting in a park on their furniture. A few meagre items – a sofa, a lamp, a couple of chairs. Heartbreaking and bizarre in equal measure.' He says of the image,

Paul photographs Lucian for the cover of The Blue Hour.

'Long before we shot the sleeve, I had a strong visual image of a small figure lost in a hostile landscape.' Even in their absence, the family from all those years ago was the inspiration for the image.

All imagined things change in the making. That said, it's striking how many of the original March 2016 notebook intentions can be mapped onto *The Blue Hour*. The choral intro was delivered, on 'As One's opening, with that 'aggressive chant'. 'Eleanor Rigby' influenced 'Mistress', and it went in a similar place in the track list to that song on the Beatles' *Revolver*. They didn't make it to fifteen minutes, but 'Flytipping' was the most expansive thing they'd done since reunion, by some distance, counting also as that 'big ending' they envisaged. There's nothing quite like 'Big Louise' on *The Blue Hour*, though Scott Walker influenced

'All the Wild Places', while 'pure atmosphere' was a key touchstone for the sound throughout. The 'radio ballad' was clearly 'Life Is Golden'. Okay, so 'no repeating parts' might have been too much of a stretch, but that's a lot for one notebook page. No matter what happened now, they could say they'd done what they set out to do.

Between the completion of *The Blue Hour* and its release later in the year, Brett's memoir, *Coal Black Mornings*, was published in early 2018, accompanied by a full UK-wide promotional campaign. The Suede hard core attended every reading, treating it like a bonus tour, just one happening in bookshops. At the Piccadilly event in March, Brett happened to say, 'I love fanzines ... fanzines are great.' So the Insatiable Ones fan group started one, immediately. Sam says, 'We went to the pub after the event and we made a team there and then.' In an interview for issue one, editors/fan club leaders Sam, Amanda and designer Rachel Apps asked what was coming next. Brett suggested that after this album trilogy, 'Maybe we'll surprise everyone and do a *volte-face*.' He described the art of songwriting as being like 'Theseus, following Ariadne's thread', a process of searching, curious for the next thing. Of course, he described the as-yet-unreleased third reunion album as, without qualification, 'the best thing we've done for nearly a quarter of a century.'

Coal Black Mornings was reviewed ecstatically, and at this point the Insatiable Ones group began to have an impact: 'Something changed ... there was a new level of respect between fans and Brett,' says Sam, reflecting on the fan campaign to get the book into the top-ten bestsellers. (It did.) The book surprised many who thought, based on Brett's old persona, that he was likely incapable of humour, self-critique, humility or reflection. Also, many who thought they knew Suede simply didn't realise his background, assuming the only kind of working-class identity available to young men in the '90s was old-school macho posturing in parkas. The idea that it was possible to grow up in penury with two artistic parents was enough to surprise some reviewers, thinking the foppish identity of Suede's early days suggested a rich boy slumming it for fun. This is a fundamental misunderstanding of Brett's origins and motivations.

Few musicians simply turn themselves into good literary writers in middle age, though Brett seemed to carry the lessons of songwriting into writing prose with ease. *Coal Black Mornings* was written fast. It was clear-eyed but bleak, ignoring Brett's years as a public figure in favour of a series of thoughtful portraits of a long-forgotten England, the most affecting passages focusing on his mother's death when he was a young man. This loss, he wrote, 'nearly destroyed me.' *Coal Black Mornings*' finest moments are those describing Peter, Sandra and Blandine Anderson. Here, as in 'Life Is Golden', all masks were discarded. The entire book might be seen as a tribute to Sandra. Brett writes his mum was 'a remarkable woman: incredibly creative and practical and stoical, and in her own way hard as flint.'

'WALKING THROUGH TREACLE': *THE BLUE HOUR* CAMPAIGN

Everyone knew selling *The Blue Hour* would be tough: here was a dark record about child abduction, featuring two spoken-word pieces about dead animals. So everyone had a sense, from the start, of the challenge. But once the band selected the first single, 'the whole process,' Didz says, 'became like walking through treacle.' 'The Invisibles' was an elegant indicator of the spare, wintry beauty of *The Blue Hour*. Also, the band felt there were plenty of recent examples of alternative artists of Suede's ilk who'd launched acclaimed albums with ambitious, unexpected or outlier songs. Beck's *Morning Phase* led with the mournful, string-laden

'Wave'; no one called it a pretentious misstep. Joanna Newsom's hugely celebrated second album *Ys* featured a 29-piece orchestra and dominated end-of-year best album lists. Why couldn't Suede attempt something similar? More recently, Gruff Rhys put out a left-field soundtrack, *American Interior*, its title track securing heavy rotation on 6 Music. Even the Manics had changed things up, their acoustic album *Rewind the Film* playlisted, too.

At this time, 6 Music was the only station really playing Suede records. The band thought that if they put out 'The Invisibles', 6 Music would probably play it. Despite this, the Suede office still believed 'The Invisibles' was 'an absolutely ridiculous choice of first single'. It had hardly any drums. It was slow, subtle. It didn't sound, to the passing ear, like Suede. The management wanted 'Life Is Golden', the most uplifting song on the record, and stronger in isolation. Though they might have said so more strongly to the band.

With hindsight, the management acknowledge they might have done more, early on, to identify 'Life Is Golden' as the first single. But everyone knows that *both* strategies – leading with the most obvious single, or holding it back for later – can work. Buoyed by the critical success of *Night Thoughts* and credited with 'reinventing the gig', they 'thought they could do anything ... and quickly learned they couldn't.' They'd been immersed in making what they wanted to, for its own sake. It's one thing to enjoy stretching out, quite another to sell the results. 'There were lots of capable people involved in trying to promote the album,' says Didz. 'But none of us were capable of rescuing it.'

Band insularity was compounded by a sense of absence at record label Warners – absence of staff, resources and interest. When Suede first got back together, the industry wasn't yet in an age where bands of that era were reforming, never mind making new music: 'This wasn't the mature area of business that can be furrowed by everyone now,' says Didz. Initially, Warners signing Suede had been a hopeful, calculated risk. After the promising *Bloodsports*, another two-album deal followed. The *Night Thoughts* idea was big enough to impress; when they saw the Roundhouse shows, Warners were blown away by it and, though 'Outsiders' may or may not have 'saved the reunion', it certainly saved the campaign. As Didz puts it, 'You had this brilliant single that could be put in the canon with other great Suede singles'. That meant they got away with making an uncommercial album while gaining plenty of attention for doing so, in part because one or two songs promised something more palatable.

But Warners first took Suede on in 2012, and five years is forever in the music business. By *The Blue Hour* the band had virtually no one at Warners advocating for them. During the lead-up there were many red flags, and these might have been spotted sooner. First, the people they knew in radio plugging and promo had their priorities realigned elsewhere. (Suede brought in their own plugger, Kevin McCabe.) Staff changes followed, and by the time the campaign was underway Suede's management were working without access to the promotional heft you might expect from a company of Warners' size. The success the label hoped for in 2012 hadn't transpired, and when they heard the new music, they switched off.

For the campaign, Didz was on his own but for two people: product manager Julie Eldridge, who helped with delivering artwork, masters, commissioning videos, building out a box set. (Another instrumental version of the album, like *Night Thoughts*, and a series of band commentaries.) The other was Victor Aroldoss, a close friend of the band from the '90s who, by chance, went on to find a job in the international division at Warners. By the reunion, he was running that department. There'd usually be fifteen or twenty people doing label jobs, pitching in, a contact linking up with people for shoots, artwork, video directors. But now they had to lean harder on people they knew and trusted, often patching together things late and on the hoof. Paul and Dean Chalkley, for photos. Mike and Roger for videos, all of which were busked. (When singles go to radio, videos should be ready too, but they weren't.) The band chose not to appear in videos themselves. That was intentional but came across as curious for a record so personal. For some, it contributed to the sense of there being something missing at the heart of the campaign.

The album's great Scott Walker moment flattened expectations. DJ Steve Lamacq had the first exclusive play on 6 Music ahead of release on 3 June. 'Make of that,' he drawled, as the song finished, 'what you will.' And that, it seemed, was that. Of all the disappointing moments from the reunion era relayed to me by the band, this is the one that was most often repeated, something that seemed emblematic. But what would fans make of 'The Invisibles'? In mid-July, the next taster was 'Don't Be Afraid If Nobody Loves You', a more conventional-sounding song released as an instant 'grat' track. (That is, free in advance, downloadable when you bought the album online.)

The camp still hoped 'Life Is Golden', due 15 August, might rescue the campaign. Maybe 'The Invisibles' made all the difference. 'Perhaps people had already made up their minds they weren't interested in the new Suede record,' recalls Didz, 'if that's what it sounded like.' But when it didn't get picked up some wondered if 'Life Is Golden' was too slow for radio. Too edgy for Radio 2, not edgy enough for 6 Music, it rather got lost. The Mike-directed video for the song was spectacular, though. It was filmed in Pripyat, Ukraine, initially as part of his racing documentary on Amazon Prime, *The Road to Gymkhana*. Mike secured rare access to the devastated post-Chernobyl landscape, getting unheard-of permission to fly a drone above the area, taking in empty high-rises, the infamous abandoned Ferris wheel and access to buildings not entered in decades. At Chernobyl, he took enough footage for Suede, too. (If you watch the documentary closely, you can see a couple of familiar shots, duplicated in 'Life Is Golden'.) Despite its bleakness – or because of it – the video got a lot of views (1.5 million and counting). So, radio isn't everything – but it felt like the verdict, at least in terms of reaching new people who'd buy the album, was in. All this before it was released. It's foolish to judge any song on immediate response alone. What can you learn after just a few weeks about a song's future life? But by the end of the summer of 2018, it already felt like the chances of *The Blue Hour* doing well were slim.

THE COLD BLUE HOUR

The Blue Hour was released on 21 September. A shot of encouragement: it landed at number five in the UK, one place higher than *Night Thoughts*. The hard core who bought hard copies were more organised now, and Suede were lucky with that week's releases. (Eminem's ninth number-one album in a row, *Kamikaze*, held on for another week, with Christine and the Queens' glorious French–English standout *Chris* at number three.) This meant a continuing upward trajectory. But reviews were coming in, and far from being hailed as their great art masterpiece, *The Blue Hour* left some cold.

In an age of fast-turnaround reviews and increasingly instant thrills, the band felt this album rewarded repeat close listening. Others wondered if it was the framing. Before release they'd talked with John Doran, tasked with doing the press pack, using the phrase 'folk horror' as a tag, pointing to something that sounded dangerous, dark, exciting – rather than leading with the thornier child abduction narrative. Now, Brett regrets not clearly badging this Suede's 'folk-horror album'. Had they put 'SUEDE DO FOLK HORROR' in big letters at the top of the press pack with a cover featuring, say, menacing, shadowy trees spattered with blood, journalists at home and abroad would have largely reviewed the album within that context.

Every album release is a dice roll, and there are multiple factors you can't control, even with a big budget, supportive label and great music. It's hard to know, years later, what mattered, and what's remembered simply because it hurt. *Night Thoughts* got Suede multiple broadsheet newspaper lead reviews (meaning a large article or a page). In the digital age, these still have huge readerships. Pre-internet, hundreds of thousands of people might read a review, having a big impact on reception and sales. By 2018 the landscape was vastly different, many of those publications scrambling to adapt to a new model in which much smaller numbers of people subscribed, but some articles were shareable online, meaning casual observers might read them on their phones. Now that's the norm, and fans share, celebrate or react to every review in fan groups and online, meaning similar reach, just in a different way. In 2018, that wasn't quite as common yet, so when Suede landed fewer prime review inches, it was noticed.

You're also responding to competition, sometimes from long-established or heritage acts. In September 2018, Minnesota's Low, featuring husband and wife duo Alan Sparhawk and Mimi Parker, released their universally acclaimed, radical *Double Negative*. This wasn't a commercial hit but did swallow column inches; *Double Negative* was so full of dread that it made *The Blue Hour* look positively conservative. It was hard to work out what instruments, if any, were being used. Static and distortion peppered the record. It sounded utterly unlike anything else, undoubtedly the band's masterpiece, twenty-five years into their career. Given the choice, some places lauded Low, relegating Suede to the sidebar in the same week. *Double Negative* was *Uncut*'s number-one album of 2018, and made the *Pitchfork* top ten. In the *Guardian*, for example, reviewer Ben Beaumont-Thomas gave *Double Negative* a rare five stars, compared the record to the work of writer Cormac McCarthy (author of *The Road* and *No Country for Old Men*), calling it 'a document of contemporary social collapse'. You have to remind yourself that he was describing not a political movement, but an album. Meanwhile, Suede were nowhere to be found in any of the top albums of 2018 listed by the *NME*, 6 Music, *Pitchfork*, *Rolling Stone*, *Billboard*, *Q*, Fopp, *Mojo*, *Uncut*, the *Independent*, Rough Trade, Radio X, *PopMatters*, *Stereogum* or many more. Sure, there's a hugely various body of opinion out there. Coverage in any single publication doesn't say anything for certain. But the overall picture is hard to deny.

During the writing of this book, several members of Suede sent me specific reviews they found hurtful or felt contributed to a sense that *The Blue Hour* didn't land. Some are fair. Some feel like the reviewer heard a different record. That's music: what moves you leaves me cold. What makes me cry makes you reach for the off button. Okay, maybe *The Blue Hour*'s strongest songs appeared in its second half. (Brett certainly thinks so.) It was meandering. It *wanted* to be hard work: 'Roadkill'? 'Dead Bird'? They're haunting pieces that take you deep into Suedeworld. You're not supposed to sing along. Still, in my view *The Blue Hour* contains half a dozen of Suede's very best songs: 'As One'. 'Mistress'. 'Life Is Golden'. 'Tides'. 'All the Wild Places'. 'Flytipping'. The response to these was sometimes baffling. That doesn't just hit a nerve or cause upset, it materially changes what the band feel they can do next. It changes the songs they write, what they prioritise, how they self-select in future.

The response closed a door that at the time of writing, eight years later, remains firmly closed.

But Suede were still an excellent live band, heading out on tour. This presented challenges, too. With no orchestra, this meant they'd have to make do, patch up, Neil charged with approximating some parts on keyboards, using loops and interstitials from the record to reproduce or adapt. They only played *The Blue Hour* once in full: at the DR Koncerthuset in Copenhagen, on 10 October. Denmark was safe, the band were loved, and whenever they were booked for two shows, it made sense to present differently on each night. But they never repeated it. This was part of a European tour where Suede looked like a band at the height of their powers. Not just to fans, either. That tour saw the band play across Europe in grand venues with Gwenno, who sings in Cornish and Welsh. Not needing to engage with a record company pushing for them to accept certain acts as support, or dependent on support acts to help sell tickets, Suede simply choose artists they like. Admirers of her Mercury-nominated second record, *Le Kov*, the band approached Gwenno directly to support them.

To Gwenno, Suede's behaviour on tour seemed like a model of how to act, a status worth reaching for. This definitely wasn't how they felt – while they were travelling, a lot of the lukewarm reviews for *The Blue Hour* were dropping back home – but they came across as having all the benefits of experience, being unburdened by their own past (setlists leaned heavily on reunion material and they might play seven *Blue Hour* tracks a night), while remaining humble, good humoured, appreciative of their position – what Gwenno, charmingly, calls 'the art of not being a knob'. This was evident in the way Suede treated their crew, each other, fans before and after shows. Being welcoming. Lifting up, rather than pushing others down. All the work that remains hidden, but affects an atmosphere. She recalls: 'The whole 2018 tour really worked for us, partly because of Brett's showmanship. It was this huge lesson in how to communicate with an audience. No matter the song, he holds the whole room. It's incredible. In these beautiful rooms Brett was making everyone stand up and it was creating this lively, chaotic, anarchic vibe in the crowd, everyone just really going for it, in a space where traditionally that wouldn't happen ... He was able to change the atmosphere.'

2019's TOUGH CAMPAIGNS

The UK tour ran through April 2019, with further shows over the summer. The management remember 2018–19 as a period of multiple, tough campaigns. Richard's Artmagic album was organised by him and Sean, but Brett's book, the twenty-fifth anniversary edition of debut album *Suede*, the filming then release of Mike's documentary *The Insatiable Ones* in November 2018 and *The Blue Hour* itself meant that by the time of the UK tour many in the camp were knackered. Not just from promoting the many releases, each given their own space, but also due to the nature of each one. Bleak, arty album. Bleak, arty memoir. 'There was a lot of bleak, arty Suede around in those days,' Didz says now, laughing.

This exhaustion might explain the approach to tour set design, which was not quite as clear in concept or bold in delivery as for *Night Thoughts*. They used 'some shadows and lights', almost like puppetry, with Brett as the puppet. He remembers: 'We ended up with a load of sheets, not symmetrical on the stage, and it could have been more powerful.' In among these shows, the band played two nights at the Apollo in Hammersmith, a Friday and Saturday night. These were celebratory, a good balance between arty Suede and good-time Suede. By the summer, shows were less *Blue Hour*-focused, setlists for middling festivals from Poland to

Croatia, Spain to Russia, drawn from the back catalogue. Invitations were less regular. No wonder. If you create a wintry album about child abduction it doesn't scream summer festival circuit. In Didz's words: 'Well, if you make an album that's largely uninviting ...'

Over this period Richard sometimes toured with two bands at once, Artmagic trailing Suede around the UK. He loved these shows, despite the small audiences, while he and Anna were now fully committed to each other. She proposed to him on 1 October; they were looking forward to getting married, talking about living as a family in Sweden. Meanwhile, Brett already had another book out – just eighteen months since *Coal Black Mornings*, he'd spent the winter of 2018 doing what he said he'd never do: writing about the '90s, drugs, Bernard, fame and all, in *Afternoons with the Blinds Drawn*. Again, the book was received extremely well.

By the end of 2019, everyone was tired. Focus had long moved to Suede #9, which would be a very different beast, but a sense of frustration lingered. For years, one of Brett's most used lines in the press has been: 'Suede are at our best when we have something to prove.' That's code for: when they feel misunderstood, rejected, or suspect they've failed on their own terms. *The Blue Hour* was a gorgeous record, but after it, Suede were on the defensive. That sense of frustrated urgency, and how the band responded, would define the next few years, radically changing their fortunes.

CHAPTER 5

autofiction

'shadow selves'

'As they get older, lots of bands slow down. We felt Suede needed to go the other way, playing faster, throwing ourselves around more, getting more connected.'

—Neil

'A BAND FOR A NIGHT OUT'

In public, Brett sometimes called the first three reunion records 'a loose trilogy'. Pretty loose. What, if anything, tied *Bloodsports* and *The Blue Hour*, except being made by the same band? Either way, after completing a trilogy, you get a new start. One day in 2019 Brett and Ian were in the car when Ian said gently, 'It would be great if people could have a good time at a Suede gig again.' At those recent Hammersmith shows, the crowd were primed for it. Neil saw a lesson there, too: 'Though the TBH stuff went down well, it was the older and more "up" stuff that went *really* well – it reminded us of what we'd gradually begun to lose over the last two tours. Being a band for a night out.' Could Suede still make an album for a night out? Music for jumping around and roaring along to? If so, what would those songs be about?

This time the first meeting was at Brett's London flat in June 2018, in that strange window after the first song goes to radio. 'The Invisibles' was out, Richard saying, 'We had a slight inkling that it might have been a wrong step, but no more ... We thought, let's do something less conceptual and demo-based. Be a band in a room again, trying to excite each other.' Mat describes this as a natural response to *The Blue Hour*'s final note: '"Flytipping" was clearly the end of a line,' he says. 'We had to snap back, somehow.' For years, writing sessions happened at Neil's; now they switched to Richard's, in west London. Change of scene, change of sound. Brett, Richard and Neil would try to do something, in Brett's words, 'more visceral'. He meant musically and lyrically. Brett's always feeling his way in a record's early days, looking for patterns. But this time, after an album based on outward fear, he now wanted to train the microscope on himself.

Shortly after the first meeting, on 6 July, the family had a huge shock. Brett and Jodie were involved in a brutal crash that sent their car spinning on the main road close to their home. Jodie was driving and was badly injured. As Brett recalls now, 'I had to carry her away from the wreck of the car to a grassy verge to await an ambulance because she was unable to move. For a few bleak minutes I thought she was permanently paralysed. Thankfully it was just shock, but she still had to go to hospital for treatment as the impact had ripped open her knee. I could see the white of her bone through the gash.' A split second either way and it could have been fatal, for one, or both. The car was smashed beyond recognition.

Mike was around that day and saw the impact, Brett witnessing his cosy rural life in new perspective. Now in his fifties, and after twenty-five

Jodie's car after the crash.
Photo by Mike Christie

years as a public figure, who was Brett Anderson, and what did he want to do with his remaining time? What was he afraid of? What had he hidden about himself, from himself? What had he flinched from, and was it too late to face it? Brett's notebook listed things he wanted to explore on the next album. In fact, these would influence the next *two*, and some of his notes would be set aside for a while. But themes of hiding and revelation were about to become important.

Suede's inner circle know well that there's a 'Brett from Suede' persona, then the person they know in real life. All musicians need to balance public and private, protecting each identity from the other by degrees. It's the same for Mat, Simon, Neil, Richard. It's the same for many creatives. My own partner, the horror writer Elle Nash, frames this in terms of safety: 'Persona is how an artist protects themselves from the public.' Creating distance between the image and the person makes

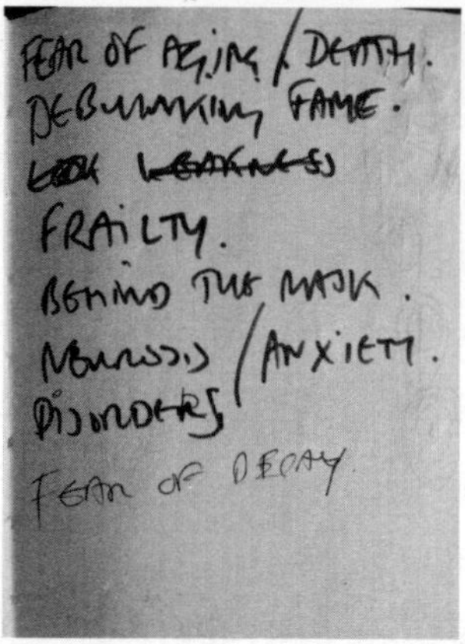

Brett's notebook: 'Fear of Aging/Death / Debunking Fame / Look [struck out] / Weakness [struck out] / Frailty / Behind the Mask / Neurosis/Anxiety / Disorders / Fear of Decay'.

for more protection. But there's something uniquely complicated about being a band's *singer*. More attention, focus, responsibility.

If, as Richard describes it, 'Suede is a five-brained monster, and the monster has Brett's face', the face presents an idealised version of itself to the world. Confident, assured, filing away self-hate and shame – avoiding, in interviews, anything genuinely painful. Ring-fencing what's acceptable interrogation. Not mentioning recent, private, personal trauma. In reuniting the band, repairing its legacy, and in writing books reflecting on early life before and during stardom, Brett got used to channelling vulnerability positively.* That's what making new art can be. Trying to face yourself, repeatedly. Finding your fear and articulating it. But might Brett reach down into himself and dredge up unknowable fear he'd not yet faced, something rawer, something genuinely difficult? As he's told

* Times change. In 1999, when Suede's *Head Music* was voted *Melody Maker*'s album of the year, Brett declared he didn't read at all and that music was a higher art form than literature, dismissing many of his contemporaries and presenting in peacock-like form. Twenty years on, Tariq Goddard said Brett wrote his own books with such a 'vulnerable and careful voice' in *Afternoons with the Blinds Drawn*. Same guy.

me, 'You often don't know what you've unearthed until many years later. But you have to unearth it anyway.'

Suede wanted music to reach beyond the hard core, drawing on the spirit of their live performances as a guide. Richard had been disappointed by recent festival offers; these encouraged him to consider where he wanted the band to go next: 'There are different ways of being challenging,' he recalls now. 'TBH challenged us musically – next we wanted the challenge to come from the direct power of the band. We didn't want it to be difficult to understand but did want it to have a confrontational spirit.' When I spoke to Johnny Marr about this period, he felt there was something essential about Suede live that fed into the next moves on record:

> I could see, backstage at festivals or just talking to other bands, people were *surprised*. So many reunited bands go through the motions ... but Brett wrings every bit of energy from any room, like he's trying to win each person in the crowd over to the band before the last song. Most rock stars act like they've done the work already and just show up to be applauded for what they made years ago ... [But] Suede behaved like they were just *starting* work. Like they'd just realised it was this great thing they could do.

That sense of starting again chimes with Brett's own take. When I asked him what he made of Marr's observations, he responded by focusing on his changing attitude to performance:

> It might sound strange, but yeah, [after *The Blue Hour*] I felt I was just starting to get the hang of playing live ... after thirty years! [laughs] What I mean is, understanding each song is a kind of tool. The things I do in each song, the ways I communicate ... I realised I could use those tools to manufacture a response, try to move a gig

forward. Working towards the atmosphere I wanted. The feeling, in the room.

The tools metaphor is one he returns to repeatedly. Which songs, in which order, done in what form, might produce results? As Brett puts it, 'Of the early songs, "Animal Nitrate" is a tool, you know. "Beautiful Ones". "Trash". "Saturday Night". This one's a ... [laughs at himself], *wrench*. This one's a ... *screwdriver*. I wanted new tools, to complement those I already had, to let me work, more effectively, to that end.' That's also about go-to tricks – a leap here, a sinking to the knees there. Movement, across the stage. One-liners to the crowd, where and how to deliver them. All of which, considered together, made the band's live energy. Could Suede take what Marr noticed and bottle it? The sound of Brett, off-mic, yelling to the back row, while clinging to hands at the front? Could they intentionally set about writing for that context, music that didn't sound overly earnest or clichéd?

In a sense, Suede's live identity had been disguised by the curated sounds of *Night Thoughts* and *The Blue Hour*. Now, the band wanted 'direct, immediate, catchy' material. In Mat's words, 'Next time round, we couldn't afford to have nothing for radio.' These songs for a good night out couldn't *only* be that, either. Even when partying, Suede fans were interested in finding ways to survive darkness, shaking off their own hidden pain. New songs had to contain hurt, then, too. If you could get both, you might hit the sweet spot. Enough to prove people wrong, once more.

IN SEARCH OF 'PUNK'

This time round, the mountain of material grew and grew, with more than 120 demos produced and more than 60 songs written. Neil described this, particularly given they were engaged in a conscious, renewed effort to find a specific type of song, as 'a bit mind-numbing after a while'.* Week on week, songs getting chopped up and reshaped. Songs discarded from previous albums reappearing, then disappearing again. Things speeding up, slowing down, dropping or gaining sections. Titles being recycled or modified. As we've seen, the more material there is, the more disorientating that can be. Also, given their difficulty finding floor-filling bangers, they might need to roll the dice more times to get a few sixes. If you don't want to get lost in all that half-finished music, you have to hold tight to your compass.

By now, Suede's working method – so different from most bands, but so familiar – had become uninteresting to them. They just cracked on, reshaping once more, Neil tucking into something more like his pre-*Blue Hour* role. As he's said, 'Suede are at their best when Richard is at his best.' That's typically self-effacing, but Neil's role was changing again, with less keyboards, less ranging across instruments. With Richard's greater maturity and happy, stable personal life, others wondered if he might lead more, especially on such a guitar-heavy record. He'd done this fitfully many times, a song or clutch of songs at a time – but not consistently across a whole album since way back when he and Neil were 'New Boy' and 'New New Boy' respectively.

By now, the band were settled on making a 'punk record'. Not trying to recreate the sound of 1976, exactly; that world was gone, though references to the Pistols and Iggy Pop were more relevant. Rather 'punk'

* Neil, on the *Autofiction* writing process: 'Until lockdown it was quite monochromatic, rather one-paced: simple, edgy, no flowery guitar passages ... It took until lockdown when Richard came up with "Drive Myself Home" and "What Am I Without You?" to broaden things more.'

was, says Brett, 'Code for something new, ours, that harnessed the *spirit* of punk ...' Brett and Mat talked this over. Mat recalls:

> We've been obsessed for years now with breaking down barriers between audience and band. The whole Dogme thing.* When you're younger ... You look down on people, you know? Literally, from big stages. Like kings. But as we've gotten older, I think we're more interested in how we can connect to our fans. Be on the same level. It's a sign of insecurity to rely on props. [During] 2018 and 2019 we started to consider how we could harness that punk spirit. Yes, in the songs. But also in the delivery, recording, everything in and around the music. We wanted to reach out to people.

Mat laughed here because he knew reaching out was about to become impossible – but of course no one knew that was coming. If this album was to be anything, they thought, it was an attempt to level the ground. In Neil's words, 'Punk rock is an attitude as well as a musical genre.' They set about finding both.

An early breakthrough was '15 Again', demoed as 'Salt and Vinegar', on 27 February, music by Codling–Oakes, with Brett's vocals added in early March.† It's a funny case study. Initially it wasn't even rehearsed, the poppy demo outshone by others in the mix, with Brett unsure. But Simon, Mat and Ed responded to the 'scrappy' version with enthusiasm, then Richard went back and wrote the lead intro, 'making it more confrontational, less whimsical. Suddenly, '15 Again' was on the A list.‡

* The Dogme 95 movement, led by film-makers Lars von Trier and Thomas Vinterberg, was designed to strip away artifice and reliance on special effects.

† Brett added to that original February 2019 demo on 6 March, rewriting his verse part the following day.

‡ Originally, this was a response to the Gary Numan song 'We Are Glass', though the demo doesn't sound anything like that.

Lyrical territory began to emerge. '15 Again' sounded hopeful, reckless, letting Brett celebrate youth without pretending to be youthful. The 'So Young' band obviously weren't kids any more, but listeners might relate to *feeling* young, even just for a moment. Because you're in love all over again. Because life, once deadened, feels exciting again. Because you forget what you look like in the mirror, or how others might see you. This was what the band saw up close at gigs. Ageing doesn't mean you lose desire or potential. As we've seen, the age range of Suede's audience varies radically. But in the UK, those people calling in favours so they could make it down to the barriers just one more time – they were older now, their Suede obsession part of a desire to reconnect with previous selves. When you're in the crush in a sweaty club, reaching over the hands of many other grown-ups to grab the same body you fantasised over when you were a teenager, back when he presented as both feminine *and* masculine – you're not an office worker, parent, or survivor of many mundane, reducing defeats, the kind experience inflicts on us all. Once more, you're a kid, for whom too much is not enough.*

The '15 Again' lyric did something different with yearning: this was yearning for losing yourself, outside the body, outside time, the song's subjects itching to move beyond the boredom of daily life: 'Nothing is as bad as the time we kill', goes the opening line, 'sitting in the bathroom, in kitten heels'. In the chorus it's not 'I', but 'we', who feel fifteen again. The teenage 'we' who are 'stained in our hearts'. 'Sometimes you get a song that's a guiding light for what follows,' says Brett. '"15 Again" was a pretty good light.' The guitar part had potential, seeing Richard drawing from different traditions. Mat confesses:

* Neil: 'People want to be reminded of when they were teenagers – this is partly our relationship with nostalgia.'

> We had rather force-fed [Richard] the Suede set of influences when he joined the band, and we never really gave him space to explore his own. Amazingly, that never seemed to stop him coming up with brilliant ideas, for whatever we were working on. But now, here was the evidence of all these guitar players he'd always admired, coming through.

It's extraordinary that Suede should be on their ninth album, Richard the guitar player for seven of these, without him operating squarely on his own territory. Richard wasn't raised on Bowie the way Mat and Brett were, in Ed's words, 'listening to *Hunky Dory* a thousand times in their bedrooms'.* Teenage listening shapes you. For Richard, a decade younger than Brett – nearly three years younger than Neil, too, though they're often lumped together – it was influential guitarists of the punk and post-punk eras, the distinctive playing of people like Magazine and Siouxsie and the Banshees' John McGeoch, also Keith Levene, founding member of both the Clash and John Lydon's Public Image Ltd., that came most naturally. Richard was a toddler when Magazine were formed. He discovered them via his older sister's record collection, that fondness for spiky, distilled melody hiding in plain sight even in his earliest Suede recordings. Here was more of it, delivered with fresh intent.

SUEDE #9, PRE-COVID

There are few people Brett trusts more than Ed Buller. For this next move, maybe it was time to go back to him once more? In spring 2019, Ed was working in LA. He's usually weighing options. He'd just been

* This admiration survives, even now. On 9 January 2026 Brett hosted a BBC 6 Music show with Craig Charles and Tilda Swinton, in tribute to *Hunky Dory*.

invited to teach masterclasses at the San Francisco Conservatory of Music and was toying with moving back to London. When Brett emailed to ask if he fancied doing another Suede album, Ed said he'd love to. In a phone call, he asked, 'Are you ready to do that punk record, then?'

They began to scope out approaches. Suede were busy touring and there was much more to do before Ed was confirmed. But in the coming months they shared music-in-progress, ideas, Ed a good sounding board for Brett especially. As he recalls now, 'Early on, they had the punk label, but didn't really have enough songs to match it. So that's what we were looking for. Songs to match the idea.' This was Ed's specialism: responding to what the band said they wanted, then encouraging them to get there.

The next demo excited everyone. This was the Stooges-like 'White Boy on a Stage', another Anderson–Codling–Oakes composition demoed on 25 March as 'Dark Non-Triumph'.* (It was slower at first, like Iggy Pop's 'Nightclubbing', before speeding up.†) As Neil recalls, the music was 'written to be an angry adjunct to the more contemplative "Sunrise over the Care Home".' Two days later, the top line was emailed round. How can you be sure of a song's potential? Neil says, 'Everyone knows it when they hear it. '[White Boy] was one of the ones on *Autofiction* where everyone went, oh yeah, this is going on the album, everyone gets it straight away. These moments are rarities, but they're a high for everyone, and they can suggest the direction of a record.'‡

---

* Suede avoid demo titles that sound cocky. They liked this song from the start. It might have been called 'Dark Triumph'. But of course, you don't want to jinx anything ...

† Mat, on 'That Boy on the Stage': 'When [Richard] first joined the band there was a line that had to be followed, there was a history to the band, but also by playing things that we did he was learning the kind of sounds we liked. With this one, you can hear John McGeoch. We'd been talking about the Fall for about thirty years but here it finally was ...'

‡ Neil, interview with Wayne Imms, the Space, Brighton, January 2024.

Following '15 Again', with its magic of lost youth regained, here was a song about performance itself, for an album with an emerging theme: the relationship between person and persona. If it hadn't been jettisoned already, the subtlety of folk horror Suedeworld seemed all but swept away with the first lines of 'White Boy on a Stage' delivered in lazy, boisterous *Sprechgesang*, Brett shouting over the guitars. 'WE. USE. WORDS. AS WEAPONS.' The verse moved across few alternating notes: 'He speaks of love and power and all those pretty things / You know the voice that flatters you, is not the voice that sings'. The 'he' is 'Brett, the 'voice that flatters' the voice of a band's frontman. These versions sound like the pre-*Bloodsports* songs of 2011. The difference is: they're *better songs*, written with more confidence and experience. Whisper it, but the song also seemed to contain a little self-mockery. Humour, too. The swagger of 'White Boy on a Stage' felt like another light. That was two, then. Two songs about being in Suede, then and now. Neither was *punk*, exactly. But the band could imagine both being played loud, hollered back by some future crowd.

When they returned to writing later in the year, Brett felt this record needed to be 'much more in your face'. The demo 'Big Popper', then retitled 'The Prey', was another ballad – though they were pushing for more aggressive stuff. 'Fag Packet' had sinister potential.* Richard wrote the bass line himself, resurrecting a part he'd toyed with during the recording of 'Electricity' twenty years earlier. Within a day this became 'Black Ice'. In the late '90s, when lyrics became a stick to beat Brett with, this was, in part, because he seemed to be forever returning to familiar

---

* Via Neil, to the Insatiable Ones: 'Working title: "Fag Packet" because Richard played the bass line on the demo through a Smokey cigarette packet amp designed by Bruce Zinky.' This is apparently one of the world's smallest, cheapest amps. Zinky was an engineer who developed it in the '80s.

territory, producing a cringing imitation of what had gone before. Come the reunion years, then, the prospect of another song with a driving metaphor at its heart might have been rejected. So too, one featuring the falsetto emblematic of early Suede. But in 'Black Ice', Brett made both sound forward-looking. When Mike heard the song, his first thought was Brett and Jodie's crash.

Control might be the most commonly used, commonly disguised theme of Suede songs; it's a bottomless pit of a subject, with no end of possible variations. Control in love. Self-control. Control, or lack of it, through drugs. Initially I thought 'Black Ice' explored parental desire for control of a growing child: 'Well you made me a father / And I gave you my name / And we call it reality but somehow it feels like a game', father and son forever bound, by name, by blood. I thought I heard Brett in an impossible competition for influence against bigger, stronger forces, his hands scratching across the metaphorical wheel as he tried to regain control over his child's future.

Sometimes while writing this book I've shared my theories with the band. Each person responds differently. Brett is mostly hands-off, believing interpretation belongs with the listener. He rarely corrects me and doesn't complain when criticised. But I welcome details I might learn from, and Brett's response made me rethink the song. It speaks to 'Black Ice', but also to the challenges of writing about long-term love as you get older:

> 'Black Ice' was intended as a rumination on marriage rather than parenthood. I suppose in many ways the dynamics are interchangeable, they're both about fealty and loyalty and overcoming the itch of quotidian life ... It was actually Jodie who 'made me a father' and me who 'gave her my name'; seems like a fair swap! Ha! I guess it's

> about the need to embrace the danger, the unknown, to take your hands off the wheel and relinquish control in order for things to stay alive, that sense that a relationship is a paradox that must somehow contain both stability and excitement and that it's the constant interplay between these two opposing forces which as partners you are constantly negotiating and re-negotiating ...

Brett remembered writing this, thinking that songs about marriage and long-term commitment were rare, 'as concepts like duty are extremely hard to make cool ... The rock lexicon is always about fleeting, tragic romances rather than the long-term grind of life that stable relationships can tend towards, the routine and repetition peppered with occasional moments of joy.'*

The unfortunately titled demo 'Balls of Clayderman' became the more Suede-typical 'The Only Way I Can Love You', or 'TOWICLY' in band circles.† This might sound like a song to a lover, though the idea was inspired by paediatrician and psychoanalyst Donald Winnicott's concept of 'good enough parenting'. Brett was interested, he said, in Winnicott's idea that 'You don't have to be a world-class parent, just a good enough one and that, in a way, "excellence" in parenting is a slightly contradictory idea, inspired by the parent's ego rather than any actual practical goodwill towards the well-being of the child.' Brett applied this to the relationship in the song – 'the only way I can love you' being a kind of 'good enough love', 'less glamorous than the romantic kind but real and just as worthy

---

* BA email to RG, 24/12/25.

† Describing the song later to the Insatiable Ones fanzine, Neil said, tongue firmly in cheek: '"TOWICLY" is a song about someone who can't quite act on their feelings and succumbs to inaction and indecision. So it's basically *Hamlet* in 4 minutes and 8 seconds, which is about 60 times shorter than watching the Shakespeare play.'

In Richard's attic, writing Autofiction, *27 November 2019.*
Photo by Neil

and strangely noble.' (In Brett's draft the chorus was more desperate: 'Our future is fucked and life's a mess'.)

'TOWICLY' went through quite the evolution. It was first sent to Ed in November 2019; when the band started pre-production in January 2020, Ed says, 'I mentioned the chorus was one of the best things [Brett had] ever written but the verse wasn't up to par. He flatly disagreed. It took a while for him to come round.' The verse was droney and downbeat, soon to be replaced with something celebratory, 'matching the energy and poppiness' of the chorus. They'd return to it in the new year.*

* After November 2019, the whole track sped up. The band re-recorded the demo at Ed's, Brett writing the new verse on 16/3/20.

The next standout demo was 'Karen E', influenced by 'Woman' by Karen O of the Yeah Yeah Yeahs, an early, partial version of what became 'Personality Disorder' already including Brett's vocal and the Motown drumbeat that Neil played on Richard's electronic drum kit. This was a conscious attempt, Neil says, 'to come up with a Suede song as driving and insistent' as Karen O's. Neil described 'Personality Disorder' to the Insatiable Ones fanzine as a 'true collaboration', Richard writing the main riff's first nine notes, descending, Neil delivering the last eight, scaling back up again. It was aggressive, shouty, catchy, provocative. Ed felt they were trying to 'boil down to the essence' of what made the band worth listening to in a room.

Brett has repeatedly told interviewers he doesn't know what 'Personality Disorder' means. He often speaks in pull quotes, knowing how the music press works – it's not quite true he has no idea, more that he's not saying what he knows. It was written using his version of the William Burroughs cut-up technique, to see what emerged: 'like a painter throwing paint at a wall and hoping it makes interesting patterns, then using those patterns as a basis for something more concrete and narrative.' Often, Brett would jot down phrases, words and stolen ideas, mixing them together to see if word combinations, as he puts it, 'acquired a life of their own.' If they did, he'd go back to expand, hone and polish 'until they become something else.' Sometimes, the juxtaposition of lines charged them.

In part, Brett's recycling habit can be explained by his increasing use of this cut-up method. He's often looking for the best home for a phrase he already likes. Discussing this now, he believes 'Personality Disorder' has a sense of 'the inevitability of one's own demise'. Brett thought of the chorus lyric in 'Personality Disorder' as a 'pay-off' of the idea explored in 'Black Ice'. There's always been bleed between Suede songs, a strong

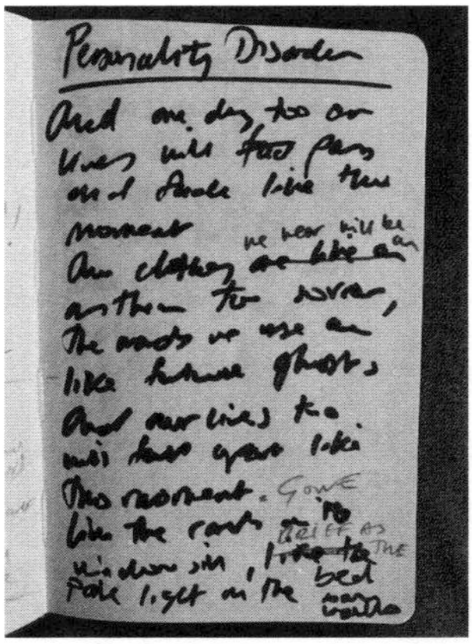

Brett's 'Personality Disorder' lyric draft, including slightly different, alternative line, 'Our clothes we wear will be an anthem'.

sense of lyrics being part of a wider Suede vocabulary, but now this was going into overdrive. In songs like 'Personality Disorder', Brett felt like he was exploring 'that symbiosis of conflicting elements that make a relationship work, an acceptance and celebration of the flaws of yourself and your partner.'

On 11 December, the full-throttle demo 'Offsiders' was written by Neil and Richard, becoming 'The Sadness in You, the Sadness in Me', the following day. Title and sentiment were inspired by the famous Mark Rothko quote, from an interview in *Time* magazine: 'You've got sadness in you, I've got sadness in me – and my works of art are places where the two sadnesses can meet, and therefore both of us need to feel less sad.' Richard remembers this one 'was a great way to sign off the year.' By the end of 2019, they felt they had a whole album, with only two ballads On the list. It's a mistake to make too much of any list – there were many, constantly going around at any given time, and Brett often obsessed over options. In a sign of sheer scale, there are several songs here I'd not heard mentioned before Brett shared this notebook page with me. Management didn't recognise them either.

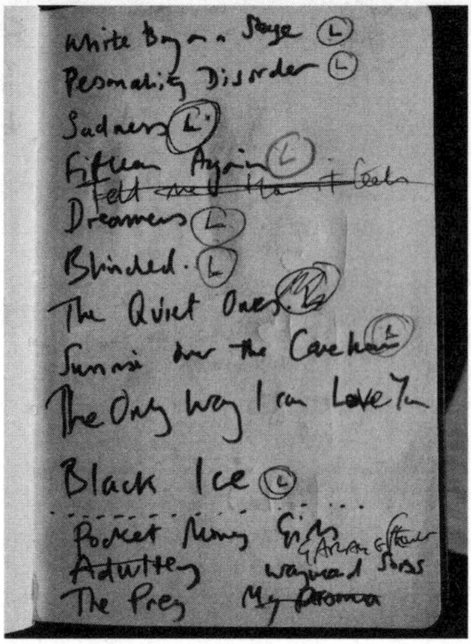

One of Brett's many draft 2019 track lists for Suede #9, with some in reserve. These include lost songs like 'Pocket Money Girls', 'Adultery', 'Garage Flowers' and 'Wayward Sons'. Crossed out is 'My Persona'.

It's impossible to know what would have happened if Suede had released this version of their new album, or something like it. But few artists did as they planned to in 2020. The business of being in a band at all was about to seem trivial.

THE RETURN OF THE IMPERIAL THUMB

Throughout this time, Ed was an integral part of conversations around not just what but also *how* the music would be recorded. The term 'back to basics' was *verboten* – that suggested old-fashioned. But no orchestras this time. No frills. They wanted something that shortened the distance between band and listener.

As we've seen, Ed's connection to Suede is as much emotional and historical as practical – he wasn't officially signed on as producer for Suede #9 yet. Meanwhile, other options were explored: bands often scout around, skin is thick, and diaries are often bursting. Also, living on different continents had made working together tricky last time out. Ed was working on multiple projects anyway. Endless writing, schedules ever-shifting, deadlines ever-moving, are essential elements of Suede's survival. But it makes planning hard. They couldn't be sure everyone would be available.

This is forgotten now, but as Richard recalls, 'Plan A was to go with someone else ... though we still wanted him as a critical arbiter, either way.' Richard says Ed 'may have hated' being hired as tastemaker but not record-maker and might have refused to be involved. Anyway, in October 2019, when the record was starting to cohere, there was a meeting with James Ford, the hugely in-demand producer of Arctic Monkeys and Blur, among many others. James was sent demos, though his meeting with Brett, Richard, Neil, Mat and Didz was tentative, exploratory and lukewarm.

Brett reacts poorly if he thinks he's working with someone for whom Suede is just another gig. Suede is his life's work, and he needs people who care as much as he does whether the next thing works. At the time, Ford was fast becoming one of the hottest producers in alternative music. But there was a delay in getting the demos to him, it was early in the writing and the album's best songs weren't part of the picture yet. Hence the muted meeting. Nobody's fault. Next, the band raised working with Alan Moulder again. Alan had a great time on *The Blue Hour* – though he really did prefer mixing anyway and was friendly with Ed, who he thought best placed; maybe they could come back to him for mixing? What the band suspected they needed again was their enthusiast, their agitator. Working on behalf of the band, untroubled about challenging people, but also deeply invested. Ed was still the producer who had recorded much of their best work. Richard recalls Ed 'bouncing off the walls, wanting to make that punk album'. (Again, no one was paying Ed yet. Few others would provide such support.) This was the enthusiasm they were looking for. Around Christmas 2019, the decision was made: The Imperial Thumb was back.

Since *Night Thoughts*, Ed had worked on movies in the US – *Dunkirk*, *Pacific Rim*, *The Little Prince*. Now it looked like he was returning home, either side, potentially, of working with White Lies again. They'd start work afresh in the UK in the new year. As Ed recalls now, '*Autofiction* was perfectly timed for me. And I couldn't wait to get started.' Unfortunately, Ed and band would have to wait a little longer.

COVID TIMES

The year 2020 was supposed to be when Suede released their ninth album. Management had March to April 2020 slated for pre-production, with rehearsals booked at the Joint. One early plan was to record songs with a studio audience, with ICP reserved for the session in May. But the plan was about to be torn up.

News of a spreading virus began to surface early in the year, Covid-19 making its way into Europe, then the UK, as life continued for many in some kind of denial. On 1 February, the band played the Maya Music Festival in Pattaya, Thailand, a set featuring only three post-reunion songs: 'As One', 'Life Is Golden' and 'Outsiders', in their last gig before Covid. Later that month, Richard and Anna bought a new house in Sweden; they planned to marry later in the year. Mat's debut novel was published on 11 February, with events planned either side of the Atlantic, the book also released in the US. The idea that societies might shut down, in whole or in part, at first seemed ridiculous. Then unlikely. Then possible. Then suddenly, horribly, inevitable.

All industries must react to changing circumstances, and in spring 2020 the music business was in panic. How to sell music without live music? How to promote? To record? The way individual acts responded was often influenced by their album/promotion cycle, also the financial might behind them. For many, it was too late to change releases anyway. At the end of March 2020, Pearl Jam, Skepta and Dua Lipa all put new albums out, as planned. Some with release dates later in the year decided to hold firm. (Bob Dylan's *Rough and Rowdy Ways* didn't shift, for example. Though it helps if you're Dylan.) Others tried to second-guess the pandemic, in the hope of delaying until this was over. Many guessed and lost. Meanwhile, listening habits were changing, with so many out of work or working from home. Millions were reflecting on life anew in the wake of 2020's horrors, turning to their old favourite records for comfort. That meant charts were more full of 'greatest hits' albums and re-entries than ever. Decades-old records by Amy Winehouse, Queen, Elton John and Fleetwood Mac were the year's bestsellers.

Suede were frustrated. Concerns for family, vulnerable individuals and wider society aside, suddenly the band's whole future had shut down, indefinitely. Meanwhile, after so long working up to it, most of Mat's book tour was cancelled too. (He did get one great launch in San Francisco just before lockdown, and you can't catch Covid from review coverage. But Covid severely limited his ability to promote *The Ruins*.) Still, the timing did mean Suede weren't, say, about to release an album into a world in which promotion and touring were paused. In fact, post-*Blue Hour*, Suede didn't have a record deal at all. Maybe they were lucky they hadn't started recording yet. Maybe it would all work out. But for now, those over-full diaries emptied out.

The band kept writing, but meeting up became impossible. Email it was, then. Working individually, then sending each other the latest ideas.* Band and management met online to take stock. They postponed recording, switching back to more writing instead. How long for? Well, no one knew. If they came up with better material in the meantime then great, maybe some of that would stick. If not, nothing was lost. They'd keep talking to Ed in the meantime. It's obvious to say this was a dark time, but it was destabilising even if you weren't directly impacted by the virus. Like many bands, Suede's entire business model was predicated on being able to travel. The practicalities of this new world were confusing enough, while emotionally everyone in the band had different challenges too. Families, relationships, distance, health.

Given the attitude to Covid there Richard was able to go to Sweden and back freely throughout 2020, setting up a family home, enjoying the first summer of a new life all together. Reflecting on it now, shaking his head, he says, 'I could have spent all that time in the attic, feeling lonely.' Same pandemic, different societies, different rules. During this time Simon was living in his mum's attic in Stratford, unable to return to Thailand for months. (Lockdowns were more severe there and he happened to be in the UK rehearsing when it hit.) Having had TB in the past, Simon, who smokes like a chimney was medically vulnerable and understandably scared. According to Richard, 'all of us were afraid of getting it'. During lockdown Brett was with the family in Somerset, home-schooling Lucian:

* In March 'Polly & Esther' was demoed, later becoming 'There Is No Me If There Is No You'. The week after, 'Jesus Pig' followed, becoming the spare, haunting 'Drive Myself Home', music and vocals landing the following day. Brett wrote the vocal line on 1 April 2020. Amy Langley played cello on the final version of 'Drive Myself Home', recording herself at home exactly a year later during lockdown. Neil 'had high hopes' for this song, and, as he told the *Insatiable Ones* fanzine, he 'abandoned the album aesthetic to layer it up with synths, a violin and viola section, and a solo cello. The icing on the cake was the French horn beautifully played by Meredith Moore.'

> I'd been finding the balance, between this quiet existence at a remove sometimes, being in the city sometimes [in London, or away]. Somerset worked because I had this other outlet, you know, this other place where I could be feral and wild and shout and scream on stages, with the band. One made the other one possible. But when lockdowns came, suddenly that was over.

I asked Brett if he was also fearful – of not being able to perform, not keeping the Suede show on the road, on which so many people relied now. He wasn't sure about the word 'fear', though perhaps 'concern' is fair, a kind of vague, bubbling anxiety. You can't plan. You can't tour. You can't record. You can't let rip on a lockdown walk. For someone like Brett, who needs to shriek and clasp hands, lockdowns hit hard.

All the more reason, then, to throw himself into music.

'SHE STILL LEADS ME ON': LOVE SONG IN DISGUISE

It's tempting to make a connection here between the weird beginning of Covid and the first great Suede song written under lockdown. You never know exactly how circumstances feed into what a band makes, how the times apply pressure. Whether the era somehow influenced a song in which the protagonist feels 'like screaming' in a time of seemingly endless grief, or if that's just coincidence. What we do know is, Richard wrote a backing track he recorded on 3 April, the 'slick demo' of 'Kaspar's Elbow' becoming 'She Still Leads Me On' when Brett added a vocal the very same day.

This version got fired around, Ed, Ian and Didz responding fast, celebrating what they instantly all thought *had* to be the first and lead track on the next Suede album. (Hardly any changes were made to the song after this.) It wasn't *punk* exactly either, though it was uplifting, had a driving rhythm from the start, felt urgent, and had a soaring vocal that transcended the usual fare. There was more confessional here, another attempt to rip off the mask: Brett sang of 'all the feelings I hid' and, as in 'White Boy ...', not being able to control emotion. 'She Still Leads Me On' provided a vital boost when the idea of playing the song, together, in a room, was a bitter joke.

What's special about 'She Still Leads Me On'? It's not the most musically distinct Suede song, nor the catchiest. 'She Still Leads Me On' is special to fans because the 'leading on' isn't as it might appear – perhaps a lover 'leading on' their partner, misleading them, maybe. Rather, it's about a child being inspired, pushed forward, encouraged, 'led on' – by his mum, years after she's gone. It's a disguised love song most people can relate to. Everyone has a mother. In the real world, in memory, or in absence. For almost everyone, that love is complicated.

Brett's mum Sandra died from cancer in 1989, the year he formed Suede with Mat and Justine. He'd written about her many times. What made this time different was it being an uplifting song of tribute, rather than an elegiac ballad. To write it, Brett used a similar approach to 'Life Is Golden', inverting the relationship (now child to parent, rather than parent to child), homing in on memories that summon complication instead of sentimentality. 'She Still Leads Me On' has this singular, absolute dedication, not by way of sanitising the life once lived, but rather revelling in its difficulty. This, suggests the lyric, is what real tribute sounds like. One with the courage to admit imperfection: 'I loved her with my last breath / And I loved her with a love that was strong as death / And I loved her when she was unkind'.* As 'Life Is Golden' traded sharper observations

* This line was recycled from Brett and Bernard's the Tears, a song called 'A Love as Strong as Death'.

in the verse for a bright, hopeful chorus, so did this one: 'Sometimes when I look up at the sky / She still leads me on' is the refrain, while the Solina keyboard line descends in the background. If 'Black Ice' was facing fear of losing your partner, '15 Again' facing fear of lost youth, the retitled 'That Boy on the Stage' fear of losing yourself in a persona, 'She Still Leads Me On' concerned facing the small resentments which are also part of lifelong grief. This was the previously unacknowledged shadow, revealing itself.

With 'She Still Leads Me On' now leading the A list, the unreleased record was becoming ever more about Brett's alter-egos, identities, lives lived and unlived. It was about trying to come to terms with himself in his fifties, facing down ghosts, admitting shortcomings. If the album was to work for listeners, those admissions had to be convincing, the self-critique genuine. Meanwhile, lyrics and images repeated across the key songs made this feel less like an accident and more like a determined effort.

So, 'She Still Leads Me On' fired the writing process anew. But how would writing work in the longer term? Much of Suede's best reunion material had been written either together in a room, or by collaboration, in stages. On 22 April they tried a Skype writing session with Richard in Sweden and Brett and Neil in England, but it was a failure, the split-second delay on the call meaning they couldn't even keep in time. They decided within half an hour to write separately.

The year dragged on, restrictions being lifted and reimposed. Suede's live dates for the year – festivals in Spain, Ireland, Denmark and Norway, a rare tour of Australasia and East Asia, as well as a two-week UK and European tour – were cancelled. Getting anything organised in 2020 was 'a fucking nightmare'. Though at least they could devote all their time to the new album.

AUTOFICTION APPROACHES

'The unmentionable thing producers get told,' says Ed, 'is that a band sounds better live.' This, he says, is part of a decades-old conversation: how bands respond to the ever-expanding possibilities of recording. 'The band had these great songs,' says Ed of Suede, in 2020. 'We were on the same page musically. And we were all just glad to be doing it.' That's true, though that doesn't mean there weren't any debates. There are always debates.

In a meeting in Richard's kitchen in February 2020, just weeks before the first lockdown, he and most of the band discussed what they had so far. Music. Direction. Recording plans. Brett was keen for Ed's take on various songs. Ed recalls, with a laugh: 'It feels a bit like Dad arriving and the three kids showing off their homework, trying to get Dad's approval.' Sometimes Ed wasn't keen on individual elements. For example, with part of 'TOWICLY', where he felt the others' disappointment at his reaction, but by now he considered it his job to tell Brett what did and didn't work. 'I accept this,' Ed says now, 'that in a way, at that stage my biggest job is to stand up to Brett. To say, hey, I think there's better in you.' Ed says now that, 'by the time we were in the Joint [rehearsal studios] in March it was obvious ["TOWICLY"] needed fixing and Richard and Neil by then agreed. The new verse is fabulous, and I still think it's one of the best Suede songs ever.'

In Richard's kitchen, they discussed what it meant to be 'more direct'. Ed wasn't thinking about singles now: just the right songs. He liked '15 Again', 'Black Ice' and 'Personality Disorder' but says, 'no one had thought about what the record was gonna sound like and the mix of songs [on the demos] wasn't very punky.' Several ideas were suggested. One was recording the album live, together. Another, rehearsing lots, playing live gigs with the material in secret, before digesting for a while and working out what needed to change. Then recording in a studio, with live takes, audience in the room.

Brett and Mat were keen to make a record that sounded live, but the last thing Ed wanted to do was record with a crowd: 'Brett would say, "Blob, why I can't I do it like this?" And I'd say, "Practicalities! There'd be fluffs all over the place!"' Ed understood why the idea appealed. 'They'd had this gimmick for *Night Thoughts*, with the film, which worked. With *The Blue Hour*, they didn't. They wanted a gimmick to help sell the record.' Something that brought together the music and presentation made sense, though Ed argued recording live was a mistake. 'The Beatles did it, sure. But they weren't punk. They were the antithesis of punk!' For Ed, the ideal was to play parts live where possible, stripping back tracking overall, so recordings didn't inflate, becoming ever more complex. 'Richard was very amenable to combining what he did into one guitar part,' Ed recalls. 'We got into that level of detail, though the slow song thing wasn't faced.' The slow song thing could wait.

Ed now believes the stripped-back recording he initially hoped for was never realistic. This, in part, was because Richard and Neil had already started layering on the demos; computer software was now much more sophisticated than most studios ever used to be. Ed felt it was not just about the technology, but the fact that, to enthuse Brett about new ideas, Neil and Richard *needed* to deliver them to him in a certain way. Ed says that with Brett, 'you need to bring him something every two or three weeks, detail, colour, you need to spend time working on it, the texture, feeling, energy. That comes from overdubs, from sounds, you're trying to get [him] into it ... That layering process is part of the thing you have to do to get him interested in the first place. But once you send it to

[Brett] and it comes back it's this tapestry. You're not then gonna make it back into a pencil drawing.'

You don't need to appreciate the entire history of recorded music to get the point here; over recent decades, studios have gone from having a basic analogue set-up with few tracks to record with, to 16-, then 32-track studios (as with Suede's first album*), the digital age reinventing the process once more, making for infinite possibilities. With this change, bands have evolved how they record, meaning the distance between how a band sounds live and on record has increased. Ed says: 'Everyone used to be on the same track, in a little room, cut straight to vinyl. It's not till you get to the Beatles, the idea of what they made in a studio was more curated. Writing parts for other people to play, like, say, "Eleanor Rigby". With '70s punk, there was an attempt to simplify as much as possible. Guitar, bass, drums, vocals. *Never Mind the Bollocks*, that's perfect! Though in reality, most bands can't do that any more.'

In Ed's kitchen, most of the band said they wanted to make that distance shorter, between Suede live, and Suede on record. The question was, how? 'When Brett asks questions,' Ed says, 'you've got to have a good way of explaining why things don't work ... I said to him, you really want it to sound like you're standing in front of 8,000 people and you're listening to it through the monitors? You're fighting against that spirit [with Brett]. What is a live experience? You're prepared to strip all this down to bass, drums, keys, [guitars], vocal?' Ed believed there was a fundamental misunderstanding at work here, one he's seen with others,

---

* Ed recalls this journey over time: 'We just did fairly basic stuff in early albums. Live bass and drums, some overdubs, that was it ... Over the years Suede got more into layering, we got bored and tried different things – also, Richard thinks differently when he's making a record ... a part of what he has to do is perform Bernard's music, but also somehow keep that relationship between guitar and vocals in the music on record.'

too. What bands say they *want* is sounding live, until they hear it. What they mean, he believes, is they want to *feel* how they feel when playing live, when they listen back to the recorded versions. Which is impossible. One's emotional, the other practical. The adrenaline of the live gig can't be replicated. It's a tempting illusion.

Not all singers see themselves primarily as performers, though these days, Ed says, 'Brett gets his energy from being on stage.' It's an evolution he's observed over decades:

> When I first met Brett, the shows were a lot more paced. Now it's the energy he wants, he's become this energetic frontman. He's become much more comfortable with who he is and what he can do live. He's less mysterious and more up front. It concerns him if he doesn't have that material, and his focus in the studio has become more like: how can I make what I need to take to people live?

With this in mind, Ed remembers getting Brett on board with the approach for *Autofiction* was critical, a process that took time and patience: 'Brett is a very responsible frontman, he understands the challenge, he's respectful of Richard and Neil – but he's got to be convinced. It's like an illness, he gets the flu about something, he doesn't have the energy you need – you really just need to wait till he's revitalised.' Through 2020, almost everyone felt drained of energy sometimes and the record had several false starts. But eventually they agreed to concentrate on recording the best songs possible, more stripped back, where possible. Ed laughs now, 'It was the only thing we didn't get that I wanted [sparser arrangements]. Otherwise, they were sweethearts. I love them all. I mean, who else but Suede could make a record like that, nearly thirty years after their first?'

CHARLES AND THE PARAORCHESTRA

In 2020, in Brett's Somerset village, the creatives were all locked down together. One of these was Charles Hazlewood, a charismatic conductor, music director and curator with a long-standing interest in melding musical styles. Charles led multiple major European orchestras after becoming celebrated as a young conductor; in 2011 he set up the Paraorchestra, the UK's first orchestra explicitly designed to provide opportunities for disabled musicians, using specially developed technology to do so. Charles's own daughter is a singer with cerebral palsy; he'd been frustrated by the ways disabled musicians like her were often perceived, shut out of live work because traditional spaces were often unable to make small adjustments to facilitate inclusion. Also, having travelled widely, he wanted to lead an orchestra of his own, from home. In 2012, the Paraorchestra played the closing ceremony of the London 2012 Paralympics, alongside Coldplay. The original seventeen-member ensemble showcased disabled and able-bodied virtuoso players such as the one-handed pianist Nicholas McCarthy and jazz trumpeter Clarence Adoo. Soon the Paraorchestra became well established, with a cast of players often taking part in shows incorporating dance and performance, sometimes playing classical pieces, sometimes newly composed music. In 2019, they became the Love Unlimited Synth Orchestra for Glastonbury, Paraorchestra composer and saxophonist Charlotte Harding arranging Barry White's music for a gig featuring Gruff Rhys, Adrian Utley of Portishead and the up-and-coming Nadine Shah, her album *Holiday Destination* recently nominated for the Mercury Prize.

When lockdowns came, Brett and Charles discussed a collaboration for the times: this became the 'Death Songbook' – songs about death and dying, designed to be uplifting in a time of widespread devastation.

For Brett, it was another attempt to face the unspoken. The theme wasn't new to Charles: in 2019, he'd run a Festival of Death and Dying with his ex-wife Henrietta, 'a determined attempt to break the death taboo'.* For Brett, this kind of project was a reach. He hadn't worked outside Suede in nearly a decade, but he and Charles had become firm friends since he'd moved, and as a personality, in Brett's words, Charles was 'blessed with this infectious, can-do enthusiasm that makes anything seem possible'. Charles found his new friend 'exceptionally sweet, genuine, humble, possessing this incredible generosity of spirit.' For the Death Songbook they'd arrange songs for the orchestra, with Brett installed as regular vocalist. Brett rarely did covers. But here, when so little else was possible, he agreed. Paraorchestra projects typically had a more radical set-up, but quickly Brett saw how he could contribute, on his own terms.

Charles and Brett also discussed writing an album together, potentially, though that was more talk than work: 'We chatted about doing something atmospheric and almost ambient as a starting point,' says Brett now. 'I remember going to his swimming pool studio in Wells (he had an empty pool in his house full of keyboards) and him coming up with a handful of classical-sounding piano ideas – beautiful, melodic pieces which reminded me of the kind of stuff my dad used to listen to.' They may have chosen to focus on the Death Songbook instead, but they were getting to know each other, feeling each other out as musicians as well as friends.

The theme of the Death Songbook was loose, but taken together, the songs suggested a kind of atmosphere. They were largely drawn from a pre-Suede era, music both had known long ago. Black's 'Wonderful Life'. Japan's 'Nightporter'. Echo & the Bunnymen's 'The Killing Moon' had long been a favourite of Brett's, and Charles felt the song had orchestral

* Charles Hazlewood, interviewed for the Death Songbook livestream, 6–7 March 2021.

potential. Though not initially included, Suede songs seemed to suggest themselves, too, despite Brett's squeamishness, thinking that a conceited move. 'The Next Life' was an obvious candidate (Brett said he 'didn't see how I could leave it out'), so too 'He's Dead', both early songs much beloved by Brett from Bernard's time now rarely played by the post-reunion band. There was also a rare opportunity to resurrect the tribute to Jesse, 'Unsung', not played live in many years. Brett sent it to Charles, who loved it. This too was a way of coping, when surrounded by reminders of mortality. Soon, they were contacting collaborators. Plans moved fast, not least as Paraorchestra CEO Jonathan Harper was a big Suede fan and, in his words, delivered with a boyish grin, 'I was desperate to make something happen.' But what? How to connect with people in a time of disconnection?

Plans were set for a one-off performance on Europe's largest stage, at the Wales Millennium Centre; this allowed a skeleton Paraorchestra to perform at social distance. (Everyone in a circle. Facing each other, but not too close. Something you'd never usually have in a live gig.) Charles asked Nadine Shah to duet with Brett on Depeche Mode's 'Enjoy the Silence' and Skeeter Davis's '60s hit 'The End of the World' (a much sweeter note than usual for both artists), as well as recruiting Adrian Utley on guitar and percussionist Seb Rochford, known for his work as one of two drummers in jazz outfit Sons of Kemet. Rochford had played drums on two of Brett's solo records, co-writing songs on *Black Rainbows*. Quickly, there was a Paraorchestra rock band to complement a Covid-restricted orchestra featuring cello, flute, violin, viola, bass clarinet, recorder and percussion.

Charlotte Harding speaks insightfully about Suede's music. She's worked with the band since. This was the beginning, not the end, of something. But when she was enlisted as arranger for the Death

Songbook she brought a fresh perspective, not least because she knew very little about Brett or Suede beforehand. Charlotte recalls, 'I was too young to catch them first time around ... but I got an education fast. I devoured all the music during Covid, just listening hundreds of times, and soon I was a huge fan.' Over email Charlotte drew out the intricacies, Brett giving her free rein to interpret Suede/Brett songs as she saw fit ('he emailed me lots of ideas and very patiently answered questions, but mostly just told me it was mine and I should make of it what I wanted'). The non-Suede music was new to her, too. Mercury Rev's 'Holes' was released much later than most pieces included in the Death Songbook, being a 1998 single – when Harding was nine years old. She was able, then, to hear this music that was familiar to Brett, Charles and older listeners in a different way. As regular Paraorchestra arranger, she was also attuned to how it might be complemented by their players. 'He's Dead', for example, had been a rock song to Brett for thirty years. Now the early Suede B-side was going to be remade, woodwind and strings to the fore, with a member of Portishead playing Bernard Butler's furious guitar part.

The setlist for the Death Songbook show contained nine songs: 'We only really considered one that we then discarded,' says Brett now. 'This rare duet by Jeff Buckley and [the Cocteau Twins'] Elizabeth Fraser called "All Flowers in Time Bend Towards the Sun".' Buckley and Fraser were in an intense romance in 1994–5, demoing but never releasing the unfinished song around the time Fraser's relationship with her bandmate Robin Guthrie fell apart. 'We wanted to do it,' says Brett now, 'and I did know Jeff a little, so felt fine about singing one of his songs. But Liz [Fraser] said it was theirs, you know. To do a version of our own would have been against the spirit of the project.' Fraser rarely discussed this in public, but was dismayed when the demo leaked after Buckley's death in 1997. In a rare interview in 2009, she was still against release:

'Why do people have to hear everything?' she asked. 'It's unfinished. I don't want it to be heard.' Others have done their own versions already, and you can see why. 'All Flowers in Time Bend Towards the Sun', which *American Songwriter* called 'spellbinding' remains a favourite of Buckley devotees. It's not officially on major streaming services (though you can find it). It would have likely been a highlight, but wasn't to be. Charles and Brett continued to set plans, in between their own main projects, floating a future Death Songbook album.

KEEPING SUEDE ON TRACK

Whenever restrictions allowed, Suede rehearsed at the Joint, as they had regularly since *Bloodsports*. These studios near King's Cross were in trouble already, but Covid made survival harder. At one point, you could only have two people in one room. At others, it was the whole band, but no crew or engineers. In June 2020, when Suede were rehearsing 'She Still Leads Me On' and 'What Am I Without You?' together for the first time, the building was empty. Suede worked until 16 July, doing pre-production with Ed (Brett wanted five weeks but they could only do three) just before the Joint shut for good.

They were due to go into AIR Studios in Hampstead on 15 July starting, as ever, with Simon. (He was still in the country; he'd never left.) Ed recalls these sessions fondly, as he does much of the recording process:

> Simon's a complete diva, I adore him. You can't get things done till he's happy, otherwise you don't get the drums. Then when he's happy, he's incredible. You do two or three takes and that's it ... Of everyone [in Suede], I sometimes feel he's the most improved musician of all, and he's such a professional now. The drums always sound huge. Get those first, then you can do anything.

Ed says they got loads done at AIR. Not just Simon's parts, but also 'the Sex Pistols guitar sound we wanted. You need to get Brett excited, early on. He loved the guitar sound, day two or three.' Still, it was tricky working at AIR mid-pandemic. Didz explains, 'Every two hours in AIR they'd put on this disinfecting fog, which would mist up the room, then [we waited] a couple of hours while it settled and did its work.'

Then Anna suggested Richard, Neil and Ed might record in Sweden, where there was no lockdown. Anna has long been friends with Ludvig Andersson, son of Benny (of ABBA). Benny and Ludvig's studio, RMV, in a 19th-century naval building on the picturesque island of Skeppsholmen in Stockholm, was open and available that summer. From here Richard could return home in the evening, while Ed and Neil could stay nearby. So they switched to RMV in July. The band had guide parts down; now they could concentrate 'on replacing them with proper guitar parts, synths ...' Benny wanted to meet Richard, but couldn't because of Covid – though Neil did get to play Benny's keyboards. He recalls, 'There's an enormous Yamaha GX-1 in the studio you can see on *ABBA: The Movie*, you have to climb inside it it's so big.' Only five of these 'Dream Machines' were ever made. Neil played one of them on 'Sunrise over the Care Home', also Benny's Minimoog on 'Personality Disorder'. In mid-August, Ed, Neil and Richard returned. Brett hated not influencing guitar sounds, but he didn't want to go. So, he kept in touch from home.

Despite its lengthy gestation, the recording of *Autofiction* was largely good fun. They sometimes butted heads, but once they'd left behind 'the idea of the stripped-back thing', focusing instead on giving nods here and there to 'live' sound, there was little disagreement. Ed was comfortable with his role, everyone pulling the same way:

I like the responsibility of being in charge of making the record, but I will only make it if I have the approval of the band to make that record. Creative tension can become personal tension. The best thing about Suede is they're sweethearts, they really are ... with *Autofiction* we were all in agreement about the record we were making ...*

With Suede, it's always music first. The thing that makes our relationship what it is, is: I'm not in the band, I don't write the songs, but my opinion has as much weight as anyone else. Not more weight, but they do listen to me. Also, by this point [remember that] Richard and Neil are much more experienced. I can focus on the music. I don't need to stress on the recording. I've got a band I trust.

'Thanks so much! SUEDE' in Swedish.
Signed by both Richard and Neil.

---

* Ed says he's glad he didn't make *The Blue Hour*, in part because they wanted to pull in different musical directions at the time.

Mat also points to Richard and Neil's greater experience, saying *Autofiction* 'may have seemed an album very much about Brett, and in a way it is – though by now Richard and Neil were taking more control over how things were being done. They were both more forceful with their opinions.'

The band scheduled two weeks in October for vocals. Of all the periods I spoke to Ed about, this one stood out as a particular pleasure: '"She Still Leads Me On" was a real game changer,' he says now. 'We didn't know if it was going to be a hit, of course – I was just so proud of them for doing it, especially for Brett – to write a song like that and nail it ... I remember doing the vocals near his [London] flat. He doesn't wear his heart on his sleeve much, he's always talking via or through something, so you notice it. It's such a beautiful song.'

Recording an album designed to be performed in sweaty proximity was strange; these vocals were mostly recorded as the first, weird Covid winter approached. As Brett said, 'Performers are so defined by their persona. When that's taken away from you, you're not quite yourself.' These recordings, a real contrast to the last time Ed and Brett worked together without others present, were Brett's only opportunity to perform all 2020, except with headphones on, singing into his home mic, or miming to demos, mid-run. His only audience was Lucian, who he'd sometimes play demos to in the garden.

LABEL AND PLANNING

The band needed a record deal. The right one. Didz's diaries rarely show blank days; rather, the office was often scrambling to keep things going while navigating ever-changing rules. In early autumn 2020, band and management met with three labels: Orchard (more digital-focused, part of Sony), Virgin PMR (Clive Calder there had just launched Virgin North and done a record with Doves) and BMG. At this stage, they didn't send any demos. As Didz recalls, 'We felt the prospect of a new Suede record was enough to garner interest.' BMG 'won the meeting-off' with Alistair Norbury, president of BMG and Suede fan, and Gemma Reilly-Hammond, then co-head of BMG,* both in the room. Gemma said, 'We want to put Suede back where they belong and we know we can do it.' That was 'simple, seductive, direct, genuine.' BMG was a relatively traditional label, more familiar for a band like Suede. Neil, Richard and Brett already had long-standing publishing deals with BMG; they were co-producers on Mike's *Insatiable Ones* film. (They worked with Ian's other Quietus clients too, all with long back catalogues: the Pretenders, Simple Minds, Simply Red.) So, this brought things together. That first BMG meeting was at the end of September, with negotiations following in November, while the band talked videos, photos and artwork with Paul and Mike. Mike developed plans for a series of videos with a complex stage set-up, though as diaries kept shifting, with no deal confirmed and finance TBC, this stalled. Since *The Blue Hour*, they'd learned lessons. Initially, they'd approached Turner Prize-winning conceptual artist Gillian Wearing for the new record. She had ideas and was keen – until budgets were discussed; then she laughed. To avoid more overly ambitious ideas beyond the budget, perhaps this time the band needed to work with a video commissioner, through a label.

Plans for recording live had been junked once Covid hit, but the band were still looking for ways to connect. (In March 2020, for instance,

* In 2022, Reilly-Hammond became managing director at Suede's Quietus Management, where many BMG acts were already on the roster. Previously, she worked on chart-topping campaigns at BMG for the likes of Kylie Minogue and Rick Astley.

they'd set up a new Instagram account for something called 'Crushed Kid'. No band. No text. Just black and white images. What could it mean?) Management also put out a call via the Insatiable Ones to record fan vocals from home, Neil patching hundreds of these contributions together himself. The result was effective. Many individuals who had recorded in isolation sounded like a shouty choir, standing together. Fan vocals were used as backing on two songs that made the album.* First, 'That Boy on the Stage', the line 'shut up and hit that metal'. ('Every shout, every scream' sent in, was used, says Neil.) Second, 'Personality Disorder' – where fans provided the call and response: 'Will (will), you (you) be (be) my (my) personality disorder', then again on 'Fill (fill) me (me) with (with) your (your) personality disorder'. This was a cute trick. No need for Neil to conduct hundreds of Suede fans at a digital distance; they yelled, so there was no risk of being out of tune. In 'Personality Disorder' the back and forth made it sound like fans were with the band, which of course they couldn't be. Contributions were emailed. It also set up crowds for a ready-made feature of the set, when the tour came around. Whenever that would be.

Early December 2020 and the band were at Konk studios in north London to 'finish the record'. 'At the time,' Richard says now, with a wry look, 'it felt like we were wrapping up.' The plan was to send the record to Alan Moulder in December for mixing; Christmas was conducted in widespread lockdown, though that month, on 8 December, the first Covid vaccine was administered in the UK. Maybe Suede would be able to put their album out in 2021 after all?

* They were also used on the end of 'Blinded', later included on *Sci-Fi Lullabies Vol. 2.*

2021: 'HOLDING OUR BREATH'

Early the following year the album was mixed while Ed was moving home once more, to Highgate in north London. But band and management held off; the pandemic rolled on, wave after wave, vaccines playing catch-up with variants, everyone determined to take *Autofiction* on the road. As Neil recalls, 'In 2021 bands were doing socially distanced gigs and it looked awful, we couldn't do that, especially not for this record. Also, vinyl lead times were very long ... We thought, let's just hold our breath and wait till it's all over.' That meant more writing. In March 2021, they added two more new songs. First was the fast-paced but average 'You Don't Know Me'.* A day later, a much better piece of Richard's with a distinctive guitar part called 'Vet Shit'. Yet again Brett wrote his vocals in a day, turning the demo into 'Shadow Self'. Didz says, 'They'd talked a lot about punk and post-punk. But they still didn't really have songs that *sounded* like that, not really. Then "Shadow Self" came along, with this solid, jittery chassis of a rhythm section, Richard painting broad textures over it and Brett making wolf noises. [In practical terms] it was a pain because we were really all done, we'd been done for a long time, and now we had to work out how to record the song. But it pulled everything together.' If it did so, it did so by accident. As Richard recalls: '[It wasn't] written to go on the album, as we believed it was already finished. It was simply an experiment in something a bit different.'

---

* Demo name 'Pointed Stick', after the Monty Python sketch 'Self-Defence Against Fresh Fruit'.

DANCING WITH 'SHADOW SELF'

'Shadow Self' brought the autobiographical element of the record sharply into focus. There's no need, here, to pretend Brett is a specialist in the theories of Carl Jung, one of the most influential psychologists of the 20th-century, who came up with the theory of the 'shadow self' in 1951 in his book *Aion*. (Forgive me, but it's my job to ask if he'd gone deep into the work. He laughed: 'Err, not really! Just, you know, the shadow self thing ...') Pop music can be ruined by thinking. If people feel you're trying to educate them, you've probably lost them already. But Brett is good at reducing complex ideas to their essence, then doing something determinedly unintellectual with them. 'Shadow Self' is arguably the best example of this in the post-reunion era.

Jung called the shadow self 'the thing a person has no wish to be'. It concerns the relationship between what we know of ourselves and what's hidden, what we reject about ourselves and how we might recognise, then face it. Which was what Brett was attempting, in this music. Jung believed all of us live with a 'shadow self' where what we reject about ourselves resides. Here lies shame, repression, unresolved trauma, self-hate. Jung's ideas have increasingly resonated as Western culture's relationship with self-help evolves, especially the idea of what Jung called 'integrating the shadow'. If you're a singer in a band, the shadow is with you every time you record, step on stage, or give interviews. In public, in private. All the time.

Jung encouraged patients to 'integrate their shadow', by which he meant they should face shame, repression and that unacknowledged part we must admit to if we are to grow as people. You still look for approval, even as you accept yourself: Brett recalls sharing music with eight-year-old Lucian around this time, looking for his reactions when so few others knew it:

> I remember playing 'Sadness ...' and 'Shadow Self' back-to-back to Lucian one day in the garden in Somerset to get his response [wondering which to include]. Lucian was often the first person in the world apart from me, Richard and Neil to hear the songs on *Autofiction*. I would often write all day until my head was spinning then pick him up from school and play him stuff in the evening around bath time just to get some perspective. I love how kids respond to music, how for them it contains none of the cultural baggage and reference points that it does for adults so their responses have a purity and immediacy ... It was that kind of instinctive clarity that I was looking for in the songs on AF, songs that would bypass the logical, rational part of the brain and hit the listener hard in the gut.

When Brett was asking for feedback, he didn't explain Jungian concepts. He just asked what Lucian thought of the song.

BMG AND RETURNING LIVE

The pandemic dragged on; work was still complicated, but Suede felt confident enough to reveal the record deal they'd been sitting on. In July 2021 *Music Week* announced BMG had signed Suede for two albums. Brett had been describing *Autofiction*, most recently to the BBC, as 'nasty, brutish and short' (that was a nod to Thomas Hobbes, who wrote the line a mere 370 years earlier).* But those who'd heard it knew it was more commercial than that.

* 'No arts; no letters; no society; and which is worst of all, continual fear and danger of violent death; and the life of man, solitary, poor, nasty, brutish, and short.' From *Leviathan* by Thomas Hobbes (1651)

In Europe, some venues were allowed to open long enough for Suede to tour. Rehearsals were a reminder of what they'd missed. Richard recalls: 'When we came back together, it's like, oh yeah, this really works. It's a kind of stubbornness to try and do justice to [it] – it's worth sticking with. You have this thing which is essentially a happy accident – the dynamic you get in a room – when you all plug in together it makes a certain sound. And people will pay to see it.'

Their first gig post-pandemic was Qstock in Finland on 31 July; they opened with 'Europe Is Our Playground', then 'That Boy on the Stage'. Richard remembers 'a strange experience, seeing the crowd together … I felt worried about safety, I couldn't concentrate.' They wrote more new material at Neil's in October between preparing to play the old songs live for a future project in mind; in early November, they managed a quick-fire UK tour with Nadine Shah as support, marking the twenty-fifth anniversary of *Coming Up*. This started in Edinburgh and finished at Ally Pally. Suede rarely bring other artists on stage, so it was a sign of their respect for Shah that she joined them for a cover of her song 'Fool' in Manchester on the penultimate night, duetting 'The Wild Ones' with Brett during the last show, too. Twenty years before, Suede were the exception; now, this was industry standard: the promise of old, familiar albums played in full bringing in middle-aged crowds who might otherwise stay home. With no new album yet, this was the time to do it, though it's notable they held back new songs completely, choosing instead to intersperse non-*Coming Up* hits with mid-'90s rarities like 'Together', 'Sadie' and the brilliant, brash 'Young Men'. These were good shows, well received. It was good to be back. Though it was the opposite of what they'd been planning since 2018.

On 26 November, Brett and Charles's Death Songbook show was broadcast in full on the BBC; this on the day after total UK Covid cases passed 10 million. The following day, he emailed the band, Ian and Didz the new album's title: *Autofiction*.

'AUTOFICTION': NEW WORD FOR AN OLD IDEA

The term 'autofiction' is a modern expression of an ancient idea. Artists have always written in disguised ways about their lives. 'Autofiction', borrowed from the French (a portmanteau of the words *autobiographie* and *fiction*), is a literary genre coined in 1977 by the novelist Serge Doubrovsky when discussing his novel *Fils*.

First-person narratives mixing real and imagined life have been around as long as storytelling itself, but by the early 2020s the term 'autofiction' was everywhere, so Suede's album title felt contemporary. As writers like Karl Ove Knausgaard and Rachel Cusk blurred the line between fiction and truth, so might a songwriter. Here was Brett's determined effort to do just that. Call your album *Autofiction* and you invite fans to compare lyrics with real life. Call your songs 'That Boy on the Stage', 'Personality Disorder' and 'Shadow Self' and you only invite more attention. In a sign of the term's fresh popularity, in 2025 Penguin published *A Guide to Autofiction*. Here, author Stephen Carlick argues it's not just 'the blurring between fiction and truth' that defines autofiction, but also the writer questioning whether truth and imagination can be distinguished from each other at all. Again, that might resonate for someone who's spent thirty years plus performing a 'revealing' version of themselves, while keeping people at a distance. With autofiction, it's always about the speaker, but it's slippery. Autofiction wants you to know: this is me, undisguised. But also: it might not be. Maybe I don't even know the difference.

2022: REVEAL YOURSELF

In early 2022, *Autofiction* still wasn't out, and Suede were still writing. But for *Autofiction* at least, there was one more addition left. In January, Richard sent round 'Bovine University'. That's a *Simpsons* reference, now a meme, where the character Troy McClure, he of the information skits, dressed in a cowboy hat, tells a small child it's time for a cow to go to 'Bovine University'. By which he means, the slaughterhouse. (For anyone wondering about demo titles across this book, *lots* of Richard's are *Simpsons* references).* A day later, this became 'Turn Off Your Brain and Yell'. Again there was widespread agreement that this new song needed to be included, and Brett pushed hard for this to finish the record, replacing 'Blinded'. As Richard remembers, 'The management were a bit like, ugh, when is this [process] ever going to end? ... But the rest of us thought, yeah, it's a great song let's put it on.' According to Didz it was easier now; they'd been through this once before. Finishing the record. Then adding a song. Needing to record, across time zones, with Simon back living in Thailand.

'Turn Off Your Brain and Yell' is a final track that sounds like a first, the extended intro with driving, fuzzy bass line and thumping floor tom ideal for the start of a show. Even more explicit than 'Shadow Self', the opening line is 'Reveal yourself, in your complex ways', the refrain 'reveal yourself' repeated throughout. Brett had been changing perspectives, angles, points of view, but doing the same thing repeatedly: the line 'show me all your wounds' might be the album's whole lyrical content in one line. What charges the song is that encouragement from Brett to himself

* Pity the poor biographer chasing down this essential information, but there's also another, different *Simpsons* meme, with Ralph Wiggum declaring that when he grows up, 'I want to go to Bovine University!'

to stop suppressing, hiding, while making a screaming party of self-examination. 'Turn Off Your Brain and Yell' is six minutes of letting go.

Another way they were changing, now obvious ahead of release, was a change in their approach to guitars. This jumps out to Richard:

> When I first joined, reverb or chorus pedals were *verboten* in the studio – but when time passes, attitudes change. I can hear a lot of those John McGeoch, melodic sounds in AF now, it became a nostalgic thing and suddenly I was using a lot more of these effects. Amps like JC-120s, that era of post-punk, Bernard Sumner, icy, corrosive, minimalist – I love that approach. It was a deliberate, pointed detail of early Suede that made those records exciting – I've always tried to keep it going. Brett prefers music to be more direct and muscular now – he doesn't like too much detail in the music, whereas Neil and I do.

With 'Shadow Self'* and 'Turn Off Your Brain and Yell' added, that icy, corrosive thing was more evident. Both Richard compositions, they also weighted the album anew, meaning that though they'd often written together, *Autofiction* was ultimately made up of more songs Richard had written alone – 'Drive Myself Home', 'Black Ice', 'She Still Leads Me On', as well as 'Shadow Self' and 'TOYBAY'.

It's too reductive to say, *The Blue Hour*: Neil's album, *Autofiction*: Richard's. Though there are clear differences in process and outcome, as Richard notes:

> When I'm writing on my own I can go down a tunnel and get to the end of it – when you're with someone, sometimes you can't both fit in the tunnel. So it's quite liberating to do stuff on my own, but

* This was recorded in May 2021 at the same time as two further tracks, 'There Is No Me If There Is No You' and 'You Don't Know Me'.

the results surprise me less, and I want to be surprised. 'Days Like Dead Moths', for example, we'd never have come up with that alone. Neil is faster at editing, cutting up ... so, together we can be more spontaneous. As things went on with AF, it became obvious to me the sort of stuff we needed was what I'm quite good at doing alone. These days, I can be clear and focused, I don't need to ask others. On AF I'm not always thinking my ideas will be the best but am thinking, yeah, I know what I'm doing here. So, it's not as simple as saying apart we're like this, together we're like that.

The band recorded 'TOYBAY' with Ed at Konk at the beginning of February. On the final song of the album, the last sound listeners heard was Richard pulling the lead out of his guitar, the first him plugging in at the start of 'She Still Leads Me On'.* The finished album kept in these in-studio touches, from Ed communicating something through

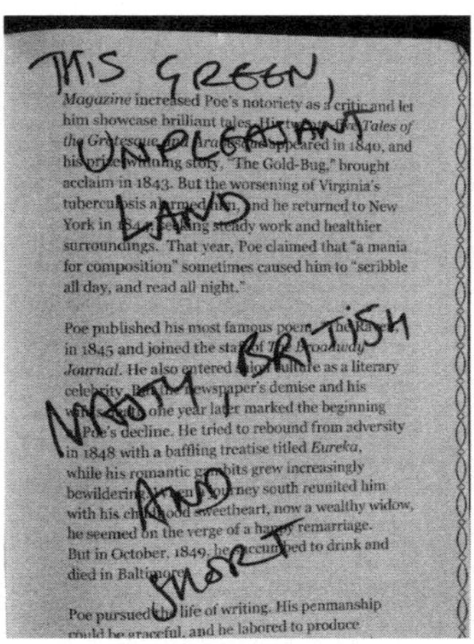

From Brett's notebook, scribbled on a page of Edgar Allan Poe's biography, from a notebook gifted by the Insatiable Ones. 'Nasty, British and short' was changed back to 'Nasty, brutish and short' to describe the album.

---

* This has been done before, of course, whenever bands wanted to give the impression of 'live' on record. Radiohead's *Hail to the Thief*, for example, starts the same way.

the talkback mic at AIR, to various coughs and squalling feedback. All this, in place of playing live, was intended to give the feel, through the speakers, of Suede in a room. Of course, they weren't. But tricks help create the illusion.

POST-COVID GOOD TIME

No one announces the end of a pandemic. It just slowly, steadily, retreats. By early 2022 the worst seemed to be over, though theories about the possibility of new, threatening strains still abounded. Live music had been on a stop–start cycle, with many venues, labels and artists struggling or already going under, and it wasn't clear when it was safe to 'return to normal'. Still, you can't go on making the same album for ever, and 'Turn Off Your Brain and Yell' was a full stop. *Autofiction* was scheduled for 16 September, when the world *might*, they hoped, be in some kind of recognisable shape, audiences desperate for that good time. In May 2022 Suede did a European tour, once again celebrating *Coming Up*. For this tour, the second set was mostly hits. It was a conscious choice, to help new songs land hardest, when they came.

This finally happened on the last night of the tour, back at Cirque Royal in Brussels on 24 May. Steve Lamacq again had first play, 'She Still Leads Me On' debuting the day before on 6 Music back home. (This time, Lamacq was much more enthusiastic.) Release day was Simon's birthday, also Brett and Jodie's thirteenth wedding anniversary. Neil recalls: 'You never know what the reception will be till it lands ... You're waiting with bated breath. I remember being in Belgium, listening to Lamacq, thinking, yeah, that sounds good on the radio. You get more of a sense of what a record is when you hear it on the radio.' In Brussels, Suede played their new single at the start of the second set, livestreaming it on their website.

'We've been writing new songs for the last four years,' said Brett to the crowd. Then once more, drawn out, unable to resist. '*Four years*. This is one of 'em, this song's called "She Still Leads Me On".' Then he started the crowd clapping. As the riff began, the album cover appeared for the first time too, an outsized, familiar-looking naked black-and-white torso their new backdrop. The body was on a mattress again, but this time, for music more naked than ever before, the body was Brett's own. (Some chutzpah, this. To put the lower back – and upper arse, frankly – of a 55-year-old man, clutching himself, on an album cover.)

Draft photo of Brett for Autofiction *cover.*
Photo by Paul Khera

Paul had previously done covers for Brett's solo albums *Wilderness*, *Slow Attack* and *Black Rainbows* with him obscured (in a field, in shadow, behind flowers). This was now a tradition.

As we've seen, Suede have a long history of picking counterintuitive first singles. This time, as Mat recalls, 'We'd had lots of chats with the record company over what to put out first, and it was the first time in a long time we just thought let's put the most single thing out first.' They did consider '15 Again', 'Personality Disorder' or 'That Boy on the Stage' instead, but in the end, in consultation with new radio plugger Kevin McCabe, they did just that. Brett says, 'We just *had* to put our best foot forward.' Lo and behold, it worked. Neil remembers: 'We were quite surprised by the fact that people had such an emotional connection to it – it moved people ... they connected with the lyric.' This worked not just in the first six weeks of BBC playlisting, but longer-term, too. Mat also noticed the response, thinking it went beyond the song itself, rather signifying a cultural change:

> I remember looking through the comments, the responses on Twitter, expecting to see lots of people laying into Brett for writing a song about his mum. Earlier in our career, I think we might have got that response. Like there was something unmasculine about it. Something inappropriate. But it just wasn't there. I saw one comment. One. You know, man up, that sort of thing. But apart from that, people just responded with love.

'She Still Leads Me On' was released on vinyl as an EP.* It didn't exactly cross over, but had more impact than anything in the whole reunion era, by a distance, piquing interest in the album. '15 Again', the second single from *Autofiction*, was released on 8 August, followed by 'That Boy on the Stage' on 2 September. No weird choices. No noses thumbed. Just three of the most immediate, representative songs.

* The lead track was backed by 'The Sadness in You, The Sadness in Me', 'Days Like Dead Moths' and 'The Prey'.

AUTOFICTION VIDEOS

In May, the band shot videos for 'She Still Leads Me On' and '15 Again' in an underground club near Waterloo station, by the South Bank. In the end they stuck to straightforward performance videos, while the label commissioned *Autofiction: A Short Film* via MrMr Films, directed by Katie Lambert. MrMr had worked with Wet Leg in their breakout year – their 2022 number-one album following viral debut single 'Chaise Longue' – also rapper/actress Little Simz, very much on the rise ahead of her Mercury Prize win.

For 'That Boy on the Stage', Lambert used a live version of the song recorded at AIR. There was a great idea in here. The film is a scripted narrative in black and white centring around a young couple. Non-binary Chris wears a *Bloodsports* T-shirt, their partner Hannah pregnant but on the edge of wanting to break up. The video shows differing perspectives on the day of a Suede gig, before they travel separately to the club to see them. Like Roger's film, it shows the same places in different moments, flashing back and forward, tracing the relationship's arc. Chris can't get through security, they don't have a ticket, only making it inside once the band have begun. (That recent live footage from Brussels was patched in here – Brett's intro to 'She Still Leads Me On's debut, saying, 'This is one of 'em.') Brett's in the distance, moving through the crowd as Chris and Hannah have an argument, then make up mid-show. Unfortunately, the script isn't sharp enough and scenes are repeated in only slightly different versions (it's intended to portray an unravelling through different perspectives). Another version of an old Suede story: big, ambitious concept; small budget, compromised result.

I love the idea here, as a companion piece to the album. But the execution jars, and when you ask band or fans about it now, it seems to have sunk without trace. At the time, director Lambert said the film explored 'the memory soup' we all swim in, the gig intended as a backdrop to a relationship's 'crunch time'. That's ripe for a film, no doubt, as are the hopes, dreams and fears of a young queer couple in London coming apart and together at a Suede gig. But watching this feels very much like hearing a band through a wall. Muffled, confusing, unsatisfying. If I didn't have to watch the whole thing for this book, I admit I wouldn't have made it to the end. And there's not much music in it. Part of 'She Still Leads Me On'. Part of '15 Again', mostly quiet, as characters pass through spaces far from the stage. In an album so explicitly about Suede's best asset, their singer, this reduced both man and music to a marginal presence. *Autofiction: A Short Film* was released on 17 August. Didz describes it now as 'the only thing in the whole campaign that didn't land perfectly'. Unlike Sargent's *Night Thoughts*, even many hardcore fans haven't heard of it. But it didn't seem to matter. The album was taking off anyway. Before it was even out.

The month of the film's release, August 2022, Richard married Anna, in Järna, Sweden, forty-five minutes south-west of Stockholm. (Mike was there, making him perhaps the only person at both Richard and Bernard's weddings.) Afterwards, the band did festivals in Norway, Portugal, England and Romania – only one new song each time – before a break, ahead of the album campaign. Though the album was already working for them. 'She Still Leads Me On' was still being heavily rotated at 6 Music. Meanwhile, the record's most accessible song, 'The Only Way I Can Love You' was playlisted by Radio 2, meaning crossover on the station with by far Europe's biggest listenership. Radio 2 had also played 'She Still Leads Me On'. The band were pushing for every pair of ears they could get. It wasn't just the BBC any more, either, but Virgin Radio, the alternative music station Radio X, Absolute Radio, and Suede were due to be back on *Later ... with Jools Holland*, too. Good will was suddenly everywhere.

AUTOFICTION: RELEASE AND RECEPTION

In the UK, the past three Suede albums had gone to number ten, six and five. This time, they had a more immediate record with traction, but also a much more engaged fanbase; organised too. When Suede scheduled in-stores for release week, some fans treated it like a Suede tour. The online fan groups went into overdrive, many of these people knowing each other well. Go to five, ten, fifteen Suede events – book launches, in-stores, gigs – and you get to know the faces of the committed. While some set about trying to source tickets, others focused on maximising sales for the all-important first week.

That week (16 September), there were releases from Japanese–British singer-songwriter, model and actress Rina Sawayama with *Hold the Girl*, also *Self-Titled* by Marcus Mumford, while the all-girl K-pop outfit Blackpink released their new album *Born Pink*. BMG were a bit blindsided by Blackpink, though management kept flagging it – in the lead-up, the main concern was a potential clash with the much-expanded reissue of George Michael's classic record *Older*. In the end, that came out two weeks later. This was Suede's best chance of finding new fans since May 1999, when they were so ubiquitous that London's flagship Virgin Megastore was retitled the *Head Music* store for release week. It was a strange time, with Queen Elizabeth having died just days before (8 September) and Britain being suddenly in the first days of Liz Truss's bizarre, 49-day premiership. (Bus stop adverts were replaced with pictures of the Queen. Society, it seemed, was at a kind of standstill.) This also had a practical impact on some of the campaign, with in-stores in

Liverpool and Manchester scheduled for the middle of release week being postponed owing to the Queen's funeral.

When *Autofiction* landed, fan groups descended, buying up all the vinyl stock and sending it by post to Suede fans abroad or unable to travel who'd asked for signed, reserved copies in the first week. The machine went into overdrive: Suede signed all they could, travelling the country in a van, working flat out all week. Sawayama was on the same in-store schedule, until she got ill and had to pull out of her final appearances.

In the 2020s, hot takes on new albums land hard and fast, online. Journalist Claire Biddles, writer for the *Wire* and a DIY Suede fanzine creator, got her copy of *Autofiction* and took the record out of the bag, 'feeling a small twinge of dread' when she saw the second song was called 'Personality Disorder'. 'I have borderline personality disorder,' she says, 'which is well known for being one of the more misunderstood and maligned mental diagnoses. One or two compassionate examples aside, I'm used to seeing crass and cruel cultural representations of my condition: villains, murderers, crazy exes in tacky films … I was pretty certain I could trust Suede but I was trepidatious.' It soon became her favourite song on the new album:

> The song is deeply evocative: I recognise its hard edges … ['Personality Disorder'] really embodies the feelings of emotional extremity that comes with BPD, and the harshness and brashness that you can both cause, and are attracted to, as someone with the condition. It's also kind of goofy – its lyrical form is silly, it's a bit cartoonish and over-the-top, which your view of yourself as a BPD sufferer can absolutely be. It recognises that the obsession and extreme desire that comes with something like BPD can be dangerously alluring.

What Claire spotted was a fresh focus for Suede – though it was a version of something they'd explored before: taking potential slurs, attacks or perceived weaknesses and delivering them in tribute, claiming a 'personality disorder' as dangerous, fluid, beyond cold medical diagnosis. A come-on.

At the in-stores, the band noticed fans they hadn't seen for a quarter of a century. People who approached the signing table with enthusiasm to share how they'd only just got back into Suede again. How they didn't even know they'd reformed but they did now. They talked animatedly about what they'd loved about the band, having no knowledge at all of anything they'd done since the '90s. Neither *Bloodsports, Night Thoughts* nor *The Blue Hour* had troubled their timelines – but they'd fallen in love with 'She Still Leads Me On', or heard something on the radio, and just bought *Autofiction* and OH MY GOD. For a chunk of fans in the signing queues in, say, Southampton or Portsmouth, this might as well have been Suede's first record since *Head Music*. Guys! So glad to have you back! Hey, what have you been up to all this time? Twelve years into their second life, they had finally found these people again. In one emblematic moment, Richard's dad gave blood that week and got chatting; his phlebotomist mentioned the new Suede album. That had never happened to him before.

By now, they were optimistic about beating *The Blue Hour*'s first-week placing – these days there are daily updates, with sales figures – though nothing is ever guaranteed. (It's common to start out number one early in the week and not make the top twenty by the end.) At first Suede were number one, then they got pushed to two by Blackpink, with Rina Sawayama making a late charge as the weekend approached. Whole vinyl stocks were bought up in indie record shops across the UK. Fans were sure their system made a difference. When the news came in, it was a huge boost. K-pop is all powerful. But number two was yet another big step up.

The impact was immediately noticeable: this is what it felt like to have a record that lands with both listeners and critics, their first since *Coming Up*. Responses were widespread and full of praise, at home and abroad. In his review, long-time fan Andrew Trendell, now *NME* editor, wrote that Suede's second act was 'one of the greatest comebacks of the 21st century'. Yes, *Autofiction* was being well received on its own terms, but also having four quality albums since reuniting was considered part of the picture now, too. Trendell's review was headlined, 'Indie icons reborn as "raw" and "nasty" punk rockers'. Survive for long enough and you become survivors. People like survivors. Survivors are resilient, adaptable, tough. You can't keep survivors down.

In the press, Brett came across as more confident that second-era Suede had now delivered an album to stand alongside the first era's best. He could still be catty, still dismissive about '90s peers who enjoyed more success. But he was also more self-aware, owing in part to the long wait, and the books written in those Somerset winters before lockdowns came. As he wrote in *Afternoons with the Blinds Drawn*, 'A band has to accept what kind of band it is and work within those limits and, if they're clever, use them to their own ends.' Reflecting on his memoirs, Brett told the *Irish Independent*: 'It's an amazing way to get to know yourself a bit better. I don't have soundbites to deliver to say how I got to know myself better, but I just feel as though I'm more familiar with myself. That sounds like a weird thing to say, but sometimes you go through life and not really know who you are. All of these things are in your head, but it's not until you have to structure them and order them [that true self-knowledge emerges].'*

* 'Suede frontman Brett Anderson: "Writing about my parents and the death of my mum dredged up some feelings that have fed into this album": Interview with Brett by John Meagher', *Irish Independent*, 17 September 2022.

Later that same month, Brett took the Paraorchestra show back to Wales, with an audience this time. They didn't have the funding to do a conventional record, but live recordings were good enough to do something with, and a label was interested. (The Paraorchestra had just released a collaboration with composer Hannah Peel, *The Unfolding*, a classical UK number one.)* The 2021 lockdown set was expanded, with new arrangements of 'She Still Leads Me On', strings giving the song a new depth, also a pedestrian version of Depeche Mode's 'Enjoy the Silence' alongside one new, utterly gorgeous Anderson–Hazlewood composition, a piano and vocal song called 'Brutal Lover'.

CRUSHED KID

This time, the campaign for Suede's new album was clear, clean and effective. Lots of ideas had come and gone through the various recording stages, most abandoned as unworkable. Repeatedly, the band had been foiled in their attempts to get up close to fans. Many of the shows they'd done since things opened up again had only demonstrated that so many shows and festivals were, to use Mat's words, 'designed to keep fans and the band from ever coming into contact.' How were they going to get closer? Since the start of 2020, one idea had stuck: pretend they were a brand-new act. Here was a simple idea that would show exactly what they wanted to project: that Suede were 'reborn', as punks. Visceral, close-up, impossible to ignore. The band worked with Dave Palmer, associate director at DawBell, the PR and comms company with a slew of high-profile clients (Harry Styles, Paul McCartney, for starters), drawing

* Hannah Peel won an Emmy for her score for *Game of Thrones: The Last Watch*. She's also collaborated with Paul Weller, and won an Ivor Novello award for her score for the Sky series *The Midwich Cuckoos*.

together a strategy: 'As soon as Mat mentioned the band appearing under an assumed name, they immediately loved it.' The Crushed Kid Insta account had been posting sporadically since March 2020 without fans making the connection.

DawBell loved the idea so much that it overtook all others. In August 2022 Crushed Kid posted on their Insta story about the new band's debut single, 'Shadow of My Former Self', the one-track online preview being a section of 'Shadow Self' (not too hard to work that out) with Brett's voice pitched down, unrecognisable. Meanwhile, 'blurred Instagram photos of five sultry, yet naggingly familiar figures' gave further clues – these taken by Dean Chalkley, who'd photographed the band for *The Blue Hour*. The *Quietus* (the music magazine, not the management company) even did a preview, pretending the band were real. Long-time supporter Luke Turner, who'd reviewed those first reunion gigs back in 2010, wrote: 'New group Crushed Kid have shared debut single "Shadow of My Former Self". The track is a curious mix of the likes of Killing Joke, Simple Minds and vocals yelled through an Argos megaphone and straw pillow. It caught our ears after arriving in tQ's inbox this past weekend, and is available to listen to above. If you're a fan, you might like to note that Crushed Kid play live at London's MOTH* Club on September 5.'

When that first gig by 'Crushed Kid' was announced at the MOTH Club in Hackney (capacity 300), the price of tickets suggested maybe this wasn't some student debut, though to be sure of filling the room, the gig was part of the regular club night run by Suede fan and bass player of the Horrors, Rhys Webb. Why Crushed Kid? Well, suede is crushed goat leather. If you put 'Suede' into a Mandarin translator, that's the transliteration that comes up. So: whenever Suede HQ wanted to read their

* This stands for 'Memorable Order of Tin Hats'.

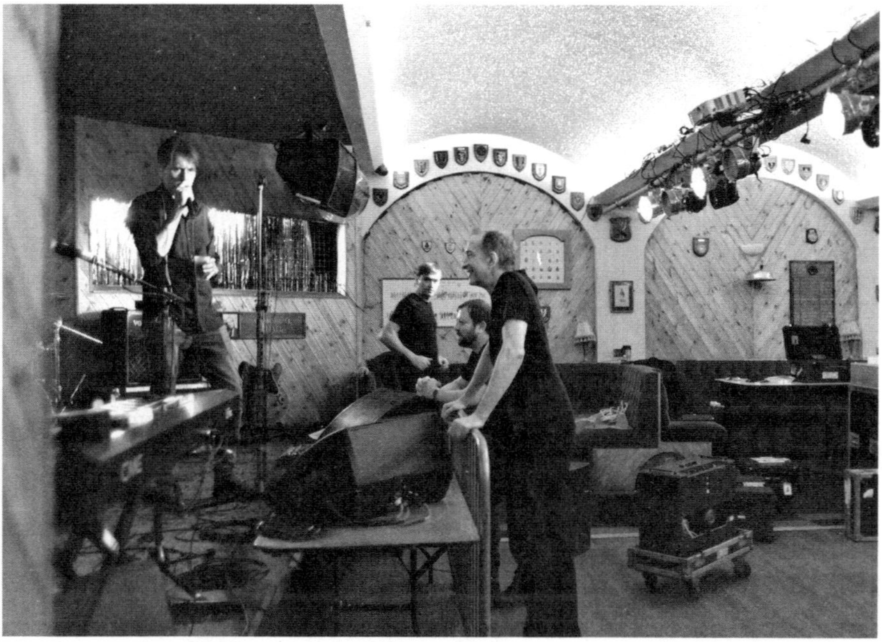

Pre-gig at the MOTH Club. Erstwhile Suede drummer Justin Welch second left.
Photo by Paul Khera

Chinese press, 'to see how we've gone down', they searched for 'crushed kid'; now that's who they became. For a while.

The MOTH Club stage is small; members of Crushed Kid huddled in close to each other while the singer addressed the crowd. 'A lovely greeting for our debut gig,' he said, unable to hide his pleasure. The band being 'new', they had only their 'debut' album to draw from. That meant a gig entirely of *Autofiction* songs. Reflecting on the band's image post-pandemic, Ed says now: 'No one ever smiles in promo shots, they want to look cool and interesting. But on stage, Brett's grinning ear to ear.' That contrast was very much in evidence now. Neil reflects: '*Autofiction* partly landed because it was about reaching out and personal connection at a time when people had been denied it. The Crushed Kid gigs seemed to exemplify that.'

The crowd that first night was nearly all made up of Insatiable Ones, hardcore fans and journalists given the tip-off. This time, even the red tops and popular newspapers whose culture sections usually never go anywhere near a band of Suede's age or reputation reported on this as an event. Full-page splashes, with tiny 100-word reviews. Photos of Brett raging into the front row. The full works. Mark Beaumont reviewed the gig for the *Evening Standard*, praising '[Crushed Kid's] lithe, feral hellcat of a singer', noting these songs moved between 'bursts of seductive and seditious glam rock, soaring indie bombast and babbled autobiographical poetry.' As several of the band and management have put it to me since, 'It landed perfectly.'

By the time they arrived at Manchester's Deaf Institute the following night, any pretence of secrecy was abandoned. Back on a tiny stage, the atmosphere charged by all that waiting during Covid times – Brett wanted much more of this. His only regret was, he didn't say at the end of the second gig, 'That's it, we're splitting up!' Looking back now, Neil recalls the novelty: 'It was nice to have a kind of persona as a lot of *Autofiction* is about fractured identities ... to hide behind a different band name was a lot of fun. You could see the whites of people's eyes. It's a pleasure to play places the size of the O2, but perhaps we're better suited to smaller venues.'

After four long years, what Suede finally delivered, with bells on, was a great album for that night out, exactly when people needed one. *Autofiction* gave Suede new life, and a reunion-era high. It had been coming, slowly, through thousands of micro-decisions, by the band and Suede HQ, for so long. 'It felt pretty good,' says Brett now, with offhand understatement, as if it doesn't mean very much. 'We'd worked for it. In a way, we *were* a new band. Just one who got to learn from our mistakes. Our many, many, mistakes.'

Crushed Kid on stage at the MOTH Club.
Photo by Paul Khera

CHAPTER 6

antidepressants
'the anti-nostalgia band'

'Pain is temporary, art is forever'

—Brett, by text, to Rodge, *Antidepressants* release week

THE *AUTOFICTION* AFTERGLOW

Autofiction announced Suede once more as a major British rock band – a living one. Big profiles. International invites. Word of mouth. Glowing reviews noticed 'a palpable sense of the band enjoying themselves' (the *Guardian*) while being 'simultaneously forward-looking and nostalgic' (*Clash*). Once again, they graced album of the year lists (*Mojo, Uncut, Record Collector*), the sheer length and consistency of their unlikely second life now given more prominence in coverage. The new record's sound was hardly 1996 all over again; rather, it was very 2020s, our nervous decade's glitchy, modern, therapy-speak anxiety fed through a 1970s sound machine. In language, sound, delivery, this was a different Suede from the one last widely noticed. Less shiny. More gritty. More noisy, too. All things are relative, but progress was real.

At first, setlists drew lightly or not at all on other post-reunion albums. Instead, Suede played most of *Autofiction* wherever they went. The reaction encouraged Brett to give back more energy to crowds, making for a virtuous circle, band to crowd, crowd to band. Mat says this was partly about familiarity: 'The thing with *Autofiction* was not just that they were really good live songs – it was that, straight away, people *knew* them. We were on the radio. You don't need the whole audience to know [everything], but there's a tipping point.' When Brett threw the mic out, yelling, 'Sing it!', people knew the words. And not just to 'Trash' or 'Beautiful Ones'. That call on 'Personality Disorder', with the response delivered live by Neil and the crowd. 'Shut up and hit that metal', yelled back, like a protest, in 'That Boy on the Stage'. The chorus of 'She Still Leads Me On', hundreds of faces, cast upwards, echoing the line 'when I look up at the sky'. That reception was as satisfying to Brett as anything he'd experienced live in years. Meanwhile, the intention in the depths of lockdown – making *Autofiction* sound like 'indie greats getting back in the garage to make a racket' (Andrew Trendell's *NME* review namechecked Iggy's *Lust for Life*) was even, partially, true. Okay, they weren't quite in the garage. And some of *Autofiction* was written when they were literally isolated. But that distance fired the sound too.

As ever, the process for 'Suede X' began long before the latest album's release, and this time they were backed up with new material: the Covid delay contributed to *Autofiction*'s success, but it also made for a creative traffic jam. Before writing time, though, there were shows. Suede followed an appearance at the Singapore Grand Prix on 1 October with two celebratory nights at the Electric Ballroom in Camden – in the crowd, manager Ian 'couldn't believe how far Brett had come' since they first began working together – then a quick-fire skip through Amsterdam, Paris, Cologne, Hamburg, playing *Autofiction* in full, like it was a classic album already. The furious energy of the shows was noticed, the reviews were excellent, and Brett seemed focused as never before. The gimmick of being a new act was just that: a gimmick. But being re-energised, relishing performance for its own sake, like kids, after thirty-plus years on the job? That was all very real.

'A SHARED DNA': NORTH AMERICA, NOVEMBER 2022

In November Suede embarked on a rare North American tour in a double-header with the Manic Street Preachers. The bands first toured together in 1993, and this was their first since 1994, back when the Manics' sensitive, intelligent guitarist Richey Edwards was still with them and Suede were a four-piece fumbling through Richard's earliest days. Back then, the Manics were the lesser-known band. (That didn't last much longer. Soon they got huge, then gradually came closer to Suede's level, as Suede came back up.)

The press announcement saw Brett and the Manics' James Dean Bradfield trading compliments. James marvelled at Suede's ability to incorporate Richard in the years following Bernard's departure, thriving after so many predicted the band's demise. (That prediction was also made of the Manics after Richey disappeared in February 1995. The dates were close. And both bands went on to mainstream commercial breakthroughs in 1996–97.) In a much-used quote, James told the *NME* the Manics and Suede 'share[d] a DNA'. Both pre-dated Britpop but were co-opted into it. Both traded on their outsider status. Both were allergic to the self-congratulatory, flag-waving culture of the mid-'90s. And both were still pushing, decades after many peers had given up or resorted to occasional victory laps. (The Manics' 2021 album *The Ultra Vivid Lament* was their first UK number one since 1998.)

This new joint tour, twenty-eight years on, was Suede's first visit to the States since that Mat-less Coachella gig in 2011, twelve travel-heavy gigs over twenty-one days. Didz remembers: 'On the plane, they felt good. This album has been a massive success, and now, after all this time, we're doing something successful international rock bands do. Tour North America.' They started in Vancouver and finished in Toronto, taking in places like Seattle, San Francisco, Austin, Chicago, New York and Boston. With neither band having a larger audience in any city, they took turns to headline one night, support the next. Sets were shorter, Suede playing about two thirds first-era music, with *Autofiction* highlights sprinkled in. Neither was used to doing support slots, but the mutual appreciation society seemed genuine and crossover between fanbases real, with the Manics hard core likely to be Suede-curious and vice versa. The Manics tend to be quiet, insulated by their long-established crew. (Unlike Suede, they don't greet fans at gigs. They largely go unseen, even by their co-headliners.) The chaos of both bands' early days was far behind them now, anyway. It was just good show after good show.

How unusual to see two bands formed in the 1980s starting again this way, after so long. For different reasons, both had struggled in North America. The Manics enjoyed success pretty much *everywhere except* the US, their confrontational politics making it hard to make inroads. (Imagine hearing 'IfwhiteAmericatoldthetruthforonedayitsworldwouldfallapart' on the radio, if you can...) In their early days, the Manics wrote protest songs attacking major banks, wore home-made clothes and make-up, slogans like 'Culture of Destruction' stencilled across their chests. Richey infamously carved a bloody '4 Real' into his arm, mid-interview, an act of self-harm jarringly celebrated in the UK music press. Their anthem 'A Design for Life', an ode to the power of the written word, became ubiquitous in the mid-'90s and remains timeless. Inoffensive MOR fare for US radio this was not, though occasionally the music sounded like it.

Suede, meanwhile, were eternally the London Suede in the US. They tackled this issue over the decades by avoiding it, often going the other way across the globe instead, becoming popular in countries many Western bands ignored. Japan, China, Singapore, Thailand. Their relationship with the US was also clouded by their 1993 tour, embarked on shortly after Bernard's dad's death, when they should have cancelled, and didn't.* For years, Suede considered the US too big, too complicated, too hard. But now, armed with *Autofiction*, they embarked on their longest trip there for decades. Success changes attitudes.

There's plenty in common between the Manics and Suede. High and low art, in conversation. Literary references. Goth sensibilities. Though as Claire Biddles points out, there are differences too. Claire's a huge fan of both bands (she's seen the Manics over forty times) but was too young to catch either first time around:

> Obviously, the glamour was what drew me in [at first], but there was something about how Suede used 'glamour' in the magical sense too: as a way to dazzle the listener/viewer, and cloak the meaning of their work. There was an essential mystery to Suede – as opposed to the on-the-sleeve earnestness of the Manics – that I found, and still find, extremely beguiling.

Perhaps that contrast helped disguise the commonality – you'd never catch Brett scrawling a slogan on a T-shirt. The politics usually come via

* Mat states this to camera in Mike Christie's documentary *The Insatiable Ones*.

the personal with him, especially these days. By 2022, though, despite those differences, the two bands suddenly seemed quite similar. With Brett trading that haughty cool for genuine, straightforward enthusiasm, Suede were more on-the-sleeve than ever.

The tour was received well. US magazine *Under the Radar* covered the Philadelphia show, where Suede went on second. Brett's antics – lassoing the mic stand, going walkabout in the crowd, screaming, shirt unbuttoned, hollering, whooping, singing off-mic when the spirit took him, berating people down the front filming on their phones or standing still – these were standard fare for Suede shows now, though these tricks seem new when arriving in new places and US audiences hadn't seen him up close since Suede's first life. Mark Redfern's review said Brett 'proved he's still one of the most dynamic frontmen of his era'. Redfern finished with an overheard comment from the long merch queue: 'I've seen them five times and this is the best [so far].' Reactions like this were common. Sure, they were occasionally messy, but they weren't selling themselves as polished, rather as a band with a furious spirit, marking themselves out by refusing to do the obvious. (Even the Manics were doing that, delivering a straightforward 'greatest hits' set every time.)

Back home, they were in demand. They finished the year on 7 December by playing the top of the News International building next to the Shard as part of a live session for Virgin Radio, a noisy show in the centre of London that led to complaints from other occupants of the office building. It was a one-off, but also typical of the period, band and audience either side of a room, seventeen floors high in the sky. Brett's grin was almost permanent throughout the show. Suede were on another new high.

THE PRE-*AUTOFICTION* VACUUM

One more time, let's scroll back to go forward.

Before all this – before *Autofiction*-in-full shows, before North America with the Manics – there was another record, made when all this adulation might have seemed a distant, near-impossible dream.

In early 2021, *Autofiction* supposedly finished and lockdowns still in effect, Suede's writing team were kicking their heels. This was a unique time for musicians, with lockdown uncertainty widespread, long processing delays for vinyl in particular, little happening live, and Suede needing to wait until *Autofiction* could be released. Aside from the *Coming Up* tour, there was an unheard-of nine-month gap. Maybe they couldn't get away with a full-on ArtSuede record again – but they'd spent years writing this full-throttle, direct music now, and maybe there were more experimental things they could do? Sure, they hoped *Autofiction* would land, but then you always do, and at this point they had little evidence of that being likely. They were, for a while, in a strange vacuum, creatures of habit who were *always* writing, no matter what. It's often hard to unpick one Suede album from another, but this was muddier than usual. From March 2021 until August 2022, they were mostly doing three things: 1) writing for Suede X, 2) adding extras to *Autofiction*, and 3) writing something else. Richard remembers: 'We had done the "band in a rehearsal room" album, so the idea was to do something quite different.'

It had been nearly a year since Brett, Neil and Richard had written together, and they were itching to get back to it. The first session saw Brett and Neil together at the beginning of March, Neil regularly coming over to Richard's. For six long months, Richard was unable to see Anna or the family, stuck in the UK, pre-wedding, when restrictions changed. What did he do with his days, I asked? 'The Capital Ring Walk,' he tells me, 'which you could do in sections, during lockdown. That, and write an album for a ballet, with Neil and Brett.' Well-timed pause. 'That naturally, we then put in the bin.' He also catalogued those demo tapes and started learning Swedish (but soon gave up). Almost immediately, they wrote 'Shadow Self', the most *Autofiction* song of all. This mattered not just for Suede's ninth album, but also for their tenth. But they'd already begun something else, too. This was 'Suede 9.5', as titled on Richard's laptop.*

SUEDE 9.5

With that gap in the schedule in front of them, Brett, Neil and Richard discussed possible new approaches to writing and performance. Richard recalls how conversations evolved: 'Gradually, the ideas came together – it would be avant-garde, it would perhaps have instrumentals. Then the idea came that we'd have a ballet troupe. We'd perform the show in a one-off event somewhere special, and we'd be the backing band.' (Not all the inner circle believed Brett even enjoyed *sitting through* a ballet, but Jodie was a huge fan, so he'd found himself going more often, recently. Then getting ideas.) Maybe the ballet soundtrack could be released as a limited-edition recording, the show premiering somewhere like the Southbank, Suede in the orchestra pit or at the side of the stage.

Perhaps this was that ArtSuede side of Richard and Neil looking for an outlet again, that self-expression emerging after years of looking for three-minute bangers. Didz recalls:

> After *The Blue Hour*, rather than release something experimental and bleak like that and have it go through the same critical and

---

* When Neil sent this file to Brett and Richard, it was titled 'Suede 10 Maquette 1'. They expected further iterations, as the project developed.

> commercial mincer as, say, *Coming Up* ... To be judged against that when it was nothing like it and wasn't supposed to be, there was this idea that we could try another way, with the time they had spare. [We thought] it would be good to put out something differently, with more protection from commercial judgement.

Despite the musical possibilities, this wasn't about art alone. In a world where acts were forever dropping individual songs, guest appearances, remixes and extras, the algorithm keeping those Spotify and YouTube numbers ticking over, perhaps Suede might be able put something significant out between major releases, too? (They have, according to Didz, 'a disastrous relationship with remixes – they're best avoided, these days'.) Richard again: 'The idea was, we'd record it at Neil's house, with him essentially being the producer.'

A Suede ballet may seem a wild notion for a rock band who'd just spent years discussing how best to reconnect with fans. Still, what was the *Night Thoughts* film if not a way to take attention away from the band? What was *The Blue Hour* if not a sign of their sonic potential beyond guitar, bass, drums? The ballet may look like a handbrake turn from the outside, but it didn't feel like one for the band. Neil says now, 'We've always had multiple energies in the same line-up, so that's nothing new. You don't need to change the singer to have a different vibe.'* Also, they were using Neil's production skills, as before – by now, that was just one of their ways of working. Meanwhile, because of the time lag, Neil says, 'We could do the next thing and come up with something esoteric.' But hadn't they just learned there was limited appetite for that? Neil again:

---

* Neil continues: 'Pretty much we do a good job of that in a live gig, but I've always thought with a few more changes you could put in different songs, a few more nods, different colours and textures, so things are less one note.'

'If we took three years to come up with a weird record and it went down badly there would be six years between "proper" Suede records, but we thought that in a year we could come up with and release something ... but still get on with "proper" records.' The deadline provided focus. The ballet would be whatever they came up with before *Autofiction* came out, with any release being, in Neil's words, something 'we would put out within a year of AF'. This might be online. It might not be with BMG. Anyway, it might also have a life in a theatre.

Initially, I wondered how much space to give this music, whether to talk it up or down. At times I've thought of it as a more formalised version of what Suede have *always* done – that is, written lots for every record, the music's identity cohering over time. (A reminder of scale: when Richard first shared this music with me in March 2024, he and Neil had already written eighty-seven pieces of music for Suede X. And they had a long way to go.)* At times, I've considered the ballet an album with an identity of its own – an abandoned, complete statement with a couple of songs reused later. Speaking to Richard, I notice he never talks it down as a side concern; rather, he says the ballet 'represented the writing work for most of 2021 and 2022', calling these 'songs we worked on a lot'. Certainly, the sheer distance travelled – between where they started musically in 2021 and where they ended up in 2025 – is unusually stark. But let's assess the ballet on its own terms, and see what we see.

I think it's fair to say this wasn't a Suede *album*; after all, Mat and Simon hadn't even heard it. (They still haven't.) In 2021, Mat was working hard on his ambitious follow-up to *The Ruins*. This focused on a very different kind of performance – theatre in the Elizabethan era; also,

---

* At this time, the band were yet to write the final version of 'Disintegrate', the third and final version of 'Sweet Kid', with new chorus, 'Broken Music for Broken People' and 'The Sound and the Summer'. Almost half the record.

he was developing his art book *England on Fire* with Stephen Ellcock. Simon, meanwhile, was back in Thailand. Over that year or so, aside from recording drums for two *Autofiction* songs, his contribution was at gigs. The fact that Brett, Richard and Neil didn't share the ballet music suggests maybe they thought of it purely as an *experiment*? But that's not the right word, either. These weren't just fragments of sound. This was forty minutes of music, complete pieces running into each other. In 2026, Richard said calling it 'Suede 9.5' suggested this was 'an art project, rather than a follow-up album proper', though Neil points out it was conceived of as a 'ballet score'.

There are fans of the Fall in Suede. Suede's ballet idea was similar to *I Am Kurious Oranj*, their 1988 album conceived of as accompaniment to the ballet *I Am Curious, Orange*, produced by Michael Clark. That featured classical ballet, post-punk and performance art, all in one show. The Fall weren't Suede's only example, either. The Pet Shop Boys scored a contemporary ballet, *The Most Incredible Thing*, in 2011. Pink Floyd once toyed with this too, in a one-off 1972 performance in Marseille, where they collaborated with choreographer Roland Petit. (Rather than develop the idea afterwards, they got back to writing *Dark Side of the Moon*.) I was struck by just how energised Richard was about the ballet, even now. He described in detail the various ideas they had for how it might work, how the band might even wear masks to hide their faces (this too an echo of early conversations planning *The Blue Hour*). He wanted something 'that would allow them to experiment with remaining a band, but not being the entire focus of a performance'. Not all members of Suede, of course, like the spotlight.

After March 2021, the ballet score developed fast, despite Richard sometimes writing alone in Sweden; Neil and Brett in England. These pieces ranged between conventional songs with typically Suedey titles and moody instrumentals suggesting space being made for a story to play out on stage. Eventually, that would mean working with choreographers and a libretto, if they could find a theatre. And collaborators. And funding. There were a lot of ifs here. Songs would have London itself as a focus, the intention being to perform it in London, too. If, if, if.

LISTENING TO THE BALLET SCORE

When Chinese fans asked at a recent video Q&A if the ballet would be released, the answer from the band was definitive: no. As we'll see, the project is not completely disconnected from *Antidepressants*, but almost all this music will likely remain unheard. That said, as the band have often referenced 'the ballet album' in interviews, fans are curious. For that reason alone, it's worth investigating here. Neil emailed me a version of the whole score in 2024, the one he sent to Brett and Richard in June 2022. There was much more music written – though this was the first and only version in this form. Brett came up with the track listing, then Neil compiled it. I've been able to return to the ballet score repeatedly, doing so afresh once we all knew how *Antidepressants* played out. That changed it for me, too.*

The lyrical focus of the ballet score is Brett's changing relationship with London as he ages. In fact, Brett never left completely, but rather found himself a more occasional visitor, a kind of tourist, after all

* Track list June 2022: 1 'Life Is Endless, Life Is a Moment' (0:00); 2 'Under My House' (3:57); 3 'You're Not Afraid of Life' (5:36); 4 'One Last Spring' [note different to eventual title 'One Less Spring'] (11:26); 5 'Mystery Meat' (14:07); 6 'Broken Music for Broken People' (15:58); 7 'Why Do I Always Feel So Sad?' (17:21); 8 'Icy Guitars' (20:40); 9 'Shatter Life' (22:36); 10 'Young Men Gone' (25:13); 11 'Somewhere Between an Atom and a Star' (28:36); 12 'Ravens' (31:04); 13 'London Rain' (34:40); 14 'Scatter My Ash in the Long Grass' (37:30); 'end' (39.28).

this time. In songs with lyrics like 'London Rain', 'Brutal London' (not included on the initial version, but a contender Neil sent me direct) the promising, evocative 'One Less Spring'* and 'Young Men Gone' (a kind of mournful partner to bold, witty '90s Suede standout 'Young Men'),† lines about valuing the moment amid the long stretch of life dominate.

In instrumental pieces as well as whole band songs, there's plenty of space in the sound. Pieces without Brett such as 'Under My House' feature spectral, unlikely chord changes, while 'You're Not Afraid of Life' is a six-minute number starting with hypnotic guitars and little accompaniment but for a simple, second, fluttering guitar line. There are several more conventional-sounding Suede songs too, with verses, choruses – 'Ravens', 'London Rain', 'One Less Spring', also 'Broken Music for Broken People' (a different song to the later one on *Antidepressants*‡) – but across the record Brett often flits in and out, a line here, a line there. Opening track 'Life Is Endless, Life Is a Moment' is loping, slow, has tons of space and is drenched in reverb, Brett scrawling in his notebook at the time that it sounded like 'early Pink Floyd' to him. 'Great, stately post-rock from Neil,' he told me. Verse three has just eight words:

---

* The verse lyrics here are borrowed almost wholesale from Christina Rossetti's poem 'When I Am Dead, My Dearest'. As it develops, 'One Less Spring' sounds reminiscent of 'Learning to Be' from *Night Thoughts*. Repeating the phrase 'green, green grass above me' (Rossetti's lines are: 'Be the green grass above me / With showers and dewdrops wet; / And if thou wilt, remember, /And if thou wilt, forget') it's a low, slow piece of piano and sinister echoes. It unfolds gently, lyrics focusing on getting closer to death as the seasons roll around, each year: 'one less spring, one less winter'.

† 'Sit with me and count the daisies', sings Brett, 'sit with me and count the stars'. Lyrically, 'Young Men Gone' was a nod to the Pete Seeger folk classic 'Where Have All the Flowers Gone?' It might be delivered in a graveyard. 'Oh and where have all the young men gone?' asks the chorus, 'Melted like the snows in summers long', comes the answer, before an extended trumpet solo redolent of the flugelhorn solo on 'The Big Time'.

‡ This is more of a stomping, glam-sounding band song in demo form. The 'broken people' line is good, and it'll get reused. But that aside, this is the weakest thing so far.

Formless
as a cloud
Weightless
as a sound.

It's a collage of abstract images, slightly different to the length and amount of syllables you'd find in a haiku. Brett felt the title 'neatly sums up that paradox of age where life feels both fleeting and endless, when you feel both creaking and decrepit and simultaneously the same as you did as a teenager.' In a way, it's shorthand for the whole ballet score.

Several songs stand out. One is 'Why Do I Always Feel So Sad?' This opens with a memorable, spidery Neil piano figure that establishes an unsettling mood. The verse sees Brett sounding exhausted and weak, almost like a chanteur in some grand, tragic, self-pitying monologue. Suede chords revolve below the verse melody, the big chorus moving in and out of falsetto as the question repeats: 'If love is always a miracle, then why do I always feel so sad?' The 'miracle' line gets chopped up and repeated, like it's all Brett has to say. It sounds like someone who's achieved what they want to in life, then finds, as so many do, that external validation doesn't inevitably lead to internal peace. A gorgeous, fluid bass line opens out towards the end of the song. I visualise the choreography accompanying it, the encore, the bows. It manages to be both an identifiably Suede song, while also sounding appropriate for a ballet.

'Somewhere Between an Atom and a Star',* also calls back, in its first line, to the score's opening – 'Life is just a moment, and words are just a trick'. There's not quite the grandeur of future versions evident

---

* Originally this was 'Gift Tag', written by Neil and Richard on 24/1/22, Brett adding a top line three days later.

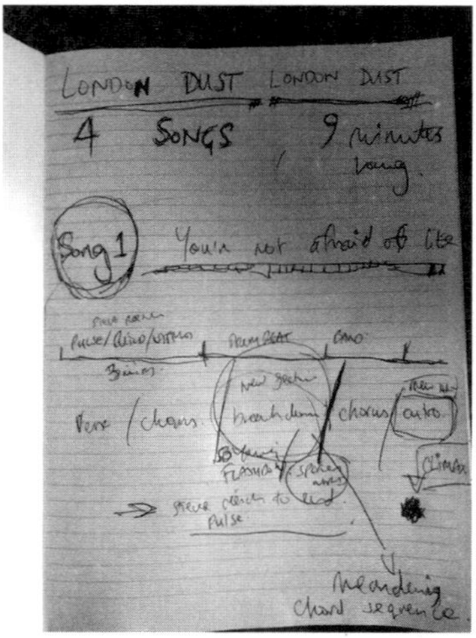

Brett's handwritten notes for the ballet score, 2021, titled 'London Dust, London Dust'.

here – sometimes you really feel Mat and Simon's absence – but there's a hint of that 'cosmic beauty' Brett wants from it, and a sense of the ballet's theme: time running out. 'I wish there was more of life than was given to us', he sings, 'Like the rain that's washed away, it's almost gone now'.* Where earlier songs lament our insignificance in the grand scheme of things, this one accepts that smallness, the final lines looking to 'find a way to float away ... between an atom and a star'.

---

* Brett lifted the title from a chapter title in a novel he'd read recently, then forgotten, Sarah Winman's *Still Life*. 'Somewhere Between an Atom and a Star – 1946–1953' is the title of the second chapter of Winman's novel. Brett also read *The Blue Hour* by Paula Hawkins, author of the 2015 bestseller *The Girl on the Train*. *The Blue Hour*, published in 2024, was a psychological horror set on a remote Scottish island. He reads books with Suedey titles. Brett says of the title of 'Somewhere Between an Atom and a Star', 'I thought it was a lovely description of the physicality of a person and a sense of one's own scale and insignificance. I love how that sense of insignificance can be strangely freeing and give you a feeling of security rather than fear, that feeling of awe and comfort you get when you stare up at the stars.'

SUEDE 9.5 AND THE BALLETBOYZ

In early 2022, there'd been talk of working with someone Brett knew from Somerset on the ballet. When that came to nothing, Quietus had a contact. In the days of socially distanced gigs – every other seat empty – Chrissie Hynde played the Royal Opera House, with a company called the BalletBoyz producing the livestream.

Though they're also producers, the BalletBoyz are a multi-award-winning (mostly) male dance company led by artistic directors Michael Nunn and Billy Trevitt.* They'd previously worked with Michael Clark, who made *I am Curious, Orange* with The Fall.† Didz approached the BalletBoyz about potentially collaborating with Suede. As Richard recalls, there was a lot going on at the time. (Aside from anything else, this was also shortly before his wedding.) Though they focused on the ballet, at one point the three albums crossed over: 'There were only a few weeks between writing the backing track for "Turn Off Your Brain and Yell" in March 2022 and "Car Screaming",' he recalls, which would one day morph into the first track on Suede X.‡ On several fronts, this felt encouraging. Richard remembers multiple 'ballet writing sessions at Neil's', with a focus on instrumentals and songs specifically about London.

Ian set up a meeting with the BalletBoyz at John Henry's, the band's post-Covid rehearsal studio, to discuss ideas with Michael and Billy. (Outside, at the courtyard picnic tables. The courteous way to do business

---

* Nunn and Trevitt met as students at the Royal Ballet School and first came to prominence as the subjects of the Channel 4 documentary *BalletBoyz*, which focused on the ordinary lives of ballet dancers, before setting up a company of their own.

† The title was taken from the Swedish films *I Am Curious (Yellow)* and *I Am Curious (Blue)* from 1967 and 1968.

‡ 'Car Screaming' was written on 23 March 2022.

at the time.) Though Mat and Simon hadn't heard the music and none was played on the day, the whole band were there, Ian and Didz too, another indicator this wasn't some ghost project, but rather something being taken seriously as a next move. Didz remembers the meeting being tentative, Simon wandering around outside smoking fags. Richard 'wouldn't normally come to a meeting about a video treatment or visual presentation' either. But of course, this was a musical project, and if it was about music, he wanted to be there.

I asked Didz how serious these discussions were. Could they really make a ballet happen? Did they have the contacts, the knowledge, the budget? 'This isn't our world,' Didz acknowledges. 'Neil has an awareness of what's hip in ballet cos it's Neil. He's a polymath and he soaks up all this stuff like a sponge. But the others don't really know that world. It was a decent medium for what they were trying to achieve musically, but I think we realised at the meeting what this would mean in practice.' This wasn't the last time the management worked with the BalletBoyz, but it was the only meeting for this project.*

Brett, Neil and Richard continued working on the score between the *Coming Up* anniversary tour, the odd festival, and Richard's wedding. But their nine-month window was up and Brett now says he was 'having second thoughts anyway'. He told Richard and Neil this, simply saying he didn't want to 'an album of ballads', and that was that. After all these months of waiting, the rest of the year was suddenly looking busy anyway. It would have taken much longer to do well – in Richard's

---

* They collaborated on the video for the Pretenders single 'I Think About You Daily' in 2023. Quietus booked Michael Clark himself to dance, as Chrissie Hynde wanted someone 'older, lithe, but rough in the face'. Michael Nunn starred eventually, Chrissie talking him out of retirement to play the part. This was the last song on *Relentless*, for which Jonny Greenwood wrote the strings.

words, 'I need to get everything just right, no matter what I'm doing, and that takes time' – which meant it could no longer squeeze into that space between 'proper' Suede releases. And they didn't want to do anything half-baked.

Shortly after Mat and Stephen Ellcock's art book *England on Fire* was published in May,* the BalletBoyz set about converting it into an elaborate theatre production. Like *I Am Curious, Orange*, this also included a band. Mat says he didn't even know about this, wasn't involved in the libretto, and only learned about it when they announced the show: four nights at the Sadler's Wells Theatre in 2023 (where the Pet Shop Boys put on *The Most Incredible Thing*). The eventual production melded the book with a novel by early Suede collaborator Derek Jarman. A very Suede reference, outside a Suede context.

Scroll forward.

RESTARTING SUEDE X

By early 2023, the emphatic reception to *Autofiction* was clear. Didz recalls how the temperature in the camp changed:

> *Autofiction* landed as well as anything since *Coming Up*. It was a unanimous win. That's seductive. So, the thinking changed. Suede had never consolidated a victory before. After a success, they'd always taken a left turn, making life more difficult for themselves. Yeah, *Autofiction* took a long time ... but it was a rock album, they knew how to do it. It was their territory.

---

* *England on Fire: A Visual Journey Through Albion's Psychic Landscape* by Stephen Ellcock and Mat Osman (Watkins Publishing, 2022).

Suddenly releasing the ballet score, or anything like it, felt risky. From his place on stage, Richard saw the reality: 'Over the course of that [period], everything changed. We realised how well the new songs were going down live, we'd recaptured an energy we'd not felt for years at gigs, the reviews were fantastic and it made everyone (Brett especially) realise we needed to follow *Autofiction* with another "band-based" album.' So: no left turn, no low-key release. Neil recalls: 'We thought we might mine some of those songs in the future – songs like "One Less Spring", for example.' But Neil's June 2022 version was set aside, for now.

When the band met up in January 2023, it was once again new year, new start. Brett told me: 'I realised Suede needed to change direction.' As I approached my last few weeks drafting this book, the band were on their 2026 UK tour, Brett emailing from the tour bus. Context is a factor here – after all, we're talking about a move they didn't make, while the one they made instead has since done well enough that Brett now wants to push that even further. That influences perceptions. But three years on, this is how he sees it:

> For me the ballet thing was very different intentionally from what became AD. It's misleading as two songs survived and made it onto the album, to be frank not because they chimed with AD but in a way because they didn't – they added a change of feel and pace I thought the album needed. The most important role for [the ballet] was not as a progenitor for AD but as a kind of antonym, a direction to avoid.

If this sounds like Brett disowning the material, that's not quite how he sees it. There are songs on here he rates; he's still keen to come back to 'Young Men Gone', for instance, when we talk this through. But after *Autofiction*, Brett says:

> [I]t slowly dawned on me that we were just trying to be too bloody clever, that Suede are a great rock band and there is nothing wrong with just embracing that and being the best version of that we can. As I get deeper into my career I'm less interested in being a Jack of all trades than I am in being a master of one – honing what I do to a cold, bleak, efficient perfection hwwwwoooooooowaaaaAAAAA-HHHHHHHHHHHHH!!!!!!!! If you want a vision of Suede's future imagine a boot stamping on an art-rock face FOREVER!*

For Brett, then, this was an intentional change of musical direction, though his notebooks from the period suggest he was including multiple ballet score songs like 'You're Not Afraid of Life' in what he calls his 'early, forlorn and hopeful album list' for Suede X several months after this realisation, so perhaps it's never that clear cut.

When I put Brett's take to Richard, he said Brett alone decided they should 'start afresh'. Richard also wrote to me mid-UK tour, putting it this way: 'At first it was going to be shelved as a project for later consideration, but more recently Brett has disregarded it completely and now thinks we were mad to pursue it. I disagree ... [at this point] the idea of recording at Neil's went out of the window, we went back to writing sessions at mine in January 2023. That's when *Antidepressants* began its life.' Richard's language here disguises some discomfort. The band may usually present as one, and even sometimes be as one. But ultimately, if Neil and Richard want to finish off the ballet score they've been working hard on for most of year, they can only do so if Brett agrees. Sometimes he'll make a decision for everyone. Even if he knows the others don't like it.

---

* The 'jackboot' is a riff on George Orwell's *1984*, repurposed for noisy 2020s rock albums. The end of this paragraph in an email from BA to RG reads: 'Well that's how I feel in January 26 and that's what we're heading towards with XI. When XI falls flat on its face I expect I'll come crawling back to art-rock's door, tail between my legs.'

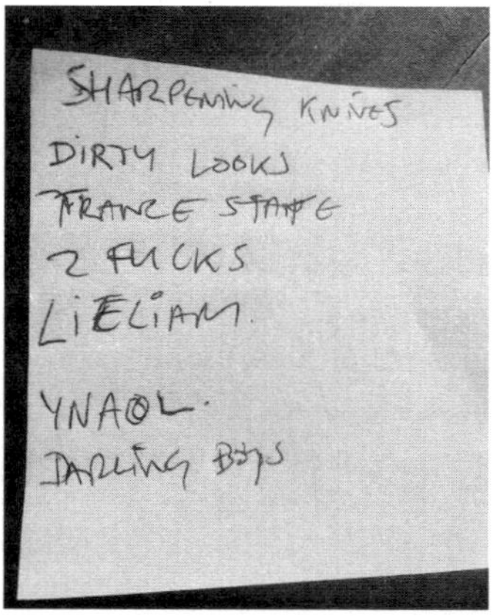

Brett's 'early, forlorn and hopeful album list' for Suede X from Spring 2023. 'YNAOL is 'You're Not Afraid of Life'. '2 Fucks' and 'Darling Boys' never made it over the next hurdle.

My discussions with Neil revealed a different story. At the time there was a ballet score in progress, then it was junked, then they did something different. Though now he looks at the making of Suede's tenth album as being part of a pattern: 'There were three sessions for *Night Thoughts*. There ended up being three sessions for *Autofiction*. And with this one, too ... It's part of the process to find a song's level – you have to do it or else you sit around waiting for twelve songs and you haven't even started.' Neil was being honest, presenting this as a normal Suede recording process – and in a sense, it is. Though also, it's not. For Neil, not getting the ballet score to a releasable state has been a source of lingering regret. Having given all of himself to *The Blue Hour* and feeling the result misunderstood or maligned, it was difficult, the next time he led a Suede project, to learn it would not have a life at all. Finding the whole ballet score project over once Brett declared it so affected Neil's sense of his place in the band. Was Suede stronger when he contributed less? When Richard was more to the fore? Was there room for him to exercise his creativity in Suede in a way that went musically beyond

Brett's 'cold, bleak, efficient perfection', that boot stamping on art-rock's face? Neil was also, of course, an essential part of *Autofiction*'s success, but with more focus finally on Richard as a songwriter post-*Autofiction*, Neil's own often ignored or unnoticed contribution left him doubting himself. In our extensive conversations about the ballet, Neil shared not just the music but the journey of this score, walking me through the whole timeline step by step when he could have flinched from doing so. This must have been frustrating; we were documenting something abandoned that he clearly wanted to see through to a conclusion. At this point, it's worth flagging that it wasn't just Neil who was disappointed here. Richard says now that he was 'fully behind Neil's vision' for the ballet score, feeling a 'sense of regret that it was never finished. Even behind the pride in *Autofiction*'s success. As he wrote to me recently, 'It's unlikely anyone will hear this, as when Brett abandons material, he abandons it.' When we discussed the ballet score, Richard pointed to how it fascinates so many who follow Suede. He says, 'It's already become a lost gem for the fans, the ultimate "what if" for people that aren't into the more brutal, primal side of Suede. The people that rate *The Blue Hour* as our best post-reunion album.'

There are plenty of those people out there, plenty more who see the evident value of Neil's contribution to Suede, not only because of his versatility, but his interest in music of nuance and depth. But despite *The Blue Hour* doing just as well as *Night Thoughts* commercially, the perception was that it was *owned* more by Neil, and that people didn't want it. (As I've tried to show, I think that's untrue. Though perceptions have a material impact on decision making.) The more Brett moves towards that primal thing, his own personal need for connection at live gigs pushing them into desiring more full-throttle music, the less chance there is, perhaps, for Neil to express himself fully.

In other words, the more Richard leads, the better things are for Suede. Certainly, the success of *Autofiction* suggested what people wanted was three-minute bangers. I thought long and hard over how to write about this, not erasing Neil's feelings or his contribution, and I'm choosing not to quote directly here, rather drawing more broadly on my sense of how he regarded it as a personal failure. I considered saying nothing, but it's important to the band's story. Neil now considers his inability to get the ballet score done a personal failure, an indictment of his contribution to Suede.

Because he couldn't make it work, they stepped away from it, Brett feeling that if they went ahead if would be seen as another mistake. There's also a broader frustration at work here: Neil and Brett moving away from each other, in terms of the music they wanted to make, and how they wanted to make it. Neil and Richard don't see themselves in competition, though. Rather, they look out for each other, pointing to the other's contributions, both hidden and seen. Anyway, it's possible for Neil to wish to do better personally without feeling envy or being jealous of Richard.

Mat, meanwhile, was finally getting something he'd been working towards for two decades: the publication of a novel of his, along with the ability to promote it properly. *The Ghost Theatre* was published by Bloomsbury in May 2023. This was rooted in an idea he had in those early days of tentative writing practice before Suede reformed. Initially, he wanted to write the Sex Pistols story 'but set it in an anachronistic timeline', with the idea that 'certain archetypal groupings of people might recur over the centuries'. So: he sketched out a novel with the story of the Pistols' rise and fall 'but having them as Elizabethan minstrels or balladeers'. Mat recalls: 'Everyone I mentioned the idea to *hated* it, so I shelved it, but when I saw Katherine Rundell's *Abducted*, about children kidnapped to appear on Elizabethan stages, I knew it was the way in.'*

In the 2000s Mat wasn't ready to realise this novel but, now more practised and able to secure a larger publisher, he could tackle the concept with confidence. Look closely at *The Ghost Theatre* and you might spot the odd throwback to the original germ – the character Nonesuch's slogan T-shirts are 'pure punk' Mat says. The names Daltry and Jagger also appear, the kids' enemies being named after the rock dinosaurs punk usurped. It feels relevant that Mat was returning to his Pistols obsession when Suede's music was about to move back in that direction too. *The Ghost Theatre* was well received internationally as a historical novel about performance, just a different kind from *The Ruins*. It was simply a much better novel and took Mat's work independent of the band to a wider audience.

THE SOUTHBANK IDEA IS BORN

In early 2023 the band began to think ahead towards what they'd do for the launch of the Suede album they'd just agreed they hadn't started yet. Mat recalls the thinking now:

> It's curious that so few bands seem to associate themselves as London bands, but that's what we are. And we had this idea of doing this takeover of an iconic London venue, where we could do a residency that allowed us to do all these different things. Yes, launching an album. But also drawing attention to Suede's sheer variety ...

* This BBC documentary, *Abducted: Elizabeth I's Child Actors* (2018, directed by Susie Attwood), hosted by children's writer and academic Katherine Rundell, explored the true history of what Mat would make the basis of his new novel: children abducted then made to perform on Elizabethan stages.

> It's incredibly rare to get two songwriters like Richard and Neil in the same band. They can do anything. They could be session musicians, they're so versatile [laughs].* You don't get many rock bands with that kind of range, and we wanted to show it.

But where could host? Somewhere not so cavernous as to be exposing, but big enough to cope with a Suede residency, across multiple nights, in central London. Well, there was somewhere only yards from where they'd shot footage for the *Autofiction* film, under the bridge by Waterloo station, the venue for the annual Meltdown festival. In 2002, Bowie had invited them to appear there the year he curated it. How satisfying it would be to return, a quarter of a century on, as if they were running a Meltdown of their own? A 'deliberately artsy flex' entirely made up of Suede shows?

With half a plan formed, in January 2023 Brett, Mat, Didz and Mike Christie had their first meeting with Mark Ball, artistic director at the Southbank Centre. As Didz recalls, 'They asked, when would we be ready? You never really know but we guessed we could work to September 2025. By this point, we'd done everything enough times [making an album] to be able to make a prediction ... If we were running behind it could be a pre-launch like *Night Thoughts* at the Roundhouse. But from the start they [the band] didn't want to wait that long.' They toured the various contrasting rooms, Mat suggesting making each show a response to each individual space. So: strings in the 950-capacity Queen Elizabeth Hall, the 'ultimate Suede gig' in the 2,700 capacity Royal Festival Hall, a 'spit and sawdust show in the round' in the 650-capacity Clore Ballroom, and even an off-mic show in the tiny 300-capacity Purcell Room, too. They

* This was very much delivered as a compliment to their musicianship, though it may not look like it to those who may consider session musicians 'below' bona fide rock stars.

also floated a show at the 'Undercroft',* the room behind the skatepark made up of ledges, pillars and stairs that's been home to skater culture since the early '70s.† BMG and DawBell were supportive, while the Southbank said they'd hold the space. What exactly for, though, shifted. Mat recalls: 'As with most Suede projects we went in grandiose then scaled back. We were keen at the beginning to use as much of the Southbank as possible. There was talk of using the Hayward Gallery for artworks, showing films at the BFI and using outside and rooftop spaces. But even finding a week where we could commandeer all the traditional music venues was hard.' Liaising with cinemas and theatres meant further delays, so the idea shrank a little. The most important thing, perhaps, was ensuring the gigs themselves showed radically different Suedes, while giving them the chance to get closer to fans. Mat again: 'The Clore and the Purcell Room both played into an ongoing Suede obsession, breaking down the barriers between audience and band.'

BLAME IT ON THE MIRTAZAPINE: 'TRANCE STATE'

The first new music of 2023 put down a marker. This was a Neil and Richard demo called 'Comachrome', which Brett turned into 'Trance State'. In demo form, it featured synth more heavily though it was missing Mat's standout bass line – which wasn't in the song yet. Lyrically this was fresh, had attitude, and it *moved.* It was confrontational, aggressive,

* There was some discussion over whether this would be instead of, or as well as, the Clore show.

† 'The Undercroft wasn't designed as a skatepark. As described on the Southbank's website, 'This patch ... was left open to the public by architects when the Queen Elizabeth Hall was built in the 1960s, but as early as 1973, the city's skateboarders adopted it as their own. It now lays claim to being the world's oldest continually used skate spot.'

direct. At first this had not one but two bass lines on the demo by Richard. Though they were deemed 'not very Suedey' sounding more like the Cure's Simon Gallup, the song overall was encouraging. The task, after all, was to capitalise on *Autofiction* without making *Autofiction 2*.

If 'Shadow Self' 'showed the way for Suede X', for Mat, 'Trance State' 'helped clarify its concerns', the line 'I'm in a trance, I'm in a trance state' repeated to the point of comedy. But the shiny surface distracts from the song's darkness. Encouraged by the reception to *Autofiction*'s unflinching self-examination, also the fact that it was cathartic to sing so directly about his life, Brett doubled down, writing what hurt, and harder. Though he rarely discussed personal vulnerabilities with the band, Brett described himself to me as being in 'the depths of despair' at the time Suede were having this renaissance, battling with recurring 'dizziness and [the effects of] medication'. To understand the song 'Trance State' and those written in its wake, you need to know a little about Brett's personal circumstances.

The initial trigger was heavy touring. Brett keeps a very strict regime on tour to manage its pressures. Running. Sleeping. Resting. Soundcheck. Gig. And go again. With as little as possible in between. He's done this since kicking drugs, and it's been critical to Suede being able to do so much, for so long. But, struggling with sleeplessness in the early 2020s, Brett started to take Valium to manage it, then became dependent. Sleeplessness was worse on tour, going to bed after ninety minutes of a high-energy Suede gig often difficult. How do you give everything, late at night, to thousands, then simply lie down and close your eyes? When Brett stopped taking Valium he got withdrawal symptoms, including dizziness and panic attacks – for which he was then prescribed antidepressants. Touring is a deeply physical business. It takes a toll not just on the voice, but the whole body, especially if you make a living from being much more of a physical performer in your fifties than when you were young. At once, he resented being suspicious of his medication, but feeling like maybe he needed it, too, though he wouldn't have needed antidepressants in the first place if he hadn't been struggling to sleep on tour. This wasn't some nebulous mental illness, some vague ennui. Writing can be a way of coping, as performing is a way of coping. So: Brett used his situation, which felt oppressive and inescapable, turning it into an asset by writing about its physical and mental effects, in a thinly disguised way.

'Trance State' was the first time Brett wrote about our modern obsession with the medicalisation of 21st-century experience. In language, in action, in thought. On one hand, he agreed to take the 'help' of medication in a time of need, having been struggling since lockdown. (He'd been drinking more, too.) But on the other, he was deeply suspicious of the value of doing so. In 'Trance State', he wanted to write about what he described to me as 'covert state oppression, hiding behind the fig leaf of safety-ism' while celebrating the trance, too. Imagine thousands of fans singing, 'I'm in a trance!' to each other. Commentary on covert state oppression, perhaps. Or a simple expression of the pleasure of a transfixing night out? In music, of course, we can have both.

Once you hear what's hiding in 'Trance State', it's hard to unhear it. Compared to the cloaked, image-laden lyrics of Suede's earliest years ('Pantomime Horse' is a good example), the contrast is stark. In verse one: 'If I'm unsociable it's fine, I'll blame it on the Mirtazapine* / hope I'm going somewhere nice'. In verse two:

* The NHS describes Mirtazapine as 'an antidepressant medicine' used 'to treat depression'. It works by 'increasing the amount of mood-enhancing chemicals called noradrenaline and serotonin in your brain.' It's only available on prescription. Common side effects include headaches, dry mouth and feeling sick. It's not a sleeping tablet, but can make some people feel sleepy.

I think you know me much better now
Since my emotional breakdown
Riding the fear instead of projecting myself back to me better
We're all trying to stay alive on this emotional baseline.

It reads like a diary. Like prose. Mirtazapine is the widely used antidepressant Brett was on at the time. In 'Trance State', medication provides temporary escape, but at what cost? This gave him the germ of an idea for how to link the songs on Suede X.

The theme stuck in Brett's mind. Only a week later he wrote 'Dirty Looks' to Richard's fast, hard demo 'Dynamo':* 'I love when you're feeling violent and whenever you're pissed it's so nice / I took my medication, it made me feel worse'. 'Dirty Looks' also explores the thrill of dancing, but in a different way, sounding furious throughout. It's full of yips and yelps and contains the unimprovable couplet: 'I'm glad I'm not your husband, I'm glad I'm not your wife / We both would be insulted, so I won't touch the merchandise'. Still, what leaps out now, looking at band diaries and Brett's notes, is how much the word 'medication' kept appearing in lyric drafts. The more it came up, the more it shaped the album.

LIVE IN 2023: THE SPIRIT OF *AUTOFICTION*

In early February Suede did a radio session for Steve Lamacq's 6 Music show, followed by a gig at Stereo in Glasgow as part of Independent Venues Week, an initiative to put big bands in small venues. Stereo is an old-school underground club. Suede played to about forty mostly middle-aged, stubbornly unmoving blokes. Still, they played like a new band

---

* Written by Richard on 24 January 2023. Became 'Dirty Looks' on 27 January.

doing their first radio session. Later that month they recorded another session for Radio 2's *Piano Room*, a very different vibe. (For 6 Music it was grimy, noisy Suede. At Radio 2, they played 'She's in Fashion', 'The Only Way I Can Love You', and covered Patti Smith's 'Because the Night', replete with the BBC Concert Orchestra.) This showed they could do both audiences, both stations, by showing different faces.* Shortly after, they wrote 'Sharpening Knives' (the titles were getting more biting, like the music), based on Richard and Neil's demo 'Noddy'.† This one sounded positively angry, the song's narrator protesting too much as they detail a list of complaints, while claiming not to 'give a toss': 'I shout your name but the more I repeat it the more I hear the sound of sharpening knives'. It went on the draft list. That list was expanding.

In March, the band embarked on a nineteen-date UK tour, with venues chosen to keep band and fans close. It wasn't exactly the MOTH Club, but then, as Richard puts it, 'We could have pushed ourselves into bigger venues, riding the wave.' Instead, they chose to stick to clubs where possible, forgoing a bigger payday (or smaller loss) to keep with the spirit of *Autofiction*. Even after a more successful album, Suede were working on a different scale from other bands of their era who were routinely playing arenas or stadiums.

On the UK tour, Suede often played seven or eight songs from the new album to a couple of thousand people at a time, ignoring most of their best-known songs, preferring to lift out different deep cuts each night. They could have had it easier. No matter how well the new material went down – and it did – there was still a significant portion of the crowd who'd always love the hits more. Just look at when those phones came

---

* Suede at Radio 2's *Piano Room* was broadcast several times, February–March 2023.

† 'Sharpening Knives', completed on 23/2/23, was demoed as 'Noddy' the day before.

out, filming the moments fans wanted to remember. But by now it was clear: Suede's choice was to lead every show with new things, dipping into a handful of old singles here and there, Brett taking the chance literally to climb into the throng, going on a long walk, taking in hugs and kisses as he went walkabout deep into the crowd during 'The Drowners'. Sticking with the same start and end, varying the rest, represented what Mat calls 'the spine' of a tour setlist.* In between, they'd sweat and sweat, and keep resisting the obvious.

Much of this was well received, even by those who had previously been sniffy about the band. (The lack of Suede drama at this point is notable. When things happen, big or small, Richard says, 'The old Suede would have thrown a strop. The new Suede carries on as if nothing's wrong.') The only gig cancelled was for a tragic reason: the London date, at Brixton Academy, was pulled after two deaths in a devastating crowd crush. This happened during a show by the Nigerian Afrobeat artist Asake in December 2022, leading the venue to close for eighteen months. It devastated not just the people at the gig, but the community of Brixton more widely.

At the Glasgow date of the tour I was in the crowd, my Suede pal with me.† It wasn't a memorable show for the band, though the crowd around me were giddy. Afterwards we chatted to Mat and Richard.

---

* Between 2023 and 2026, this might likely see 'Trash' and 'Animal Nitrate' played early in the set after a trio of new songs from the newest album, with 'So Young', 'Metal Mickey' and 'Beautiful Ones' held off till the end. The variety goes in the middle, with different songs added in places where particular albums did better (e.g. *Head Music* and *A New Morning* might get more play in Europe or China).

† This is my friend Alan Bissett, to whom this book is dedicated. Alan and I were, for many years, the only person the other knew who was at all interested in the band. As the reunion years played out, we shared enthusiasms, went to gigs together such at the Roundhouse for *Night Thoughts* and an outdoor gig in Glasgow around the time of *The Blue Hour* before the one documented here.

Poor Mat could barely stand up straight in the low-ceilinged corridor at the side of the stage; he ushered us, several friends and booky types from the local Waterstones who knew him as an author through into a modest backstage area. Here, Mat waxed lyrical to me about *Get Back*, the documentary about late-era Beatles, in which they try to work out how to carry on, together – just before they fall apart. 'There are only twelve notes,' Mat told me. 'All new music responds to old music. It's the same for us. It's the same for everyone'. Close-up. Watching. Seeing how things are made. The Beatles documentary lasts for eight hours. It's like one, extremely long close-up. 'Doesn't matter who you are,' said Mat. '*Get Back* shows how every band is shaped by its past. Especially as it scopes out its future.' That's how four Liverpudlians found themselves blown around by the January cold, on a windy rooftop in central London in 1969, surprising pedestrians below with new material. Lennon quipped, 'I hope we've passed the audition.' Then the police shut the whole thing down.

I like that story, not least because it's a cheeky nod to the need for approval – a usually relevant, often hidden, factor in the making of new music. Years into the most unlikely evolution, across from each other in rehearsal studios week after week, 1969's version of the Beatles were looking for a way to return to themselves, while also seeking fresh ground, in the hope that it might be received well. Few manage it. Anyway, what does *managing it* look like? How do you know when you've succeeded or failed? When, and how, can you be sure? I looked around the backstage area, thought about the gig Suede had just played thirty-five years into their life, and wondered. Compared to the Beatles, *everyone's* a failure, right? Then, I was prompted to rethink.

Peeling off from my own chat I noticed my friend deep in conversation with the band's guitarist. At first, it was just compliments, my friend 'highlighting how good the work they were doing was', telling Richard he'd felt a wee bit of trepidation when the reunion was announced, wondering, given *Head Music* and especially *A New Morning*, were they going to be as good as they once were? Richard told the truth: that when Brett asked him about the Albert Hall, he'd suggested giving Bernard a call. My friend isn't backwards in coming forwards. He answered, 'Not gonna lie, I'd have been up for that!'

At this, Richard's facial expression changed. He listened, nodded. Possibly he'd heard this kind of thing before. Maybe he was waiting for the usual bingo card – what a genius Bernard was, how amazing the band were in those early days. Richard was not objecting, nor was he doing anything very obvious with his face. And yet, he looked somehow disquieted. Now, I've seen my friend in a few hairy situations. He's got an infectious, warm enthusiasm, but also, I've seen him threatened with murder for complimenting an army veteran's shirt. So I recognised the tone and suspected what was coming, knowing his devotion to reunion-era Suede. But could he get to the end of his speech without Richard asking him to please, for God's sake, leave me alone if you can't be nice? Richard winced, looked at the floor. 'Mmhm,' he said. 'Mmhm.'

'However,' my friend continued, face full of delight. 'Given the last four albums, *nobody* wants Bernard Butler back in Suede now. *You're* the guitarist in Suede.' This reminds me of the blindingly obvious: the quality of the comeback era has put to bed any serious hankering Suede fans have for the Butler era. You can cherish those early years, as my friend and I do. You can love the songs and appreciate Bernard's essential contribution to what they were, and still are today. The fan groups celebrate this every day. But you don't need to imagine one man replacing the other. Anyway, you don't hear Suede fans complaining this isn't the 'real' band. I've never once overheard a single comment deriding Richard or Neil's presence. They are the band, and have been now, forever. Richard's shoulders loosened a little further. The politest man in rock then thanked my friend, with what looked from my vantage point like a small bow. Then my friend asked him what he thought of Guns N' Roses: in short, not much. The conversation fizzled out, but it was complete anyway. In the background, I noticed the Scottish-themed gifts from the fan club to the band. Irn-Bru. Tunnock's Tea Cakes. Shortbread. Along with a message, delivered in person, just one of many signs of devotion.

This, I thought, may be what success looks like. Not because it denigrates or erases the work of anyone else – you don't have to choose between Bernard's era in the band or Richard and Neil's any more today than you did in 1996 – but rather because, for Richard especially, any recognition on his own terms has been so long coming. On the *Autofiction* tour of 2023, there were plenty of people like my friend – long-time fans, then doubters, then enthusiasts, then evangelists – who could see the band's long walk, and Richard's place in it. So few musicians have this trajectory. So few grow, later in their musical life. In confidence, as well as recognition. At the end of every gig these days there are usually crowds of the hard core waiting by the stage door for photos and signatures. By this point, though, there were just a handful of us, filing out at the end of the night. One family, with a young child, who'd come from the US to see their favourite band. In talking to them, as he'd talked to my friend, Richard said something similar: 'It's okay. I'm happy to talk to you. To listen. Really.' Another mini-bow. 'It's all just part of my job.'

Neil's job was still evolving. It might have seemed from the outside like he was less prominent now, though his versatility kept serving the band, still finding those gaps, on and off stage, to fill. After the tour finished, he spent most of April going through live recordings from the last month to work on iterations of each song for a future *Autofiction* live album. With barely a word about it, Neil spent weeks going through the recordings they'd made from the sound desk on the UK tour.

IDEAS PILING UP: WRITING IN 2023

It's different every time. Every time, it's the same. You keep going and keep going. You don't feel you've got very much at all, until suddenly you think, is this an album?

By May of 2023 the ideas were piling up. There were a couple of quick breakthroughs, the demo 'Avenues of Anger' written by Richard and Neil becoming an early version of 'Sweet Kid'. This was a potential second song for Lucian, no longer a small child, but somehow, already, a ten-year-old in his last year of primary school. It had a placeholder verse and chorus.* It would take more searching, Brett looking for a lyric that took its lead from 'Life Is Golden' – sweet but not too sweet, sour but not too sour – though a couple of pieces were in place, and the idea of writing something for a new stage of Lucian's life began to percolate.

The second idea that week was 'June Rain', which started life as Richard's demo 'Pipistrelle' a day later, Brett's part added the same day. Brett recalls, '[at first] it was a fairly ordinary little mid-tempo '60s sort of number'. That's underselling it, even in this early incarnation. 'June Rain' had obvious potential, a lovely guitar part interacting with a memorable melody – but the band didn't quite know what kind of a song it was yet. The highs didn't go high enough. The lows didn't go low enough. The lyric was great, though.

---

* 'Sweet Kid' first version, 4/5/23. 'Sweet Kid' 2, with new verse, was written on 28/2/24. 'Sweet Kid' 3, with new chorus, 10/9/24.

Brett initially sang the first verse: 'I'm an alien at the opposite side of the road / And you wave to me despite the fact that I've let myself go.' When we first discussed this song, after writing but before recording it, Brett told me, 'I wasn't sure about the imagery at first. You know, the alien thing, that's Bowie ["Space Oddity", "Starman", "Loving the Alien"], and I didn't want to stray too close to that. But in the end, I figured I could get away with it once in a career [laughs].' The word 'alien' is misleading anyway. We're not in the realm of literal aliens here, but rather alien as in feeling other, outside, or abject. It's a decent sleight of hand, hiding a song about suicidal ideation in plain sight, but this is Brett facing his darkest thoughts, playing out what it might be like for his loved ones, should he 'let himself go' completely. 'God only knows it's hard to say goodbye' goes the lyric, and this mini portrait of two people who can't reach each other hits hard.

With festival season coming, Suede were now in more demand, with a slew of dates across Europe and beyond, while the (yet again) expanded thirtieth anniversary version of the debut album was repackaged, with an album playback at the Curzon in Soho on 5 July. Home and abroad, shows went on through the summer – Suede didn't seem to be invited to major UK music festivals, it was usually the regional ones – with more high-profile appearances at Flow in Helsinki, the ever-popular Smukfest in Denmark, and a one-off show in China, the Xiami Festival in Qinhuangdao. There were also a couple of late-summer festivals.

A EUROPEAN SUFFERING

The first of these was 1001 Musicas at the Auditorio del Generalife by the Alhambra, Granada. A few days before travelling there, Richard wrote a demo called 'Ne Pas de Boys' and shared it with Brett. On arrival,

Brett was struggling. He was 'feeling very unstable around this whole time', 'experiencing dizziness and panic attacks' backstage. But as he puts it now, 'You never cancel. You always find a way.' What exactly Brett's doctors would make of this approach we cannot know, though something about being forced to push through the discomfort when he instinctively wanted to retreat spurred him on. As the opening of 'Turn Off Your Brain and Yell' sounded, Richard hitting the guitar with the palm of his hand, Brett decided to chuck himself into the show, and the show gave back: 'I remember this distinct feeling,' he tells me, 'of being healed by the energy of the crowd and the feeling of connection.' Though the band knew no different – he always performed well, these days, and didn't share his feelings – Brett felt like he had come through something, being reminded once more of the joy and fear of the live gig, which both manifest at once, so fast you can barely think. You just have to stop thinking, and do it.

After the gig at Visor festival in Murcia the next night, Suede travelled home and, the communal feeling of the Alhambra still fresh in his mind, Brett picked up that 'Ne Pas de Boys' demo, starting to draft the lyrics to 'Dancing with the Europeans'. He loved the 'beautiful arpeggio riff' Richard had written – 'very much in Johnny [Marr] territory but never pastiche, still his own thing' – and out poured this response, a version of the song finished just four days after the Granada show. Immediately, they sent it to management.*

For Didz, Ian and the back office, this was déjà vu all over again. In Didz's words, 'It was like they'd seen what happened with "She Still

* This version had a further repeat of 'run like a river' several times at the song's end; a darker, more inclusive 'your ghosts are my ghosts' eventually replaced it. But that aside, the song was there.

Leads Me On" then written something on spec that could do a similar job for the next album.' Not a copy, but rather something catchy, immediate, uplifting and communal, like that song was. Something you could imagine being played on the radio (2 and 6, that is), hummed in the shower, sung in the car. That could be about anything, anyone, and another song to suit Suede X's emerging themes. The highs and lows of medication. Panic. Mortality. The need for connection. All wrapped up in a call to come together and have a bloody good time. 'It doesn't have the same personal emotional resonance as "She Still Leads Me On",' says Didz now, 'but it's much more tribal, universal. You know, that "run like a river" thing, it's the kind of language that would work at any time in the last thousand years.' He laughs at himself, but he means it, too. 'There were songs in medieval Germany that talked about the rolling of the river!'

Perhaps it's the very familiarity of that 'run like a river' line that leaves me cold – so much of what appeals to me about the lyrics in Suede's second life are their very freshness. But there's no denying the effectiveness of the line, nor the unifying aspect of the glorious chorus lyrics: 'I've got a European stain within me and a European suffering,' Brett sings, 'I want to be dancing with the Europeans.' The words 'stain' (last heard in '15 Again') and 'suffering' stand out. I'm flawed, struggling. My openness is a weakness, the songs seems to say. But here we are, embrace it, and let's go. Take this, the rolling river, Richard's guitar line and the 'Shadow Self'-style dancing reappropriated for Suede X, and you've got this song that is, in Didz's words, 'at once Suede-typical [outsiders, coming together to find joy far from home], and new for them, too. Not a retread of anything, really.'

Writing continued towards the end of the year. As ever, there were many more songs in contention than most remember now. (The band diaries flag, for instance, the writing of a song called 'Mental Life' I've never seen or heard of anywhere else.)* The mountain was as big as ever; it just went unmentioned. Most things went unmentioned, these days. It's not that tensions didn't exist between everyone. They did. Nor that this was soulless plodding on as if in some tiresome office job – more that they were just so *used* to the band dynamics now, everyone knew each other's personalities, foibles, needs and habits so well, and they'd largely found a way to manage these without derailing the band. They had, by now, such long experience of each other that almost any challenge that came up, well, they'd seen a version of it before, and had a sense of how to minimise it. (I'm not saying this is always healthy. There's still a great deal of avoidance that goes on. But still.) In three whole years of hanging around I've heard critique, sharp jokes, a dig here or there, occasional catty or mean-spirited remarks – but never once heard a raised voice or truly vicious put-down. The band accept mistakes will be made and laugh at themselves, but also take the work seriously. No one freaks out or pulls rank in some pointless, destructive way. Mutual respect is real. Richard might ask on the tour bus if they could drop 'So Young' tonight – before Brett says, 'Sorry, it does a job.' Instead, they'll drop another old song, replacing it with something newer. Then everyone carries on, just fine.

RETURN TO BRIXTON

The tour of late 2023 started out as simply a replacement for the Brixton Academy gig from March, with three nights at the smaller Electric

* Music written 25 October, Brett's part written 29 November 2023. Richard: '"Mental Life" had an amazing chorus but we couldn't decide on the best verse for it. Neil and I both had a go separately.'

Brixton round the corner making for a whole weekend in London, the band able to stretch out across three different performances, some international fans travelling for all three nights. But on home turf, getting the production team up and running for three gigs – crew, travel, sound and lighting, catering, the whole shebang – is expensive, and there was more demand for dates. So the tour expanded, making for a roundabout trip through England – Eastbourne, Wolverhampton, a great reception on a Monday night in Portsmouth. Aspects of this were standard, but several moments suggested something had changed. On arrival at the Engine Shed in Lincoln (the city of Neil's first ever paid gig, pre-Suede – £30 cash in an envelope, since you ask) I found people in the queue *ten hours early*. As Neil said to me over dinner, looking utterly bewildered, 'There are bands ten times bigger than us who don't have fans as dedicated as ours.'

Old and new fans mingled more than ever, people took photos and looked out for each other in the winter cold. They took toilet breaks, holding the place for others in the queue. Some were doing the whole tour. Some did the whole of *every* tour now, entire social lives being made up of these trips with others they'd found through love of Suede. Others were local and wanted to make the most of their one night off. Several fans were dispatched to get supplies or locally themed gifts for the band. (On that date, the Insatiable Ones delivered Neil a present of a huge cake for his fiftieth birthday, replete with cake topper in the shape of a stack of books, the word 'ULYSSES' painted across the centre.) I was there to work, but working is talking. Why were they here so early, I asked people? A nice woman from Switzerland with a handbag illustrated with a photo of her cat didn't exactly answer my question, but she did explain very politely that *all* her cats were named after Suede songs. Specifically, post-reunion songs. This one, she showed me proudly, was called 'Flytipping'.

So: thirty years since their debut, Suede were back in clubs in out-of-the-way places, tightly packed in and playing to adoring crowds, with confidence. Only now, they had nine albums to draw on. These ranged wide and weird. *Autofiction* songs dominated heavily, though they were as likely to pull out some random B-side from the late '90s, delivered on piano and vocal. (Neil was often told in the morning what they'd be doing as a duo that night, then spend the day rehearsing a song he might not have played in years.) Once again, Neil was willing to play these piano versions of usually early Bernard material ('The Asphalt World', 'The 2 of Us', 'The Big Time'), while Richard took a break. In all the gigs I saw on this tour, Brett said a version of the same thing every night: 'Everyone knows *Autofiction* is Suede's best album. Everyone agrees.' Some nights he delivered this either side of 'Shadow Self' or 'That Boy on the Stage'. Some nights he delivered it from the front of the stage, brandishing an acoustic guitar. As the tour went on, he added an extra line, at first delivered like a half-meant aside: 'I've got the graphs to prove it and everything.'

At these moments, you sometimes got a wry smile from Richard or Neil, looking down at their instruments. It reminds me of that line I've heard so many times: 'Brett has to sell it to everyone else. He has to sell it to himself.' At the start, this graphs thing was made half in jest; maybe he was a little unsure of the response. But by the tour's end, he was declaring this boldly – 'I've got the graphs to prove it and everything!' – knowing he'd get a roar. Across the Brixton shows, many of the Suede extended family attended, Brett dedicating a song to Jodie on the Saturday when she was present. Many of the people quoted in this book were there. Fans. Friends. Inner circle. After every show there were group photos taken at the barrier of literally hundreds of fans, so many of whom seemed to know each other from on- and offline. Many said they'd come on their own, or travelled alone from their home country, but knew they'd find friends in the venue. I spoke to people who said they were at their twentieth, fortieth or seventieth Suede gig.

The Electric Brixton was even smaller than the usual clubs Suede were playing for *Autofiction*. Brett found the venue frustrating, and he wasn't alone in thinking it a downbeat way to finish a rare year. But none of the band gave away a thing. Big festivals are different; plenty of people only want to hear old music. But as I chatted to people in the Mild Ones fan group, also to those who'd travelled across the world – from Singapore, Hungary, Argentina, Australia, South Korea – it all felt very celebratory. To make music for that long and know you can lead with your newest songs without draining the atmosphere in the room. To mix up the set each night, drawing out songs you've not played for years, only playing them because you choose to. It could be much worse.

As usual, most press responses were positive, though one hit a nerve. The *Observer's* Kitty Empire, one of the UK's most esteemed and experienced music critics, reviewed Brixton's first night, publishing the following day. This meant that, unusually, the band read a review of their previous night at one venue, before doing two more in the same place. Empire's highly perceptive review was a reminder the band aren't indifferent to outside critiques, even when full of praise.

The article, titled 'No Mere Nostalgia Act', did two uncommon things at once. First, it pinpointed the singularity of Suede's long-earned 'victory'. Second, it noted the success of the Codling–Oakes line-up. There's also a very fair overview of the comeback albums, asserting that *Autofiction* has become 'the cherry on the cake that Suede were both having and eating.' You couldn't hope for better. In a sense, any gig is what it is to the night's highest-profile reviewer, as it's read by so many more people than are in the venue. This one gave eight full paragraphs of praise before qualifying.

The review bothered the camp because it quietly suggested all this wasn't enough. It wasn't enough to be a great live band, *and* make an excellent record thirty years after their first, *and* reconnect with fans, *and* have people singing along to the new stuff, while meaningfully changing your sound over time. On top of this, Empire yearned for more 'sonic variety ... more space between the instruments, some bpm variation.' Deep down, some of the band *did* want more sonic variety. After all, hadn't they just spent nine and a half months working on an actual ballet? Though Empire wanted more risk, the review ended on another positive: 'It would be ridiculous to deny Suede, beloved standard-bearers for anti-machoism in the face of Britpop laddishness, their continuing success.'

EARLY 2024: NEW FRUIT, IN AND OUT OF THE BAND

Early in 2024 Suede reconvened in good spirits, with several members of the band busy between writing and demoing. Neil accepted an invitation from the Space in Brighton to discuss his life in Suede with host Wayne Imms. This was so rare that the fan groups made a pilgrimage of it, squeezing a hundred fans into a tiny underground room.* Neil was relaxed and open, cracking jokes over an unusually long interview at which he took questions for hours. When asked for his favourite Suede song, he picked one from before his time. Asked about the past, he was gracious, but when asked about how the band make imagined things, he gave more. 'A lot of bands stop because it's difficult to recreate that first flush of youth,' he told Imms, 'to make your tenth album as interesting as your second – but the fact that we want to keep trying to make music,

* This evening was even the beginning of a future Suede-related marriage. There are more of these than readers might imagine.

I think that's what drives us. We're just really obsessed and I don't think we want to do anything else.'

Mostly, January and February were dedicated to writing. 'Anti-depressants', and 'Medication' came quickly. For anyone glancing across the band planners at this time, which include song titles for works in progress (e.g. '"Medication" written today') the lyrical focus of the album was increasingly obvious, though Richard points out there's no plan as such here, 'we just work on the songs that need the most work'.*

There were extracurricular activities going on too. Richard contributed to the next Alison Moyet album *Key*, with Artmagic collaborator Sean now Moyet's musical director and producer. Richard played guitar on six tracks, one of these, 'Such Small Ale' with Sean on bass, a Moyet–McGhee–Oakes co-write. (*Key* went top ten when it came out, and 'Such Small Ale' was a Radio 2-playlisted single.†) At forty-eight years young, this was a first writing credit for Richard on someone else's record, a further sign of growing confidence, another step forward after he played guitar on five songs for Emma Anderson's solo debut, *Pearlies*, released in October 2023.‡ Also, in February 'The Killing Moon' was released from the forthcoming *Death Songbook* record with Charles's Paraorchestra,

* Other songs that didn't survive long, but whose titles stand out, include 'Drunk', earlier title 'Your Body Is a Battleground' – a reference to Barbara Kruger's iconic feminist artwork about the politicisation of women's bodies – and 'Strangehold'. Around this time, Richard penned 'Call It', soon to become a new 'Broken Music for Broken People'. A couple of days later, 'Grit Bank' became 'Medication', while later that month 'Fade to Black' was demoed, with 'Sweet Kid' #2 rewritten at the end of February.

† A version of *Key* contains conversations between each song, with Alison Moyet and Sean McGhee discussing Sean and Richard's contributions on 'Such Small Ale' and more.

‡ Emma Anderson was in the '90s dream pop band Lush, whose *Sweetness and Light* EP, way back in 1990, had a pre-Suede Ed Buller on engineering duties. The ever-connected drummer Justin Welch, once of Suede and Elastica, played drums in the re-formed Lush in 2015–16.

the album proper coming that April. Early in 2024, Mat was busy doing events for *The Ghost Theatre*, with the paperback released in March, including a bonus essay, 'The Blackfriars Boys'. In April, he'd even do a *Ghost Theatre* tour of Elizabethan London for fans, taking in parts of the city featured in the novel.

Several members of the band, then, now had creative outlets outside Suede. For Richard, his partnership with Sean was bearing new fruit. For Mat, writing was now effectively his full-time job. Each member of the band was finding ways to balance their ongoing lives in Suede with a life outside it, finessing their own role. 'These days, they're an efficient machine,' says Didz. This didn't mean they'd suddenly found a way to communicate effectively; Richard insists 'it's still impossible for us to communicate with each other'. But they'd at least found an effective way to manage that inability.

ED AGAIN: EIGHTH TIME AROUND

This time, there was little anguishing over production duties; with Ed back in London full-time, the decision was simpler. There are always debates, but this time they were shorter. Soon, they'd all be driving each other mad again.

By March 2024, a schedule was emerging for the rest of the year. Several weeks of pre-production in April, recording in May, then off once more on tour with the Manics, followed by the summer circuit. Around this time the band and Ed discussed returning to including fans in recording. One idea was to book a fan club gig in May at London's ICA – the venue that hosted the five-night Suede residency in 2003 – using the recording as part of the album to come. Another was to record live in the studio but invite fans in. Some feared the studio approach would be necessarily stand-offish – not like a gig at all. Too sensible. Too reserved. Others thought it too hard to control. Also, how would the actual recording work? Would they use those live recordings, warts and all, with the sound of a crowd, or feed them into the standard studio set-up, ending up with some kind of hybrid? They might have been looking for an *Autofiction*-esque gimmick, but none of these options was quite right. So, after initial meetings and dates were pencilled in at the ICA, then scrubbed out, the moment passed.

SUEDE IN CHINA

At the end of this month Suede travelled to China for the TikTok Star Nation festival on 31 March, in Wenzhou. Their curious, ballooning reputation there gave the band a boost. In this part of the world, word of mouth was doing the work, especially among young people, who Mat notes have a very particular relationship with the band: 'The way Chinese fans simultaneously see us as pretty, anime androgynes and haggard old fifty-somethings,' he says, 'is utterly modern and unique to bands like ours, I think.' Why was this happening? Didz notes the Chinese market is changing as it matures, but points to Suede being the third Western act to spend time in China, after Wham! and Elton John. (There were many more after, of course, though the regime was much stricter when it came to permissions.) He says, 'Unless you're Olivia Rodrigo or Ariana Grande, or were there early, it's tricky for Western acts to break through.' There are also practical barriers, and limits on what you can play. 'You have to supply authorities a list of songs you'll play and lyrics,' says Didz. 'It's never the ones you think. "Animal Nitrate" and "My Insatiable One" are fine, while "Saturday Night" and "By the Sea" aren't, for some reason.' Clearly, the timing of Chinese fans' first exposure to Suede's music was a factor, but it wasn't the only one, with that popularity still growing – especially among younger fans – in just the past few years. The mixture of emotions regularly found in their late-'90s/early 2000s lighter music resonates with aspects of Chinese culture. This means that, having made a dent at an important time, they've been well placed to benefit since. And the more they return, the more it grows.

In April, Simon flew in and Suede began sixteen days of pre-production at John Henry's studios in London, with Ed in the room, to rehearse, hone, teasing out which songs were on the A list. Each day Brett, Mat and Richard all cycled in, band and producer facing each other, stress-testing the songs between Simon's fag breaks. By now, Ed was giving his view more: that's partly what he was there for. Where there were gaps, where there were issues. Where songs were too similar, or not good enough. This made for plenty of back and forth between Ed and Brett. In a session, they might try each song a few times, working on some particular aspect. Mat kept his notes nearby, on the floor, sitting close to Simon. Richard and Neil were on opposite sides of the space, instruments at their backs. Brett faced inwards, Ed at his side. During the John Henry's sessions, which Neil recorded then compiled after, fifteen songs were rehearsed. In between sessions, the band and Ed sat outside on benches in the spring sun speculating about what was sounding good, and how many slower songs they needed. The A list was always changing. In part, because pre-production showed up the weaknesses of some songs, but also because newer material was always coming. It's not like they were working with a static list. Like the writing period was over. The writing period is never over.

This was when Ed began to think more about how best to develop 'June Rain'. In rehearsal he focused more on the lyrics, being able to hear them very clearly in the room, 'and I thought that opening line deserved something a lot less angry and insistent than they currently had.' The harmony and the melody of the song were good; he just felt it began with far too much aggression. This kind of conversation can be hard, not least because the point of rehearsal is to make the songs work ahead of recording them, though Ed felt this song 'required pretty much the opposite treatment ... it needed to be created in the studio.' This meant building the song carefully, relying on overdubs. In Ed's words, 'careful application of textures and parts to sculpt and shape the track.' He was surprised to find there wasn't much resistance: 'Brett was very keen to have a look at it and was able to sing or speak the first verse an octave lower, then the first chorus. There seemed to be an obvious point at which you could go up the octave and pick up the drama of the song enormously.'

After pre-production, Ed and most of the band decamped to ICP in Belgium to start recording, Brett joining after playing with the Paraorchestra in April. When these dates came round Brett had been frustrated at the timing, keen to get on with Suede recording, but in fact the shows were joyous, well received, their dynamics different from Suede shows. They had the air of an improvised, laid-back good time, despite the theme of mortality, as seen when Charles tried to get the crowd to sing nine notes, and it all fell spectacularly apart. 'I've been trying to get people to sing "la la la" for thirty years!' Brett laughed in response. At ICP, much of the discussion with Ed centred on how to avoid making *Autofiction 2*. Partly this was about song selection. Partly it was about sound. But to have the sound, you need to have the songs.

LOVE LIKE A WEAPON: BRETT, BACON AND 'DISINTEGRATE'

If the album needed one more lead song, maybe 'Disintegrate' was it. Certain songs can appear anytime. Others can only be written at the end of a cycle, when the territory of an album is already set, intentions clear. With a clipped, urgent, four-on-the-snare beat and fuzzy bass line, the post-punky 'Disintegrate' brought together Suede X musically and lyrically.

Artist Francis Bacon's work is a growing influence on Brett. Bacon's take on art's relationship with death is useful here. Bacon talked often about the violence of life being undeniable, it being something that's often turned away from, but must be faced if we are to be true to ourselves. Birth being a violent act. Sex being a violent act. Death, too. For Bacon, this was ordinary: 'I never go through a day without thinking sometime about death,' he said. 'It just comes into everything that you do. Into everything that you see. Into every meal you eat. It's just part of nature.' In the documentary, *Francis Bacon and the Brutality of Fact*, Bacon said of his own work, 'I may bring in very strongly this quality of mortality. Because the more violently, more strongly you feel about life, the more strongly you must be aware of death.'

Bacon's influence on Brett is evident elsewhere, but no more so than on the themes of *Antidepressants*, so many of which seek to face mortality head on. Soon Brett would literally remake a photo of Bacon, itself a response to one of his own paintings, with himself in the artist's place, reproducing it as a set backdrop. It doesn't matter that one's a visual artist, the other a musician. Consider them both makers of the imagination who are interested in the violence of life and death, and the commonality becomes clear.

Brett's experience of ageing wasn't the only inspiration for 'Disintegrate'. In Somerset, he lives within walking distance of Mells churchyard, where he regularly visits the grave of Siegfried Sassoon, the anti-war First World War poet and soldier also known as 'Mad Jack' owing to his bravery. It might seem a surprising reference but in fact

Brett makes regular visits to the Imperial War Museum when in London, especially in school holidays with Lucian. He knows the place by heart. Of the 'Disintegrate' lyrics, Brett told me 'The poppies imagery was a conscious reference to the War Poets, people like John McCrae [the Canadian physician and soldier-poet]. I love "In Flanders Fields" [McCrae's famous poem that imagines "We are the Dead"*] and the one by Rupert Brook about the "corner of the foreign field that is forever England" ["The Soldier"].' Brett admires the likes of Sassoon, McCrae and Wilfred Owen because, as he puts it, 'somehow their poems are never schmaltzy but stirring and heartfelt and full of a kind of noble pain that our pampered, cynical generation will never be able to achieve.'

These poets engage fearlessly with the spectre of death, and so does Bacon – every work of his is loaded with it. It's that spectre, in its different forms, that Brett's chasing as he walks the rooms of the Imperial War Museum, peering at portraits, imagining what it must have been like to stand tall, knowing the end has no meaning and your end will make no difference to war's outcome. It's through facing death, according to Bacon, that you get to the true joy of existence. Many observers notice the new Brett, on stage, seems to be determined to enjoy himself no matter what. It's less commented upon, perhaps, that this joy of the moment is charged very much by mortality. Brett and I discussed his on-stage persona making its way more into his writing:

> Usually the persona is something that only comes out of its box the moment you step on stage (mask as protection etc). But when writing AD I locked myself away with my headphones in the remote north wing of my house and just let rip ... it's a process very far from

* From 'In Flanders Fields': 'We are the Dead. Short days ago / We lived, felt dawn, saw sunset glow, / Loved, and were loved, and now we lie / In Flanders Fields.'

the 'man sitting soberly at a piano' vision that most people have. I shout and scream until I find 'the note', that sweet spot between music and noise that contains both melody and tension. It's both musical and deeply unmusical. Kind of like me, I suppose.

SUMMER MANICS TOUR 2024: STAY BEAUTIFUL, BEAUTIFUL ONES

'We're confident,' says Didz, 'that when people see Suede live, they're impressed. No matter who they've come to see. No matter the venue.' It makes sense, then, that Suede would commit to another big tour with the Manics, again jointly headlining, across the UK in summer 2024. As Mat notes, 'the Manics still play arenas on their own – we don't'. In other words, this partnership allowed Suede to play venues, especially in the UK, above their usual level. T-shirts and merch labelled 'Stay Beautiful Beautiful Ones', in reference to the Manics' 'Stay Beautiful' and Suede's 'Beautiful Ones', gave a sense that this was a more backward-looking tour, though it also reinforced the sense that Suede and Manics fans were, or could be, one and the same.

This time around, it was a different test. No more dirty little clubs of one or two thousand people, no more darkness. This was 'the most night-time band ever' (Didz' wording) playing in the height of summer, outside. Like at, say, a festival, there'd be thousands of people at the back. It's one thing trying to force a reaction when everyone's up close and you're the only focus. It's quite another when you're in broad daylight, the stage is high, security stands between you and the front row, and a portion of the far-away crowd might only be half listening for songs they know, texting pals, ordering food or waiting for the other act. On this tour, Suede were playing *literal castles* – in Cardiff and Edinburgh. They'd also be doing more gigs in Wales, where the Manics were royalty. Suede needed to strike a different balance between older and newer material for those big stages, making every movement larger, like in theatre, as opposed to the close-ups of TV. Richard enjoys the bigger scale, but at this point in the band's evolution he often felt like the one pushing hardest for less-expected material and more breadth from their mushrooming back catalogue:

> Brett has a very particular idea of how the shape of a setlist should be, how the energy flow in the room should be managed. This will be something we always disagree on. I see songs as songs [not tools], and believe if a song is good enough to make an album then it should be played live as a statement, to show our pride in it, whether or not it 'goes off'.

For Brett, his belief in reusing certain 'tools' is partly a way to avoid playing other songs he doesn't want to touch, but also, to buy himself space to do a couple of things each night that show Suede have forward momentum. This, more than anything, is important to everyone.

The best way to do that is to play unreleased music, though it's a risk, especially in big venues – the very definition of not knowing if something will 'go off'. Suede were now well used to trailing songs from future albums live, though which one to do, here and now? At the Isle of Wight Festival on 22 June, where they headlined the second stage, they planned to play a new song for the first time. Backstage beforehand, talking to Absolute Radio, Brett sometimes evaded questions, and sometimes talked about how his lyrics had been poetic and veiled in the past. All standard fare. But he also road-tested language for the next album campaign. In this interview he used 'raw', 'unhinged', 'honest', 'direct', 'noisy', 'strange', 'desperate' and 'neurotic'. Words that would soon become a kind of script. Then he slipped into saying something revealing: 'There's no poetry on it [the next record's lyrics]. It's just ... saying the way I feel about things.'

Perhaps the song that most nakedly displayed this approach was 'Antidepressants', debuted at the Isle of Wight. Pleasantly surprised by the reaction, they kept it in the setlist, through places like the Eden Project in Cornwall, Llangollen, Dublin and Edinburgh Castle. The tour also saw two consecutive nights at Cardiff Castle, a stunning backdrop where Suede went on first. Didz remembers seeing the song performed live there:

> We'd heard a demo of 'Antidepressants' and it was good, but when they started playing it, it was much better. When new songs are played live it puts them in a new light. It exposes them. If they're good, they'll emerge – and if they're bad, they'll shrivel. This was a really successful version of that. Maybe because it's so simple. And Brett's *Sprechgesang*, the words are so clear. It being so clear what he was singing and what the song was about, being struck by the lyrics for the first time [in Cardiff] – we knew it was going to be quite easy to convey to people.

'Antidepressants', a post-punk thrash with an insistent, fuzzy bass line reminiscent of Siouxsie and the Banshees' 'Halloween', had a huge chorus. When I asked why he chose this song for this tour Brett initially gave a throwaway answer, which he can do sometimes: 'It's just easy to get and people can clap along. With a new song, that helps.' Sure, if you can get a big crowd clapping, they might forgive you for playing a song literally no one knows, but that likely wasn't the only reason. In a context where Brett hadn't discussed being on medication, this gave him permission literally to declare 'I'm on antidepressants' in full voice, repeatedly, without having to answer questions (a performance is not an interview), delivering the line, 'Singing a song while I'm happy' while inviting crowds to do the same. This is very on the nose: I'm a mess, the song tells us, I don't know why I'm on these things, I don't like living in a world where human experience is so medicalised. But also: it's working, here we are together, and come on. The act of singing itself is Brett's way of accessing freedom in the moment, no matter what. Here it was, hiding in plain sight. When Brett stood on the monitors and yelled down at the crowd the first night in Cardiff, he often pointed hard as he did so, as if trying to insist people understood.

Before the second night, instead of taking part in the whole of soundcheck as usual, Richard went for a walk for a while, leaving the rest of the band to play without him. 'Sometimes I just need to get out for a bit,' he says now. This gave him a chance, for once, to hear how the band sounded from a distance, outside, the sound washing way beyond the venue. 'I remember hearing them playing "Antidepressants" and got chills,' Richard says now. 'I just thought it sounded huge. I got to be a fan, listening in, thinking wow, what's that sound?' Whole chunks of tours can quickly be forgotten by performers, so many memories lost in the fog. But this moment stayed with Richard, long after his wander in Cardiff.

On most nights of the tour, as if chattering to himself, between songs, Brett modified his previous claim, now saying both *Autofiction* and *Dog Man Star* were 'the best two Suede records we've ever made'. Once he gets a phrase in his head, he'll repeat it across multiple tours. As if trying to win people over not just to the band, but to the version of the band he prefers. It's kind of relentless, kind of irresistible. Sometimes, I find myself shaking my head at this stuff or wincing, wondering what Richard or Neil make of him saying 'we' made *Dog Man Star* thirty years ago. But it's part of an obsessive approach to performance that works, an essential part of why, on this summer tour, the reception was so good.

THE FERAL ONES: BRETT'S ON-STAGE PERSONA

Anyone coming to see Suede for the first time in years might have been surprised by Brett's on-stage persona. Long gone were the foppish affectations, also the expectation that everyone should simply turn up and accept Suede's evident greatness. Rather, these days Brett is driven by the chance to earn admiration, one show at a time. By summer 2024 he was mixing a more aggressive mid-song delivery with humility between songs.

In Suede's early days the influence of the Sex Pistols may not always have been obvious, but now there was no denying it. Brett's more mobile now than Lydon ever was, even in his youth – crawling, falling, getting up, jumping down, battering his palms on the stage floor – but the way he attacks every line is so evocative of Lydon or Mark E. Smith these days, it's spooky. His increasing use of *Sprechgesang* is a sign of that influence too. No word falls out of the mouth unplanned. Everything's considered, then spat out, with as much venom as possible, in a specific, intentional rhythm.

Lydon is one of only a small handful of performers Brett admits to being influenced by. He's more appreciative of younger bands these days, and his influences are so widely documented and obvious as to be yawn-inducing (Bowie, the Smiths), but he's surprisingly dismissive of other *performers*. When I pressed him, Brett admitted this 'probably sounds arrogant', but I've only ever been able to get three names out of him as touchstones for his own style. One is Lydon. Another is Siouxsie. 'Even Bowie was a bit am-dram for me,' he says, 'and someone like Jagger is a bit too choreographed.' (But aren't Suede choreographed? Right down to specific moves in specific songs, at specific moments?) Still, one thing makes sense to me, something I saw in action throughout the 2024 tour, where Brett might reasonably have delivered these gigs in third gear, but never did. 'I like performers with a bit of madness in their eyes, the feral ones, the lunatics,' Brett tells me, though he has to go back over twenty years to come up with an example of being genuinely moved by someone live – the Yeah Yeah Yeahs at the Southbank, in 2002, the year Suede featured on Bowie's bill:

> I was blown away by Karen O ... Most [artists] seem to misunderstand the point that in the live arena one's music needs to be performed rather than just delivered, that there needs to be a new dimension breathed into it. She was one of the few people that I thought really got that and one of the few I thought had anything to teach me.

Considering these three together – Lydon, Siouxsie, Karen O – there's a connection evident in Brett's performances. All three can appear wild-eyed, confrontational. Karen O especially gives a sense of being lost in performance, a hypnotised stage persona, as if she's on the verge of losing control. Lydon and Siouxsie were in their prime long before Brett was old enough to go to gigs, so she's the only one he's seen in person like this, impressing him, while he's in the crowd. Learning.

At the Leeds date of the Manics tour Claire Biddles was in the crowd. As a fan of both bands – 'this was basically the tour of my dreams' she says – I wondered what she saw, in terms of performance. Reviews so far were glowing, though often comparing the Manics unfavourably to Suede. She answered:

> They [the Manics] were great that night [in Leeds] – but Suede absolutely blew them out of the water. I think Suede's energy was so

> high the Manics couldn't reach it. Their stage presence felt more low-key and their moves more practised. On the other hand, Brett was freewheeling, whipping his mic all over the stage. The stakes felt high throughout the set, but there was also that trademark Suede loucheness, in all the members, not just Brett. I got the same feeling as I did first listening to *Autofiction*: the feeling of something so vital, so visceral – which is rare, and I couldn't expect the Manics to match that.*

Claire wasn't alone. Some of the press verged on the embarrassing: 'the most visceral live act on the planet today' (*Evening Standard*); 'provocative and potent' (the *Guardian*); 'Their music is ever forceful, and their live show spectacular' (*i Paper*); 'Manic Street Preachers played a fine show, but Suede are operating on a different level' (*Mojo*); 'Every corner of their music is inherently magnificent' (*Uncut*).

Over ten gigs, the band played 'Antidepressants' ten times. By the time they got to Alexandra Palace, the biggest gig of the tour, where Suede were on second, their confidence made 'Antidepressants' seem like an old song, the chorus emblematic of where they were headed next. It also contributed, along with the heavy representation of *Autofiction* and sprinkled one-off appearances of different songs each night, to an overall sense that Suede were looking forward, whereas the Manics played near-identical sets, featuring only a few songs written in the 21st-century. Ally Pally was a very different kind of triumph from, say, the Electric

---

* I've chosen to focus on comparisons between the two bands here, as Claire's well placed to comment, though she was equally effusive when it came to describing aspects of Suede's individual band members' performance styles. Claire, on Neil, Leeds 2024: 'For "Trash", he had his legs crossed, one hand on the keys, the other arm draped over his knee, looking out into the crowd with a kind of glazed, alluring stillness. In the same way that Brett is astonishing in all his exuberant physicality, Neil is equally astonishing in his elegant movements and vampiric grace. Two perfect poles of glamour.'

Brixton, or the MOTH Club. Suede's audience is big in London and, as Richard says, 'it's about as close to a home gig as is possible for Suede'. It drew more heavily on *Dog Man Star* and featured more singles: 'New Generation', 'We Are the Pigs', 'Saturday Night', 'Filmstar'. Though the crowd and backstage party were full of the excitement of an unusually good show, the band themselves were the same as always. If anything, on reflection, Brett considered Ally Pally 'a bit too easy now'.

FINISHING SUEDE X: 'A TRIED AND TRUSTED PROCESS'

There wasn't much writing time in September, but there was progress. First, a brand-new song with the title 'Broken Music for Broken People', which Brett wrote in the first week of the month.* Brett now says this was the latest demo he 'kind of became obsessed with'. He describes the first few rehearsal run-throughs as 'thrilling'. 'For a while, I thought it was an anthem to rival "Trash", a song both about the band itself and its connection with the fans.' That is, a version of what the band had produced before, but more explicit. It may have seemed like familiar Suede ground, but this time Brett considered the 'broken' to be everyone, in a 'the-weak-shall-inherit-the-earth song of defiance'. Brett remained shy of making grand claims for 'society', but was also more willing to point to the problems of our times. Fracturedness. Dislocation. Disconnection. The medicalisation of everything. The all-consuming spread of alienating tech. Dependence on our phones. The kind of thing everyone might experience in their little digital bubble, not just gothy Suede fans in the mosh pit. Preoccupied by the changing nature of modern life, very much

* Another song, 'Best Years', was written the day after. Though it's mentioned on the planners, it doesn't seem to have been a contender for long.

influenced by Orwell's *1984* and its common ground with the world of that novel, Brett adapted 'hope lies in the proles' to 'hope lies in the broken'* who will, as the lyric goes, 'save the world'. That line, 'It's broken music and it's broken people who will save the world' made Didz wince – 'simply too direct' – while it also makes me baulk in a way I've rarely felt in the band's second era. It's hardly 'she live in a house, she stupid as a mouse' but it's too distracting for me to lose myself in the song. That said, I can see why the big, anthemic chorus and the theme – at once traditional Suede, also very of the now – felt like a breakthrough.

Energised by 'Broken Music for Broken People', Brett finished 'Sweet Kid', a third version with a new chorus finally getting the balance right. The struggle, as usual with lyrics about family, had been how to avoid ruining any emotional impact with too much soft focus. The answer, as usual, was darkness. '[The final version] is inspired by one of the core themes in Cormac McCarthy's *The Road*,' says Brett now. 'That fear every parent has of not being there to see your kid grow up. I was ruminating on the parent's paradox – preparing your child for a life without you. The Man has to prepare the Boy for his inevitable death in that book and it's such a bleak but powerful way to describe parenthood.' The sound of 'Sweet Kid' matches the title. The chorus, 'Sweet kid, this life belongs to you', does stray close to saccharine, though the verses tell a different story, the influence of *The Road* evident: 'If my body belongs to the worms, oh well, my blood still belongs in your veins'. To me, this sounds as much about Brett as Lucian, though Brett routinely labels it his second explicit Lucian song. Here, once more, is mortality, the approaching grave in all its coldness. The best the song's narrator can hope for in the face of

* 'Hope lies in the broken' is the sentiment of the song, rather than the exact lyric.

ageing is to be 'there when you think of me', a kind of life after death, 'There like a beat at the back of your skull.'

They had so much material now. This meant they could over-record, then cut down to the very best. There was only one more key song to come, 'The Sound and the Summer'.* If the album's best moments so far – 'Disintegrate', 'Antidepressants', 'Dancing with the Europeans' – suggested a sense of *carpe diem*, then this sounded made to fit those. Sometimes interpreted as a J.G. Ballard-esque song about two lovers getting it on during a car crash – there is some Ballard in there, for sure, and Brett's called it 'J.G. Ballard meets *Thelma and Louise*'– really, it's about Brett's personal relationship with driving. The sense of power you get behind the wheel, the control, the freedom. 'I don't have a fleet of Ferraris, just a crappy family car, but I just love driving, watching the world zoom past, the stereo blasting out "She Sells Sanctuary", flicking the Vs to the world.' 'The Sound and the Summer' has a real thrill about it, the sun shining and Brett, anonymous, singing along to the Cult, feeling invincible. More defiance, more celebration, more *carpe diem*. When Mike heard the song, his first thought was Brett and Jodie's crash. Last time out, 'Black Ice' used driving to write about embracing the unknown. This time, it was for joy.

Over October, November and early December, the record was put together between several studios: Belgium, Sweden and the UK, Brett recording vocals closer to home. By early December Richard and Neil were at Ed's doing tie-ups. If this sounds more straightforward than previous records, it was. They'd made progress at ICP earlier in the year, when the songs that didn't fit were, as Richard says, 'quickly abandoned'.

* Neil and Richard's summer demo 'Neon Dogs' (30/7/24) and parts of 'Trigger Warning' became 'The Sound and the Summer' on 26/9/24.

Meanwhile, they worked better with Ed, though they still argued, and were back once more in the time warp – old nicknames, dynamics and all. Everyone knew what they'd be getting; this was simpler than almost any previous Suede record. No pandemic. A clear sense of direction. Good songs. A tried and trusted process. The 'same gear, same techniques, same studios and same producer,' in Richard's words. And no more talk of 'live' recordings. Having resisted the live ideas last time out, Richard was determined not to get drawn back into talk of this approach: 'The adrenaline, the audience, the energy and sweat of live shows, you can only experience that at a live show. Recording an album is an almost completely different experience.' Still, if so much of the approach here was similar, how could they avoid repeating themselves?

Throughout the process, Ed had, as he says, 'forefront in my mind that we needed to find ways to be different to *Autofiction*. They couldn't be too comfortable, with all these other elements the same.' That counted for himself, too. Aware he'd recorded with this band, this line-up, so many times, he was looking for ways to unsettle himself. On arrival at ICP, Ed was struggling: 'Every Suede record I've ever worked on,' he tells me now, 'has been different than the one before, sometimes dramatically so. I knew this record wouldn't be that different, but I wanted to avoid repeating myself at least.' Between recording drums and bass, he often went for long walks in Brussels, daydreaming:

> I imagined I was working with this strange German band called Bürogebäude that had once been prog. They'd reformed as the lead singer had recently appeared in a hit film, and there was a chance of them having a hit. Crazy, I know, but I needed some distraction in my head on these walks. This was just for me. It kept me sane and

> allowed my imagination to run a little and think of different ways of doing things.

Ed never mentioned this to the band, though when I chatted to him about *Antidepressants* after recording, he was energised by his secret approach to keeping it fresh. Everyone in his imagined band had alternative identities, different names. Perhaps the impact on the actual sound was minimal, but this was quite developed in his mind. 'Neil was Matthias Menelaus,' says Ed with a grin. 'Though there was a serious side to it, too. I was trying to find a way to think of the band as new, not this familiar group of people I had these set ideas about ... who they were, how they played.'

By now, the idea was crystallising that this would be Suede's 'post-punk' album, a partner to, but different from, last time out. But again, they had the challenge of making sure the songs matched the tag line. The band had survived so long by obsessing over quality control. This time around, with so many good songs in the mix (I counted more than twenty serious contenders in autumn 2024), selection was going to be crucial.

When I spoke to Mat about this period, I noticed sometimes he was talking as if he was outside the recording process. He laid down bass parts with Simon's drums in the first week at ICP, then after doing his bit his role was simply to hang around, antennae up. Though he continued to bring a particular skill set:

> Every now and then I can hear when something has gone slightly awry. There comes a moment when some kind of idea has been there from the very start and can't be fitted in and you're still trying to squeeze it in because it was there right at the start, so I think I'm

> occasionally good at saying that doesn't work. But so much of what we do now, especially me and Simon, is done in the rehearsal room, because everything is so well constructed. We don't go in with half-baked stuff any more.*

That's true, but sometimes you need to advocate for a particular song, done in a particular way, saying what *does* work, too. Or what could. 'Trance State' stands out to Mat as an example of that in action, after Ed expressed his unsureness, especially over the sheer amount of times the title was repeated. Mat recalls:

> 'Trance State' so nearly fell through the cracks. Ed never really got it, which I understand. It's not as immediate as lots of things on the record, but you really need those slow-burn tracks which only reveal themselves over time if an album is going to be three-dimensional. It was only that all five of us knew there was a great track in there that we kept plugging away. I think we got too hung up on making the music have the same trippy, woozy feel as the lyrics. That dumb fuzzed-up bass line, inspired by the kind of simple but melodic lines that Peter Hook plays, just gave it the kind of drive and immediacy it was missing.

When Mat came up with that bass line – 'so super-last-minute!' says Richard – the song took on a new life, and the five of them kept advocating for it.

---

* Mat continues, on Richard and Neil's contributions: 'Cos Richard and Neil are both great multi-instrumentalists it means that we don't really go in stuck for how we are gonna, say, do strings or anything – Neil's string arrangements are incredible. Properly scored and written out, it's like having a whole load of extra musicians in the band, but Neil especially can play loads of instruments. He's a really good bass player.'

Elsewhere, songs Ed advocated for were set to one side. The whole band liked 'One Less Spring' from the ballet score; Ed loved it. As Brett tells me, 'I like juxtaposing flowery, romantic poetry with dark modern music, something I did with that Byron poem in "Heroine" ["She Walks in Beauty"]. … "One Less Spring" was a very strong contender but I felt it interrupted the momentum of the album too much.' He recalls now, 'It would have been the centrepiece of a more left-field record', and he envisages it 'being revived at some point'. Instead, they decided to include songs like 'Broken Music for Broken People'. Brett thought of the title as a great slogan, as well as being the 'core lyrical message of the album.'

As with the live arena, some songs shrink in the studio, others grow. 'June Rain' is perhaps the best example from *Antidepressants* of a song that grew because of Ed's input. That earlier version had the verses and choruses in place, the lyrical focus too, though the song hadn't quite achieved lift-off in demo form. Brett acknowledging that Ed's reshaping of 'June Rain' 'was a fantastic idea which completely transformed it … When Ed gets it right, he really gets it right.' Suddenly, it felt like the album had its standout ballad.

TOO MANY STRIKERS SYNDROME: *ANTIDEPRESSANTS* STRATEGY

By early November, the band had enough music in good shape to take it to the label. On 11 November they had a meeting with Alistair Norbury, the head of BMG, playing him tracks at Westpoint Studios in Acton. His response was ecstatic. The day after, a strategy meeting with BMG focused on potential singles and order of release. Schedules began to crystallise, as did the idea of announcing the album *and* the Southbank residency at the same time as dropping the first single. At the end of the month, they played the Clockenflap Festival in Hong Kong, tight in among the skyscrapers and the waterfront, high on a bill headlined by Jack White, Air and rapper Central Cee. *Rolling Stone* has called this 'one of the most unique festivals on the planet', reviewer Ben Jolley reporting that on arrival Suede were 'mobbed by selfie-pleading fans who hand them armfuls of gifts and worship them like gods.'

Around this time, Neil wrote to me of the album-in-progress, 'It's a load of ingredients and we can't taste the dish.' There was still plenty to talk about. Ed was 'determined for it to be poppier', while Brett 'wanted to double down – [asking] what would happen if you went down that *Autofiction* road but more primal, more brutal, more raw?' Late in 2024

Suede at Clockenflap 2024, 30 November 2024.
Photo courtesy of Anissa

Neil and Brett sent me their preferred album track lists. Brett only felt sure of seven songs.

At the end-of-year meeting they also discussed potential mixers, with Alan Moulder, now largely retired, on a boat to Antigua, and the band searching for someone new to trust. Before signing off for Christmas, Neil told me, 'Everyone's impatient, but we've been through this before. We know we won't be able to tell what the record is for another couple of months.'

In the new year, the band returned, fresh, trying to work out what dish to make from what ingredients. (Richard's own fresh start, his new year's resolution, was to learn Swedish properly. This time, he'd stick with it, growing more fluent in the year to come.)* By the end of January, they were back in the studio, Sleeper Sounds in west London.

The atmosphere was jocular at times, Brett chivvying the others along like a military commander, announcing the next song, the next recording task. By this stage in the process, the outside world was starting to encroach on their cocoon of making. For months or years, you *imagine* what others might make of the music, without being able to test it. Then you get feedback. On the 27th, Alistair at BMG emailed Ed, sharing his enthusiasm for the five songs he was listening to on repeat.

The following day, radio plugger Kev and Brett were in discussion about possible singles, specifically the lyrics on 'The Sound and the Summer'. (For the 'don't fuck with me' line, Brett wanted silence, like '90s rap tunes aired on MTV, though Kev wondered about 'mess with me' as an alternative.) Kev saw multiple potential singles: 'Sweet Kid', 'Dancing with the Europeans', 'Antidepressants', 'Trance State', 'The

* Swedish update, April 2026: Richard's now started making jokes in Swedish. Anna wants to make a list of the best.

Sound and the Summer' and 'Disintegrate' were all possibles, and the band wanted to send him 'Broken Music ...' too. At the following day's campaign meeting, Didz shared the 2025 plan with the band. Kim from the office and Charlie were also there. Mat and Brett floated 'Disintegrate' as a first single as it gave a sense of how the album was immediate, celebratory.* Didz wondered whether Kev might be suffering from 'too many strikers' syndrome.

These weeks weren't without tensions, costs rising the more time they spent on the songs, discussions over who might mix the album becoming fraught as work continued into February. At this stage of the process, Ed got frustrated with Brett, whom he used to be able to influence more. These days, Ed felt, Brett more often got in his own way. As far as Ed was concerned, the 'stars were aligning' for Suede to have their most successful record in decades, even more than *Autofiction*; he feared Brett's preferences ruining things. Those preferences sometimes came down to differing approaches to technical details.

Ed and the others listened to Andrew Scheps's mix of 'Dancing with the Europeans' on the studio monitors in early February. Neil wrote in his notes, 'We listen. It sounds GOOD. For a first pass, and given Andrew's not worked with us before, it's really close. This is something of a relief. Ed, who has pushed for Andrew all along, feels vindicated.' Listening at home on his laptop, though, Brett was less enthusiastic. Ed found it maddening Brett always preferred demos to proper recordings, his £70 home mic and GarageBand sound to the vintage preamps and mixing desks worth thousands. The others listened on high-end audio

---

* The date for taking first single to radio was initially tied to the album announcement on 9 June, with single number two due to be released mid-July. They had the Radio 2 in the Park invite by now (see Southbank chapter) and the Southbank residency was pencilled in. The initial album release date was 26 September.

equipment in an expertly treated room; Brett listened through a pair or earbuds or on his phone. The mix was 'objectively good', agreed Didz, but Brett didn't like what he heard. The following day Neil and Brett discussed control over mixing on the phone, Neil feeling it was more about *relinquishing* control at this stage. Richard agreed. As he put it, 'We've been sitting on these songs for years' – why not let someone else bring their own fresh approach? While Brett wanted to hold on to as much control as possible.

INTERSTITIALS: 'HUMANITY AS WIDGETS'

They were also thinking more about how to link the songs. Contrasting with the *Autofiction* impersonation of live performance, this time it was all about finding ways to give the sense of a world in which AI voices speak from the ether, sound is generated rather than made by humans, and you don't know what to trust. Brett had become interested in voices and various bits of automated 'safety advice' that clutter day-to-day experience, what he calls 'that sense of suppression and dread and coercive authoritarian control that a citizen of the 21st-century feels. Covert state oppression hiding behind the fig leaf of safety-ism. Everyone neatly in their box. Humanity as widgets.' How to render that, though, in an album which was constantly working towards real human connection but kept finding alienating modern disconnection in the way? The band couldn't use real recorded bits of, say, the sounds of the London underground – 'If you see anything suspicious, please report it to ...' for example, as they could run into rights issues.

As so often, restrictions forced the band to come up with better ideas. Brett turned to Jodie, asking her to deliver these parts herself. With 'Disintegrate' slated as the first track, the first sound listeners heard would be Jodie's voice saying, 'connected, disconnected' repeatedly, like a Bluetooth connection slipping on- and offline. If you listen closely, you can hear Jodie elsewhere too, most obviously in 'Trance State'. As the song ends, she intones, deadpan, 'Do not drive, do not operate heavy machinery.'* When you know whose voice it is, it adds something. After all, this is the wording on the side of Brett's medication. But even if you don't know, it contributes to a sense that this record grapples with what it means to be human in an age of technology infantilising us at every turn.†

MIXING ANTIDEPRESSANTS: 30 SECONDS OF GOODNESS

Four-fifths of Suede joined Andrew Scheps in RAK Studios for two full days of mixing in early March as well as a third without Brett (so he could see the family before the band headed off to Chile the following week). As Andrew told me, in a short break, he never met Adele when working with her; they only had a quick hello, once, at the Grammys. Unusually, Suede want to be present for the tweaking of each song. Increasingly, they seem very old-school in a world where many prefer to work at a digital distance. It's a shame so few value that personal connection. You can see Andrew's worth in the room immediately. He's an understated,

---

* Jodie's contribution was added at the end of the recording process. The first time Brett spoke this part was when the band performed 'Trance State' live, at the Clore Ballroom, on 26/8/25.

† Just before mixing, the band had a photo shoot at the 'sound mirrors', RAF Denge in Kent, the location featured on the cover of their B-sides and rarities album *Sci-Fi Lullabies Vol. 2*. Covering 1997–2023, this was a nineteen-track partner to the still-essential *Sci-Fi Lullabies*, which traced 1992–97. The cover image for *Sci-Fi Lullabies Vol. 2* was taken by Richard Reader, showing the large 1920s/30s acoustic mirrors, sometimes called 'concrete ears', built to detect sound waves from enemy aircraft. One of these is visible on the cover of this book, too. It's from the same photo shoot.

relaxed, assured presence. Years of navigating big egos has taught him how to read people, how to get the best out of them. This encouraged me to see the band as he might see them. After all, they didn't know each other.

- RICHARD: Humble but sharp, with a sarcastic, self-critical sense of humour. Easy-going, confident, upbeat. Prone to the occasional eye-roll. Glad to be here.
- NEIL: Dirty laugh, laptop permanently open, taking notes. Able to bring up details at a second's notice. Most animated when something is a fraction off. Irritated by little details. Knows precisely what he's asking for and able to articulate this in language Andrew understands.
- MAT: Band raconteur, lightening the atmosphere, telling tales between fixes, from way back when. How they'd used so much reverb on *Dog Man Star* that they then 'banned the word' when Richard joined. 'We called it "spring"!' Of everyone, the most likely to comment on something he actually likes: he loves 'how stark the guitar is on "Life Is Endless ..."'
- SIMON: The drummer. Elsewhere.

Brett, meanwhile, sat at the edge of the group, sometimes relaxed, sometimes restless. In the end, Brett has the right to call for any changes: that's what mixing is, and he's the singer. He's been through this many times before. But on the other hand, as he stands against a kind of academic musicality – he and Ed clash over this – he might tune out when tiny changes are being discussed. The first thing he did on arrival on the second day of mixing, when I attended, was play a version of 'Disintegrate' through his tiny phone speaker while everyone else had to sit and listen. He wanted to know how it would sound when he listened on the move.

For Brett, mixing was sometimes a waste of his energy, though he clearly enjoyed listening back to what they'd made and when he had a view on something, his instincts were usually good. (He pushed for 'more clanky, post-punk' bass on several songs, for instance.) On 'Trance State' and 'Criminal Ways', it really sounded like the band were having a good time. Mat told me, eye twinkling, 'Well, you *can* occasionally have fun if you like, in a band. You just can't *look* like you are.'

Mixing is very details-orientated, the language clinical. Turn this up, please. Can we get a bit more of that? Patterns. Low eights. What sits with what. Above. Below. Attack. It's also an exercise in seeing how musicians collaborate without picking up instruments. As Mat says, 'We communicate through making music.' But also, through talking about it. If you complain constantly, people switch off. If you get too insistent, they switch off. Rather, gently suggest. Ask to hear this or that, open-minded, then listen to what others say when they hear it. Over eight hours, I only heard one person ask to turn themselves up, once. At one point, Neil moved a chair to the centre of the room for one more listen of 'Trance State', trying to work out how to make the song sound clearer – something at the high end or mid-range was too cluttered. The crash cymbals stood out, so Andrew turned them down. Neil was not thinking about his place in Suede, but rather Suede as one single entity. After this moment, Mat turned to me: 'People that say you can't describe music mean you can't replicate a *feeling*. But much of what you do in a studio *can* be described.'

They moved between songs, calling out 'Print!' or 'Printage!' when a song was complete. (Little is as satisfying as being able to call for a song to be 'printed', finally complete after years of work.) By now, they were nearly done. This allowed for more joking than during tenser recording times, where it can still all fall apart. There was also, I think, a great deal of confidence. I never got the sense the band were unsure about the songs chosen. No one mentioned one that hadn't made the cut, while Andrew praised this or that section, celebrating parts others had obviously heard so many times they could barely recognise their beauty. Brett felt confident enough to leave early. This revealed, even in jest, Richard's freedom to direct more. Once Brett was gone, Neil said, after a beat, 'Richard, the floor is yours ...' With perfect comic timing, Richard tagged in, leaning forward and half whispering nasally to Andrew, 'Just a *few* small changes if I maaaay ...' The laughter echoed through the small space, and they carried on.

One other moment stands out. I remember watching Neil leaning forward, long hair dangling down in front of him, listening hard for something that might not be there, playing air drums while listening to 'Life Is Endless ...' Richard, giving context for my benefit, said, 'We stopped working on "Life Is Endless ..." for about six months after the initial recording at ICP [in 2024] as it was too rocky, too sludgey, and we couldn't get it right. "June Rain" was going to be the final track, then in November '24 we decided to give it a go again. Once we had the idea of making it the final song on the record, once it's not going to be followed by anything, that changes things.' Shortly after, they were working on the very end of the album, that wash of sound, which they stretched out, then stretched out further. 'Ahhh,' said Andrew, pulling on his long beard and smiling. 'Thirty seconds of goodness.'*

* On the Friday night, Andrew and Ed went for dinner, meeting in person for the first time. The following day, Ed turned up unannounced at the studio with his now grown-up daughter, a toddler when they were recording *Coming Up*, asking her dad to play 'Ones' so she could dance along. At the end of the third day, Andrew told Richard, Mat and Neil this was 'the first time he'd finished a mix with the band in the room (well, 60 per cent of the band) for ten years.' He says email couldn't work for Suede, given all they want to try in the room.

On Sunday the 9th they heard from Ian, who'd been listening to the mixes: 'Sounds epic to me ... possibly my favourite Suede album so far. Even feels like a step up from *Autofiction*.' The following day it was Alistair at BMG's turn, emailing Ed to call the new record 'magnificent'. With this gratifying feedback fresh, they packed for South America, discussions still ongoing about mixing. Should they ask Andrew to mix 'Emotionally Unavailable' as well? The extra tracks too? Was it too late for 'Emotionally Unavailable' to go on the record? If so, what got pushed off, or moved around?*

DRUMMERLESS IN CHILE

From one extreme to another: the band got on a plane and headed to South America. They'd considered a longer tour including São Paulo, Buenos Aires and Mexico, but couldn't make it work financially. Two gigs in a week, though, made sense – one headline Suede show at the Movistar Arena in Santiago, with a second at the Rock en Concepción festival alongside Garbage and legendary Chilean band Los Tres. As Neil

* From Neil's notes to me by email, on 10 March: 'Over the last week we've been considering getting Andrew to mix "Emotionally Unavailable", with an eye to including it on the record. Brett suggests putting it after "Somewhere Between an Atom and a Star".' Brett is rather superstitious about the seventh track on Suede albums and always wants it to be a favourite track of his. 'Emotionally Unavailable' is a favourite, and – not entirely by-the-by – Lucian's favourite of the new songs too. 'Perhaps "Broken Music for Broken People" could be moved to the end of the album, after "Life Is Endless, Life Is a Moment". Even if "Emotionally Unavailable" doesn't make the record, or we can't find a gap in Andrew's schedule to get it mixed in time, Brett's considering having "Broken Music for Broken People" as the last track on the album.' In the end, band and management opted to hold back 'Emotionally Unavailable' as a standalone 'single' to be released at the same time as the announcement of an *Antidepressants* expanded edition. The first play of this song was 5 p.m. on 8 June 2026, on Lamacq's 6 Music show again. It was tied in with the announcement of the publication of this book: same day, same time.

wrote to me, 'The free festival would be a forward-looking thing to do: there's potential for the band to reach new people in South America still. The last time we played Santiago in 2012 we played to 3,200, but this time we played to just shy of 5,000.'

The gig in Chile's capital, no small matter, was made to look tiny by their next gig, Suede's largest audience yet. Before this, their biggest was probably headlining Roskilde Festival in Denmark in 1999, to something like 75–80,000 people. I used to live in Chile, so I know a little about these free festivals, having attended a few. The context matters. In Chile, free festivals are huge in scale, mixing household-name Chilean acts with cross-generational appeal alongside international visitors, as part of wider cultural celebrations. Often in massive open areas, most of a city – or of a whole region – may attend, meaning audiences of more than 100,000 are possible. At this gig in Concepción, the promoter claimed there were 175,000 present. Promoters are inclined to exaggerate, especially with numbers so vast – 175,000, even in a Chilean context, is unlikely. That said, the evidence of the day proves this was, by a distance, Suede's largest ever audience, and a great opportunity to find new fans far from home, playing in one fell swoop to many more people than they would on a whole UK or European tour. The Santiago gig went off without a hitch and featured new music, as recent shows elsewhere had done. For Concepción, the plan was different anyway, but in the end the band had to think fast, under pressure, for a different reason.

Apart from one spell of TB years ago, Simon has rarely been ill in decades of touring, so it was troubling to find him ill on the Chile trip. He got through the Santiago show just about, but by the morning of the 15th it looked like he might not make the festival. Well, you never cancel a show. But what could they do? Surely not play acoustic, to all those people? They considered several options, rehearsing songs they could play with Simon's drum tech Martin Oldham, if they needed to, also ones where Neil could play the drums instead of keyboards or guitars. They rehearsed in a garage-cum-studio on the day of the show, with photos showing Richard looking worried. The band changed the middle of the setlist for playing more easily without Simon if he couldn't perform, or if he had to stop mid-gig. Martin learned 'Turn Off Your Brain and Yell', 'Trash', 'Animal Nitrate', 'Metal Mickey' and 'Beautiful Ones'; if necessary, Neil could do the rest. All this felt high pressure, with concern for Simon on one hand and the approaching biggest-Suede-gig-ever on the other, Simon's usually invisible drum tech about to be thrust into the limelight, and much asked of Neil too. Fortunately, just before showtime Simon got the medical all-clear and he played the gig, though by now they'd rejigged the set so much that it was 90 per cent pre-reunion material. These were, in the end, two memorable shows, with wonderful, enthusiastic Chilean audiences, many of whom had never been exposed to Suede before.

Rehearsing without Simon. Neil on drums, Collao, Concepción, 15 March 2025.

On return from Chile, it was back to more prosaic concerns. Richard, Neil and Brett began writing for Suede #11 in earnest later in March, with a great deal of momentum and enthusiasm in the camp driving things forward. By the time *Antidepressants* was released, they wanted progress on its follow-up. But, ahead of that announcement, there was another release coming first.

Sci-Fi Lullabies Vol. 2 came out on 12 April for Record Store Day and was received well, reflecting positively on the reunion years as well as drawing attention to Suede's long-standing reputation as a band whose extras were worth searching out. Much of the chat online was about the previously unreleased 'Blinded', another song to Brett's mum, a sort of ambient, inverse 'She Still Leads Me On'. This sees a young Brett stunned by his mother's kindness, each of the verse lines concentrating on childhood observations:

The way she looked when she was happy
And with her majesty, she'd see through everything
The way she talked, just like a girl sometimes
A rose in a paperweight, she'd stop the turning tide.

Elsewhere, reviews praised the song selection. 'Twenty-eight years in the making,' wrote Kevin Harley in *Record Collector*, 'not all sequels are created equal, but this one assuredly is.'

ALBUM ANNOUNCEMENT

On 19 May the album announcement dropped, along with the Southbank residency announcement and first single, 'Disintegrate'. 'Dancing with the Europeans' was slated as the second single proper – 'that's the big one,' said plugger Kevin – and plans were set to release different songs to different stations at different times, as well, with 'Trance State' going to Radio 2 as a kind of half-single. The 'Disintegrate' video directed by Chris Turner was fantastic. A simple black-and-white performance encapsulated the new album's aesthetic, from the image of the fast-rotting flowers to the sight of Neil throwing guitar shapes in a way that's rarely been seen in all his years in Suede. (On Spotify, the reel that plays during the song sees Neil thrashing and re-thrashing, every few seconds, like he's in an old-school metal band.) Brett was at his most aggressive, light and shadow used smartly throughout in between lyrics flashing up, glitchy and disconnected, on the screen. The video even managed to make Richard look cool and sinister. No small feat.

When I asked Didz how they sought to avoid *Autofiction 2* with the *Antidepressants* campaign, he laughed. 'Well, they sort of *did* make *Autofiction 2* ... I mean, the songs were different, and there were a couple we could sell as "post-punk". But the approach was the same. *Autofiction* did so much of what we wanted it to, I think we were looking to repeat it, but not look like it.' 'Disintegrate' was one of those post-punk songs, and it was certainly a different approach, not releasing the more obvious 'Dancing with the Europeans' first. '"Disintegrate" is quite pounding, in this brutal, industrial way,' says Didz now, 'It was intended to let people know there was an album coming that was different ... But it really over-achieved. It got more airplay, more streams, more views than we expected. A million, in no time. The photos worked, and it set up the album perfectly.' What exactly did it set up, though? What does it say? Didz's answer was immediate: 'Well, the track says joy, death and violence. That's what you're going to get. It lays out the album's stall in a way that "She Still Leads Me On", for all its success, couldn't really do for *Autofiction*.'

With 'Disintegrate' out, the Southbank sold out in seconds. The campaign was humming. The title worked, too. Though obviously associated with mental health, in fact the word 'antidepressants' itself suggests the opposite, that joy in the moment, that temporary relief from pain. It works as a symbol for the album too: each song is an antidepressant, pumping you full of pleasure, despite the decay that comes with the passage of time. It reads like Suede themselves are an antidepressant, the title oddly uplifting, as well as dark. Joy, despite it all. Because of it all.

CHAPTER 7

the southbank diary, 2025

NOSTALGIA SUMMER

A successful *Antidepressants* campaign requires multiple elements working together. Gigs. Timing. Image. Tag line. Reviews. Videos. Then there's interviews, socials, radio, tour announcements. All this presenting Suede as a forward-looking act in an age drenched in nostalgia. Though as we've seen, you roll the dice every time. You finish a record not knowing what world it will arrive into, months later.

Nobody says it directly, of course. But the context in summer 2025 is the all-conquering Oasis world tour in which the entire setlist, except one song, is drawn from 1994–97, the Gallagher brothers setting aside sixteen years of estrangement to play to vast audiences worldwide. Thirty years after Britpop, everyone's cashing in. In the last week I've heard impromptu conversations in cafés, on trains, in pubs, across generations. It's staggering how the Oasis reunion dominates. There are precious few topics that make for national conversation in the 2020s, even fewer where music is the centre of that conversation. And yet, here we are. Are Liam and Noel really talking? Have they really had 'secret beers' on tour? All this as 'Wonderwall' plays for the millionth time. My fellow Suede fan likes Oasis too. I listen to him chat to waiters, waitresses, taxi drivers, strangers at the bar. He's going to one of the gigs. Obviously, only to hear the early stuff. They've just done five nights at Wembley. Yes, this is a different world from Suedeworld.

To tie in, multiple ranges of questionable 'Britpop revival' fashion and merch are launched in summer 2025, Britpop-tagged tours are embarked on, with everyone who was anyone (except, praise be, Elastica*) dusting off their old semi-hits, taking a deep breath and giving it one more go. The exception is Blur, Damon Albarn having a 21st-century renaissance in Gorillaz as well as occasionally reforming the old band for huge shows and a new album. But in 2025, other members of Blur are on the nostalgia train. Just a few weeks ago Alex James did his first Britpop Classical show at his own Oxfordshire Big Feastival (a pun for the foodies, there) in the Cotswolds. This featured himself on bass, a band with multiple singers, an orchestra, classical interpretations of Blur songs as well as Oasis, Supergrass, the Charlatans and the Verve. (No, no Suede. Can you imagine? But then, in 1995, you might not have foreseen the Blur bassist covering Oasis on his personal farm, either.) Soon, there'll be a full UK tour. The distance between these approaches to music feels vast to me as I prepare to document the Suede residency. I look at the words 'bassist and cheese maker' in the Britpop Classical announcement, and wonder at the world we live in.

In a sense, it was always this way. Suede are usually upstaged by someone, though in summer 2025 there's a lot of competition for that title. Pulp release their first album since 2001, returning to number one with *More* and reprising their famous headlining Glastonbury set, thirty years on. The music is well received on its own terms, Jarvis Cocker (a Suede fan,

---

* Justine is retired from music and doesn't engage with this stuff at all.

incidentally, currently doing media rounds calling 'Animal Nitrate' 'the best song of the '90s') is articulate and grounded, though even he says their sound hasn't changed. On the Mercury Prize red carpet, drummer Nick Banks, asked whether they'd make another album, says, 'It's a big undertaking ... You have to do all this kind of malarkey.' Some *More* songs were written before the band split, their 'new' single 'Got to Have Love' first demoed in 1999. In the album promo, cut-outs of Pulp members circa 1995 are used, with a cheeky wink. The lead single is 'Spike Island', a song about the legendary Stone Roses gig, looking back on that event thirty-five years on. *More* is a witty, warm record, and in one fell swoop Pulp have had more impact than Suede in sixteen years of graft. But it's hardly anti-nostalgia. Meanwhile, two days before Suede's album is released on 5 September, Radiohead nearly crash the internet by announcing a twenty-date tour across Europe, their first shows in seven years, nearly a decade after their last album. No new music, just shows, and no promise of more. You can try and escape this framing, but the '90s doesn't care what you think. In summer 2025, it's back, bucket hats and all, only this time it's your kids in the front row. I know because I've seen them at Suede gigs. Of these examples, Pulp perhaps stand out most, if only because they *are* making new music, but with such a determined nod to the past.

There's no contest, in terms of popularity, between these behemoths and Suede, so consistently credited as starting the Britpop 'movement'. (Of course, they didn't *start* anything. Music is ongoing, always.) But for those interested in a different approach to time's relentless march, the Southbank residency has an outsized impact, way beyond the relatively small number of tickets available. The poster – SUEDE TAKEOVER – Brett, Mat, Simon, Neil and Richard, looking downward from their concrete Southbank perch at the viewer, provides a focus, suggesting there are many Suedes worth seeing. (An alternative title for the residency was 'Yesterday and Tomorrow', before they decided against any looking back.) Meanwhile, in this nostalgia summer, Suede will have their first UK magazine front cover since 1999, for *Mojo* – the headline 'A great British band seize their moment'. They'll give the album five stars, an indicator of the across-the-board critical acclaim to come. Whatever praise Suede may have dreamed of in the past, they're about to get more than they can process. At home. Abroad. Everywhere. End of year 'best ofs'. *Antidepressants* is about to become the most instantly acclaimed Suede album since their debut.

Across five gigs, they'll play over sixty different songs.* Only one is due to be played at every show, and according to draft setlists, it's the latest single 'Dancing with the Europeans'.† Then there's the wider 'takeover'. Film night, with Mike Christie, Neil, Mat and journalist Miranda Sawyer, for a showing of Mike's *The Insatiable Ones*. Monochrome footage is projected onto the side of the building featuring the flowers from the 'Disintegrate' video, clips from the band's past and present lighting up Waterloo at night. There are Suede fan after-parties planned, too. All this sets up the campaign for the year ahead, gives a sense of what's distinctive about Suede around the time of maximum attention for *Antidepressants*, and says something that has the added advantage of being true: Suede are stronger than ever. It's the anti-ICA from 2003. Back then, they were at a low ebb, about to split. Twenty-two years on, it's a very different picture.

From the outside the campaign seems like it's aiming for a number-one album, their first in twenty-six years. Sam Hand and the Insatiable Ones, as well as José and Sara's Mild Ones, go into overdrive in the weeks before the first Clore Ballroom show, Sam telling Didz she's sure

---

* Sixty-two different songs, in fact, and 108 in total.

† They ended up playing 'The Only Way I Can Love You' at each gig, and in the end didn't play 'Dancing with the Europeans' at the Purcell Room show.

that this time, they'll get that top spot. She does believe it. Advance CD and vinyl sales are worth more, and months of these contribute to the first-week figures. There's a monumental effort ongoing. DawBell, who led the *Autofiction* campaign, know how to portray the band. That is: the antithesis of enormodomes and choreographed nostalgia, all of which seems designed to prevent reality breaking out. When Noel and Liam hold their arms aloft for the crowd, it's because everyone wonders if this is all a pretence. They stand in the same position, unmoving mid-song, poses identical to 1994, and the money rolls in.

Meanwhile, Suede perform in venues where they can touch the hands of every fan, sweating themselves into a puddle every time they play. No, they're not the centre of anything. Yes, it's worthwhile. Is a number-one album ever likely? For those who want to see the band succeed, it's tempting to think so. Ten, six, five, two. One? Well, why not? The fanbase feels it's no more than they deserve. It's tempting to see this all as a potential 'happy ending'. The main run of Southbank gigs will start the day after the chart announcement. Christ, say the comments on socials, even Shed Seven have had a number one since *Autofiction*. Two of them! In a single year! (Yes, this has been noticed by the camp, too.) So why not, once more, our band?

ANTIDEPRESSANTS IN THE ROUND (ALMOST)

The Clore Ballroom show is the band's attempt to play in the round, close to fans; though in reality it's more like *two-thirds* in the round, they've rarely been so exposed.* Wires are everywhere. The whites of people's eyes? You bet. Between songs, you can hear everything people say, too.

---

* Perhaps the 100-capacity Southampton Joiners Arms gig in 1993 might compete for this title. The MOTH Club *Autofiction* show in 2022 was also exposed. But this is right up there.

Tonight, Suede debut *Antidepressants* in full. Especially with bigger shows, Mat resents the number of things put in the way between the band and the audience. Usually some at the front are holding up phones. Because of health and safety, crowds are being pushed further back, too – that increases the spectacle, but lessens the connection. Usually, every gig is similar to the last. Tonight is about reducing that gap, where possible. There's a lot of positive energy, many people know each other. 'Wherever you look,' says Sam Hand, 'you can see a familiar face. A friendly face. One of our own.'

Approaching the performance area, Mat can see behind the amps, the pedalboards. Tonight there'll be no mystery apart from the noise. Already he's enjoying himself, having the unusual sense, almost like a kind of vertigo, that he can move between the band's space and the audience's, as they jostle for position. When 'Disintegrate' starts, the ground shakes. This first show is a couple of weeks before the main run, the wonky scheduling owing to the album release date getting moved. So this feels a little strange, too. It's part of the residency, but not. It's less pressured, with a kind of rehearsal room feel. The night was billed as '*Antidepressants* and Other Post-Punk Pick-Me-Ups', so they can do what they like. In front of the most home of home crowds.

Almost immediately, they lose the beat in 'Disintegrate'. Brett's in a different place from Mat, Richard and Neil – they take it in turns to chase a solution. This happened in rehearsal too. Simon shifts to where Brett is, then the others are confused. Eventually, they fall back into the same place, relief washing round the room. A few seconds later, it's repaired. It's a small moment, but enough to distract Richard for the next half an hour. During the second chorus, Mat looks out and wants to be among the people singing along: 'Come down and disintegrate with me ...' Brett belts out. That line's going to work well live.

In theory, you can change the rules of a gig, but in practice, it's hard, and they've made compromises. This results in an *almost* no-holds-barred show. 'We are the anti-nostalgia band,' Brett says, at one point, in a line he's been practising for weeks. He hasn't mentioned he'll be saying this to the band. Something else he hasn't mentioned is his preferred next move; mid-gig he announces *Antidepressants* as 'the second in a trilogy of "black-and-white" albums'. At this, Richard hears an audible groan on his side of the stage, which he feels proves what he already suspects: that some fans 'yearn for the more artistic, experimental side of the band, the expansive, soulful, maybe even softer side of Suede. The ballads, the soaring, the sensitivity, the heart.' It's not that Richard doesn't want Brett having his own artistic vision or drive. He does. But if Brett has a specific musical aim, he's going to need to rely on Neil and Richard to make it a reality.* If that's an aim they have reservations about, it makes the task more complicated than the way Brett presents it to the public. But anyway, Brett's said the line about the trilogy now, knowing full well there are press here, who'll report this as fact.

And they do. In an *Uncut* review posted online the following day, John Lewis writes: 'Playing your new album in full, to an audience who've not had a chance to hear it all yet, could be seen as a sign of arrogance or bloody-mindedness. But ... this was a triumphant statement of intent. In a month where their Britpop peers are playing entire setlists that are thirty years old, with barely a nod to the 21st century, Suede have their focus on the future.' Then he quotes Brett, on anti-nostalgia. The article is titled 'A band embracing the future'. The review also mentions almost everything Brett wants to flag: 'post-punk', 'the black and white

---

* This in contrast to *Head Music*, where Brett ended up saying he'd write the music he wanted himself.

trilogy', 'Public Image Ltd.', even Greenock's finest, John McGeoch, gets a mention. It's the full Suede 2025 bingo card. After the gig Richard will ruminate on Brett's language. He wishes he hadn't said the trilogy thing. He does this sometimes, like the band is his alone to steer. Maybe not all of them want three albums like this. Tonight was supposed to be enjoyed for its own sake. Now it's the start of the next thing, a decision taken without him. But there are also some lovely moments: Anna is here from Sweden tonight, it's the first time she's heard 'June Rain' live, and she cries when they play her favourite song on the new album.

The Clore Ballroom encore is ten songs. They've tinkered with the setlist, putting 'Tides' in at the last, thinking it fits the 'post-punk' billing better. If they can't do it for pleasure tonight, when can they? Before 'Snowblind' Brett says, 'We're going to get in a time machine and take you all the way back ... to 2013, when the world was a very different place.' It's another line he's used before, but tonight it lands different as it's as far back as they're going to go. The band finish with 'Outsiders', then depart through the back. It's not breaking down all the barriers, Mat thinks. But it's as close as they've come so far.*

RELEASE WEEK

It's been all go ahead of release week. First, a radio session at BBC's Maida Vale studios on 1 September. The next day, another trip up the News International building, revisiting the site of their Virgin Radio *Autofiction* show, three years later. On the 5th, they play the Camp and Furnace in Liverpool. It's another 100 per cent post-reunion set, the only lull a ten-minute break when the PA breaks down.

---

* NB: Biographer not present for this gig. (Biographer's daughter's birthday.)

On Sunday the 7th it's a rare, high-profile TV appearance, Suede playing at Radio 2 in the Park, at Hylands Park in Chelmsford, where they headlined V Festival in 1999. It's on BBC iPlayer, Suede bizarrely sandwiched between '90s pop star Louise and Soul II Soul, with Def Leppard headlining – surely a first time for that sentence. There's much setlist negotiating beforehand. With a half-hour set for mainstream TV and 65,000 in the crowd, they can't just play what they like. They play four old ones, four new ones: 'Trash', 'Dancing with the Europeans', 'Animal Nitrate', 'Trance State', 'She Still Leads Me On', 'Saturday Night' 'Metal Mickey' and 'Beautiful Ones'. (Radio 2 wanted 'She's in Fashion', one of Suede's most popular songs. But they don't play it.)* 'Fresh off stage, Brett does a giddy interview with DJ Jo Whiley, saying the odd glass of wine is his only vice these days. It's another one of his lines, and it's not quite true. But he does seem genuinely delighted, even surprised, to find such gigs possible once more. Whiley first played Suede on the *Evening Session* in 1993 and is still an enthusiastic supporter. The day after the gig, *Antidepressants* is announced as Radio 2 album of the week – huge for reaching new people – and it feels like something is working. Both 'Trance State' and 'Dancing with the Europeans' have been B-listed by the station, and being on the Radio 2 in the Park bill sees the BBC getting behind Suede even more. Across the whole week, tracks are on heavy rotation. 'Album of the week' is bigger than any review, or any playlisting, anywhere else.

After the alternative universe of Radio 2, they switch to small-scale record store signings and gigs around the country. At Circuit in Kingston

---

* Mat says: 'Radio 2 is strict with what you play on TV – "She's in Fashion" is Suede's second-best known song around the world, it made it across into pop radio, not just alternative radio. It's still big in Europe, in particular. We struggle to do it justice live as it's so compressed, it's not really a live song – which is why we try to do it acoustic. It's also a very simple song which is almost the same all way through.'

upon Thames on the 9th they play post-reunion songs only. The same day, Simon posts the midweek official chart on his Facebook page, with Suede at number one. If they weren't before, the fan groups are beyond excited now, many of them feeling number one is inevitable. When you're putting in all that effort, it feels like it *has* to happen. Like it's *supposed* to. Fans push every physical sale they can. They buy multiple copies. They try to game the system by streaming *Antidepressants*, continuously, for days.

On the 11th it's a gig at Signature Brew, the 'Brew Hall' in Walthamstow, along with a signing for Rough Trade. Local MP Stella Creasy is in the audience, loving the show.* During 'She Still Leads Me On', Neil is surprised to find he can still be moved by the song, even after playing it so many times. These gigs are like a party, they're fizzing with energy, while reviews are beginning to land. Honestly, they feel a little taken aback. It all feels a little *too much* praise. Do they really deserve it? In-band, there's plenty of self-deprecation among anyone who isn't named Brett. Richard tells me, 'You tend to get the praise you deserved for your last one when the next one comes out. Remember what happened with *Head Music*?' They can't know the long-term reception yet. But the immediate reception is excellent, higher profile, more international. As if everything last time out had been used to work out how to do the same, bigger, next time. Then it actually worked.

THE INSATIABLE ONES PLAYBACK

It's quiet at the venue this morning, though beyond the Southbank, on and offline, the fan groups are humming. Early, Brett texts me. I've

* Not exactly news, this. Also spotted at the *Night Thoughts* show at the Kentish Town Forum, among others.

messaged something bland and encouraging, wishing him good luck for later, but he says there's absolutely no chance of making number one in today's chart and there's no point thinking about it. 'We can't compete with that behemoth any more.' He's blunt, downbeat. You get the sense that, as much as Brett might not want to care, he does. Late afternoon, backstage, no one is waiting by a phone or refreshing their browser. By tonight's film showing, Sabrina Carpenter's *Man's Best Friend* will be number one; Suede: number two; number three: Oasis, *Time Flies: 1994–2009* (released sixteen years ago). They're also at numbers thirteen and sixteen. That's normal. Four: Ed Sheeran. Five: Fleetwood Mac. This is what you're competing against, no matter when you surface. There's little anxiety about the wider picture. The band's future feels secure, and there's plenty of optimism around. Just not about this.

It's been a strange journey this week, with fan optimism inflated by two things. The first is common knowledge. In those first few days the pre-sales from the last six months all showed up; these give acts who sell hard copies an advantage over those whose fanbase is all about streaming or racking up YouTube views. For Suede, that gave them a misleading lead, given everyone knows the sheer size of Carpenter's following. The second thing is less widely known. It's not public knowledge yet, but Spotify had a data outage for several days, meaning its figures didn't feed into the chart for a while: Spotify represents about 47 per cent of all streaming in the UK, so it makes a difference. Sabrina Carpenter's sales are 85 per cent streams, 15 per cent physical, Suede's the reverse. So the outage made it look like Suede had more of a lead than they did. Either way, the number one was deeply unlikely as soon as Carpenter's record was scheduled;* though fans'

* NB: had Carpenter's record come out the same week as *Antidepressants*, there would have been no tension at all. It would have outsold Suede five to one.

optimism is real, there are always weeks where there's less competition or things play out strangely, and it is possible to get lucky. That luck can then make a material difference – a number one changes perceptions – so it's not nothing. Just look at how perceptions of *Bloodsports* were changed by creeping into the top ten. But in a world where a genuine global pop princess has over 25 million monthly listeners on a single streaming platform, does it really matter if an old rock band can have the illusion of being able to compete with that for a few days, because the equation used by the chart company makes them feel like they're 'on top'? Brett was brought up in a very different chart world and feels like once upon a time he was able to compete, an outsider with a baby record label 'poisoning' the big bad mainstream. That makes it harder to accept that bands like Suede can't compete with, to use the term he texts me with, 'pop slop'.* After this, I hear nothing else for the rest of the day. The chart position isn't even the only announcement today. Mat's next novel, *We Are Starting Our Descent*, is announced by his publisher Bloomsbury for 2027. So too the Suede European tour, tagged, of course, 'Dancing with the Europeans'. No brief skip this time: nineteen dates, in ten countries, over twenty-six days. A big part of the campaign.

Tonight's room is the Purcell Room, the small venue where Wednesday's off-mic gig will happen, too. But tonight, it's a showing of Mike Christie's Suede film *The Insatiable Ones*. Fans might imagine tension in a week like this, a kind of manic energy – but I've rarely seen the camp more low key. It shows how far the band have come; with *Autofiction*, number two was considered transformative enough to

* This isn't something the whole camp agree with. Some members of Suede believe Sabrina Carpenter and Brett have plenty in common, both being articulate, acerbic, witty lyricists and fantastic singers, also both having success in taking risqué songs high up the charts in their day. Though perhaps we are all entitled to be a little catty when beaten to number one.

change their direction in response. The same result today barely raises a shrug. Before the event, sitting around chatting with host of tonight's post-film Q&A Miranda Sawyer, Didz and Dave from DawBell, we discuss longevity in bands, the art of communication (Miranda thinks it's not just Suede, but all bands of that generation that don't really communicate). I'm reminded of Mat's one-liner 'Well, musicians communicate through music.' Very effectively, too.

In the green room, the film plays small on a nearby screen, silent, with subtitles. Once Mat and Neil arrive, we chat about the adaptation of Mat's brother Richard's book *The Thursday Murder Club*, now a major film. I ask some questions about *Night Thoughts*, trying to tie up loose ends. I only ask once about the atmosphere, though Mat thinks I'm talking about the film screening, not the chart position. (I genuinely don't think anyone apart from Brett is even thinking about it. And as Mat says later, 'If we really cared about number one, we'd release every album in January.') While we're chatting, an email from Kim at Quietus lands, with an avalanche of quotes, reviews, interviews and stats on how *Antidepressants* is being received around the world. That's the bigger picture.

After the film, a short video from Brett plays, in which he apologises for not being here as he's 'taking a night off from talking about myself'. On stage for the Q&A are Miranda Sawyer, Mike, Mat and Neil. It's not always comfortable, as much of Mike's film looks back to such a different time. Still, Mat and Neil are eminently quotable. 'The sense of chemistry and connectedness when it just works it's just right ... just because it's not a spoken thing, I don't think it makes it any less moving.' ... 'Quality control and mental health – it's the only way we can make good records.' ... 'Every time we set out to make a particular kind of album we have always failed miserably ... It's not cynical, it reveals itself over time.' When someone asks Neil if his illness changed his relationship with music, he answers, 'It was the one thing that stayed the same. When that's the way you've chosen to express yourself, it's the one thing that stays constant when everything else falls apart ...' Neil takes a breath. 'It's just really difficult to talk about.'

Once you've been to multiple Suede events, you begin to hear things for the second, third, fourth time. The best stories are recycled, for a big laugh. Mat's so practised at this – speaking for everyone, at ease with the 'we' even when reporting something he wasn't present for. But in between repeats, there's new information, and the atmosphere is different from even a few years ago, as Suede's reunion now has *five* good albums behind it. Miranda notes Mat saying, in Mike's film, that the band have made so many mistakes they've started to learn from them. What have they learned, then? 'That certain lessons are eternal. The biggest one is against complacency and cynicism. There's this daily thing, of reminding yourself that this is an incredible thing to do [to make music together]. These days sometimes I forget that we ever split up. It's not inevitable that we are doing this, we could be off doing other things. It's going to sound terribly Californian, but you just have to appreciate every day.'

Neil has much to think about. He's a little tense. Not quite present, though he's trying. Mat always looks comfortable in his own skin, though seeing him contrasted with the film that's just played, where he reflected on those mistakes – not noticing how bad things were with Bernard, expressing regret – it looks like that discomfort occurred in another life. In a way, it is another life. The next thing can always go wrong, and it might. But they carry themselves with confidence. Knowing it'll get a laugh, Mat says, 'We're past the *New Morning* phase of the reunion now, so I think we're safe.' If there's any unsureness about *Antidepressants* or

Suede's ability to carry off this residency, Mat doesn't show it. There's a limit to how much they can focus on the reunion after a film that largely concentrates on the '90s, though the panel give it a go. Mat tells the crowd: 'Everything was reset after the reunion, everything was far more equal than before, the five of us starting from scratch. Everything's much more meritocratic now.'

Mike describes the film, once backstage, and again on stage to Miranda Sawyer, as 'an exorcism' – he means for him personally. Clearly, the moments that excite him in his own film, even now, are the moments of drama and healing. The band are more interested in keeping on going and making fewer mistakes, Mat and Neil both stating in public what they've told me in private – that they didn't feel they needed this exorcism the way others did. (That exorcism was most evident in one key scene that saw Brett apologising for splitting the band up in 2003, and another where he was pushed to face the consequences of his drug addiction, head on.) Mike, meanwhile, feels he knows what viewers want: 'the stories of young people getting everything they want and fucking up'.

'ANYONE CAN FIT IN': THE ROYAL FESTIVAL HALL, NIGHT 1

Today, the area around the Southbank is dominated by over 100,000 protesters marching from Southwark to Whitehall via Waterloo as part of a 'Unite the Kingdom' rally. When I get off the tube the streets are full of them, some wearing 'No One Cares If You're Offended' T-shirts. There are Union Jack skirts, hundreds of flags and people collapsed on the ground drunk, all while multicultural, multicoloured London weaves through the procession, heads down. Women holding hands scurry by underneath the mural between the station and the Southbank, a large Paddington Bear in bright blue duffel coat alongside the words, 'Mrs Brown says that in London everyone is different, and that means anyone can fit in.'

The smell of booze wafts across the river and a series of chants against Keir Starmer goes up, also shouts of 'Stop the Boats'. Above us all, the Suede logo flashes. As I weave through, past a group of volunteers in 'Unite 4 Humanity' vests handing out newspapers made for the day, I head towards the venue entrance by the market. At the stalls selling food from cultures around the world – Bangladesh, Korea, China, India, Afghanistan – the anti-immigration protesters queue politely for their lunch amid the smell of these rich aromas. Then they head back to join the chanting.

Inside the building, it's as if there's no noise outside at all. In the quiet of mid-afternoon, in one of the many side rooms designed for the orchestras that often play here, Mat is folded into a low couch practising a song on an unplugged bass. He's leaning in, listening to a song on his phone; it rings out tinnily into one of the band rooms. 'Do you know this one?' he asks, in a voice that suggests he doesn't quite know it himself. (It's 'Crackhead', a B-side from the *Head Music* era they've never played live before.) Down the hall, Neil's on the Steinway piano, playing something sweet, major, intricate. Starting and stopping, worrying over a couple of changes. The piano faces out onto the 1960s brutalist Hayward Gallery, where Gilbert & George adverts pepper the space. Simon pops his head round the door as Richard hangs his three items of clothing on dressing room hangers, muttering, 'Ah yes, black, black or black? It's always so difficult to choose.'* Whenever Simon spots me he gives me

* When I shared a draft of this section with Mat, it reminded him of one of his favourite ever tweets: 'Sentences you never hear on a Suede tour: "Who's got stuff for a white wash?"'

a charming, 'Wotcha, Rodge,' then scarpers before I can ask him any questions. Very wise. I have plenty.

At 4.30 it's soundcheck, Brett fussing over the monitors, as usual. Primarily, if he can stand on them without falling off. They do 'Criminal Ways', 'Crackhead' – Mat's getting the hang of it – then they do 'This Time', the song Neil's been rehearsing. (He got the call from Brett early, and here he is, refreshing the memory. A B-side in 1997, he hasn't played it since the Electric Brixton.) During 'Disintegrate', sitting in one of the central seats in a near-empty hall, Didz is properly rocking out in his seat. He turns to me and says, '"Europeans" was always a bolt-on, that was obvious; but "Disintegrate" was a punt. We didn't know how it would go, but it's really landed.'

Once Suede are done, support band Bloodworm, goth-punks from Nottingham, take their turn. George, Chris and Euan are several decades younger than their headliners and tonight's a big show for them. Contacted by management in a short, mysterious Insta message, drummer Euan followed up and was asked if they wanted to support Suede. At the Southbank. No, really. His parents thought it was a scam and Euan could barely believe it, but Richard saw them play his local music festival in west London – 'between several awful dad rock bands' he says – and he told the management to make the booking: 'Sure, they only have two or three songs online, but they're great, let's get them on.' It's not long between soundcheck and the gig, many fans streaming in early. After their set, George, Chris and Euan 'come off stage buzzing ... Brett and Richard shaking our hands, very impressed.' It's surreal. Working with a proper team, the largest dressing rooms they've seen so far, and more beer than they could ever want.

Paul Khera's shot of faceless Brett framed by carcasses hangs huge above the middle of the stage like a threat. It accentuates his bones.

It makes his head a shadow. There's a chessboard of cream-coloured posh seats either side of a low stage. Neil's pre-stage music is a distorted, filtered version of Mat's 'Disintegrate' bass line that breaks out into a kind of punky house beat as the band enter the stage in near darkness. Brett's out last, as usual. As usual, his appearance triggers a roar.

The start of the gig is blistering. The opening trio of 'Disintegrate', 'Dancing with the Europeans' and 'Antidepressants' shows just how aggressive they've become. The venue is seated and that's hard – full throttle all the time is all very well, but it's harder to make work when only the most devoted are standing. From his place at the back of the stage, in a brief, distracted moment, Mat thinks they should have started the week with the orchestra or the acoustic night.

In places like this, Brett has to work overtime. The first thing of any import he says is, 'Shall we play an old song? Let's play an old song,' – it's a line he's been trying out. That's a joke, because they break into 'Personality Disorder'. Ed's in the crowd tonight. When a few real old ones follow, he's unbelieving. Was it really thirty-two years ago, he thinks to himself, since they recorded 'Animal Nitrate' and 'So Young'? The band don't announce or draw attention to the new album at all. Rather, they lead with it, presuming, each time Brett throws the microphone out, that fans already know the words.

When they dip into 'older songs', it's mostly from reunion records – 'It Starts and Ends With You', 'Outsiders'. Then comes the deepest of deep cuts, 'Crackhead', written and recorded in the early days of Brett's recovery from heroin addiction. Did he expect he'd still be alive twenty-six years later? And clean? 'Can't stop, won't stop', goes the rasping chorus, though he *did* stop before writing this, and playing it all this time later feels like a conscious callback. Then comes a trio of songs about family, the first of which, 'Life Is Golden', is dedicated to Jodie, here tonight too. Brett climbs into the audience, hugging friends, fans he recognises, saying their names aloud, at one point taking a seat in the middle of the auditorium, singing up to the ceiling while people wave phones in his face, disbelieving. On his way back to the stage, Brett rests his head on the raised black block where his foot has been for half the gig, at the middle of the front row.

At the end of 'Trance State', Brett delivers Jodie's lines from the record on his knees – 'Do not drive. Do not operate heavy machinery. Avoid ... al-co-hol.' By now, Simon's already off stage, sparking up (he has to hurry, or he'll run out of time). Richard and Mat are gone too. Brett takes a breath, then introduces this as a moment to 'enjoy Neil tinkling the ivories'. He gets a warm round of applause as the afternoon's practised piano part rings around the Royal Festival Hall. Brett's always fiddling with the toolbox; tonight, it's the switch to piano at the last (even the on-stage setlists read 'THIS TIME – Richard acoustic'). For the second verse, Brett drops the mic entirely and sings to the room. He looks shattered. It's a lot, this. All energy, all the time. At one point he trips over a black box on stage and smiles, pulls up his jeans. They've been threatening to slide off all night. Moving between the up-close seats they've been given and the side of the stage towards the end of the gig, Bloodworm watch on, drummer Euan thinking the energy is unreal. This room full of thousands of people going mad, leaving their seats and going to the front like it's a standing gig. Euan thinks, did we really just play on that stage? Brett is drenched in sweat. The crowd lap it up. Standing next to me, Paul – who's seen Suede more times than most – says it's one of the best Suede gigs he's ever seen, though Mat feels differently, as he tells me later:

> The trouble with playing a lot is that you fall into routine, you fall into doing the show. It's exciting for crowds, but from on stage I

> know exactly when Brett's gonna get on his monitor, I know the moves. The show works, there's a reason people keep coming. But part of the point was to try and get away from the traditional idea of a reformed band or even an older band. Constantly trying to not be one of those bands, not repeat ourselves, trying to put these restrictions on ourselves. The plan for this residency made us look at our material again which was good. But in the midst of all the fuss, suddenly you're thrown back into quite a traditional gig. You can't really go crazy and half your mind is on the next week. I can't help thinking the first two gigs might have worked better as a victory lap. Meanwhile, we're still rehearsing for the off-mic and orchestral shows, so there's that too.

When Suede come back for a one-song encore it looks like Brett's about to say something about the protests of the day, or maybe something else – 'We don't need to say anything,' he says, eventually, before trailing off. Then they play 'TOWICLY'. Mat says, 'People keep telling us it's a special song. We didn't really think of it as a live song, then we realised it has this swagger to it.'* Of everything they could finish with, they finish with this. Ten of Suede's best-known songs are missing tonight. Are they determined to ignore them, or have they just not noticed? Mat describes doing these gigs, which look hard to outsiders, as 'like shooting fish in a barrel'. You can do anything. Suede aren't overwhelmed by fans demanding individual songs. It's not Springsteen, people holding up requests on signs. Rather, most people take what they're given and love it.

You'd think there might be a celebratory atmosphere afterwards, and for fans, there's much giddiness – though for the band, management and crew, it's business as usual. Not like they're avoiding the fuss and

---

* The other example of this Mat gives is 'June Rain', which gets an especially warm reaction tonight.

excitement, rather they just see things differently. Overall, there's a sense that *Antidepressants* is different enough from *Autofiction* to avoid accusations of laziness, but similar enough to build on that success. They need to look different; this year of all years, that's easier to do. But a gig is just a gig, and for the likes of Mat, today's been a bit underwhelming.

After a couple of beers in their own dressing room, Bloodworm go along to the Suede after-party. Euan chats with Mat and Richard, 'sliding in a couple times how cool it would be to do their UK tour'. Meanwhile, the fan after-party is more raucous. American superfan A.J. Radd, here for the duration, leads a big singalong of his favourite, never-played-live Suede song, 'The Sadness in You, the Sadness in Me'. A dedicated traveller to shows across the globe, A.J. has been at the barrier since the early 2000s. He's been asking for this song, outside venues, by stage doors, in queues and online since it was released, pitching to Brett directly by pointing to its popularity on streaming platforms. Self-made T-shirts, requesting it. Social media posts. Sure, most people take what they're given. But A.J.'s never stopped asking for his favourite song.

GIG IN A CONCERT VENUE: ROYAL FESTIVAL HALL NIGHT 2

On my way in the following day, I spot Neil under an umbrella, walking towards the Southbank, deep in thought. I say something clumsy about enjoying last night's gig, but Neil's frustrated by things he wanted to do better. He's sharper than usual. The rest of us are here to have a good time – for thousands, this feels like a moment of triumph for Suede – but Neil's reaction is a useful reminder that the band can only survive as a going concern by obsessing over what he calls 'the hair in the gate', focusing on the debris that might cast a shadow on the film. For the band, these gigs aren't so much about the applause, as the lessons for next time.

At soundcheck, Richard's playing a Led Zeppelin riff when Brett asks someone to give Neil a shout. 'Criminal Ways' is half-sung, with a few off notes. Running through songs in the afternoon can be like this, and it's rarely a clue to that night's performance, but Brett's voice does sound tired. Tonight's piano duet is 'The Asphalt World', Brett and Neil running through the song as Richard sits, arms crossed, on the drum riser. Brett's still a little wobbly but he's warming up now, standing right at the front of the stage. This version ends with a melancholy minor 9 chord, filling the empty auditorium.

Backstage, after soundcheck, some of the team are watching Man City beat Man United in a side room. Richard appears and asks what people thought of last night. Didz says 'Shadow Self' was the standout. Tour manager Charlie appears, giving his own feedback. There's plenty of mention of 'June Rain', Mat reporting that of the new songs, it's the one fans keep mentioning to him the most. A song about suicidal ideation, done well, hits many nerves. Richard is once again in black. What, I ask, would happen if he went for pink? He doesn't miss a beat. Of everyone, Richard seems the most peppy today. 'Chaos would break out!' he answers, giving it jazz hands for a moment and widening his eyes. 'Among exactly two fan groups!' Across the room, Brett and Neil recline deeply, Brett studying his phone behind thick, black-rimmed square glasses.

As folks filter in and out for food or drink, offering the occasional line of support or commentary on the football, Mat's in full storytelling mode, reaching for online portraits of Osman the First, 14th-century Turkish ruler and eponymous founder of the Ottoman Empire. There's some resemblance, you've got to admit. Yes, the proliferation of Usmans and Osmans in the present day has continued to make travel tricky, post-9/11. But no – when I ask if he has any Turkish in him, he laughs. 'Alas, about 99 per cent Haywards Heath, I'm afraid ...' As I leave the backstage area to chat to fans out the front, I hear some of the band joking about dropping a song from tonight's setlist. Though a certain person would be disappointed. And you couldn't do that to them, really. Could you?

On night two, the set is moved around. 'Criminal Ways' is moved up to follow the opening trio of 'Disintegrate', 'Dancing with the Europeans' and a brutally joyful 'Antidepressants'. 'Criminal Ways' is playful and rambunctious, Simon's speedy snare rolling as they wind up to the ending with Brett on the monitors, provoking the crowd. Tonight, he's determined to combat security, who keep telling people not to go down to the front. 'Ignore him, ignore him!' Brett calls, pointing, when security staff try to follow orders. 'Ignore him! Come on! Come on down here!' As Brett directs the human traffic, I'm reminded of Mat's joke the other night at the film screening: 'The Southbank is a concert environment, not a gig environment ... In the Royal Festival Hall we're just going to ignore what it's intended for ...'

The band is tighter tonight – usually a second gig in the same venue means more comfort, more familiarity – and they've overcome last night's sound issues. But Brett's a little more ragged, there's no doubting it. A few more top notes are missed or not attempted. There's more *Sprechgesang*, including where he's singing on record. The Johnny Rotten sneer is there, yes. But also, he's not trying to be cool about it. Meanwhile, no fewer than eight songs make their debut appearance of the week. The first is 'To the Birds', double A-side to 'The Drowners' and one of just a handful of pre-reunion songs. (This set is even more weighted to new stuff than last night.) Between songs, Brett keeps returning to his preoccupation with getting people out of their seats; any reasonable onlooker might wonder why they've booked a seated venue. 'Fucking security,' Brett mutters, 'Fucking security ... ignore them!' Then it's back to the off-mic 'Come oooooooooon', repeated thirty or forty times per show.

Tonight's never-before-played highlight is, yes, 'The Sadness in You, the Sadness in Me'. Before the start, Brett's looking for someone. 'This song,' he says, '*this* song, is especially for ...' – he points to someone on the front row – 'that man there, it's especially for you. Let's do it, we've never played this before.' Brett reaches for A.J.'s hand. When he realises what's happening – it takes a moment – it's a 'tremendous feeling of disbelief', for A.J., 'mixed with overwhelming joy to finally hear the song live.' A moment that's only previously lived in his imagination is suddenly happening, feeling the appreciation coming back from a band he's loved most of his life. For A.J. and fans like him, 'The Sadness in You ...' helps him feel invincible: 'let's start changing our lives ...' He sings his favourite, typically Suede lyric that empowers people to join hands and conquer the world together: 'It's time to step from the page / let's rip up this perfect day.' A.J.'s going to be forever grateful, and from now on the song will have new meaning too: for him, it's a reminder that dreams can 'step from the page'. From my spot above the side of the stage, I can see him and his friends clearly. It's hard to think of a band of this size who know so many of their fans and will pinpoint the person they know appreciates a particular song most, then celebrate them. Okay, the song's off-key in places (that's discussed online, when the video instantly appears on YouTube). Okay, Brett speaks the chorus, avoiding the falsetto. But does it matter? What matters is: Suede might notice you and play the song you want to hear most. Even if – especially if – it means little to people outside the hall.*

* From A.J., on appreciating Suede in the here and now: 'These songs are about a world that is not always pretty and pristine, but hidden in these songs is the seed that even in these grimier moments, we can still celebrate, feel love, and be happy.

Soon after, Brett spots superfan couple Charlotte and Andy – who met on his *Afternoons with the Blinds Drawn* book tour – dancing away on the balcony. That's above stage right, the arrangement of the hall giving them an unusually close place above the heads of the band. Brett focuses on the two of them for a full minute. He'll do anything to charge the song, and anyone he spots in the crowd is likely to get pulled into the action. He draws everyone's eyes to this loving couple whom some down at the barrier recognise. They get their moment, too. Charlotte feels the 'time-stopping thrill' of realising the two of them are suddenly 'protagonists in the drama of Suede'. It's all-consuming. It's theatrical. Well worth escaping the security, shifting from their seats to a place where they feel like Juliet up on the balcony as they sing to Brett and he sings back, 'I don't know how to reach you!' (Reaching, unable to reach.) What a ham Brett is, but it's infectious.

He's back in the crowd for 'Life Is Golden' and a rush of recent favourites follow before tonight's piano-and-vocal-only song is unveiled: 'The Asphalt World' the only *Dog Man Star* song played across the two nights. Neil interprets it as understated chords, barely touching the keys to reduce the volume when Brett goes off-mic for the second verse. After all this, the back end race-through of 'So Young' and 'Metal Mickey' feels positively trad. 'Beautiful Ones' is usually last, but rarely is Brett in the crowd for it, extended mic stand threaded through multiple hands as he tries to embrace as many people as possible. It feels like he's spent as

---

Suede has this niche for taking darker elements of life but revealing even in these low moments, that we can find a cause for hope and celebration. None of this should be happening thirty odd years on – the fact that it is after all this time is a gift. It's all a little miracle to me ... I know it someday has to end – like all things do – but when it does – it won't have done so quietly – and without leaving beautiful fiery marks on those that were lucky enough to experience Suede in their life.'

much time in the throng as he has on the stage tonight. Again, the encore is 'TOWICLY', like they're trying to make a tradition of it.

REHEARSING AT RICHARD'S

Today, Richard, Neil and Mat are in Richard's top-floor studio. They've had a couple of days at Richard's already, without Brett, as well as rehearsals at John Henry's, with him. A singer naturally slips into a different key, responding to the music, where songs have been changed to suit the setting. But for those playing instruments, it's more complicated.

For all these Southbank gigs, discussions about setlist happened further ahead of time than usual and have been more collaborative. They want to represent every stage of the band's life, giving songs that wouldn't usually get an airing a chance to be heard. But they also need to change the songs to work stripped back. 'Europeans' and 'Trash' are right at the top of Brett's range. To get up there, he needs to be LOUD. But loud is no good for the Purcell; it'll drown everything else out and sound weird. So they're bringing certain songs down so Brett can croon them instead. 'Life Is Golden': different key. 'Tightrope': different key. 'Dancing with the Europeans': that's been difficult to get right. 'Trash', too. If you've been playing 'Trash' for decades one way, it's hard to retrain your brain to do it another way, given the muscle memory.

Other songs stay in key but still allow for subtle reinvention. All now feature double-acoustic interplay that wasn't necessarily there before. Neil learned the flugelhorn solo in 'The Big Time' on guitar; Richard encouraged him to play it, though every time so far, they've all fluffed the missing chord at the end. I sit watching them interact. Mat is on Richard's seat by his computer. Richard's on the futon by the window, Neil on the couch, facing the other wall. This gig is a bit of a risk, though that's energising, too. Neil, Richard and Mat don't snap at each other or make demands. Where there are challenging parts, they work out a solution together. Occasionally, after a run-through, Richard says, 'Well, whether that one's any good is rather dependent on the vocal!' As if in surrender to the fates. Neil's keen to keep running through everything. He wants rehearsal time at the venue tomorrow too: 'The more we do it, the better it gets,' he says.

I like to see how Mat contributes in these contexts. He's less likely to worry over a particular technical detail, but more likely to think of the pacing of a song. The feel. He won't comment on a specific line or part but will say if he thinks something is 'sprightly' enough. His presence also changes the atmosphere. Neil is serious and focused. Richard is self-deprecating, friendly. Mat is gregarious in a way the other two aren't, between songs, also over food, in breaks. He likes to tell a tale, to hear a tale. He knits everyone together, that invisible, essential skill that's all too easy to take for granted. You don't hear him badmouth anyone. When Paul Khera comes up in conversation over lunch, as they show me the old-school DIY fanzine they've put together to go with the vinyl edition of *Antidepressants*, Mat celebrates Paul's many polymathic, hidden skills. 'He's a jeweller, you know. He once spoke on the subject of happiness to the United Nations!'* Mat asks about Richard's old, out-of-date birthday cards that are still on his shelf, months on. He wants to know how famous Anna is in Sweden these days (she's been starring in a long-running theatre show called *My Name is Agneta*, touring for months at a time. Richard's pride is evident. A magazine with her on the front cover sits on his coffee table).† Mat makes everything go so

---

* In fact, it was the European Union. But let's not quibble.

† The magazine focuses on *My Name is Agneta*, though in a small insert on the magazine cover there's a photograph of a young Richard playing guitar along with a headline about Anna and Richard's love.

smoothly. He leads, he fits in. The afternoon passes and they run through as much as they can, once more. 'It'll be fine!' Mat beams, after the last note of the afternoon rings out. 'Well, *probably*.'

'WELCOME TO OUR BEDROOM': OFF-MIC IN THE PURCELL ROOM

Tonight is happening, in part, because Mat and Brett discussed doing an acoustic show somehow, but making it different – how rare it was, they said to each other, to hear a naked human voice sing, unamplified. (Brett's been doing more of this himself, recently.) How could they make it more real, more disarming? Then the two of them went to an art gallery in Beijing between shows in China, where the artist went round asking for a gift, then sat you down next to an opera singer, who sang to you direct – with everyone watching. Mat was struck by this experience. He thought, Suede go through this mass of electronics, and it's taken for granted. Seeing how impactful this was in Beijing, Mat and Brett wanted to find a way to do it with their own band.

In recent weeks, they've have gone back and forth about whether to do without mics completely, as it's harder for Brett to sing at that projection all the way through. Initially, Simon wanted to play drums quietly, too – bit by bit, he got his drum kit reduced, until there was almost nothing left. Did they want him to just skip the gig, he asked? No, they wanted him – but how? Mat went down to the venue with Neil, a bit concerned, tour manager Charlie recording on Neil's iPhone from the audience while Mat played tambourine and shaker, Neil guitar. Clearly, everyone either needed to be a bit amplified, or no one. In another visit, Mat was eating sweets while listening and Neil said, 'Shut up, I can hear you!' There's a 'certain bloody-mindedness in Suede,' says Mat. 'The hardest way is most rewarding.' It's easy for him to say. Brett, Mat and

Didz agreed to bill the gig as 'off-mic', though it's largely Richard and Neil that must make it work. In soundcheck there's some discussion over having mics visible on the stage. Usually they record gigs, for who knows what. To bank. To use, in future. But Brett doesn't like the look. Isn't this supposed to be off-mic? They've turned Mat's bass up a bit so it doesn't get lost at the back of the room. That makes sense, though it's also not 'off-mic'. When running through 'Life Is Golden', Brett likes it when the band drop down in the second verse. The more they can make space, 'less jing-a-jing-a-jing', he says, the better. I look around at the set. There's a rug. A lamp. A couch, for Simon. Not much else.

There's much that's different for the band here. Usually, it's so loud on stage, something crowds don't realise. There's usually a delay effect added to Brett's in-ear monitors, for example, that can't be added here. At every single Suede gig, Mat says, he has no idea what Brett says to the crowd between songs. Ever. He watches Simon, occasionally Richard's feet, earplugs in, and keeps going. But tonight, they'll be able to talk to each other on stage. Hear each other. Hear everything. They'll be able to warm the atmosphere by making jokes. Giving, showing love. Being gentle, fragile. Mat admits to nerves, knowing there's nowhere to hide if you make a mistake. They put the instruments down and shuffle off, Richard taking a long look at the Purcell Room after soundcheck finishes, before he ducks behind the curtain. It holds a couple of hundred. If someone's crunching toffees, they're all going to be able to hear.

'Hello,' says Brett. 'Welcome to our bedroom.' Simon sits, tambourine and a couple of shakers within reach. The three guitars, two acoustic, one bass, are centre stage, Brett to their side, stage right. They took the mics away in the end. In a sign of how niche some of tonight is going to be, they start with *Head Music* B-side 'Since You Went Away', Brett's arms folded as if he's not quite sure where to put them. The room's so quiet that Richard hears someone knock something over – a drink maybe? – and this puts him off for a few songs. It's hard to lose yourself when you can see faces, hear bums shuffling. A subtle, intricate 'Life Is Golden' is followed by 'Obsessions' from *A New Morning*. For 'TOWICLY' Brett wanders to the back row of cinema seats. Is it too cheesy to ascend the spiral stairs? He climbs a few steps then realises he can't get any higher because the barrier on the stairs won't open – so he goes back to standing for the chorus, as the entire audience turns around, craning their necks. Kim from the Quietus office, who thought she was safe, tries to fold up, disappearing out of the light once she realises she's now caught in the spotlight with Brett, the focus of the room. When Brett walks back down one aisle singing, hands in his pockets, he spots Didz in the fifth row and can't keep a straight face.

You don't often associate Suede's public face with laughs. Determination, yes. Energy, yes. But jokes? Brett's not usually a quipper; he tends to plan and reuse the few lines he has between songs, ones he's confident will work. Over time, they get finessed. Tonight, though, with so little in the way of a barrier, it's all very human, very warm. Much more like being in the room with them when there's no gig happening. Sitting on the edge of the stage, legs dangling, Brett introduces the next song as being written pre-Suede, not long after he and Mat started their first band together in the mid-1980s. 'When was that, again?' 'In the mists of time,' Mat replies, and you realise how rare it is to hear anyone but Brett speak at a Suede gig.

There's no reason to play 'God's Gift' tonight (recorded during the *Head Music* sessions, over a decade after it was written), except that they want to. It's that kind of night. Beginnings and endings. Tributes and dedications. Memories and celebrations. They go from the oldest song in the set to the newest, 'June Rain', and already that feels undroppable.

In rehearsals, they wondered whether people would be quiet or not. But as Brett talks the verses, barely making a noise, there's not a sound. A wisp of smoke drifts under the spotlight he's lit up by. He's missing quite a few notes; some high ones feel delivered in hope, rather than expectation. Is he going to be able to make it through the whole set? But he always does. When the song finishes and someone sneaks out in front of him, Brett asks the room, 'It wasn't that bad, was it?' At one point, he confirms the band's availability for weddings and bar mitzvahs. Others leaving the room address Brett directly as they go.*

Many songs work well delivered with their barest elements. Mostly, the strummy jing-a-jing is minimised and the whole exercise feels like there are alternative lives for these songs worth hearing on their own terms. The version of 'Breakdown' is a case in point. Before playing 'Simon', Brett says he's only just realised they put the two songs for his friend from those early bedroom rehearsal days back-to-back. This is another opportunity to remember, value, dedicate, and the song itself is a highlight. This is Mat's favourite moment of the night. He only comes in for the last eight bars, so he just gets to listen. During the most intricate part, Mat holds his breath. It goes off just fine. When the song finishes, the Simon in the band stands and shimmies off stage, tambourine aloft, disappearing behind the curtain, accompanied by playful whoops. He may have felt inessential in advance, but now it's happening, it looks like he's having the best time.

By this point in the gig it's pantomime season. 'High Rising' is both ruined *and* enhanced by Mat seeming to be completely distracted by a sound coming from behind the curtain. Turns out Simon is shaking his tambourine back there so we can hear him but not see him. Brett takes

---

* One of these is Paul McCartney's son, the musician James McCartney.

it in good heart, but mid-song he doesn't understand why people are laughing and says, 'I had no idea that song had so much comedy in it ...' 'High Rising' is about Alan, Brett's old flatmate from his hard-partying days, and Alan gets a mention before Brett moves on to Jesse. This feels like a coming full circle, of a kind, to the first gig back in 2010, only this time 'He's Gone' is delivered bare bones, vulnerable, spare. The thinking wasn't immediately obvious to me, but now it's clear: tributes, memories, celebrations. On the front row, John Brandham is sitting with a wide smile next to Sam Hand.

Simon remains off stage, and some speculate. Has he wandered off, forgetting he's mid-gig? During 'The Big Time' Brett leans on the railing at the side of the stage then disappears during the instrumental coda – is he going to get Simon? Is it an act? That gets a giggle too. Neil plays the flugelhorn solo from the record on the acoustic guitar. It's quite beautiful. Another first: when the song ends, Richard, looking on proudly, can't help himself – he holds out his hands towards Neil and encourages the audience to respond, which they do. Both Richard and Mat begin clapping their bandmate. It's vanishingly rare to see anything like this at a Suede gig.

'This has been fun actually,' says Brett, who's back on stage now. He sounds surprised. 'And we did a song off every album!' cuts in Mat, in case that was missed. Even that is a set-up: 'Yeah,' Brett answers, making himself laugh. 'Even the shit album! We did the good song off the shit album.' They can joke about that now, of course, confident *A New Morning* was an aberration, not the end of anything after all.

The encore is 'Trash'. The encore is never 'Trash'. 'We had to finish with this,' Brett tells the faithful. 'It's a song about me, a song about you, a song about all of us ...' He knows the next line is even cheesier, but goes for it anyway. 'Don't mess with the Suede army.' Shorn of its muscle and crooned in that lower key, 'Trash' sounds like a simple song of several clear, charming images, its upbeat togetherness foregrounded. Brett doesn't do the 'ooohs' himself, but the audience give it a go. It's kind of comical, kind of half-hearted and rubbish, in a way that's also sweet. The lamps in Suede's pretend bedroom shake ever so slightly as the band stand, wave, and go.

In the bar afterwards, the warmth is overpowering. Strangers hug, sharing the moment. The band don't ever get to witness this. What people say, in the venue, in the minutes right after a show. For this one, fans had to remain quiet while it all played out.

Now they want to talk.

PARAORCHESTRA REHEARSAL

There's little time for reflection; the band now move from almost no noise to *all* the noise. In Production Park near Wimbledon AFC's ground in Earlsfield, the rehearsal room is about ten times the size of Suede's regular space. It's an eighteen-piece orchestra, plus the band, and I count twenty-five more looking on. Arrangers Charlotte and Liam, pacing with clutches of annotated music. Jim, Simon's regular driver, filming video, as usual. Paraorchestra chief executive Jonathan (caught singing along, quietly delighted.) New faces behind big sound desks, headphones in. The usual gathering of Suede's focused backline techs: David and Jef on guitars, and Martin, Simon's bearded drum tech, in shorts.

They have one day to make this work – half a day on the Thursday, another half on the Friday, including pre-gig soundcheck. The musicians play everything in Suede pitch – a semitone down from concert pitch, meaning the orchestra are in keys that are harder to read and play. (In the earliest days of the band, Suede played in concert pitch, then later detuned guitars a semitone so Brett could hit the high notes more easily. Guitars for *Head Music, A New Morning* and *Bloodsports* were tuned to concert pitch, but they've reverted again since.) The orchestra get a few hours before the band arrive. They run through 'She', 'Everything Will Flow', 'Dancing with the Europeans'. Then it's an acoustic-with-orchestra 'The Wild Ones', for which the room leans in. It's lush, rich, and a reminder of what Suede can do when they have the chance. Or budget. By the time the ensemble play 'Breakdown', people in the production office have come down to the main room, heads bobbing as they peer into laptops.

Today, Neil is the most visibly animated, relishing the range of sounds, the possibilities, the responsibility. At one point, he's fairly hopping along to 'TOWICLY'. No wonder. He's been working with Charlotte and Liam closely for months – they speak the same musical language, and he's been deeply involved in adapting the set to suit the Paraorchestra while also suiting the band. When they go back over the end of the final 'da da DA' at the end of 'Life Is Golden', he conducts. Everyone is used to onlookers with their phones out, but you know it's something when the band get *their own* phones out. When the orchestra practise the instrumental interlude from 'The Invisibles', Richard videos it himself, to share with Anna. Sometimes, the orchestra find the written music is different from what the band are playing. Usually, Suede operate by a look here, a nod there. When they play an extra two bars, it throws everyone out. Charles conducts the band, Richard checking his movements for when to change.

The last time the Paraorchestra played live – in the Clore Ballroom, as it happens – it was as part of an off-book, immersive performance where the orchestra moved among the audience. Co-directed by Kyla Goodey, choreographed by Tom Jackson Greaves and commissioned with

Oliver Vibrans reimagining Mozart's fortieth symphony, it was about as demanding as live performance gets. Maybe that explains why everyone is so relaxed today. Here, they're all sitting. With music in front of them. For the Paraorchestra, this is an easy, pleasurable gig. There's not much time for messing around, and it's a long day of preparation, but everyone can hear what a difference the orchestra makes. Everyone can see how Suede suit this set-up. It's rare and it sounds just right.

SUEDE × PARAORCHESTRA: THE QUEEN ELIZABETH HALL

The final day of the residency is sunny and warm in Waterloo, and the food stalls are back out in force, though this time there are fewer flags. For Suede, tonight represents the end of seventeen days of back-to-back promotion, gigs, pressing the flesh with fans and getting trains here, there and everywhere. Soon, they'll get a brief rest. A few days, before filming *Later ... with Jools Holland*. Then on to the Busan International Rock Festival in South Korea.

Inside the Queen Elizabeth Hall the orchestra are rehearsing while the band eat, Charlotte and Liam taking notes on what they hear, feeding back quickly between numbers. (When the band arrive, they'll be able to hear much less, so now's their chance for any last-minute messages to Charles and the musicians.) During the run-through of 'Still Life', the guitar goes out of step with the orchestra, so Neil jumps up again, emphasising the beat. When they go back through the song, he bounds up through the seating at pace to listen from the back. During the sound-check of 'Indian Strings', one of the sound crew has a little weep, in the quiet of the hall.

The campaign finishes in the same green room the band used at the album launch back on 3 March, when they did the photo shoot for

Mat, Brett and crowd, Queen Elizabeth Hall, Southbank Centre, 2025.
Photo by Paul Khera

the Southbank takeover. The album was announced on 19 May. Here we are, 19 September. Backstage busier than ever.

Tonight, the stage is deeper; tighter too. The band are up front, the eighteen-strong Paraorchestra – eight violinists, three viola players, two cellists, two on woodwind, two on French horn, and one percussionist – scattered around the back. They're in all-white, as is their distinctive-looking conductor. Charles Hazlewood gives off an air of a man determined to have the time of his life. 'We are Suede and this is the Paraorchestra!' says Brett, all in black for tonight's final gig. Paul's here, taking photos. Saul Galpern's here – the Nude Records label boss who first signed them, way back when. Fans from across the world. 'It's a Suede gig,' says Brett, 'but not quite a Suede gig ...'

Very little in a Suede setlist is coincidence, so it's notable that they open with the same song as the Albert Hall in 2010, when this whole journey began. The contrast is striking. Then, they had no idea if anyone wanted to hear it. Now, 'She' – reborn with bold, bright strings giving it a bone-shaking depth – is rarely heard live, as there's so much else to pick from. This is the only time it's aired this week, and it's one of just six songs played tonight also played in 2010.*

By the end of the first song Mat knows he's never been part of a gig where he can listen to the music this way. Every time he plays a note he hears something different in the arrangements around him. It's different for Neil; he knows them inside out. But Mat's mostly thinking about the bar count. He realises how crucial Simon normally is at Suede gigs, holding everything together – as the bass player, Mat just follows Simon. Here, the orchestra need the bar count right. This makes for a weird experience, sometimes obsessing over pace more than usual, then experiencing periods really enjoying listening and not thinking about playing at all. It's all very physical. He keeps turning around. The Paraorchestra musicians are so watchable. The percussionist is fantastic, he thinks. That's Harriet Riley. Mat watches Charles a lot too. A band takes its lead from the drummer, he thinks – but now you have this guy to your side going duh-DING duh-DING, a vibe merchant on stage, kind of like a posh Bez.

'Everything Will Flow' is another one of those songs with a different life now as, along with 'Life is Golden', it has become hugely popular in China, years after release.† As the strings play, the *glissandi* sliding up and down, up and down, Charles is as hypnotic as anyone on stage.

---

* The songs played at both RAH 2010 and QEH 2025 were: 'She', 'Everything Will Flow', 'The Wild Ones', 'Trash', 'Pantomime Horse' and 'The 2 of Us'.

† Fans led a campaign in recent years to hold up thousands of golden lights during 'Life is Golden', that colour having particular cultural resonance in China. Meanwhile, 'Everything Will Flow' is one of the top three Suede songs on Chinese music apps and is known even by many Chinese people who don't know Suede's music at all.

He's so expansive in his movements and expressive, too; his grey hair, rich moustache and playful air giving him the look of some First World War general dropped into his happy place, in a new century, in a new costume. Charles is invested in every note. In the orchestra, Tilly on viola loves the 'slidey fun bit'. Usually, she can't hear the other players when they're on with a rock band, they just have to trust what they're playing is right. At times, IEMs (in-ear monitors) can feel unnatural, but tonight Tilly has a slightly different mix in her ear – they all have individual mixes, individually curated – and Tilly has more violin in hers, which helps her stay on track. This helps her feel respected as a person and as a player, and it allows her to relax. With Suede, the rules are different and she's got more freedom in how she sits, plays, moves. She can bop her head along if she likes. Hers in an underrated instrument, she feels – not as high as a violin or low as the cello, meaning it sits nicely with a male singer with Brett's range – indeed, she gets to double up some melodies with the vocal.

When 'Everything Will Flow' finishes, Charles collapses his fingers with a flourish, as if drawing the sound into his palm. 'Dancing with the Europeans' is welcomed like an old favourite; like many songs tonight it's given greater weight, depth, but also greater lightness. It's a shame they can't take this show on tour, so people around the world could hear these songs, in this way. Though it also makes the night more special. 'Life Is Golden', appearing for the fourth time this week, feels like it's finally getting its deserved place in the band's oeuvre. It's another attempt at connection, between Brett, Jodie and Lucian. 'Look up to the sky and be calm' is a line that only grows with time.

'We've done this song once before,' says Brett, after the strains of 'Life Is Golden' fade. 'We should have put it on our first record when we reformed. It was a big mistake.' Here we go, with the corrections

– making sure everyone knows what Suede records should have sounded like. It's hard to argue with, though. Tonight's the night 'Dawn Chorus' was written for. So long neglected, the strings sound incredible; the song has attack, clarity and sharpness. 'Not many of you will know that,' says Brett, at its close. 'But it's never stopped us before.' You might have paid to be here. But he's campaigning for your attention anyway.

A full two weeks after release, 'June Rain' sounds like a Suede classic, Brett on his knees as he sings, 'God knows it's hard to say goodbye,' single spotlight on him come the end. How many Suede songs look death in the eye? How many are tributes to lost friends and wasted lives? After 'June Rain', he's back up again, pacing. 'Even though we *are* the anti-nostalgia band,' says Brett, with a wry smile, 'we *do* play old songs sometimes.' Then it's back to the first album with 'Sleeping Pills', followed by the moment for all the focus to be on the Paraorchestra, as the band go off, leaving the rows of musicians to play 'The Invisibles'. What an exquisite arrangement it is.

By 'She Still Leads Me On', Charles is fairly bobbing on his heels like a boxer. Of all the reunion-era songs, this gets the most rousing reception. On bass clarinet, Lloyd looks out at the faces of the audience from his spot above and behind Simon, those he can see at the front 'belting out every line'.* It's not something he sees in traditional orchestral music. As he holds his instrument he feels 'a tremendous energy and drive'.

* Lloyd Coleman, associate musical director of the Paraorchestra, 2018–25 and clarinettist: 'It's so satisfying that Suede do things "old school" and don't use a click. Very often when an orchestra merges in this way with rock and pop acts it's decided that everyone must play to click, and that can be a restrictive and strangely antiseptic experience. Without click, the tracks all have much more give and take, push and pull, rhythmically, so we can go with the vibe of the moment.'

From my spot I look around during the final chorus and see just how many people of different ages are yelling out the line, 'a love that was as strong as death!' That's Suede in one, these days, as much as 'litter on the breeze' used to be. Love and death, in conversation. After 'Sometimes I Feel I'll Float Away' Brett has more record-straightening he wants to do. The audience has just been treated to, in his view, 'the best song off the debut album, followed by the best song off *Autofiction*, followed by the best song off *Bloodsports*.' Then he reaches for that line again: 'If you don't believe me,' – cheeky grin – 'I've got the graphs to prove it.' Another point of contrast with the Albert Hall is 'The 2 of Us', then part of the encore, played stripped back, given a lush iteration tonight. During 'TOWICLY' Brett's up on the monitors, in front of those who escaped security, as the flutes flutter in the background. He's straining for more, increasingly desperate to turn this into a Suede gig.

'Flytipping' is Richard's moment. If ever I've been moved at a Suede gig, it's now. I think of Richard meeting Anna again after all those years, and what it's like to find someone, finally, who loves you for who you are. I think of Neil and Richard working on the extra end section, when the song might have been finished. The initial scepticism of others, then overcome. I think of the way this looks like Richard's moment – and it is – though shouldn't it be Neil's too? How much he's hidden, even tonight. That, of all things, is what catches in my throat. As the climax of 'Flytipping' winds up into a barrage of sound, I think of the song's standout images. Nettles. Roundabouts. Waste. Abandonment. Worms in the ground. Crows, circling. Images that are so Suede, so evocative. There are many differences between now and the band's early days, but one commonality is Brett's ability to take mundane English life and give it an air of impossible beauty, not despite its ordinariness, but because of it. For Tilly, the extended instrumental section of 'Flytipping' is especially satisfying. When the strings join in with the solo and she's playing along, as the melody swoops upwards and hits the top notes with the guitar it makes her feel for a moment 'like the musical version of a fancy tie – adding a pop of colour to an already pristine and fabulous suit'. By the song's end, Brett is off stage, leaving Richard playing the solo as the dry ice billows all around him. The reluctant rock star, in a vanishingly rare spotlight.

As the gig moves towards its end, I want Brett to say something to cap off the week, the year, the last sixteen years. 'It's been an unusual experience,' says Brett, 'but a good, unusual experience. Hope you've enjoyed it as much as we have.' This strange bashfulness that occasionally overtakes him in the bigger moments.

For years Brett's delivered a mini-speech to the opening of 'Trash', growling and pacing as he goes. But tonight it's different. Mat, Richard and Neil melt from the stage, Richard picks at the Hummingbird acoustic like a couple of nights before, though this time plugged in, and Brett speaks the lines. 'It doesn't matter how many times they grind us down,' he says, 'we always come back.' Is it too sickly sweet? Maybe it's because I've now heard it so many times before, and this feels like the end of something. In the past, I've winced at this speech. Not now. After it finishes, the band and Charles go off but the orchestra stay where they are, in low light. Everyone knows there'll be an encore. They haven't yet played 'Still Life'.

And they do, in all its expansive splendour. There's no nice, neat tying up of anything and they finish with 'Because the Night', the 1978 song written by Patti Smith and Bruce Springsteen. Mat says they've never really been a band for covers but they played it in rehearsal and with its slight theatricality, the way it switches from piano to guitar, it felt like a lost Suede song.

At first, I think it's a shame they're not ending with something of their own. Like this is throwaway, somehow. There are so many songs they haven't played. But it *is* fun, it's different, and the orchestra are having a ball. When they come off stage, Mat says to Charles, 'I'd quite like a conductor on stage from now on!'

AND ON THEY GO

It won't last forever, all this, but they're still going, stronger than ever.

On the first night of the UK tour in 2026, Brett will test out a line or two about welcoming people into Suedeworld. The next night he'll expand it, and they'll play a new song for the first time, 'Tribe'. It namechecks Haywards Heath, another in a long line of outsider songs where people come together, but it's more explicit than ever, drawing a clear line between his marginal upbringing and the band's life today. Hearing it for the first time in Portsmouth, I write down the standout lyric: 'You are my tribe / I am your saint / No one gives a fuck about us, no complaints.' Another night, Brett will tell the crowd the writing is nearly done for Suede #11: 'It's going to be the noisiest fucker yet.' Richard's not sure about the new direction – harder, more extreme, relentless in rhythm and pace – at least not yet. Though they'll work through it. These days, they always do.

It's just part of the process, and the Suede process, these days, works. My last question to Richard is, what's he most proud of in the reunion era? He emails me from the tour bus: 'We've developed a respect for each other artistically which I'm not sure was there in the '90s, when egos, front covers and giant publishing cheques defined how we thought about ourselves ... But working so hard to make *Bloodsports* work as a comeback has really paid off, we're now acutely aware of our own very different roles in the band, and we're developing our skill sets album to album ... We are five incredibly different personalities, but when we work together, be it on stage or in a studio, the pieces fit. The team achieves its goal.' This reminds me of why I wanted to call this book 'As One'. Because it's worthwhile, but it is hard work. Not this effortless thing, but rather a sustained, determined reach for the best they can be. Together.

After the UK, it's the big 'Dancing with the Europeans' tour, supported by Edinburgh's excellent swim school. Then a tour of China. Then another with the Manics, in big arenas. Suede, one of the truly great British rock bands of recent decades, will sweat through the next moment, and the next, pushing forward, no matter what. There are always future challenges, though they must keep living with their past, too. No artist gets to leave that behind.

OLD THINGS, NEW THINGS

All new music is made from old music. Didn't Mat say that? There are only twelve notes.

Suede take things that are tatty, marginal, dank, dirty, and make them beautiful. They've always done this, even in the early days. Finding the romance in 'the condom under the bed'. Finding beauty in mundane, daily life. In family, in friendship, in love.

When he was young, Brett's mum foraged in the woods, creating new things from what she found. Valuing what she had to work with. Adding her own contribution. Years later, Brett took that as his approach to songwriting. She still leads him on today. The whole band do. In the reunion era, Richard and Neil forage freely in the Suedeworld woods, bringing back tasty ingredients. Brett works with those ingredients, adding his own contribution, while respecting theirs too. It's what's given Suede this long, strange, special second life.

New Suede is made from old Suede. It was found broken, and they've fixed it, not once, but five times. You have to keep on fixing it. Finding new ways to remake the band.

The members of Suede are old things themselves now. That's okay. Through repair and resilience, they can keep on making it new.

Suede at the Queen Elizabeth Hall, Southbank Centre, 2025.
Photo by Paul Khera

a biography is a joint effort

Interviewees

BRETT ANDERSON. NEIL CODLING. RICHARD OAKES. MAT OSMAN. (And **SIMON GILBERT**. One day. Maybe.)

JODIE ANDERSON (naturopath, Brett's wife); **RACHEL APPS** (designer of the *Insatiables Ones* fanzine, author, *The Illustrated A–Z of Suede Lyrics*); **DAVID BARNETT** (author of *Love & Poison*); **CLAIRE BIDDLES** (journalist, Suede zine-maker); **ALAN BISSETT** (fan, author); **AMANDA BLAZIER** (fan, Insatiable Ones); **BLOODWORM** (support band, **GEORGE CURTIS**: vocals/guitar, **EUAN STEVENS**: drums, and **CHRIS WALKER**: bass); **JOHN BRANDHAM** (Brett's ex-driver and close friend); **ED BULLER** (producer of *Bloodsports, Night Thoughts, Autofiction, Antidepressants*); **MIKE CHRISTIE** (director of *The Insatiable Ones* documentary, Suede videos and more); **TILLY CHESTER** (viola player, Paraorchestra, *Death Songbook*); **LLOYD COLEMAN** (associate musical director, clarinet player, Paraorchestra); **EVER DUNDAS** (fan, novelist); **JULIET ECKFORD** (fan, Insatiable Ones, New Zealand); **MARIANA ENRIQUEZ** (novelist, short story writer, journalist); **IAN GRENFELL** (Suede's manager, reunion era); **GWENNO** (musician, Paraorchestra *Death Songbook* collaborator, support on *The Blue Hour* tour); **ANNA GRANATH OAKES** (actress, director, writer, Richard's wife); **DIDZ HAMMOND** (Quietus Management); **CHARLOTTE HARDING** (arranger, Paraorchestra); **SAM HAND** (Insatiable Ones); **JONATHAN HARPER** (chief executive, Paraorchestra); **CHARLES HAZLEWOOD**

(director, Paraorchestra); HAGAR ITZIKSON (fan, Insatiable Ones); TEDDY JAMIESON (journalist); PAUL KHERA (band photographer and designer); AMY LANGLEY (Dirty Pretty Strings, *Dog Man Star* shows, plays on 'Drive Myself Home', cellist with Brett in solo years); ALEX LAKE (photographer, *The Blue Hour*); ALEX LEE (musician, ex-Suede, Placebo, Goldfrapp, currently Massive Attack); JOHNNY MARR (musician, the Smiths, solo); SEAN McGHEE (Artmagic, Richard's collaborator, musical director for Alison Moyet); THE MILD ONES: MELISSA WATERFIELD, JOSÉ DUARTE, SARA BONA and DEANJEAN PHNG (Suede fan group members from Spain, USA, Indonesia, China); LESLIE GAO, ELIZA WANG (Chinese fans); ALAN MOULDER (producer, *The Blue Hour*, mixer, *Autofiction*); DES MURPHY (Penguin Cafe, Teenage Cancer Trust); JIP NIPIUS (lighting designer, Suede live); SIMON PRICE (journalist and fan, author of books on the Cure and Manic Street Preachers); A.J. RADD (fan, Insatiable Ones); FERNANDO RENNIS (Italian music writer); CHARLOTTE RODEN and ANDY PRICE (fans); JUDE ROGERS (journalist); ROGER SARGENT (director, *Night Thoughts* film, 2015); ANDREW SCHEPS (mixer, *Antidepressants*); LIAM TAYLOR-WEST (arranger, Paraorchestra, 2025); LUKE TURNER (journalist, the *Quietus*); VEERLE VAN DEN BROECK (fan, Insatiable Ones, Belgium); HANNAH WILLIAMS WALTON (programme director, deputy CEO, Paraorchestra).

acknowledgements

Special thanks to Quietus Management (IAN GRENFELL, DIDZ HAMMOND and KIM HORTON), CHARLIE CHARLTON (Suede tour manager 2010–present, Suede manager 1993–2003), DAVID PALMER (associate PR director, DawBell Productions), AILIE DEBONNAIRE (Paraorchestra, producer), and especially PAUL KHERA, for such valuable photos from his Suede archive.

Thanks for everyone who talked to me, on and off the record.

Thanks to the many interviewees whose quotations I had to cut at the last minute to avoid this book being too big to print: your words are the essential underpainting of this book. I'm sorry I couldn't include more of your voices direct.

Thank you to ALAN BISSETT, who supported me from first idea to final page of this book, a constant cheerleader for my work over twenty years. Also to EVER DUNDAS, an interviewee but also a friend and excellent close reader as the manuscript was developing.

Thanks to my long-serving, wonderful agent JENNY BROWN, with me since day one.

Thanks to the whole New Modern team for bringing this book into the world. Publisher PETE SELBY, who worked so hard for years to make it happen, editor JAMES LILFORD, editorial assistant ELEANOR PORTER, typesetter MARIE DOHERTY, publicist DUSTY MILLER, designer PAUL PALMER-EDWARDS, copy-editor SEÁN COSTELLO and proofreader JOE BARNES for their keen eyes and essential attention to detail at the last, and to all those who go unseen but bring books to readers.

Thanks to ALASDAIR WATSON for author photos: www.alasdair.photography.

Thank you to MY DAUGHTERS – I love you always and forever. Thank you to ALL MY FAMILY, OLD AND NEW. Thanks especially to MY PARENTS for raising me to ask questions, also for listening to me talk about this band for several decades. (With some gaps.)

Thank you, ELLE, for every day together, and for true support at every stage of this process. Our love is real.

And thank you Brett, Mat, Neil and Richard. For your time, energy, patience and openness. I hope this reads like a story you recognise.

www.rodgeglassauthor.com

The team at New Modern would like to thank the following individuals:

Seán Costello for copy-editing

Marie Doherty for typesetting

Joe Barnes for proofreading

Paul Palmer-Edwards for cover design

Dusty Miller for publicity

Marie Lecouturier, Charlotte Rose, Andreina Brezzo and the team at Simon & Schuster UK for sales and distribution